KARL MARX

Early
Writings

Introduced by Lucio Colletti
Translated by Rodney Livingstone
and Gregor Benton

Vintage Books
A Division of Random House
New York

FIRST VINTAGE BOOKS EDITION, June 1975
Selection and Notes copyright © New Left Review, 1974
Introduction copyright © Lucio Colletti, 1974; translation © Tom Nairn, 1974
Translations of *Critique of Hegel's Doctrine of the State*, Letters from the
Franco-German Yearbooks, James Mill's 'Elements of Political Economy'
and *Critical Notes on the Article 'The King of Prussia and Social Reform'*
copyright © Rodney Livingstone, 1974
Translations of *Economic and Philosophical Manuscripts, On the Jewish
Question, A Contribution to the Critique of Hegel's Philosophy of Right.
Introduction* and the Glossary copyright © Gregor Benton, 1974
Translations in the Appendix copyright © Lawrence & Wishart, 1973, 1971
All rights reserved under International and Pan-American Copyright
Convention. Published in the United States by Random House, Inc.,
and simultaneously in Canada by Random House of Canada Limited,
Toronto. Originally published in England by Penguin Books Ltd., in 1975.

Library of Congress Catalog Card Number: 74-29156
Marx, Karl
   Early Writings
Vintage Books   New York
June 1975
   11-25-74
Manufactured in the United States of America

Contents

Introduction

I

The writings contained in this volume were produced by Marx during the two years 1843–4, when he was little more than twenty-five years old. Some were published at once: *The Jewish Question*, for example, and the *Contribution to the Critique of Hegel's Philosophy of Right. Introduction*. Others, like the *Critique of Hegel's Doctrine of the State* and the famous *Economic and Philosophical Manuscripts*, were published only posthumously, in 1927 and 1932 respectively. When it is remembered that the complete text of *The German Ideology* was not printed until 1932 and that *The Holy Family*, first published in 1845, rapidly became a collector's item, the reader will understand why Marx's youthful philosophical work was for the most part only discovered comparatively recently.

It is true that Mehring reprinted some of Marx's early published work in 1902 (in his *Aus dem literarischen Nachlass*). But the more important writings remained unknown. And in any case by that time the whole first generation of Marxian interpreters and disciples – including Kautsky, Plekhanov, Bernstein and Labriola – had already formed their ideas. So the Marxism of the Second International was constituted in almost total ignorance of the difficult and intricate process through which Marx had passed in the years from 1843 to 1845, as he formulated historical materialism for the first time.

Up to the end of the last century (and even later) little more was known about this process than what Marx had said of it himself, in a few sentences of the 1859 *Preface* to *A Contribution to the Critique of Political Economy*. Apart from this, the only basic authority to hand was Engels's *Ludwig Feuerbach* (1888): a work in which one of the original protagonists of Marxism provided (or seemed to provide) a most authoritative account of all that was essential, all that was really worth knowing, about their relationship to Feuerbach and Hegel and the part these men played in the formation of Marx's thought.

A whole generation of Marxist theorists knew next to nothing (through no fault of their own) of Marx's early philosophical writings: it is vital to keep this fact firmly in mind, if one wishes to understand one decisively important circumstance. The first generation of Marxists approached Marx via *Capital* and his other published writings (mainly economic, historical or political), and were unable to understand fully the philosophical precedents and background underlying them. They could not know the reasons, philosophical as well as practical, which had induced Marx to give up philosophy after his break with Hegel and Feuerbach; induced him to devote himself to the analysis of modern capitalist society, instead of going on to write a philosophical treatise of his own. The few available texts on this theme, like the *Theses on Feuerbach*, the *Preface* (already mentioned) to *A Contribution to the Critique of Political Economy*, and the *Postface* to the second edition of volume I of *Capital*, taken on their own were quite inadequate for this purpose.

This fundamental unease is revealed clearly in the Marxist writings of the Second International. Why had *Capital* been given priority? Why had Marx devoted all his efforts to the analysis of one particular socio-economic formation, without prefacing it by some other work expressing his general philosophical conceptions, his overall vision of the world?

The urgency and significance of these questions may be better grasped if one reflects upon the cultural and philosophical climate of the time. Kautsky, Plekhanov, Bernstein, Heinrich Cunow and the others had grown up into a world profoundly different from that of Marx. In Germany the star of Hegel and classical German philosophy had long since set. Kautsky and Bernstein were formed in a cultural milieu dominated by Darwinism, and by the Darwinism of Haeckel rather than that of Darwin himself. The influence exerted upon them by Eugen Dühring is, from this point of view, particularly significant. Plekhanov too was at bottom rooted in positivism – think of the place he accords Buckle in his *The Monist Conception of History*, for example. The cultural mentality common to this whole generation, behind its many differences, reposed upon a definite taste for great cosmic syntheses and world-views; and the key to the latter was always a single unifying principle, one explanation embracing everything from the most elementary biological level right up to the level of human history ('Monism', precisely!).

This is (in barest outline) the context which enables one to understand the remarkable importance of the philosophical works of Engels for this generation of Marxists: *Anti-Dühring* (1878), *The Origin of the Family, Private Property and the State* (1884) and *Ludwig Feuerbach* (1888). These works appeared in the later years of Marx's own life, or not long after his death in 1883, and they coincided with the formative period of the generation to which Kautsky and Plekhanov belonged. Furthermore, Engels not only entertained close personal relations with the two latter but shared their interest in the culture of the period, in Darwinism and (above all) the social extrapolations to be made from it, down to the most recent findings of ethnological research.

Thus, while a philosophical background or general conception could be glimpsed only occasionally and with some difficulty in Marx's prevalently economic works, in Engels it stood squarely in the foreground. Not only that, it was expounded there with such simplicity and clarity that every single disciple of the period praised him for it.[1] The leading intellectual figures were all in the most explicit agreement on this point: they had all been drawn to Marxism principally by the works of Engels. Commenting on his own correspondence with Engels, Kautsky emphasizes the fact in more than one place: 'Judging by the influence that *Anti-Dühring* had upon me,' he wrote, 'no other book can have contributed so much to the understanding of Marxism.' Again: 'Marx's *Capital* is the more powerful work, certainly. But it was only through *Anti-Dühring* that we learnt to understand *Capital* and read it properly.'[2] Later, Ryazanov, too, observed how 'the younger generation which began its activity during the second half of the seventies learned what was scientific socialism, what were its philosophical principles, what was its method' mainly from the writings of Engels. 'For the dissemination of Marxism as a special method and a special system', he continues, 'no book except *Capital* itself has done as much as *Anti-Dühring*. All the young Marxists who entered the public arena in the early eighties – Bernstein, Karl Kautsky, George Plekhanov – were brought up on this book.'[3]

1. See, for example, K. Kautsky, *F. Engels: sein Leben, sein Wirken, seine Schriften*, Berlin, 1908, p. 27.
2. F. Engels, *Briefwechsel mit K. Kautsky*, Vienna, 1955, pp. 4, 77–9, 82–3.
3. D. Riazanov, *Karl Marx and Friedrich Engels*, London, 1927, p. 210.

Not only the first generation was influenced in this way. The Austro-Marxists who followed also recognized their special debt to Engels, and underlined no less explicitly the significance his work had had for them. Of the two founders of historical materialism, it was Engels who had developed what one might call its 'philosophical-cosmological' aspect, its philosophy of nature; it was he who had successfully extended historical materialism into 'dialectical materialism'. Indeed, he was the first to employ this term. Even such a sophisticated thinker as Max Adler – a Kantian as well as a Marxist – could write in 1920 that Engels's work contained precisely the general philosophical theory whose absence had been so often lamented in Marx himself. Marx had not had the time to provide such a theory, having spent his whole life on the four volumes of *Capital*. 'The peculiar significance of Engels for the development and formation of Marxism' lay much more, in Adler's view, in the way in which he 'liberated Marx's *sociological* work from the special economic form in which it had first appeared, and placed it in the *larger framework of a general conception of society*, enlarging Marxist thought, so to speak, into a world-view by his prodigious development of its method and his effort to *relate it to the modern natural sciences*.' A little farther on, he concludes: 'Engels became the man who perfected and crowned Marxism,' not only in virtue of his 'systematization' of Marx's thought, but also because his 'creative and original development' of that thought has 'given a *basis* to Marx's analyses'.[4]

Thus, Engels's theoretical works became the principal source for all the more philosophical problems of Marxism during the whole early period corresponding (approximately) to the Second International. They were vital to an era which was in every sense decisive, the era in which Marxism's main corpus of doctrine was first defined and set out. As well as the oft-mentioned merits of simplicity and clarity, they were full of the limitations inevitable in popular and occasional writings. Nevertheless, their influence was immense. The relationship between formal and dialectical logic, between Marxism and the natural sciences, Marx's relationship to Hegel – these were only a few of the many problems posed and supposedly answered with exclusive reference to statements (often quite casual) in the pages of *Anti-Dühring* and *Ludwig Feuerbach*.

4. M. Adler, *Engels als Denker*, Berlin, 1920, pp. 48–9.

This was (naturally) particularly true for problems which had become remote from the general philosophical taste and outlook of the period, and so lent themselves easily to passive acceptance and mechanical repetition: the Marx–Hegel relationship, for example, or the problem of dialectic. Plekhanov is typical in this respect. Although one of the few Marxists of the time with some direct knowledge of Hegel's original texts, he never tried in his own writings to go beyond illustrating or commenting on Engels's judgements on this topic.[5] It was a subject, in fact, where Engels's authority seemed even more unchallengeable than usual. Not only had he personally lived through the experience of the Berlin Left (or 'Young') Hegelians, the group Marx originally belonged to, but more recently he had written a review of a book by Starcke on Feuerbach for *Neue Zeit*, vividly evoking these youthful years and their atmosphere of *Sturm und Drang*.

However, it was precisely during those years that Engels and Marx had followed quite different intellectual paths. Only the more historical criticism of recent decades has been able to piece together this divergence with any accuracy. Yet it was undoubtedly important. In 1842, when Marx had come under Feuerbach's influence and already assumed a clearly materialist position, Engels published a pamphlet entitled *Schelling and Revelation* under the pen-name 'Oswald'.[6] The attitude to Hegel expressed in it was that of the young radical Idealists of the Berlin *Doktorklub*. They held that there was a contradiction in Hegel between his revolutionary principles and his conservative conclusions. Hegel had chosen to come to a personal compromise with the Prussian state, against his own principles. Once liberated from this compromise, the essentially revolutionary principles of his philosophy were destined to dominate the future.[7]

Engels also agreed with the other Young Hegelians at this time in seeing Feuerbach exclusively as a continuer of Strauss's work on religion – even to the point of stating that the former's critique of Christianity was 'a necessary complement to Hegel's speculative doctrine of religion', rather than its radical antithesis. Like

5. See particularly G. Plekhanov, *Zu Hegel's sechzigstem Todestag* in *Neue Zeit*, X Jahrgang, I Band, 1891–2, pp. 198 ff., 236 ff., and 273 ff.

6. *Marx–Engels Historisch-Kritische Gesamtausgabe (MEGA)*, 1, 2. The rediscovery of this and other youthful writings of Engels against Schelling was made by Engels's biographer, Gustav Mayer.

7. *MEGA*, I, 2, pp. 183–4.

the other members of the *Doktorklub* (and unlike Marx) he had not yet grasped the connection in Feuerbach's work between his criticism of religion and *materialism*. As his most important biographer has observed, in those years 'Engels greeted Feuerbach's work with joy, but without suspecting that it called into question Hegel's world dominion'.[8] Even after the appearance of Feuerbach's *Grundsätze der Philosophie der Zukunft* (*Principles of the Philosophy of the Future*) in 1843 – as one scholar has pointed out most acutely – except in the case of Marx 'it was not Feuerbach's materialism which determined the new outlook of the Young Hegelians', not his critique of Hegel but his ethics, in other words the most banal part of his work, and the one most laden with Idealist residues.[9]

The difference between these positions is clear. For Feuerbach 'the historical necessity and the justification of the new philosophy [i.e. the 'philosophy of the future'] therefore spring principally from the *criticism* of Hegel', not from further development of his ideas, precisely because 'Hegelian philosophy is the completion of modern philosophy' and no more than that. 'Hegel is not the German or Christian Aristotle – he is the German Proclus. The "absolute philosophy" is the resurrection of Alexandrianism.'[10] For the Young Hegelians, on the other hand, the future lay in working out the 'revolutionary' principles of Hegelianism itself. They are insistent upon the theme of Hegel's 'personal compromise' with the Prussian state. And this is a position decisively rejected by Marx, not only in the closing pages of the *Economic and Philosophical Manuscripts* in 1844, but even previously in a note to his Doctoral Dissertation of 1841.[11]

This is not the place to try to consider in depth the complex question of the different ways in which Marx and Engels arrived at theoretical communism. However, the evidence suggests that Engels made his transition to it primarily on the terrain of political economy, rather than by continuing his critique of Hegel and the old speculative tradition. It was Marx who pro-

8. G. Mayer, *F. Engels, Eine Biographie*, The Hague, 1934, Vol. I, p. 101. See also A. Cornu, *K. Marx und F. Engels (Leben und Werke)*, Berlin, 1954, Vol. I, p. 137.

9. See M. G. Lange, *L. Feuerbach und der junge Marx*, in L. Feuerbach, *Kleine philosophische Schriften*, Leipzig, 1950, pp. 11 and 16.

10. L. Feuerbach, *Sämtliche Werke*, ed. Bolin and Jodl, 1905, II Band, pp. 274 and 291.

11. *MEGA*, I, 1/1, p. 64.

ceeded in this way – that is, by pushing his philosophical critique of Hegelianism to its logical conclusion. This may well be why, when Engels turned again to write about philosophy forty years later, he was, in doing so, partly to reproduce the ill-digested notions of the early years. He returned, for example, to the idea of a contradiction between Hegel's principles and his actual conclusions, between the 'revolutionary' dialectical method and the conservative system. But there is no documentary evidence at all that Marx ever accepted this idea of the radical Idealist left.

During the era of the Second International (and even more so after it), full and total identity between the thought of Marx and Engels became established as an article of faith. Hence, this concept of a contradiction between the method and the system ended by absorbing and obscuring another one, which looked similar but was in fact quite different. This is the idea expressed by Marx in the *Postface* to the second edition of *Capital* (1873), where he distinguishes not the revolutionary method from the conservative system, but two different and opposed aspects *of the Hegelian dialectic itself* – that is, two aspects of the 'method'. These are the 'rational kernel' which must be saved, and the 'mystical shell' which should be discarded.

Later, still another factor contributed to the success of Engels's thesis. In 1842, the youthful 'Oswald' pamphlet defending Hegel against Schelling became known to Bielinsky (who warmly approved) through some important passages the Russian critic Botkin had transcribed from it.[12] In the same year it was read by Alexander Herzen, then living in Germany, who knew the Left Hegelian milieu well and instantly took over all of 'Oswald's' most significant ideas and made them his own.[13]

These seemingly quite minor events were destined to have important consequences. Bielinsky and Herzen were among the most representative figures of the Russian 'democratic revolutionary' movement. And Plekhanov and many other Russian Marxists were originally schooled in this tradition. When they later went on to embrace Marxism, it was to rediscover in the writings of Engels an interpretation of Hegel very similar to the one they had already learnt from Bielinsky and Herzen. Since Plekhanov alone had any serious knowledge of Hegel during the time of the Second International and was for long acknowledged

12. *MEGA*, I, 2, 'Einleitung', pp. xlvi–xlix.
13. A. I. Herzen, *Textes philosophiques choisis*, Moscow, 1950, p. 340.

by all Russian Marxists (including Lenin) as an indisputable authority on philosophical matters, it is easy to see how his work helped consolidate this kind of interpretation.

It should not be forgotten either that Russian social-democracy differed from the German variety in one relevant respect: whereas the Germans were never too deeply concerned about strictly philosophical issues, the Russians paid the most serious attention to them and actually made them the chief criterion, the test-bed, of Marxist 'orthodoxy' (particularly after the turn of the century and Bernstein's revisionist attack). First Plekhanov and then Lenin carried the definition of this 'general' philosophical theory to its logical conclusion. It was henceforth definitively labelled 'dialectical materialism', and seen as a necessary preliminary to the more 'particular' theory of historical materialism. Dialectical materialism in this sense was extracted from Engels's writings on the basis of the assumption (now axiomatic) that the two founders of historical materialism were one person on the plane of thought. To understand what this came to mean historically, it is salutary to consult the heading 'Karl Marx' in the 1914 *Granat* encyclopedic dictionary. The item was written by Lenin, and later on served as a model for Stalin's celebrated treatise *On Dialectical Materialism and Historical Materialism*. Both the paragraph on Marx's 'philosophical materialism' and that on his conception of 'dialectic' consist entirely of quotations from the works of Engels.

The reader ought not to conclude that any very dramatic meaning attaches, in itself, to this difference of outlook on some points between Marx and Engels. It was only natural, and the absence of such differences would really have been extraordinary. Given that contradictions are often met with in the work of a single author, it is hard to see how they could fail to emerge between two authors who – making every allowance for their deep friendship and the many ideas they shared – remained two distinct people leading very different lives on the basis of different inclinations and intellectual tastes. The fact may seem almost too obvious to be worth mentioning. Yet the rigid identification of the two fathers of historical materialism and the rooted conviction that all of Engels's philosophical positions reflected Marx's thought were to have notable repercussions when, at last, Marx's own youthful philosophical work was published.

This happened, as we saw, largely between 1927 and 1932. The major early works – the *Critique of Hegel's Doctrine of the State* and the *Economic and Philosophical Manuscripts* – were printed at that time. By then the crystallization of 'dialectical materialism' as the official philosophy of the U.S.S.R. and the European communist parties was already far advanced and free debate was encountering increasing difficulties, even at the most theoretical level. These were to have a definite influence upon the reception accorded Marx's early writings over the next forty years.

The immediate reasons for the resistances and perplexities they aroused in Marxist circles were certainly of a theoretical nature. It would be needless exaggeration of the case to ascribe the reaction directly to political factors. Nevertheless, the sheer rigidity of official doctrine, the *rigor mortis* which already gripped Marxism under Stalin, contributed in no small way to the cool reception which the writings met with when they appeared, to the absence of any debate about them, and to the manner in which they were immediately classified and pigeon-holed.

They became, almost at once, 'the early writings'. The description is of course formally unexceptionable: they were composed, in fact, when Marx was a very young man of twenty-five or six. Yet this is approximately the age at which David Hume had already composed his philosophical masterpiece, the *Treatise on Human Nature*, and age was never considered a criterion in evaluating the work of the Scottish philosopher. The adjective 'early' served to emphasize their heterogeneity and discontinuity *vis-à-vis* the doctrine of the subsequent period.

This should not be taken to mean that the work of the young Marx poses no problems, or that there *are* no differences between it and his mature works. But the point is that the way in which the writings came to be regarded was really most unfavourable to them, and especially to the *Critique* and the *Manuscripts*. It meant that it was impossible to perceive the manner in which they were related (albeit embryonically) to Marx's later ideas, or how they might (therefore) throw new light on the work of his maturity. Instead, they were seen above all as the remains of a line of thought which had led nowhere, or into a blind alley (the *Holzwege* of Marx, as it were). There is no other explanation – to take only one particularly significant example – of the decision made in 1957 by the East German Institute of Marxism–Leninism (on the basis of an analogous decision by the Central Committee of the Soviet Communist Party) to exclude the *Economic and Philo-*

sophical Manuscripts from the edition of the Marx–Engels *Werke* and publish them in a separate volume.[14]

What made the writings appear so 'out of line' with Marxism was – quite independently of their own limitations – their profound dissimilarity to 'dialectical materialism'. They said nothing at all about the dialectics of nature; nothing which prepared the way for Engels's theory of the three basic dialectical laws of the universe (the transformation of quantity into quality and vice-versa, the negation of negation, the coincidence of opposites); nothing which at all resembled the latter's conception of, for example, the 'negation of negation' as 'an extremely general – and for this reason extremely far-reaching and important – law of development of nature, history and thought; a law which ... holds good in the animal and plant kingdoms, in geology, in mathematics, in history and in philosophy'.[15] Instead, the reader was faced with a trenchant critique of the philosophy of Hegel, in the shape of an analysis infinitely more difficult and complex than Engels's simple contraposition of 'method' against 'system'. And in addition, he found a discussion of estrangement and alienation, themes absent from the work of Engels, Plekhanov and Lenin alike.

Just how profound was the embarrassment produced among even the most serious Marxist scholars may be seen from the cases of Georg Lukács and Auguste Cornu. In the preface to the 1967 edition of his *History and Class-Consciousness*, Lukács recalls the 'stroke of good luck' which allowed him to read the newly deciphered text of the *Manuscripts* in 1930, two years before their publication.[16] This reading showed him the basic mistake he had made in his book (which first appeared in 1923). He had confused the concept of alienation in Hegel – where it means simply the objectivity of nature – with the quite different concept in Marx's work, where it refers not to natural objects as such but to what happens to the products of labour when (as a result of specific social relationships) they become *commodities* or *capital*. 'I can still remember even today the overwhelming effect produced in me by Marx's statement,' he writes.[17]

Now it is true that the mistake in question had invalidated some

14. Marx–Engels, *Werke (MEW)*, Berlin, 1957, Vol. I, p. xxxi.
15. F. Engels, *Anti-Dühring*, Moscow, 1954, p. 195.
16. G. Lukács, *History and Class-Consciousness*, London, 1971, p. xxxvi.
17. ibid.

of the assumptions of *History and Class-Consciousness*. But the *problem* at the heart of the book remained as valid as before: that is, the problem of the nature of alienation, which (in the author's own words) had been treated there 'for the first time since Marx ... as central to the revolutionary critique of capitalism'.[18] And yet Lukács was to pursue the problem no further – the problem which (before and independently of the *Manuscripts*) he had discovered to be crucial to the understanding of *Capital* itself. What prevented him was the habit of reasoning within the framework and categories of 'dialectical materialism', and the impossibility of reconciling this with his discovery. It is no accident that his use of the *Manuscripts* in later work was to be so episodic (like the few pages on them in the last part of *Der junge Hegel*, for instance), or that the themes of alienation and fetishism were to lose importance in his thought.

The result was a return to the state of affairs before *History and Class-Consciousness* when (again in Lukács's own words) 'the Marxists of the time were unwilling to see ... more than historical documents important only for his personal development' in the youthful works which Mehring had republished.[19] Another ultimate consequence of this unwillingness was that Marx's early works, virtually abandoned by Marxists, were to become a happy hunting-ground for Existentialist and Catholic thinkers, especially in France after the Second World War.

The other case, less important but equally significant from our point of view, was that of Auguste Cornu. Cornu's profound knowledge of the Left Hegelian movement made him perfectly conscious of the origins of Engels's critique of Hegel in the radical-liberal milieu, on the basis of positions wholly distinct from those of historical materialism.[20] Hence he was in the best possible position to understand the true import of Marx's criticism of Hegel in the *Critique of Hegel's Doctrine of the State*, and to see why (Feuerbach's influence on it notwithstanding) this study was far more than a mere 'historical document of Marx's personal development'. Yet his treatment of this major work consists of a few superficial pages, devoted mainly to Feuerbach's influence upon it. The obstacles of 'dialectical-materialist' orthodoxy, combined with a certain difficulty, common among historians, in tackling theoretical questions, simply prevented him seeing anything more.

18. ibid.　　19. ibid., p. xxvi.　　20. A. Cornu, op. cit., p. 202 passim.

This situation has changed little in recent years. Among Marxists, interest in the *Critique, The Jewish Question*, the *Manuscripts*, etc., has remained the preserve of a few specialist students of the 'prehistory' of Marx's thought. The old theoretical edifice of 'dialectical materialism' has lost much of its ancient solidity, certainly. However, the newer Marxist thought inspired by structuralism has not only inherited its harsh verdict on the early writings, but threatens to extend it to other works of Marx, now judged equally unworthy of the seal of approval bestowed by '*la coupure épistémologique*'.[21] One may say, therefore, that apart from the work of a few Italian Marxist scholars like Galvano della Volpe (still almost unknown outside Italy), Marx's youthful philosophical works have still not received the attention which they deserve.

II

The *Critique of Hegel's Doctrine of the State* was most likely composed at Kreuznach between the months of March and August 1843, after Marx had ceased to be editor of the *Rheinische Zeitung*. This was the date proposed by Riazanov when he prepared the first edition of the *Critique* in 1927 as part of the *Marx–Engels Historisch–Kritische Gesamtausgabe* (*MEGA* for short). Cornu also accepts this date. Other writers like S. Landshut and I. P. Mayer (who published the work in a 1932 anthology of Marx's early writing) have placed it earlier, between April 1841 and April 1842. However, this seems most unlikely for a variety of reasons there is not space to deal with here, and most scholars have agreed with Riazanov's dating.

The manuscript of the *Critique* (from which the first four pages have been lost) contains a study of much of the third section ('The State') of the third part ('Ethical Life') of Hegel's *The Philosophy of Right*. The paragraphs analysed are those numbered from 261 to 313 in the Hegel text (pages 161 to 204 of the standard English edition, edited and translated by T. Knox, 1942). The most immediately striking thing about the essay is that the first part of

21. A term used by Louis Althusser to denote what he sees as the 'radical break' between Marx's youthful and his more mature writings. The former express a 'Hegelian and Feuerbachian ideology'. The latter construct the 'basic concepts of dialectical and historical materialism' (see Louis Althusser's *Reading Capital*, London, 1970, pp. 309–10).

it (from the beginning down to at least the comments on paragraph 274) is much more a criticism of Hegel's dialectical logic than a direct criticism of his ideas on the state.

The logic of Hegel, says Marx, is 'logical mysticism', a mystique of reason.[22] At first glance this might seem like an anticipation of Dilthey's well-known theses of 1905 on Hegel's youthful theology, which depict him as essentially a vitalist and romantic philosopher. But actually the two positions are quite different. Dilthey sees Hegel's mysticism as a mystique of *sentiment*, so that his stance is radically at odds with the traditional idea of Hegel the pan-logical rationalist. Marx on the other hand perceives the mysticism as one of *reason*, deriving from Hegel's all-pervading logic – that is, deriving from the fact that for Hegel reason is not human thought but the Totality of things, the Absolute, and possesses (consequently) a dual and indistinct character uniting the worlds of sense and reason.

The principal focus of Marx's criticism, in other words, is Hegel's belief in the identity of being and thought, or of the real and the rational. This identification involves a double inversion or exchange, claims Marx. On the one hand being is reduced to thinking, the finite to the infinite: empirical, real facts are transcended, and it is denied they have genuine reality. The realm of empirical truth is transformed into an internal moment of the Idea. Hence, the particular, finite object is not taken to be what it is, but considered in and as its opposite (the universal, thought): it is taken to be what it *is not*. This is the first inversion: being is not being but thought. On the other hand reason – which holds its opposite within itself and is a unique totality – becomes an absolute, self-sufficient reality. In order to exist, this reality has to transform itself into real objects, has to (the second inversion) assume particular and corporeal form. Marx accuses Hegel of substantifying abstraction in his 'Idea', and so falling into a new 'realism of universals'.

Hegel inverts the relationship between *subject* and *predicate*. The 'universal' or concept, which ought to express the predicate of some real object and so be a category or function of that object, is turned instead into an entity existing in its own right. By contrast, the real subject, the *subjectum* of the judgement (the empirical, existing world), becomes for him a manifestation or embodiment of the Idea – in other words, a predicate of the

22. Below, p. 61.

predicate, a mere means by which the Idea vests itself with reality. In his notes on Hegel's paragraph 279, Marx says:

> Hegel makes the predicates, the objects, autonomous, but he does this by separating them from their real autonomy, *viz.* their subject. The real subject subsequently appears as a result, whereas the correct approach would be to start with the real subject and then consider its objectification. The mystical substance therefore becomes the real subject, while the actual subject appears as something else, namely as a moment of the mystical substance. Because Hegel starts not with an actual existent (ὑποκείμενον, subject) but with predicates of universal determination, and because a vehicle of these determinations must exist, the mystical Idea becomes that vehicle.[23]

As Marx's use of a Greek term suggests, this criticism is similar to one aspect of Aristotle's critique of Plato – as, for example, where the former writes that:

> a material differs from a subject matter by not being a particular something: in the case of an attribute predicated of a subject matter, for example, of a man, both body and soul, the attribute is 'musical' or 'white'; and the subject matter of the attribute is not called 'music', but musician, and the man is not a 'white', but a white man . . . Wherever this is the relation between subject and predicate, the final subject is primary being.[24]

In the *Economic and Philosophical Manuscripts* Marx reformulates this criticism and notes that Hegel's philosophy suffers from the double defect of being at one and the same time 'uncritical positivism' and 'equally uncritical idealism'.[25] It is uncritical idealism because Hegel denies the empirical, sensible world and acknowledges true reality only in abstraction, in the Idea. And it is uncritical positivism because Hegel cannot help in the end restoring the empirical object-world originally denied – the Idea has no other possible earthly incarnation or meaning. Hence, the argument is not simply that Hegel is too abstract, but also that his philosophy is crammed with crude and unargued empirical elements, surreptitiously inserted. This concrete content is first of all eluded and 'transcended', and then re-introduced in an underhand, concealed fashion without genuine criticism.

23. Below, p. 80.
24. Aristotle, *Metaphysics*, tr. R. Hope, Ann Arbor, 1952, p. 191.
25. Below, p. 385.

What this means may be seen from the whole argument of *The Philosophy of Right*, and particularly from its treatment of the state. In the latter, Hegel is concerned with a number of highly determinate historical institutions such as hereditary monarchy, bureaucracy, the Chamber of Peers, primogeniture and so on. His task ought to be to explain these institutions – to investigate their causes in history, find out whether they still have any *raison d'être* and demonstrate in what ways they correspond to real needs of modern life rather than being mere empty survivals from the past. But actually his procedure is very different. He does not show the rationale of these institutions by using historical and scientific concepts, concepts with some bearing on the objects in question; instead, he starts from an Idea which is nothing less than the divine *Logos* itself, the spirit-god of Christian religion. Since this Idea is the presupposition of everything but cannot presuppose anything outside itself, it follows that the logico-deductive process must be one of *creating* objects. Hegel has to conjure the finite out of the infinite, in short. But since, as Marx says in his comment on paragraph 269, 'he has failed to construct a bridge *leading from the general idea of the organism to the particular idea of the organism of the state or the political constitution*' (and in all eternity would never construct such a bridge), all Hegel can really do is smuggle the empirical world in again, in underhand fashion.[26]

What emerges is no historical or scientific understanding of the institutions of the Prussian state, but an apologia for them. They emanate directly out of the Idea or divine Spirit, they are its worldly development or actuality – being products of Reason in this sense, they can of course hardly help being totally rational in themselves. As Marx states in his résumé of Hegel's argument for monarchy, the result is 'that an *empirical person* is *uncritically* enthroned as the real truth of the Idea. For as Hegel's task is not to discover the truth of empirical existence but to discover the empirical existence of the truth, it is very easy to fasten on what lies nearest to hand and prove that it is an *actual* moment of the Idea.'[27] Hegel shows the institutions of the Prussian state to be *gesta Dei*, God's self-realization in the world. Hereditary monarchy, the state bureaucracy, the lords who sit in the Chamber of Peers by right of primogeniture – they all reappear in his argu-

ment not as historical realities of this world but as incarnations
of God's will on earth.

The state is based on God, according to Hegel. It is founded
upon religion (which 'has absolute truth as its content'). However,
'If religion is in this way the groundwork which includes the
ethical realm in general, and the state's fundamental nature – the
divine will – in particular, it is at the same time only a groundwork.' While religion contains God in the depths of feeling, 'The
state is the divine will, in the sense that it is mind present on earth,
unfolding itself to be the actual shape and organization of a
world.'[28]

Thus for Marx the conservative and apologetic character of
Hegel's philosophy is not to be explained by factors outside his
thought (his personal compromises with authority, etc.) as the
Young Hegelians had tried to explain it. It springs from the
internal logic of his philosophy. That 'transfiguration of the
existing state of affairs' which Marx ascribes to Hegel's dialectic
in the *Postface* to the second edition of *Capital* is explained by
the manner in which Hegel first makes the Idea a substance and
then has to show reality as merely its manifestation. The two
processes are intimately linked. As the *Manuscripts* say, the
'uncritical positivism' of the consequences is the inevitable
counterpart of the 'uncritical idealism' found in the premises.
In the *Critique* Marx writes of 'the inevitable transformation of
the empirical into the speculative and of the speculative into
the empirical'.[29] The formulae are almost the same, and all
refer one to the basic mystification of the subject–predicate inversion. The *Capital* passage states that Hegel transforms thought
into an 'independent subject' labelled 'the Idea'; after which
the real, i.e. the empirical world, which is the true subject, turns
into 'the external phenomenal form of the Idea', into an attribute or predicate of this entified predicate. In 1843, 1844,
and 1873, therefore, Marx's argument remains substantially the
same.

It is necessary, next, to say something about Feuerbach's
influence on the *Critique*. That he did have some influence on it is
undeniable. The phrase Marx employs where he defines Hegel's
philosophy as 'logical mysticism' must surely derive from Feuerbach's analogous description of it in 1839 as 'a mystique of

28. Hegel, *Philosophy of Right*, ed. T. M. Knox, London, 1942, p. 166.
29. Below, p. 98.

reason'. The same might be said of Marx's idea of Hegelian subject–predicate inversion. As well as in *Das Wesen des Christentums* (*The Essence of Christianity*, 1841) we find this idea stated explicitly in Feuerbach's *Vorläufige Thesen zur Reform der Philosophie* (*Provisional Theses for a Reform of Philosophy*, 1842). In March 1843 Marx wrote to Ruge telling him he had read this work and agreed with it wholeheartedly, except for the exaggerated importance it accorded problems of natural philosophy at the expense of history and politics. 'In Hegel,' wrote Feuerbach, 'thought is being; thought is the subject, being the predicate,' while on the contrary 'the true relationship of thought to being can only be as follows: being is the subject, thought the predicate'.[30]

But in itself such influence does not mean much. Feuerbach is generally a thinker of secondary importance compared to Hegel. Nevertheless in the 1839–43 period he touched a peak of personal achievement (soon followed by decline) which gives him a significant place in the critique and dissolution of Hegelianism in Germany, and so in the formation of Marx's thought. His influence on the *Critique* must not be used as an argument for underrating this work. Marxist scholars who have chosen this tactic were in reality trying to avoid the still thornier problem of reconciling Engels's interpretation of Hegel with Marx's. We have already noticed how the latter sticks to the subject–predicate inversion thesis in *Capital*. In the same place, Marx recalls his youthful studies of 1843 and the fact that he 'criticized the mystificatory side of the Hegelian dialectic nearly thirty years ago, at a time when it was still the fashion.'[31]

The problem of Feuerbach's influence is more complicated than appears at first sight. Della Volpe, for instance, insists on the fact that Feuerbach's criticism (unlike Marx's) was restricted to reproaching Hegel with 'empty formalism'. Feuerbach was incapable, therefore, of grasping clearly the necessary relationship between the 'uncritical idealism' of Hegel's premises and the 'uncritical positivism' of his conclusions. From this point of view, Feuerbach's limitations are seen as analogous to those of Kant, who reproached Leibntz with 'empty abstraction' in the *Critique of Pure Reason*.

But in trying so hard to dissociate Marx from Feuerbach,

30. L. Feuerbach, *Sämtliche Werke*, II, p. 195 and pp. 238–9.
31. K. Marx, *Capital*, Vol. 1, Moscow, 1965, p. 19 (translation modified).

della Volpe is probably too severe with the latter. Marx's critique of Hegel is certainly far the more perceptive. Nonetheless, Feuerbach too had his moments of insight. In 1841, for example, he saw very well the relationship between idealism and uncritical positivism in Hegel, when he wrote in *Über den Anfang der Philosophie* (*On the Beginning of Philosophy*): 'Philosophy which begins with a thought without reality necessarily ends with a reality without thought,'[32] that is, not sifted and critically examined by the mind. It would certainly not be difficult to find equally explicit remarks elsewhere in his writings of the 1842–3 period.

However, the question of Feuerbach's degree of influence on the *Critique* still remains a fairly marginal one. Writers who have laid too great stress on it have revealed chiefly their own naïvety. That the theme of subject–predicate or being–thought inversion is to be found in Feuerbach does not, of course, mean that it was an invention of his, or in any way peculiar to his thought. It is in fact one of the most profound and ancient themes in philosophical history, and recurs constantly in the debate between Idealism and Materialism. Della Volpe, for example, could properly relate Marx's critique of Hegel to Aristotle's critique of Plato and Galileo's attack on the defenders of Aristotelian-scholastic physics. Moreover, at the points in his *Critique of Pure Reason* where Kant does most to demolish the older ontology (for example, in the 'Note on the Amphiboly of Concepts of Reflection'), it is also possible to see a critique of 'real universals'. Hence, the only specific contribution which Feuerbach can be held to have made is a reapplication of one aspect of this tradition in the new context, the way in which he brought it to bear on Hegelianism.

I believe the vital element in this vexed question – the edge which cuts the Gordian knot – must be sought elsewhere. The true importance of Marx's early criticism of Hegel lies in the key it provides for understanding Marx's criticism of the method of bourgeois economics (and this is why he could recall and confirm it after he had written *Capital*). In Chapter 2 of *The Poverty of Philosophy* (1847), 'The Metaphysics of Political Economy', this connection is brought out very well. 'Economic categories are only the theoretical expressions, the abstractions of the social relations of production,' says Marx. While Proudhon, on the other hand, 'holding things upside down like a true philosopher,

32. Feuerbach, op. cit., p. 208.

sees in actual relations nothing but the incarnation of these principles'. In this manner, he goes on, 'What Hegel has done for religion, law, etc., Monsieur Proudhon seeks to do for political economy.' First of all by dint of abstraction he reduces 'the substance of everything' into mere 'logical categories'; then, having hypostatized these abstractions into substances, it is not too difficult to retrace his steps and present real historical relationships as the objectification, the embodiment, of such categories. Marx concludes:

If we abstract thus from every subject all the alleged accidents, animate or inanimate, men or things, we are right in saying that in the final abstraction, the only substance left is the logical categories. Thus the metaphysicians who, in making these abstractions, think they are making analyses, and who, the more they detach themselves from things, imagine themselves to be getting all the nearer to the point of penetrating to their core – these metaphysicians in turn are right in saying that things here below are embroideries of which the logical categories constitute the canvas. This is what distinguishes the philosopher from the Christian. The Christian, in spite of logic, has only one incarnation of the *Logos*; the philosopher has never finished with incarnations.[33]

So backward has study of Marx's work remained on questions like this that the connection between his critique of Hegel and his critique of the methods of political economy is usually seen as confined to this one particular case – that is, to the singular coincidence of themes which Proudhon's work provided for him. But in fact, as Maurice Dobb has pointed out in Chapter 5 of his *Political Economy and Capitalism* (1937), its significance is far wider. 'In making abstraction of particular elements in a situation,' he writes, 'there are two roads along which one can proceed.' The first is that which 'builds abstraction on the exclusion of certain features which are present in any actual situation, either because they are the more variable or because they are quantitatively of lesser importance in determining the course of events. To omit them from consideration makes the resulting calculation no more than an imperfect approximation to reality, but nevertheless makes it a very much more reliable guide than if the major factors had been omitted and only the minor influences taken into account.' The second is the road which bases abstraction 'not on any evidence of fact as to what features in a situation are essential

33. K. Marx, *The Poverty of Philosophy*, Chapter II, 'First' and 'Second Observations'.

and what are inessential, but simply on the formal procedure of combining the properties common to a heterogeneous assortment of situations and building abstraction out of analogy.'[34]

What characterizes this second method (with its indeterminate or generic abstractions, as compared to the determinate, specific ones of the first) is, Dobb says, that – 'in all such abstract systems there exists the serious danger of hypostatizing one's concepts', that is of 'regarding the postulated relations as the determining ones in any actual situation' and so running the grave risk of 'introducing, unnoticed, purely imaginary assumptions' and interpolating surreptitiously all the concrete, particular features discarded in the first place. He continues:

All too frequently the propositions which are products of this mode of abstraction have little more than formal meaning . . . But those who use such propositions and build corollaries upon them are seldom mindful of this limitation, and in applying them as 'laws' of the real world invariably extract from them more meaning than their emptiness of real content can possibly hold.

The resemblance to Marx's argument in the *Critique* could hardly be closer. Dobb observes how for some economists abstractions become independent of all reference to realities, and are then hypostatized into 'laws' valid for all situations, however heterogeneous and disparate these may be. Subsequently the same economists, trying to extract substance from their 'laws', are compelled to bring in 'unnoticed', in underhand fashion, whatever particular content their position requires.

Finally, after referring to Marx's early writings, Dobb concludes:

The examples he (Marx) cited were mainly drawn from the concepts of religion and idealist philosophy . . . In the realm of economic thought (where one might at first glance least suspect it) it is not difficult to see a parallel tendency at work. One might think it harmless enough to make abstraction of certain aspects of exchange-relations in order to analyse them in isolation from social relations of production. But what actually occurs is that once this abstraction has been made it is given an independent existence as though it represented the essence of reality, instead of one contingent facet of reality. Concepts become hypostatized; the abstraction acquires a fetishistic character, to use Marx's phrase. Here seems to lie the crucial danger of this method and the secret of the confusions which have enmeshed modern economic thought.[35]

34. M. Dobb, *Political Economy and Capitalism*, London, 1937, pp. 130–31.
35. ibid., pp. 135–6.

But it is not only in *The Poverty of Philosophy* and other early writings that Marx employs the critique so ably reconstructed here by Dobb. It is no less central to Marx's analysis of the method of political economy in his mature works. What economists do, says Marx, is to substitute for the *specific* institutions and processes of modern economy *generic* or universal categories supposed to be valid for all times and places; then the former come to be seen as realizations, incarnations of the latter. His reflections on the concept of 'production' in the first paragraph of the 1857 introduction to the *Grundrisse* are interesting in this connection. In any scientific analysis of the capitalist mode of production, Marx states,

the elements which are not general and common, must be separated out from the determinations valid for production as such, so that in their unity – which arises already from the identity of the subject, humanity, and of the object, nature – their essential difference is not forgotten. The whole profundity of those modern economists who demonstrate the eternity and harmoniousness of the existing social relations lies in this forgetting. For example. No production possible without an instrument of production, even if this instrument is only the hand. No production without stored-up, past labour, even if it is only the facility gathered together and concentrated in the hand of the savage by repeated practice. Capital is, among other things, also an instrument of production, also objectified, past labour. Therefore capital is a general, eternal relation of nature; that is, if I leave out just the specific quality which alone makes 'instrument of production' and 'stored-up labour' into capital.

John Stuart Mill, for example (Marx continues) typically presents 'production as distinct from distribution etc., as encased in eternal natural laws independent of history, at which opportunity *bourgeois* relations are then quietly smuggled in as the inviolable natural laws on which society in the abstract is founded'. And this is indeed, he concludes, 'the more or less conscious purpose of the whole proceeding'.[36]

In other words, logical unity takes the place of real difference, the universal replaces the particular, the eternal category is substituted for the historically concrete. After which – as the 'more or less conscious aim' of the operation – the concrete is smuggled in as a consequence and a triumphant embodiment of

36. K. Marx, 1857 Introduction in *Grundrisse*, The Pelican Marx Library, 1973, pp. 85–7.

the universal. Both *Capital* and *Theories of Surplus Value* develop this criticism at some length. For example, economists identify wage-labour with labour in general, and so reduce the particular, specific form of modern productive work to 'labour' pure and simple, as that term is defined in any dictionary. The result is – given that 'labour' in general is, in Marx's words, 'the universal condition for the metabolic interaction (*Stoffwechsel*) between man and Nature, the everlasting Nature-imposed condition of human existence' – that the light of eternity comes to be cast upon the particular historical figure of the wage-labourer.[37] Or else economists reduce capital to a mere 'instrument of production' amongst others, with the result that (since production is clearly unthinkable without instruments and tools of labour) production becomes unthinkable without the presence of capital.

There is no space to pursue this theme further here. Perhaps the most suggestive applications of this critical method are to be found in Marx's *Theories of Surplus Value* (the section on economic crises in Part II, and the section on James Mill in Part III). We must go on to look at the rest of the *Critique*.

III

After the critique of Hegel's dialectic, the next great subject Marx tackles is that of the modern representative state. As we shall see, his views here are substantially the same as those he expressed in *The Jewish Question* and *A Contribution to the Critique of Hegel's Philosophy of Right. Introduction*, both published in the *Deutsch–Französische Jahrbücher* of February 1844 and written soon after the *Critique*.

This part of Marx's work displays the same sharp difference from the stance of even the most radical Left Hegelians. True, Ruge had published a quite outstanding criticism of Hegel's political thought under the title 'The Hegelian Philosophy of Right and the Politics of Our Time' in the *Deutsche Jahrbücher* of August 1842. And in this article he had commented on Hegel's 'transfiguration' of the empirically given institutions of the Prussian state into moments of the Absolute. However, the main burden of his argument remained that of Hegel's personal and diplomatic 'compromise' – which had turned him, against his

37. *Capital*, Vol. 1, pp. 183–4 (translation modified).

own true principles, into the theorist of the Restoration. Marx's view is (as noted above) profoundly different.

Marx knew very well, of course, that the state as Hegel depicted it differed from the classical form of modern representative state produced by the French Revolution. *The Philosophy of Right* is full of feudal reminiscences derived from the condition of Prussia at that time. For example – as Marx never tires of pointing out – Hegel tended constantly to confuse modern social classes with the 'orders' or 'Estates' of feudal society: the former are socio-economic in nature, while the latter were also political in nature. In modern society economic *inequality* accompanies political and juridical *equality*, while under feudalism the landlord was also a political sovereign, and the tiller of the soil was a subject – that is, inequality reigned in all spheres between the privileged and their serfs. Hegel also wanted to retain the medieval corporations (or guilds), recognized primogeniture, and so on.[38]

Nonetheless, in spite of these strikingly pre-bourgeois or anti-bourgeois features in Hegel's thought, Marx does not take him to be the theorist of the post-1815 Restoration. He is seen, rather, as the theorist of the modern representative state. The Hegelian philosophy of law and the state does not reflect the historical backwardness of Germany but – on the contrary – expresses the ideal aspiration of Germany to escape from that backwardness. It is here and only here (on the plane of philosophy rather than that of reality) that Germany manages to be contemporary with France and England and stay abreast of the 'advanced world'.

In *A Contribution to the Critique of Hegel's Philosophy of Right. Introduction* Marx wrote:

We Germans have lived our future history in thought, in *philosophy* ... German philosophy is the *ideal prolongation* of German history. Therefore, when we criticize the *œuvres posthumes* of our ideal history, i.e. *philosophy*, instead of the *œuvres incomplètes* of our real history, our criticism stands at the centre of the problems of which the present age says: *That is the question*. What for advanced nations is a *practical* quarrel with modern political conditions is for Germany, where such conditions do not yet exist, a *critical* quarrel with their reflection in philosophy.[39]

38. In Prussia as in England, 'primogeniture' was the law of land inherit-ance which allowed the settlement of whole estates upon the eldest son, rather than division among all the children. It was essential to the maintenance of the landed class's power.

39. Below, p. 249.

It follows from this that Marx's purpose in criticizing Hegel's philosophy is not to help create in Germany the political conditions already existing in France and England but rather to criticize these conditions themselves, by demolishing the philosophical structure which expresses them. This interpretation of Hegel as the theorist of modern representative institutions is not only important for the light it throws on Marx's intentions in 1843. It is important primarily as the one point of view which enables us to penetrate to the heart of Hegel's problematic.[40] Hegel tends, as has often been pointed out, to contaminate modern institutions with pre-bourgeois social forms and ideas. But this must not be seen as a symptom of his immaturity, or inability to grasp the problems of modern society. On the contrary, what it does display is his very acute perception of just these problems, and of the urgent need to find corrective remedies for them.

In other words, the central theme of *The Philosophy of Right* is Hegel's recognition that modern 'civil society', dominated as it is by competitive individualism, represents a kind of *bellum omnium contra omnes*.[41] It is uniquely torn apart and lacerated by the profoundest antagonisms and contradictions. Hegel's account of it can leave no doubt on this score in the reader's mind. In modern civil society the power of egoism reigns, alongside ever-increasing interdependence:

> Particularity by itself, given free rein in every direction to satisfy its needs, accidental caprices, and subjective desires, destroys itself . . . in this process of gratification. At the same time . . . [it] is in thoroughgoing dependence on caprice and external accident, and is held in check by the power of universality. In these contrasts and their complexity, civil society affords a spectacle of extravagance and want as well as of the physical and ethical degeneration common to them both.[42]

It is precisely *because* Hegel's vision of the contradictory and self-destructive character of modern society is so lively that he tried so hard to resuscitate and adapt to modern conditions certain aspects of the 'organic' feudal order which still survived in the Prussia of his day. Hegel sees these more organic institu-

40. A similar discussion of Hegel, from a different point of view, can be found in Z. A. Pelczynski's introduction to *Hegel's Political Writings* (1964): Hegel as essentially the protagonist of 'radical, rational reform from above'.
41. The phrase originates in Hobbes' *Leviathan* (1651), Part I, Chapter 4:
42. Knox, pp. 122–3.

tions as an elementary way of compensating for the newly unleashed individualism of bourgeois society: they (the guilds, etc.) must be made to hold society together and effect a basic reconciliation of private interests among themselves. In this way they will prepare the way for the profounder unity which the state will realize between the private and public spheres.

The main purpose of Hegel's work is to explain how, on this basis, the state can overcome the manifold contradictions of 'civil society'. The task of a modern state, in this sense, must be to restore the ethic and the organic wholeness of the antique *polis* – where the individual was profoundly 'integrated' into the community – and to do this without sacrificing the principle of subjective freedom (a category unknown to the ancient Greeks, brought into the world by the Reformed Christianity of the sixteenth century). Hegel's ambition is to find a new mode of unity which will recompose the fragments of modern society. Such fragmentation assumes a dual form. On the one hand there is the separation of private interests from each other; on the other, the private interest of *each* is constantly opposed to the interest of *all the others* together, in such a way that a general separation between private interests and 'the public interest' takes place. These are two faces of the same problem. The internal divisions of the social order emerge finally as a division between 'civil society' and 'political society', or between society and the state.

It may help the reader appreciate this distinction to refer back to John Locke's *Second Treatise of Civil Government* (1690). There Locke maintains that the mutual conflicts of private interests make necessary some appeal to an 'impartial judge', located in the institution of 'civil government' (as distinct from 'natural society'). But this civil government must also serve to *guarantee* the 'property and freedom' of private individuals, and so to perpetuate the fragmentation of the underlying economic society which Locke called 'natural society', and which Hegel and Marx call *die bürgerliche Gesellschaft*, civil or bourgeois society.

Hegel obviously disagrees with Locke. As Marx says, 'The deeper truth here is that Hegel experiences the separation of the state [i.e. Locke's 'civil government'] from civil society as a *contradiction*.'[43] *The Philosophy of Right* contains a resolute attack on Locke's type of contractualist and natural-right theory. Hegel reproaches this tradition above all with perceiving the

43. Below, p. 141.

state as a *means* to an end, the means of guaranteeing private rights. It was, in his view, unable to grasp the fact that the state (the 'public interest', the *universal* properly so called) was no mere means, but rather the *end*.

However, Hegel's solution does not really overcome the separation of 'civil society' from 'political society' either. His formula for reconciling the two was of course inspired by the general method outlined above. He again turns the universal into a substance, a subject sufficient unto itself, and makes it the demiurge of reality. This implies that for him movement does not proceed *from* the family and civil society *towards* the state, but comes from the state towards society – comes from the universal Idea, which Hegel depicts as having three main internal 'moments' (the three powers of the state): monarchical power, the power of government and the power of legislation. Thus, all that seems to be a necessary condition of the state (like the family and civil society) is actually an effect or result of its self-development. It follows, as Marx notes at the beginning of the *Critique*, that while in reality 'the family and civil society are the preconditions of the state; they are the true agents ... in speculative philosophy it is the reverse. When the idea is subjectivized the real subjects – civil society, the family, "circumstances, caprice, etc." – are all transformed into *unreal*, objective moments of the Idea referring to different things.' In reality it is the family and civil society which make themselves into the state. Marx continues:

They are the driving force. According to Hegel, however, they are *produced* by the real Idea; it is not the course of their own life that joins them together to comprise the state, but the life of the Idea which has distinguished them from itself... In other words the political state cannot exist without the natural basis of the family and the artificial basis of civil society. These are its *sine qua non*; and yet the condition is posited as the conditioned, the determinator as the determined, the producer as the product.[44]

We return here to Marx's main methodological critique of Hegel. But what is truly original in the second part of the *Critique* is that, pursuing his analysis of Hegel farther along these lines, Marx ends by exposing a radically new level of problem altogether. The Hegelian philosophy is upside-down; it inverts reality, making predicates into subjects and real subjects into

44. Below, pp. 62–3.

predicates. Certainly, but, Marx adds, the inversion does *not* originate in Hegel's philosophy itself. The mystification does not primarily concern the way in which this philosophy reflects reality, but *reality* itself.

In other words, what is 'upside-down' is not simply Hegel's image of reality, but the very reality it tries to reflect. 'This *uncritical mysticism* is the key both to the riddle of modern constitutions . . . and also to the mystery of the Hegelian philosophy, above all the *Philosophy of Right*', states Marx. He stresses, 'This point of view is certainly abstract, but the abstraction is that of the political state as Hegel has presented it. It is also atomistic, but its atomism is that of society itself. The "point of view" cannot be concrete when its *object* is "abstract".' And so, 'Hegel should not be blamed for describing the essence of the modern state as it is, but for identifying what is with the *essence of the State*.'[45] In other words, in describing the existing state of affairs, he connives with and repeats its inverted logic, instead of achieving a critical domination of it.

From this insight there follows a radically new analysis. It is no longer accurate to say only that the *concept* of the state Hegel offers us is a hypostatized abstraction; the point becomes that the modern state, the political state, is itself a hypostatized abstraction. The separation of the state from the body of society, or (as Marx writes) 'The abstraction of the *state as such* . . . was not created until modern times. The abstraction of the *political state* is a modern product.'[46]

'Abstraction' here means above all separation, estrangement. Marx's thesis is that the political state, the 'state as such', is a modern product because the whole phenomenon of the detachment of state from society (of politics from economics, of 'public' from 'private') is itself modern. In ancient Greece the state and the community were identified within the *polis*: there was a substantial unity between people and state. The 'common interest', 'public affairs', etc., coincided with the content of the citizens' real lives, and the citizens participated directly in the city's decisions ('direct democracy'). There was no separation of public from private. Indeed, the individual was so integrated into the community that the concept of 'freedom' in the modern sense (the freedom of private individualism) was quite unknown. The individual was 'free' only to the extent to which he was a member

45. Below, pp. 127, 145 and 149.   46. Below, p. 90.

of a free community. In medieval times there was if possible even
less separation of state from society, of political from economic
life. The medieval spirit could be expressed, Marx says, as one
where 'the classes of civil society were identical with the Estates
in the political sense, because civil society was political society;
because the organic principle of civil society was the principle of
the State'.[47] Politics adhered so closely to the economic structure
that socio-economic distinctions (serf and lord) were also political
distinctions (subject and sovereign). In the Middle Ages '*principality* or *sovereignty* functioned as a *particular* Estate which
enjoyed certain privileges but was equally impeded by the privileges of other Estates'.[48] It was impossible therefore that there
should have been a separate sphere of 'public' rights at that time.

The modern situation is utterly different. In modern 'civil
society' the individual appears as liberated from all social ties. He
is integrated neither into a citizen community, as in ancient times,
nor into a particular corporate community (for example a trade
guild), as in medieval times. In 'civil society' – which for Hegel as
for Adam Smith and Ricardo was a 'market society' of producers
– individuals are divided from and independent of each other.
Under such conditions, just as each person is independent of all
others, so does the real nexus of mutual dependence (the bond of
social unity) become in turn independent of all individuals. This
common interest, or 'universal' interest, renders itself independent of all the interested parties and assumes a separate
existence; and such social unity established in separation from its
members is, precisely, the hypostatized modern state.

The analysis hinges upon the simultaneity of these two fundamental divisions: the estrangement of individuals from each other,
or privacy within society, and the more general estrangement of
public from private, or of the state from society. The two processes
require each other. They are seen in the *Critique*, then even more
clearly in *The Jewish Question*, as having culminated in the
French Revolution, the revolution which established juridical and
political equality only upon the basis of a new and even deeper
real inequality. 'The *constitution* of the *political state*', writes
Marx in *The Jewish Question*, 'and the dissolution of civil society
into independent *individuals* – who are related by *law* just as men
in the estates and guilds were related by *privilege* – are achieved
in *one and the same act*.'[49]

47. Below, p. 137.   48. Below, p. 138.   49. Below, p. 233.

'It was a definite advance in history,' he insists in the *Critique*, 'when the Estates were transformed into social classes so that, just as the Christians are equal in heaven though unequal on earth, the individual members of the people became *equal* in the heaven of their political world, though unequal in their earthly existence in *society*.' The transformation was carried through by the French Revolution, through which the '*class distinctions* in civil society became merely *social* differences in private life of no significance in political life. This accomplished the separation of political life and civil society.'[50]

Heaven and earth, the heavenly community and the earthly one: in the first all are equal, in the second unequal – in one all united, in the other all estranged from each other. Thus we find, already formulated in the *Critique*, the celebrated antithesis central to *The Jewish Question*, the contrast between 'political society' as a spiritual or heavenly community and 'civil society' as society fragmented into private interests competing against each other. The moment of unity or community has to be *abstract* (the state) because in the real, fragmented society a common or general interest can only arise by dissociation from all the contending private interests. But on the other hand, since the resultant general interest *is* formal in nature and obtained by abstracting from reality, the basis and content of such a 'political society' inevitably remains civil society with all its economic divisions. Beneath the abstract society (the state), real estrangement and unsociability persist.

In both the *Critique* and *The Jewish Question* we find this double-edged process analysed in the terms Marx first used to criticize the Hegelian dialectic. And in both analyses we are led to see a process comprising 'uncritical idealism' at work alongside 'equally uncritical positivism', an 'abstract spiritualism' forming the counterpart to a 'crass materialism'.

The 'uncritical idealism' arises from the fact that, in order to attain the universal equality of a 'common interest', society is compelled to *abstract* from its real divisions and deny them value and significance. Civil society, claims Marx, can acquire political meaning and efficacy only by an act of 'thoroughgoing transubstantiation', an act by which 'civil society must completely renounce itself as civil society, as a *private class* and must instead assert the validity of a part of its being which not only has nothing

50. Below, p. 146.

in common with, but is directly opposed to, its real civil existence'.[51] The contrary 'crass materialism' arises from the fact that, just because the 'general interest' has been reached by neglecting or transcending genuine interests, the latter are bound to persist as its true content – as the unequal economic reality now sanctioned or legitimized by the state. One obtains man as an equal of other men, man as a member of his species and of the human community, only by ignoring man as he is in really existing society and treating him as the citizen of an ethereal community. One obtains the *citizen* only by abstracting from the *bourgeois*. The difference between the two, says Marx in *The Jewish Question*, 'is the difference between the tradesman and the citizen, between the day-labourer and the citizen, between the landowner and the citizen, between the *living individual* and the *citizen*'. On the other hand, once the bourgeois has been negated and made a citizen the process works the other way: that is, it turns out that 'political life declares itself to be a mere *means*, whose goal is the life of civil society'. Indeed, 'the relationship of the political state to civil society is just as spiritual as the relationship of heaven to earth. The state stands in the same opposition to civil society and overcomes it in the same way as religion overcomes the restrictions of the profane world, i.e. it has to acknowledge it again, re-instate it and allow itself to be dominated by it.'[52] The political idealism of the hypostatized state serves only to secure and fix the crass materialism of civil society.

The *Critique* goes on to develop this argument that the modern representative state acts as guarantor of private property, with reference to one particular form of property: landed property regulated by the law of primogeniture (which Hegel sees as essential to the state). *The Jewish Question*, on the other hand, considers the argument in relation to private property in general (both personal and real) and also to the 'Declaration of the Rights of Man' and the principal articles of the constitutions produced during the course of the French Revolution. However, both texts arrive at the same conclusion: that the political constitution of modern representative states is in reality the 'constitution of private property'. Marx sees this formula as summing up the whole inverted logic of modern society. It signifies that the universal, the 'general interest' of the community at large, not only does not unite men together effectively but actually sanctifies and legiti-

51. Below, p. 143.   52. Below, pp. 220–21 and 231.

mizes their disunity. In the name of a universal principle (the obligatory aspect of 'law' as expression of a general or social will) it consecrates private property, or the right of individuals to pursue their own exclusive interests independently of, and sometimes *against*, society itself.

Paradox reigns, therefore: the general will is invoked in order to confer absolute value on individual caprice; society is invoked in order to render asocial interests sacred and intangible; the cause of equality among men is defended, so that the cause of inequality among them (private property) can be acknowledged as fundamental and absolute. Everything is upside down. And, as Marx emphasizes in the section of the *Critique* dealing with primogeniture, this reversal is found in reality itself, before it comes to be reflected in philosophy.

Independent private capital, i.e. abstract private property and the *private person* corresponding to it, are the logical apex of the political state. Political 'independence' is interpreted to mean 'independent private property' and the 'person corresponding to that independent private property'. . . The *political qualifications* of the hereditary landowner are the political qualifications of his estate, qualifications inherent in the estate itself. Thus political qualifications appear here as the *property of landed property*, as something directly arising from the *purely physical earth* (nature) . . . Private property has become the *subject* of will; the will survives only as the *predicate* of private property.[53]

Again, Marx returns to the form of his attack on Hegel's logical method. This time, however, what it expresses is the real domination of private property over modern society. Property ought to be a manifestation, an attribute, of man, but becomes the subject; man ought to be the real subject, but becomes the property of private property. Here we find the subject–predicate inversion and, simultaneously, the formulation through which Marx begins to delineate the phenomenon of *fetishism* or alienation. The social side of human beings appears as a characteristic or property of things; on the other hand, things appear to be endowed with social or human attributes. This is in embryo the argument which Marx will develop later in *Capital* as 'the fetishism of commodities'. In both places – the analysis of the modern State and the analysis of modern commodity-production – it is not simply the theories of Hegel and the economists which

53. Below, pp. 168, 173 and 175.

are upside down, but reality itself. In both places Marx does not
confine himself to criticism of Hegel's 'logical mysticism' or of
the 'Divine Trinity' of political economy (capital, land and labour)
but goes on to explain the fetishism of thought with reference to
the fetishism or mysticism built into social reality. *Capital* defines
a commodity (which 'appears at first sight an extremely obvious,
trivial thing') as being in reality 'a very strange thing, abounding
in metaphysical subtleties and theological niceties', and goes on
to employ phrases like 'the mystical character of the commodity',
or 'the whole mystery of commodities, all the magic and necro-
mancy that surrounds the products of labour on the basis of
commodity production'. Marx makes it clear that the 'veil' is
not added by bourgeois interpreters of 'the social life-process, i.e.
the process of material production', but belongs to this process,
which therefore *appears* to political economy as what it really is.[54]

Talking of the relationship between civil and political society
we saw how society must 'abstract from itself', must set itself
apart from its real divisions in order to attain the plane of common
interest or equality. To get man as an equal of other men, one has
to ignore him as he really exists in society. Expressions like 'society
must abstract from itself' may well have seemed metaphors to the
reader. But what Marx has in mind is a process of *real abstraction*,
something which actually goes on in reality itself. That is, a
process wholly analogous to the one which he describes in
Capital as underlying the theory of value – the process by which
useful or concrete work is transformed into the abstraction of
'equal or abstract human labour', and 'use value' is transformed
into the abstraction of 'exchange value'. This is not a generalizing
operation performed by thinkers, but something occurring within
the machinery of the social order, in reality. 'Men do not therefore
bring the products of their labour into relation with each other as
values,' he writes there, 'because they see these objects merely as
the material integuments of homogeneous human labour. The
reverse is true: by equating their different products to each other
in exchange as values, they equate their different kinds of labour
as human labour. They do this without being aware of it.'[55] To
the separation between public and private, between society and
the individual (analysed in the *Critique*) there corresponds the
economic separation between individual labour and social labour.

54. *Capital*, Vol. 1, pp. 71, 76 and 80 (translation modified).
55. *Capital*, Vol. 1, p. 74 (translation modified).

Social labour too must exist in its own right, must become 'abstract labour' set over against concrete, individual work. The latter is represented in Marx's economic analysis by 'use value' and the former by the objectified 'value' of commodities.

The process is always the same. Whether the argument deals with fetishism and alienation, or with Hegel's mystifying logic, it hinges upon the hypostatizing, the reifying, of abstractions and the consequent inversion of subject and predicate. A chapter Marx added to the first edition of *Capital* while it was being printed, 'Die Wertform' – revised and incorporated, in subsequent editions, in Chapter One, as the section on 'The Form of Value' – repeats the argument once more in its analysis of the value relationship of commodities:

> Within the value relation and the expression of value contained in it the abstract universal is not a property of the concrete, the sensuous-actual; on the contrary, the sensuous-actual is a mere hypostasis or determinate form of realization of the abstract universal. *Tailors' work*, which is to be found for example in the *equivalent coat*, does not have, within the expression of value of cloth, the *universal property* of also being human labour. It is the other way round. Its *essence* is *being human labour*, and being tailors' work is a *hypostasis* or *determinate form of realization of that essence*. This *quid pro quo* is inevitable, because the labour represented in the product of labour is only *value creating* in so far as it is undifferentiated human labour; so that the labour objectified in the value of one product is in no way distinguished from the labour objectified in another product.

And Marx concludes:

> This *inversion*, whereby the sensuous-concrete only figures as a hypostasis of the abstract-universal, rather than the abstract-universal as a property of the concrete, characterizes the expression of value. At the same time it is this inversion which makes it difficult to understand the expression of value. If I say: Roman law and German law are both systems of law, then that is obvious. But if I say: *Law*, this abstraction, is *realized* in Roman law and in German law, these concrete systems of law, then the relationship is mystical.[56]

The sense of the argument could hardly be clearer. The abstract universal which ought to be a quality or attribute of the concrete world becomes the subject; while the real subject, the concrete world, becomes a mere 'phenomenal form' of the former. This is,

56. K. Marx, 'Die Wertform', in Marx–Engels, *Kleine Ökonomische Schriften*, Berlin, 1955, p. 271.

at one and the same time, the inversion ascribed to Hegel's philosophy in the *Postface* to the 1873 edition of *Capital* and the inverted real relationship which determines the exchange value of commodities.

At this point, the full importance of the *Critique of Hegel's Doctrine of the State* becomes plain. The criticism of Hegel in that work is – as we saw – the key to Marx's subsequent criticism of the bourgeois economists. It is no less vital to the understanding of his views on the modern representative state. And it is the prelude to all his later studies, up to and including his famous analysis of the fetishism of commodities and capital. The question following on these observations is an obvious one: given that most contemporary Marxism has dismissed the *Critique* without serious consideration, what can be the level of its comprehension of even the first few pages of *Capital*? Of, that is, the sections on the 'relative' and 'equivalent' forms of value (pp. 35–60)?

Unfortunately it is not possible to pursue this argument further here. Before going on to consider the *Economic and Philosophical Manuscripts*, however, it is perhaps worth examining one of the captious objections traditionally levelled at the *Critique*. As well as accusing it of being unduly subject to Feuerbach's influence, critics have often insisted that in the *Critique* Marx figures merely as a protagonist of political 'democracy'. It is quite true that in his remarks on Hegel's theory of monarchy Marx explicitly uses this concept. He writes:

Hegel proceeds from the state and conceives of man as the subjectivized state; democracy proceeds from man and conceives of the state as objectified man. Just as religion does not make man, but rather man makes religion, so the constitution does not make the people, but the people make the constitution ... Democracy is the *essence of all political constitutions*, socialized man as a *particular* political constitution; it is related to other forms of constitution as a genus to its various species ... [57]

The few Marxist scholars who have bothered to study the *Critique* have interpreted these statements somewhat oddly. Given that the work as a whole contains a pronounced critique of the separation between 'political society' and 'civil society' and states unequivocally the relationship between the representative state and private property, it is scarcely possible to avoid

57. Below, pp. 87–8.

perceiving that Marx goes well beyond the intellectual bounds of liberal constitutionalism. Auguste Cornu, for instance, concedes that 'through his *Critique of Hegel's Doctrine of the State,* which helped him gain a clearer idea of the relationships between the political State and civil society, Marx arrived at a new world-view, one no longer corresponding to the class interests of the bourgeoisie but rather to those of the proletariat'.[58]

Yet even after recognizing facts like this, Cornu and other critics have tended to reverse their final judgement, and to conclude that after all the Marx of the *Critique* is simply a bourgeois radical. Cornu goes on to say, in fact, 'This criticism did not take Marx to communism, however, but to a still very indeterminate conception of democracy,' with the result that 'the reforms which he favours, like abolition of the monarchy and of representation by estates, or the introduction of universal suffrage, are still not substantially distinct from the reforms sought by bourgeois democracy'. The confusion is obvious. Cornu is repeating the old mistake – a mistake with deep roots in one sort of Marxist tradition – to the effect that 'democracy' and bourgeois democracy are the same thing, as if the latter could really be identified with 'democracy' *tout court.* From an apparently opposite ideological point of view, therefore, he reiterates the idea found in every bourgeois intellectual's head – that 'democracy' is parliamentary government, the division of powers, state-guaranteed equality before the law and so on.

Marx does indeed use the term 'democracy'. But the sense he gives it is almost the contrary of the one Cornu attributes to him. His meaning of the word is rather that found in the Enlightenment tradition, and as used by some leaders of the French Revolution (Marx had studied the French Revolution most intensively before writing the *Critique*). It is the sense to be found, for example, in Montesquieu and – above all – Rousseau, where it signifies the organic community typified by the city-states of Antiquity (communities not yet split into 'civil society' versus 'political society'). So true is this that Marx not only distinguishes *between* 'democracy' and the 'political republic' (which is 'democracy within the abstract form of the state') but goes on to emphasize that democracy in this sense implies *the disappearance of the state* altogether. 'In modern times,' he writes, 'the French have understood this to mean that the *political state disappears*

58. A. Cornu, op. cit., p. 433.

in a true democracy.'[59] In other words, what is really understood by democracy here is the same as, many years later, Marx was to rediscover in the actions of the Paris Commune of 1871.

Hence where Cornu imagines that Marx is demanding bourgeois reforms like universal suffrage, he is in fact formulating a critical analysis of parliamentarism and of the modern representative principle itself. He comments on Hegel's paragraph 309:

> The deputies of civil society are constituted into an 'assembly' and only in this assembly does the *political existence and will* of civil society become *real*. The separation of the political state from civil society takes the form of a separation of the deputies from their electors. Society simply deputes elements of itself to become its political existence.

Then he continues:

> There is a twofold contradiction: (1) A *formal* contradiction. The deputies of civil society are a society which is not connected to its electors by any 'instruction' or commission. They have a formal authorization but as soon as this becomes *real* they *cease* to be *authorized*. They should be *deputies* but they are *not*. (2) A *material* contradiction. In respect to actual interests . . . Here we find the converse. They have authority as the representatives of *public* affairs, whereas in reality they represent *particular* interests.[60]

At this point one sees how Marx's critique of the separation between state and civil society is carried to its logical (and extreme) conclusion. Even from a formal point of view, the representative principle of the modern state is shown to be a fundamental contradiction in terms. In so far as parliamentary deputies are elected by the people, it is thereby recognized that the source of 'sovereignty' or power belongs in the popular mass itself. It is admitted that delegates 'draw their authority' from the latter – and so can be no more than people's representatives, bound by instructions or by the 'mandate' of their electors. Yet no sooner has the election taken place and the deputies been 'sworn in' than this principle is up-ended: they are no longer 'mere delegates', mere servants, but *independent* of their electors. Their assembly, parliament, no longer appears as an emanation of society but as society itself – as the real society outside which there remains nothing but a formless aggregate, an inchoate mass of private wishes.

It is hard to avoid looking forward at this point to Marx's later

59. Below, p. 88.   60. Below, pp. 193–4.

essay *The Civil War in France* (1871). The 'commissioning' of which Marx speaks in the *Critique*, contrasting it to the principle of parliamentary representation, is the procedure which was to be observed by the Commune of Paris during its two months of power. There, Marx says in *The Civil War*, 'each delegate was at any time revocable and bound by the *mandat impératif* (formal instructions) of his constituents'. In a passage which reads like an extended comment upon point 2 cited above, Marx continues: 'Instead of deciding once in three or six years which member of the ruling class was to misrepresent the people in parliament, universal suffrage was to serve the people, constituted in Communes, as individual suffrage serves every other employer in the search for the workmen and managers in his business.'[61]

Almost thirty years later, the argument of 1871 clearly recalls that of 1843. What Marx says in *The Civil War* about the way in which the Commune used universal suffrage to choose delegates should be compared to its almost perfect pendant in the *Critique*. Discussing paragraph 308 of the *Philosophy of Right*, where Hegel had posed the alternative that either representation has to employ 'deputies' or else 'all as individuals' would have to participate in the decision of all public affairs, Marx objects that the choice is a false one. In fact:

Either the political state is separated from civil society; in that event it is not possible for *all as individuals* to take part in the legislature. The political state leads an existence *divorced* from civil society . . . the fact that civil society takes part in the political state through its *deputies* is the expression of the separation and of the merely dualistic unity . . . Alternatively, civil society is the *real* political society. If so, it is senseless to insist on a requirement which stems from the conception of the political state as something existing apart from civil society . . . [for here] the *legislature* entirely ceases to be important as a *representative* body. The legislature is representative only in the sense that *every* function is representative. For example, a cobbler is my representative in so far as he satisfies a social need . . . In this sense he is a representative not by virtue of another thing which he represents but by virtue of what he *is* and *does*.[62]

What Marx suggests is that *either* there is a separation of state from civil society, and so a division between governors and

61. K. Marx, 'The Civil War in France', in *The First International and After*, The Pelican Marx Library, 1974, p. 210.
62. Below, pp. 189–90.

governed (deputies and electors, parliament and the body of
society) which represents the culmination of the class division
within civil society; *or else* the separation does not exist because
society is an organism of solidary and homogeneous interests, and
the distinct 'political' sphere of the 'general interest' vanishes
along with the division between governors and governed. This
means that politics becomes *the administration of things*, or simply
another branch of social production. And it would no longer be
true that 'all individuals as single individuals' would have to
participate in all of this activity; rather, some individuals would,
as expressions of and on behalf of the social totality, just as
happens with other productive activities (for example, the cobbler)
necessary to society.

It is wholly appropriate that this should be the conclusion of
Marx's argument in the *Critique*: the suppression of politics and
the extinction of the state. In the context of the separation between state and society, the progressive tendency of society – the
'efforts of *civil society* to transform itself' – becomes necessarily a
wish to 'force its way into the *legislature en masse*, or even *in toto*'.
Marx goes on to state:

It is therefore self-evident that the vote must constitute the chief
political interest of real civil society. Only when civil society has
achieved *unrestricted* active and passive *suffrage* has it *really* raised
itself to the point of abstraction from itself, to the *political* existence
which constitutes its true, universal, essential existence. But the perfection of this abstraction is also its transcendence [*Aufhebung*]. By
really establishing its *political* existence as its authentic existence, civil
society ensures that its civil existence is *inessential* in so far as it is
distinct from its political existence. And with the demise of the one, the
other, its opposite, collapses also. Therefore, *electoral reform* in the
abstract political state is the equivalent to a demand for its *dissolution*
[*Auflösung*] and this in turn implies the *dissolution of civil society*.[63]

Here is a clearly formulated vision of the disappearance of both
'state' and 'civil society'. But not in the sense of Cornu's interpretation, which amounts to saying that all this follows from
universal suffrage alone. Marx's conception is rather that the
drive of modern society towards full suffrage and electoral reform
is one expression of the tendency towards overcoming the separation between state and society (though an indirect one, since it

63. Below, p. 191.

occurs in terms offered by the separation itself) and so towards the dissolution of the state.

It is a fact that (as critics have held) when Marx wrote the *Critique of Hegel's Doctrine of the State* he had not yet arrived at theoretical communism. He arrived at this goal *in the course of writing it.* The text which followed the *Critique* almost immediately (written at most a few weeks later) was Marx's *Introduction* to it, soon published separately. And it invokes the proletariat as both subject and protagonist of imminent revolution.

At this point in his evolution, what strikes us most forcibly is that while Marx has not yet outlined his later materialist conception of history he already possesses a very mature theory of politics and the state. The *Critique*, after all, contains a clear statement of the dependence of the state upon society, a critical analysis of parliamentarism accompanied by a counter-theory of popular delegation, and a perspective showing the need for ultimate suppression of the state itself. Politically speaking, mature Marxism would have relatively little to add to this.

How true this is may be seen by a comparison with, for example, Lenin's *State and Revolution* (1917). As regards the general *principles* of its strictly political arguments (criticism of parliamentary representation, theory of mandation, delegates subject to recall at all times, disappearance of the state, etc.) it advances little beyond the ideas set out in the *Critique*. Indeed, something of the latter's profundity is lost in it. Like Engels, Lenin tends to gloss over one vital part of the theory of the state developed in the *Critique* (and also in its marvellous continuation, *The Jewish Question*). Marx's conception was that the state 'as such' is properly speaking only the modern state, since it is only under modern conditions that the detachment of state from society occurs: only then does the state come to exist over and above society, as a kind of external body dominating it. Engels and Lenin, however, tend noticeably to attribute such characteristics to the state in general. They fail to grasp fully the complex mechanism whereby the state is *really abstracted* from society – and hence the whole organic, objective process which produces their separation from one another. Because of this they do not perceive the intimate connection between such separation and the *particular* structures of modern society. The most obvious consequence of the confusion is their marked subjectivism and voluntarism, based on their conception of the state as a 'machine' knowingly, consciously formed by the ruling class in deliberate pursuit of its own interest.

The paradoxical fact that Marx's political theory pre-dated (at least in general outline) the development of Marxism proper shows plainly how much he owed to older traditions of revolutionary and democratic thought. He owed much, in particular, to Rousseau (to what extent he was conscious of the debt is another question). It is Rousseau to whom the critique of parliamentarism, the theory of popular delegacy and even the idea of the state's disappearance can all be traced back. This implies in turn that the true *originality* of Marxism must be sought rather in the field of social and economic analysis than in political theory. Even in the theory of the state, for example, the really new and decisive contribution of Marxism was to be its account of the economic basis for the rise of the state and (consequently) of the economic conditions needed for its liquidation. And this of course proceeds beyond the limits of strictly political theory.

This interpretation may well give rise to some perplexity. However, it does not seem to me too far removed in spirit from the argument put forward by Marx himself in August 1844 in his short essay *Critical Notes on the Article 'The King of Prussia and Social Reform'*. Here he stated for the first time the necessity for a socialist revolution, even though essentially social in content, to have a political form: 'All revolution . . . is a political act,' and since 'without revolution socialism cannot be realized' it therefore 'requires this political act'. And it is in this writing – where Marx took the first steps towards a theory of the revolutionary political party – that he also characterizes political intelligence as the most essential requisite, the specific expression of bourgeois mentality: '*Political* understanding is just *political* understanding because its thought does not transcend the limits of politics. The sharper and livelier it is . . . the more completely it puts its faith in the *omnipotence* of the will; the blinder it is towards the *natural* and spiritual *limitations* of the will, the more incapable it becomes of discovering the real source of the evils of society.'[64] The 'classical period of political understanding', in this sense, was the French Revolution. Hence politics is the mode of apprehension of social problems most native to the bourgeois-spiritualistic mind. It is no surprise, this being so, that political theory 'as such' should have been perfected by a thinker like Rousseau.

64. Below, pp. 413 and 420.

IV

The prominence accorded the *Critique* so far should not be allowed to lead to the conclusion that it occupies a pre-eminent or specially privileged place in Marx's work as a whole (or even among his early writings). On the contrary, the conclusion reached in the previous section should serve to indicate that Marx's most *original* work began to emerge only with the *Economic and Philosophical Manuscripts* of 1844.

Yet it was necessary and desirable to emphasize the *Critique*'s importance. Of all Marx's texts dealing with politics, law and the state it is easily the most complex and – more to the point – the least read and the most misunderstood. It is also one of the most difficult of Marx's writings. However, clarification of its intention and mode of argument leads to much better understanding of both *The Jewish Question* and the *Introduction* – texts more widely read and acknowledged as important, and somewhat more accessible in style. More significant still, it is the *Critique* which connects Marx's view of the Hegelian dialectic to his later analyses of the modern state and its basis in private property. It demonstrates perhaps more clearly than anything else how his critical thought moved along a single line of development stretching from reflection on philosophical logic to a dissection of the form and content of bourgeois society. His discussion of subject–predicate inversion in Hegel's logic, his analysis of estrangement and alienation, and (finally) his critique of the fetishism of commodities and capital can all be seen as the progressive unfolding, as the ever-deepening grasp of a single problematic.

There is an obvious risk of over-emphasizing the factors of continuity in Marx's work inherent in this approach – that is, of neglecting the elements of novelty or discontinuity present in each single stage of its development. This could lead to failure to understand the very *process* by which Marx, slowly and laboriously, worked his way through towards his final understanding of modern society. It is perhaps also necessary, therefore, to forestall any such temptation by underlining again that Marxism's most specific terrain of development was the socio-economic one. The limitations of the early texts are constituted by this fact – in other words, by the *decisive* importance of Marx's own later advances in his mature economic writings, his ever more rigorous accounts of the theory of value and surplus value, of the rate of profit and so on.

Looked at in this light, the *Critique* and the other shorter writings associated with it constitute a final, near-definitive step in the general theory of law and the state, while the *Manuscripts* represent by contrast the first step forward in what was to be a long (and ultimately more important) intellectual voyage rich in discoveries. The very grandeur of the latter, *Capital* and the *Theories of Surplus Value*, was bound in the long run to make the first step appear somewhat irrelevant. But (however understandable) this judgement too is mistaken. The later work should not be allowed to obscure the real importance of the 1844 *Manuscripts*, and especially of their vital central portion – the chapter on 'Estranged Labour'.

In a fashion analogous to many discussions of the *Critique*, Marxist critics have often objected that the conception of alienation or estrangement in the *Manuscripts* is too directly modelled on Feuerbach's theory of religious alienation. The latter maintains that man objectifies his own 'essence' and separates it from himself, making it into a self-sufficient subject called 'God'; after which the product dominates the producer, the creature becomes the Creator and so on. In the *Economic and Philosophical Manuscripts* (it is claimed) Marx remains a prisoner of this schema, and gives us only an anthropological theory, a theory dealing with 'Man' in the abstract, man outside of and independent of his real socio-historical relationships. But the series of texts presented in this volume is itself sufficient to provide an initial reply to these objections. The references to the working class in the very first of Marx's articles in the *Deutsch–Französische Jahrbücher*; the historical and political themes tackled so boldly in *The Jewish Question*; above all, the *Critique*'s brilliant analysis of the differences between ancient, medieval and modern society – how can it be imagined that anybody so engrossed in this type of socio-historical analysis in 1843 could, only one year later, have relapsed into a merely 'anthropological' position?

As far as the Feuerbachian analysis of religious alienation is concerned, incidentally, it should be noted that Marx continued to make some use of the model it provides in his later work (without noticeably regressing into anthropology). He does so, for instance, in the chapter on 'The Fetishism of Commodities' in *Capital*. After pointing out how a 'definite social relation between men ... assumes here, for them, the fantastic form of a relation between things', he goes on to say: 'To find an analogy we must take flight into the misty realm of religion,' since it is in these regions, precisely, that 'the products of the human brain appear as autonomous figures endowed with a life of their own. . . . So it is in the world of commodities with the products of men's hands.'[65]

The charges brought against the *Manuscripts* by the upholders of 'dialectical materialism' (quite understandably vexed by a text treating problems about which 'dialectical materialism' has nothing to say) may be summed up in one hoary legend. According to it, Marx never employed the concept of alienation (*Entäusserung*) or estrangement (*Entfremdung*) again after the battle against the Left Hegelians was over: the idea simply vanishes from his mature work. E. Bottigelli, for example, recently gave a fresh lease of life to this view in his introduction to a French edition of the *Manuscripts*, and he is certainly not alone in his conviction. Not merely is criticism of this order incapable of grasping that for Marx the phenomenon of alienation or estrangement and that of fetishism are one and the same thing – and the analysis of fetishism or reification (*Versachlichung*, *Verdinglichung*) is, of course, dealt with at length in the three volumes of *Capital*. But even if one restricts oneself to the use of the actual terms 'alienation' and 'estrangement', the reader will find his only serious problem is to know which to choose among the hundreds of passages in the *Grundrisse* and the *Theories of Surplus Value* where they appear in key positions.

In the *Grundrisse* for example, discussing the sale and purchase of labour power, Marx points out how this exchange which seems at first glance to be one of equivalents is in reality a dialectical separation of labour from property. It amounts to 'appropriation of alien labour without exchange, without equivalent'. He goes on:

Production based on exchange value, on whose surface this free and equal exchange of equivalents proceeds . . . is at its base the exchange of *objectified labour* as exchange value for living labour as use value, or, to express this in another way, the relating of labour to its objective conditions – and hence to the objectivity created by itself – as alien property: alienation [*Entäusserung*] *of labour*.[66]

In the closing pages of the First Part of *Theories of Surplus Value* we find the following similar argument:

65. *Capital*, Vol. 1, p. 72 (translation modified).
66. *Grundrisse*, pp. 514–15.

Since living labour – through the exchange between capital and labourer – is incorporated in capital, and appears as an activity belonging to capital from the moment that the labour-process begins, all the productive powers of social labour appear as the productive powers of capital, just as the general social form of labour appears in money as the property of a thing. Thus the productive power of social labour and its special forms now appear as productive powers and forms of capital, of *materialized* [*vergegenständlicht*] labour, of the material conditions of labour – which, having assumed this independent form, are personified by the capitalist in relation to living labour. Here we have once more the perversion of the relationship, which we have already, in dealing with money, called *fetishism*.

A little farther on Marx adds;

Already in its simple form this relation is an inversion – personification of the thing and materialization [*Versachlichung*] of the person; for what distinguishes this form from all previous forms is that the capitalist does not rule over the labourer through any personal qualities he may have, but only in so far as he is 'capital'; his domination is only that of materialized [*vergegenständlicht*] labour over living labour, of the labourer's product over the labourer himself . . .

Then he concludes:

Capitalist production first develops on a large scale – tearing them away from the individual independent labourer – both the objective and subjective conditions of the labour-process, but it develops them as powers dominating the *individual labourer* and *extraneous* [*fremd*] to him.[67]

Statements like these demonstrate clearly the persistence of certain key terms and concepts formulated in the early writings: the 'inversion' or 'reversal' which turns the world upside down to give 'the personification of the thing and the materialization [*Versachlichung*] of persons'; the 'domination . . . of the labourer's product over the labourer himself' and the dominion of 'materialized [*vergegenständlicht*] labour over living labour'; and lastly, the dominion over men of all the forces and powers they themselves have created, which tower above them as entities alienated or estranged from them.

The same themes are at the heart of the *Economic and Philosophical Manuscripts*. In estranged labour – which Marx already understands as *wage-labour*, the work which yields commodities

67. *Theories of Surplus Value*, Part I, London, 1969, pp. 389–90 and 392.

and capital – the labourer objectifies and alienates his own 'essence'. 'The object that labour produces, its product, confronts it as an alien being, as a power independent of the producer,' because the product of estranged or wage-labour is not a mere natural object modified and adapted to his own needs by man (a 'use-value'). It is rather the objectification of human subjectivity itself, of the worker's subjectivity which in labour separates itself from the worker and is incorporated in the material object or use-value (the 'body' or material 'envelope' of the commodity). In this form it then confronts the worker as objectified labour, the 'spectral objectivity' which Marx refers to in *Capital*. As he writes in the *Grundrisse*, '. . . objectified labour is, in this process, at the same time posited as the worker's *non-objectivity*, as the objectivity of a subjectivity antithetical to the worker, as *property* of a will alien to him . . .'[68]

In the opening pages of the *Manuscripts* we find Marx well on the way to understanding something which his critics and interpreters would still be struggling with a century later. That is, that the object produced by estranged wage-labour is not simply a material thing but the objectification of the worker's subjectivity, of his labour-power. This means, as Marx explains in *Theories of Surplus Value*, that 'When we speak of the commodity as a materialization of labour – in the sense of its exchange-value – this itself is only an imaginary, that is to say, a purely social mode of existence of the commodity which has nothing to do with its corporeal reality . . .'[69] He reiterates the point in *Capital*:

The objectivity of commodities as values differs from Dame Quickly in the sense that 'a man knows not where to have it'. Not an atom of matter enters into the objectivity of commodities as values; in this it is the direct opposite of the coarsely sensuous objectivity of commodities as physical objects. We may twist and turn a single commodity as we wish; it remains impossible to grasp it as a thing possessing value. However, let us remember that commodities only possess an objective character as values in so far as they are all expressions of an identical social substance, human labour.[70]

But the *Manuscripts* also go well beyond this recognition that in estranged labour men alienate their own 'essence' or 'nature'. They have left behind in substance, if not yet in form, the characteristic Feuerbachian position referred to in the sixth of Marx's

68. *Grundrisse*, p. 512.   69. *Theories of Surplus Value*, Part I, p. 171.
70. *Capital*, Vol. 1, p. 47 (translation modified).

Theses on Feuerbach: 'The human essence ... can be compre-hended only as "genus", as an internal, dumb generality which *naturally* unites the many individuals.'[71] Possibly the most original single aspect of the *Manuscripts* is Marx's attempt to define what this human 'essence' or 'human nature' actually consists of, and to show that it has nothing in common with the essence of previous metaphysical philosophies.

In his *Studies on Marx and Hegel* (1969) Jean Hyppolite claims to detect the survival of 'natural law' among the distinctive themes of the *Manuscripts* – the persisting echo, as it were, of a position tied to theories of the Natural Rights of man. But this simply reveals his own incomplete understanding of Marx's evolution. To avoid such an error, for instance, it should have been enough to read through *The Jewish Question*. In reality the *Manuscripts* define 'human nature' in a radically different fashion: not as a 'nature' or 'essence' of the sort found in natural-right philosophy but as a *series of relationships*.

If the worker alienates or separates his subjectivity from him-self in the course of work, this happens because he is simul-taneously separated and divided both from the objective world of nature (his means of production and subsistence) and from the other men to whom his work-activity belongs. This means that Marx does *not* conceive of his subjectivity as a fixed essence or an 'internal, dumb generality', but as a function of his relationship with nature and with other men – a function of inter-human or social relationships. This is the key to the most fascinating aspect of the *Manuscripts*, and (more especially) of the chapter on 'Estranged Labour'. Their secret is that Marx envisages the process of estrangement as occurring in three directions or dimensions at the same time: (1) as the estrangement of the worker from the material, objective product of his work; (2) as the estrangement of his work-activity itself (he does not belong to himself at work, but to whoever he has sold his day's work-activity); (3) lastly, as estrangement from other men, that is from the owner of the means of production and of the use to which his labour-power is put. Marx writes in the *Manuscripts*:

We have considered the act of estrangement of practical human activity, of labour, from two aspects: (1) the relationship of the worker to the *product of labour* as an alien object that has power over him.

71. Below, p. 423.

This relationship is at the same time the relationship to the sensuous external world, to natural objects, as an alien world confronting him in hostile opposition. (2) The relationship of labour to the *act of production* within *labour*. This relationship is the relationship of the worker to his own activity as something which is alien and does not belong to him, activity as passivity [*Leiden*], power as impotence, procreation as emasculation, the worker's own physical and mental energy, his personal life – for what is life but activity? – as an activity directed against himself, which is independent of him and does not belong to him.[72]

The third aspect of estrangement, Marx adds a little farther on, is that 'an immediate consequence of man's estrangement from the product of his labour, his life activity, his species-being, is the estrangement of man from man. When man confronts himself he also confronts *other* men. What is true of man's relationship to his labour, to the product of his labour and to himself, is also true of his relationship to other men, and to the labour and the object of the labour of other men.'[73]

At first glance such formulations might appear a mere puzzle, a sophisticated word-game. In fact, they record one of the most important insights later to be amplified in *Capital*: that is, that wage-labour does not produce only commodities, but also produces and reproduces *itself* as a commodity. It produces and reproduces not only objects but also the *social relationships* of capitalism itself. This is hinted at in the *Manuscripts* at the beginning of the chapter on 'Estranged Labour', and we find it again much developed and enriched in Chapter 23 of the first volume of *Capital*, 'Simple Reproduction'. Here Marx comes to the conclusion that 'The capitalist process of production, therefore, seen as a total, connected process, i.e. a process of reproduction, produces not only commodities, not only surplus value, but it also produces and reproduces the capital-relation itself; on the one side the capitalist, on the other the wage-labourer.'[74]

The human subjectivity or 'essence' estranged by wage-labour, then, is no longer that of traditional metaphysics (Kant's 'transcendental ego', Hegel's *Logos*) but a function which mediates man's relationship both to nature and to his own kind. It is the 'mediating activity, the human, social act' of which Marx speaks in his notes on James Mill in 1844–5. It is the function which, after abstracting or separating itself from this simultaneous

72. Below, p. 327.   73. Below, pp. 329–30.
74. *Capital*, p. 578 (translation modified).

duality of relationships (man/nature, man/man), becomes transformed from a mere function into a self-sufficient subject, and assumes the character of an independent entity. It is transformed into *God*, or into *money*.

In 'value' or money the human essence is certainly estranged from man: man's subjectivity, his physical and intellectual energies, his work-capacity, are removed from him. But – this is the decisive insight of the *Manuscripts* – the 'essence' in question is clearly recognized to be no more than the functional relationships mediating man's working rapport with nature and with himself. His estrangement, consequently, is the estrangement or separation of *social relationships* from himself.

This argument again reproduces the general form we noted above, considering Marx's analysis of the modern representative state. The latter creates a separation between 'civil society' and the heavenly or abstract society of political equality. When real individuals are fragmented from one another and become estranged then their mediating function must in turn become independent of them: that is, their social relationships, the nexus of reciprocity which binds them together. Thus, there is an evident parallelism between the hypostasis of the state, of God, and of money.

'In this society of free competition,' writes Marx in the 1857 Introduction, 'the individual appears detached from the natural bonds etc. which in earlier historical periods make him the accessory of a definite and limited human conglomerate . . . Only in the eighteenth century, in "civil society", do the various forms of social connectedness confront the individual as a mere means towards his private purposes, as external necessity.'[75]

This is one of the high points of Marxist theory. The specific trait, the essential characteristic of modern bourgeois social relations, is that in them the social link presents itself to us as something *external*, that is as something separated (estranged) from the very individuals whose relationship it is. We live in society, within the web of social relationships; yet it is perfectly possible for social relationships to have no meaning at all for us (think of the question of unemployment, for example). The social relationship in general has become something independent of individuals, who in order to partake of that relationship have to carry out certain actions: selling their labour-power, finding

75. *Grundrisse*, pp. 83–4.

someone willing to employ them, and so on. This social relationship which has rendered itself independent of the members of society, and now counterposes itself to them *as* 'society', as something outside and above them, is distinguished and described for the first time in the *Manuscripts* as *money*. Money is the social bond transformed into ownership of things, the force of society petrified into an object.

This is the perspective in which the great analysis of money in the *Grundrisse* must be placed: an analysis condensed by Marx, at various points, in the following pregnant phrases: 'The individual carries his social power, as well as his bond with society, in his pocket.' 'Money is therefore the God among commodities. Since it is an individuated, tangible object, money may be randomly searched for, found, stolen, discovered; and thus general wealth may be tangibly brought into the possession of a particular individual.' 'Money thereby directly and simultaneously becomes the *real community* [*Gemeinwesen*], since it is the general substance of survival for all, and at the same time the social product of all. But as we have seen, in money the community [*Gemeinwesen*] is at the same time a mere abstraction, a mere external, accidental thing for the individual, and at the same time merely a means for his satisfaction as an isolated individual.' 'The special difficulty in grasping money in its fully developed character as money – a difficulty which political economy attempts to evade by forgetting now one, now another aspect, and by appealing to one aspect when confronted with another – is that a social relation, a definite relation between individuals, here appears as a metal, a stone, as a purely physical, external thing.'[76]

This analysis leads to a definition of capital as an estranged social relationship: estrangement means that it is incorporated in a stock of objects (raw materials, the means of production, etc.). It leads also to an understanding of commodities, and the sense in which the objectivity of their value is 'imaginary, that is to say purely social, having nothing at all to do with their corporeal reality' as use-values. In *Capital*, as we noticed, Marx insists that commodities acquire such reality only because they are 'expressions of one identical social substance, viz., human labour'.

What is implicit in these arguments of the *Manuscripts* is in fact the first premise of genuine 'historical materialism': that is, the discovery of the concept of *the social relations of production*. These

76. ibid., pp. 157, 221, 225–6, 239.

relations are constantly changing, because while producing objects men produce their own mutual relationships at the same time: while transforming nature, they also transform themselves. Hence Marx can affirm in the last of the *Manuscripts* that man's 'act of birth' is history, because man's 'being' is how he makes himself, how he 'becomes' historically. This statement alone, incidentally, indicates Marx's distance from Feuerbachian anthropology.

A pedantic Marxist critic might object to this that the words 'social relations of production' are not actually employed in the *Economic and Philosophical Manuscripts*. But if the words are not there, the concept is, though admittedly in a still tentative and half-obscured form. In the section entitled 'Private Property and Communism' Marx describes how 'man's relation to nature is directly his relation to man, and his relation to man is directly his relation to nature', and this should be placed alongside his subsequent remarks on industry: '*Industry* is the actual historical relationship of nature, and thus of natural science, to man . . . the history of *industry* and industry as it *objectively* exists is an *open* book of the *human faculties* and human *psychology* which can be sensuously apprehended.' That is, just as inter-human or social relationships are inconceivable apart from man's relationship to nature, so his relationship to nature (and hence industrial production) is inconceivable apart from men's social relationships among themselves.

The formulations of the *Manuscripts* are in this respect still involved and abstract. But they point forward clearly to the admirable definition of the social relations of production given, only a few years later, in *Wage-Labour and Capital* (1847–9):

In production, men not only act on nature, but also on one another. They produce only by cooperating in a certain way and mutually exchanging their activities. In order to produce, they enter into definite connections and relations with one another and only within these social connections and relations does their action on nature, does production, take place.[77]

Lucio Colletti

77. Marx–Engels, *Selected Works* in one volume, p. 80.

Critique of Hegel's Doctrine of the State
(§§261–313)[1]

[*The* Critique *was written during the months March to August 1843. In it Marx criticizes Hegel in two ways. Firstly, he criticizes the philosophical form of Hegel's work. He describes how Hegel inverts the real situation by deriving empirical institutions (the state, the family etc.) from the Idea. This method infuses social institutions with an uncritical mysticism. Secondly, he makes a detailed internal criticism of Hegel's arguments by means of textual analysis. He shows how Hegel's concern to depict the existing state and existing social institutions as 'rational' leads him into internal inconsistencies in his argument.*

Marx also develops his own historical account of the 'act of birth' of the state and its relationship to private property.

Both Hegel and Marx aimed at resolving the split between civil and political life, that is between man fighting for his individual interests and man as a citizen of the state. In Hegel's view this unity and synthesis is achieved by means of the sovereign, the bureaucracy as universal class and the Assembly of the Estates. The hereditary sovereign because he is independent of all political groups; the bureaucracy because it is paid by the state and its interests coincide with those of the state; and the Assembly of the Estates because it is a microcosm of political and civil society and can harmonize the conflicting interests of civil society.

Marx argues that Hegel has resolved the cleavage between the two spheres only in appearance. *In* reality *the basic division into the permanent war of individual interests on the one hand and the abstract, spurious unity of the state on the other still persists.*

Marx considers the bureaucracy is far from being a truly universal class. He calls instead for unrestricted suffrage to heal the schism in society. Not a small, closed fraction of society (the

1. These paragraphs are to be found in the section of Hegel's *Philosophy of Right* entitled 'The State'.

bureaucracy) but all humanity must play an active part in political
society. But when all become legislators, the state disappears.

*

This translation is based on the text printed in Marx–Engels
Werke (Berlin, 1970), Vol. I. The translator has been fortunate in
being able to consult two existing versions: the partial one by
Lloyd D. Easton and Kurt H. Guddat (Anchor Books, New York,
1967) and the more recent complete translation by Annette Jolin
and Joseph O'Malley (C.U.P., 1970). Thanks are due to Professor
T. M. Knox and the Clarendon Press for permission to reprint his
translation of the relevant sections of Hegel's Philosophy of Right.
In general Knox's text has been adhered to but changes have been
introduced where Marx's commentary made this desirable.

   Hegel's emphases (largely omitted by Knox) have been restored.
Marx's additional emphases in the Hegel text are printed in bold
type, his omissions are indicated by square brackets. Phrases in
square brackets represent additions by Knox or the present translator,
unless otherwise noted. Marx's own emphases have been slightly
reduced in quantity.]

Contents

§261. 'In contrast with the spheres of private rights and private
welfare (the family and civil society), the state is *on the one hand* an
external necessity and their higher authority; its nature is such that their
laws and interests are subordinate to it and dependent on it. *On the
other hand*, however, it is the end *immanent* within them, and its
strength lies in the unity of its own universal end and aim with the
particular interest of individuals, in the fact that individuals have *duties*
to the state in proportion as they have rights as members of it (see
§155).'

   The above paragraph informs us that *concrete freedom* consists
in the identity (supposedly two-sided) of the system of particular
interests (the family and civil society) and the system of the

general interest (the state). The relationship between these two spheres must now be defined more closely.

On the one hand, the state stands opposed to the sphere of the family and civil society[2] as an '*external* necessity', a power to which the 'laws and interests' of that sphere are 'subordinate' and on which they are 'dependent'. The fact that the state is an '*external* necessity' ranged against the family and civil society was implicit partly in the category of 'transition' [*Übergang*] and partly in their *conscious relationship* to the state. Their 'subordination' to the state is still wholly in accordance with this relationship of '*external* necessity'. However, what Hegel means by 'dependence' emerges from the following statement in the Remark to this Paragraph:

'It was Montesquieu above all who kept in sight both the thought of the *dependence* of laws – in particular, laws concerning the rights of persons – on the specific character of the state, and also the philosophic notion of always treating the part in its relation to the whole.'

Thus, Hegel speaks here of the *internal* dependence of the civil law etc., upon the state or its essential determination by it; at the same time, however, he includes this dependence within the relationship of '*external* necessity' and counterpoises it to that other relationship in which the family and civil society are related to the state as their '*immanent* end'.

The only meaning that can be given to 'external necessity' is that in the event of conflict the 'laws' and 'interests' of the family and society must give way to the 'laws' and 'interests' of the state; they must be subordinate to it, their existence depends on its existence, alternatively its will and its laws confront their will and their laws with the force of a necessity!

But Hegel makes no mention of empirical conflicts; he talks of the relationship of 'the *spheres* of private rights and private welfare, of the family and civil society' to the state; he is concerned with the *essential relationship* between these spheres themselves. Not only their 'interests', but also their 'laws', their 'essential determinations', are 'dependent' on the state and 'subordinate' to it. The attitude of the state towards their 'laws and interests' is that of a higher authority. The attitude of their 'interest' and

2. The term 'civil society' is used to designate the sphere of economic life, in which the individual's relations with others are governed by selfish needs and individual interests. Hence it is a sphere of conflict.

'law' towards the state is that of a 'subordinate'. They subsist in a condition of 'dependence' on the state. Precisely because 'subordination' and 'dependence' are *external* relationships, running counter to autonomous existence and limiting it, the relationship of the 'family' and 'civil society' to the state is one of *'external* necessity', a necessity which affects the internal essence of the thing. The very fact that 'the civil laws depend on the specific character of the state' and that they are modified in accordance with it is therefore subsumed under the relationship of *'external necessity'* just because 'civil society and the family' in their true, i.e. their autonomous and complete, development are the special 'spheres' which form the premises of the state. 'Subordination' and 'dependence' are terms that express an 'external', *forced*, specious identity and it is only fitting that Hegel should describe this as *'external necessity'*. With this 'subordination' and 'dependence' Hegel has further developed one side of the divided identity, namely the aspect of estrangement within the unity.

'... on the other hand, however, it [the state] is the end *immanent* within them, and its strength lies in the unity of its own **universal end and aim** with the **particular interests** of individuals, in the fact that individuals have *duties* to the state in proportion as they have rights as members of it.'

Thus Hegel presents us with an unresolved *antinomy. On the one hand* external necessity, *on the other* immanent end. The unity of the *universal end and aim* of the state and the *particular interests of individuals* lies in the supposed identity of their *duties* towards the state and their *rights* as members of it. (For example, the duty to respect property coincides with the right to own property.)

This identity is explained in the Remark to §261:

'*Duty* is primarily a relation *to something* which from my point of view is *substantive*, absolutely universal. A right, on the other hand, is simply the *embodiment* of this substance and thus is the *particular* aspect of it and enshrines my *particular* freedom. Hence at abstract levels, right and duty appear parcelled out on different sides or in different persons. In the state, as something ethical, as the interpenetration of the substantive and the particular, my obligation to what is substantive is at the same time the embodiment of my particular freedom. This means that in the state duty and right *are united in one and the same relation*.'

§262. 'The real Idea is mind, which, sundering itself into the two ideal spheres of its concept, family and civil society, enters upon *its finite phase*, but it does so only in order to rise above its ideality and become *explicit as infinite* real mind. It is therefore to these ideal spheres that the real Idea assigns the material of this its finite reality, viz. human beings as a *mass*, in such a way that the function assigned to any given individual is visibly *mediated* by circumstances, his caprice and his personal choice of his station in life.'

If we translate this sentence into prose we find:

The state's relations with the family and civil society are mediated by 'circumstances, caprice and the personal choice of a station in life'. Hence the state's rationality [*Staatsvernunft*] has no part in the sundering of the material of the state into the family and civil society. The state emerges from them in an unconscious and arbitrary manner. The family and civil society appear as the dark ground of nature from which the light of the state is born. By 'material of the state' we are to understand the functions of the state, namely the family and civil society in so far as they form parts of the state and participate as such in the state.

This development is remarkable in two respects.

(1) The family and civil society are conceived as *conceptual spheres* of the state, indeed as the spheres of its *finite phase*, as its *finite phase*. It is the state that is *sundered* into them and *presupposes* them. It *does* so 'in order to rise above its ideality and become explicit as *infinite real mind*'. 'It sunders itself in order to . . .' It '*therefore assigns* to these ideal spheres the material of its reality *in such a way that* this assignment etc. is *visibly* mediated'. The so-called 'real Idea' (mind as infinite and real) is represented as acting in accordance with a specific principle and with a specific intention. It divides into finite spheres and it does this 'in order to return to itself, to exist for itself', in such a way that it is just as it really is.

The logical, pantheistic mysticism emerges very clearly at this point.

The *real* relationship is 'that the assignment of the material of the state to any given individual is mediated by circumstances, his caprice and his personal choice of his station in life'. This fact, this *real relationship* is described by speculative philosophy as *appearance*, as *phenomenon*. These circumstances, this caprice and this personal choice of a station in life, this *real mediation*, are merely the *appearance of a mediation* which the real Idea performs on itself and which takes place behind the scenes. Reality is not deemed to be itself but another reality instead. The ordinary empirical world is not governed by its own mind but by a mind alien to it; by contrast the existence corresponding to the real Idea is not a reality generated out of itself, but is just the ordinary empirical world.

The Idea is subjectivized and the *real* relationship of the family and civil society to the state is conceived as their *inner, imaginary* activity. The family and civil society are the preconditions of the state; they are the true agents; but in speculative philosophy it is the reverse. When the Idea is subjectivized the real subjects – civil society, the family, 'circumstances, caprice etc.' – are all transformed into *unreal*, objective moments of the Idea referring to different things.

(2) As we have seen, the assignment of the material of the state 'to a given individual is mediated by circumstances, his caprice and his personal choice of a station in life'. However, the latter are not regarded as true, necessary and intrinsically self-justified; they are not *as such* deemed to be rational. If they are held to be rational it is only in the sense that, while they are regarded as furnishing an *illusory* mediation and while they are left just as they were, they nevertheless acquire the meaning of a determination of the Idea, of its result or product. The distinction lies not in the content but in the way it is regarded or *talked about*. It is a history with two aspects, one esoteric, the other exoteric. The content is relegated to the exoteric side. The interest of the esoteric is always directed towards the rediscovery of the history of the logical concept in the state. However, the actual development takes place in the exoteric sphere.

Rationally Hegel's statements can only mean:

The family and civil society are parts of the state. The material of the state is distributed among them by the individual's 'circumstances, his caprice and his personal choice of his station in life'. The citizens of the state are members of families and of civil society.

'The real idea is mind, which, *sundering itself* into the two ideal spheres of its concept, family and civil society, enters upon *its finite phase*' – thus we see that the division of the state into the family and civil society is *ideal*, i.e. necessary, belonging to the nature of the state. The family and civil society are real parts of the state, real spiritual manifestations of will, they are the state's forms of existence; the family and civil society make *themselves* into the state. They are the driving force. According to Hegel, however, they are *produced* by the real Idea; it is not the course of their own life that joins them together to comprise the state, but the life of the Idea which has distinguished them from itself. They are moreover the finite phase of this Idea; they are indebted for their existence to a mind other than their own; they are not self-determining but are instead determined by another; for this reason they are defined as 'finitude', the 'real Idea's' own *finite phase*. The goal of their existence is not that existence itself; instead the Idea divests itself of these its premises 'in order to rise above its ideality and become explicit as infinite real mind'. In other words the political state cannot exist without the natural basis of the family and the artificial basis of civil society. These are its *sine qua non*; and yet the condition is posited as the conditioned, the determinator as the determined, the producer as the product; the real Idea only condescends to become the 'finite phase' of the family and civil society in order that by their transcendence [*Aufhebung*] it may bring about its own infinity and enjoy it. It '*therefore* assigns' (i.e. in order to achieve its goal) 'to these ideal spheres the material of this its finite reality' (this? which?: these spheres *are* its 'finite reality', its 'material'), 'viz. human beings as a mass' (here the material of the state means human beings, the mass out of which the state is formed, its existence is explained here as resulting from the act of the Idea, as the 'assignment' of its own material; however, the fact is that the state evolves from the mass existing as members of families and of civil society; speculative philosophy explains this fact as the act of the Idea, not as the Idea of the mass, but as the act of a subjective Idea distinct from the fact itself), 'in such a way that the function assigned to any given individual' (he had spoken previously only of the assignment of individuals to the spheres of the family and civil society) 'is visibly mediated by circumstances, his caprice, etc.' Thus empirical reality is accepted as it is; it is even declared to be rational. However, it is not rational by virtue of its own reason, but because the empirical fact in its empirical existence has a meaning other than itself. The fact which serves as a starting-point is not seen as such but as a mystical result. The real becomes a mere phenomenon, but the Idea has no content over and above this phenomenon. The Idea moreover, has no goal beyond the logical one to 'become explicit as infinite real mind'. In this paragraph we find set out the whole mystery of the *Philosophy of Right* and of Hegel's philosophy in general.

§263. 'In these spheres in which its moments, individuality and particularity, have their *immediate* and *reflected* reality, mind is present as their objective universality *glimmering in them* as the power of reason in necessity (see §184), i.e. as the *institutions* considered above.'

§264. 'Members of the mass have *themselves* a spiritual existence and their nature is therefore twofold: (i) at one extreme, *explicit individuality* of consciousness and will, and (ii) at the other extreme, *universality* which knows and wills what is substantive. Hence they attain their right in both these respects only in so far as both their private personality and its substantive basis are realized. Now in the family and civil society they acquire their right in the first of these respects directly and in the second indirectly, in that (i) they find their substantive self-consciousness in social institutions which are the *universal* implicit in their particular interests, and (ii) the corporation supplies them with an occupation and an activity directed towards a universal end.'

§265. 'These institutions are the components of the *constitution* (i.e. of rationality developed and realized) in the sphere of *particularity*. They are, therefore, the firm foundation not only of the state but also of the citizen's trust in it and sentiment towards it. They are the pillars of public freedom since in them particular freedom is realized and rational, and therefore there is *implicitly* present even in them the union of freedom and necessity.'

§266. '*But* mind is objective and real to itself not merely as this' (which?) 'necessity [. . .] but also as the *ideality* and the heart of this necessity. Only in this way is this substantive universality *aware* of itself as its own object and end, with the result that the necessity appears to itself in the *shape* of freedom as well.'

The transition from the family and civil society to the political state takes the following form: the spirit of those spheres, which is *implicitly* the spirit of the state, now behaves as such to itself and becomes *real* to itself as their inner truth. Thus the transition does not result from the *particular* nature of the family etc., and the particular nature of the state, but from the *universal* relationship of *freedom* and *necessity*. We find exactly the same process at work in the *Logic* in the transition from the sphere of Essence to that of the Concept. In the *Philosophy of Nature*, the same transition can be observed from Inorganic nature to Life. It is always the same categories which are made to supply now one sphere and now another with a soul. The problem is merely to discover the appropriate abstract determinants to fit the individual concrete ones.

§267. 'This *necessity* in ideality is the inner self-*development* of the Idea. As the substance of the individual *subject*, it is his *political sentiment* [patriotism][3]; in distinction therefrom, as the substance of the *objective* world, it is the *organism* of the state, i.e. it is the strictly *political* state and *its constitution.*'

The subject here is 'necessity in ideality', 'the inner self of the Idea', the *predicate – political sentiment* and the *political* constitution. In plain words this means: *political sentiment* is the subjective substance of the state, the political constitution its *objective substance*. The logical development from the family and civil society to the state is, therefore, mere *appearance* as we are not shown how family and civil sentiment, and family and social institutions, as such are related to political sentiment and political institutions.

The transition in the course of which mind advances from 'this necessity and the *realm of appearance*' to 'its ideality', in which the soul of that realm becomes real for itself and has a particular existence, is in fact no transition at all, for the soul of the family exists for itself as love, etc. The pure ideality of a real sphere could, however, only exist in the form of a *science*.

The crux of the matter is that Hegel everywhere makes the Idea into the subject, while the genuine, real subject, such as 'political sentiment', is turned into the predicate. The development, however, always takes place on the side of the predicate.

§268 contains an able exposition of political *sentiment* or *patriotism* which has nothing in common with the logical development of his argument except that Hegel defines it as '*simply* a product of the institutions subsisting in the *state*, since rationality is *really* present in the state', whereas the converse is just as true, namely that these institutions are an *objectification* of political sentiment. Cf. the Remark on this Paragraph.

§269. 'The patriotic sentiment acquires its specifically determined content from the various members of the *organism* of the state. This *organism* is the differentiation of the Idea into various elements and their objective reality. *Hence* these different members are the *various*

3. Knox's addition.

powers of the state with their functions and their spheres of action, by means of which the *universal* continually *engenders* itself, and engenders itself in a *necessary* way because their specific character is fixed by the *nature of the concept.* Throughout this process the universal *maintains* its identity since it is itself the presupposition of its own production. This organism is the *political constitution.*'

The political constitution is the organism of the state, in other words the organism of the state is the political constitution. The argument that the different members of an organism stand in a necessary relation to each other derived from the nature of the organism is – pure tautology. Furthermore, if from the definition of the political constitution as an organism it is deduced that the various aspects of the constitution, the various state powers are related organically and rationally to each other – this too is a tautology. It is a great step forward to have seen that the political state is an organism and that, therefore, its various powers are no longer to be seen as organic[4] but as the product of living, rational divisions of functions. But how does Hegel present this discovery?

(1) 'This *organism* is the differentiation of the Idea into various elements and their objective reality.' It is not argued that the organism of the state is its differentiation into various elements and their objective reality. The real point here is that the differentiation of the state or of the political constitution into various elements and their reality is *organic.* The *real differences* or the *various aspects of the political constitution* are the presupposition, the subject. The predicate is their definition as *organic.* Instead, the Idea is made into the subject, the distinct members and their reality are understood as its development, its result, whereas the reverse holds good, viz. that the Idea must be developed from the real differences. The organic is precisely the *Idea of the differences,* their ideal determination.

(2) Hegel, however, talks here of the *Idea* as of a subject that becomes differentiated into *its* members. Apart from the reversal of subject and predicate, the appearance is created that there is an idea over and above the organism. The starting-point is the abstract Idea which then develops into the *political constitution* of the state. We are not concerned with a political Idea but with the abstract Idea in a political form. The mere fact that I say 'this organism (i.e. the state, the political constitution) is the differentia-

4. Evidently an error: 'mechanical' or 'inorganic' is presumably intended.

tion of the Idea into various elements etc.' does not mean that I know anything at all about the *specific Idea* of the political constitution; the same statement can be made with the same truth about the organism of an *animal* as about the organism of the state. How are we to *distinguish* between *animal* and *political* organisms? Our general definitions do not advance our understanding. An explanation, however, which fails to supply the *differentia* is *no* explanation at all. Hegel's sole concern is simply to re-discover 'the Idea', the 'logical Idea', in every sphere, whether it be the state or nature, whereas the real subjects, in this case the 'political constitution', are reduced to mere *names* of the Idea so that we are left with no more than the appearance of true knowledge. They are and remain uncomprehended because their specific nature has not been grasped.

'*Hence* these different members are the *various powers of the state* with their functions and their spheres of action.' The use of the word 'hence' creates the illusion of logical rigour, of deduction and the development of an argument. But we should rather ask: why 'hence'? The fact that 'the different members of the organism of the state' are 'the various powers with their functions and their spheres of action' is an empirical fact; but if so, how can this lead us to the philosophical predicate that they are the members of an 'organism'?

We would draw attention here to a peculiarity of Hegel's style which constantly recurs and which has its roots in mysticism. The whole paragraph runs:

'The patriotic sentiment acquires its specifically determined content from the *various members of the organism* of the state. This *organism* is the differentiation of the Idea into its various elements and their objective reality. *Hence these different members* are the *various powers of the state* with their functions and spheres of action, by means of which the univer-

1. 'The patriotic sentiment acquires its specifically determined content from *the various members* of the organism of the state.' 'These different members are the *various powers of the state* with their functions and spheres of activity.'

2. 'The patriotic sentiment acquires its specifically determined content from the various members of the *organism* of the state. *This organism* is the differentiation of the Idea into

sal continually *engenders itself* in a *necessary* way because their specific character is fixed by the *nature of the concept*. Throughout this process the universal *maintains its identity*, since it is itself the presupposition of its own production. This organism is the *political constitution*.'

its various elements and their objective reality [. . .] by means of which the universal continually *engenders itself* in a *necessary* way because their specific character is fixed by the *nature of the concept*. Throughout this process the universal *maintains its identity* since it is itself the presupposition of its own production. *This organism* is the *political constitution*.'

It can be seen that Hegel links his further definitions to two subjects: 'the different members of the organism' and 'the organism'. In the third sentence the 'different members' are defined as 'the various powers of the state'. By inserting the word 'hence' the illusion is created that these 'various powers of the state' were deduced from the intervening sentence about the organism as the differentiation of the Idea.

Hegel goes on to discuss further the 'various powers of the state'. The statement that the universal continually 'engenders itself' and thus maintains its identity tells us nothing new because it is implied already in their definition as 'members of the organism', as 'organic' members. Or rather, this definition of the 'various powers of the state' is nothing more than a circumlocution of the statement that the organism 'is the differentiation of the Idea into its various elements etc.'.

The statement that this organism is the 'differentiation of the Idea into its various elements and their objective reality' is identical with the statement that the organism is differentiated into various elements by means of which the universal (the 'universal' is the same thing in this context as the 'Idea') 'continually maintains itself and *engenders* itself in a *necessary* way because their specific character is fixed by the *nature of the concept*. Throughout this process the universal *maintains its identity*, since it is itself the presupposition of its own production.' The latter is merely a more detailed exposition of 'the differentiation of the Idea into its various elements'. It does not advance Hegel's argument a single step beyond the general concept of the 'Idea', or at best the 'organism' (for this is in fact his sole concern). How then can he justify his conclusion: 'This organism is the political constitution'? Why not: 'This organism is the solar system'? Because he has defined the 'different members of the state' as 'the various powers of the state'. The statement that 'these different members of the state are its various powers' is an empirical proposition and cannot be passed off as a philosophical discovery; nor is it in any sense the result of a logical argument. By defining the organism as the 'differentiation of *the* Idea', by speaking of the various elements of *the* Idea and then interpolating the concrete fact of 'the various powers of the state', the illusion arises that a *definite* content has been elucidated. It is impermissible for Hegel to follow the assertion that 'the patriotic sentiment acquires its specifically determined content from the various members of the organism of the state' by saying that '*this* organism' instead of '*the* organism is the differentiation of the Idea etc.'. At any rate, what he says applies to any organism and there is no predicate to be found which might justify the subject 'this'. The goal he hopes to reach is to define the *organism* as the *political constitution*. But he has failed to construct a bridge *leading from the general idea of the organism to the particular idea of the organism of the state or the political constitution.* Moreover, even if we wait to the end of time it will never become possible to construct such a bridge. In the opening sentence mention is made of 'the different members of the organism of the state' which are defined later as 'the various powers of the state'. The argument is simply that *'the various powers of the state organism'* or *'the state organism of the various powers' is – the 'political constitution'* of the *state*. The bridge leading to the 'political constitution' has not been constructed from the 'organism', 'the Idea' or 'its various elements' etc., but from the axiomatic concept of the 'various powers', the 'state organism'.

The truth is that Hegel has done no more than dissolve the 'political constitution' into the general, abstract idea of the 'organism'. In appearance and in his own opinion, however, he has derived the particular from the 'universal Idea'. He has converted into a product, a predicate of the Idea, what was properly its subject. He does not develop his thought from the object, but instead the object is constructed according to a system of thought perfected in the abstract sphere of logic. His task is not to elaborate the definite idea of the political constitution, but to provide the political constitution with a relationship to the abstract Idea and to establish it as a link in the life-history of the Idea – an obvious mystification.

Another claim is that the 'various powers of the state' are 'fixed by the nature of the concept' and that therefore by means of them the universal 'engenders itself in a *necessary* way'. Thus the various powers are not determined by 'their own nature' but by something alien to them. Similarly, their *necessity* is not to be found in their own essence, much less has it been critically established. Rather, their fate is predestined by the 'nature of the concept', it lies sealed in the holy archives of the Santa Casa[5] (of the *Logic*). The soul of an object, in this case of the state, is established and predestined prior to its body which is really just an illusion. The 'concept' is the Son within the 'Idea', God the Father; it is the *agens*, the driving force, the determining and differentiating principle. 'Idea' and 'concept' are here autonomous abstractions.

§270. '(1) The *abstract reality* or the substantiality of the state consists in the fact that its end is the universal interest as such and the conservation therein of particular interests since the universal interest is the substance of these.
(2) But this substantiality of the state is also its *necessity* since it is divided into the *distinct spheres* of its activity which correspond to the moments of its concept, and these spheres, owing to this substantiality, are thus real, *fixed* determinate characteristics of the state, i.e. its *powers*.
(3) But this very substantiality of the state is mind knowing and willing itself *after passing through the forming processes of education*. The state, therefore, *knows* what it wills and knows it in its *universality*, i.e. as *something thought*. Hence it works and acts by reference to consciously adopted ends, known principles, and laws which are not merely *implicit* but are actually present to consciousness; and further it acts with precise knowledge of existing conditions and circumstances, inasmuch as its actions have a bearing on these.'

(We shall postpone consideration of the Remark to this Paragraph, on the relationship between church and state, until later.)

Hegel's use of these logical categories merits a particular examination.

'(1) The *abstract reality* or the substantiality of the state consists in the fact that its *end* is the *universal interest* as such and the conservation therein of particular interests since the universal interest is the substance of these.'

5. The prison of the Inquisition in Madrid.

The fact that the universal interest both as such and as the existence of particular interests is *the end of the state*, is an abstract definition of the state's reality and existence. The state is not real without that end. This must be the essential object of its will, but at the same time it is no more than a quite general definition of that object. This end viewed as being is the state's sphere of existence.

'(2) But this' (abstract reality, substantiality) 'is also its *necessity*, since it is divided into the *distinct spheres* of its activity which correspond to the moments of its concept, and these spheres, owing to this substantiality, are thus real, *fixed* determinate characteristics of the state, i.e. its powers.'

This abstract reality or substantiality is the state's *necessity*; as its reality it is divided into *distinct spheres of activities*; these distinct spheres are rational and they are moreover fixed determinate characteristics. The abstract reality of the state, its substantiality, is its necessity inasmuch as the pure purpose of the state and the pure existence of the whole are realized only in the existence of the distinct powers of the state.

It is evident that the first definition of the state was abstract; the state cannot be regarded as a simple reality, it must be viewed as an activity, as a differentiated activity.

'Its abstract *reality* or substantiality [. . .] is its *necessity*, since it is divided into distinct spheres of its activity which correspond to the moments of its concept, and these spheres, owing to this *substantiality*, are thus real, *fixed* determinate characteristics of the state, i.e. its powers.'

The fact of substantiality is also one of necessity; i.e. the substance becomes manifest split up into autonomous, but essentially determinate, *realities* or *activities*. I can apply these abstractions to any reality. Having once considered the state in terms of 'abstract reality', I shall have to go on to consider it in terms of 'concrete reality', of 'necessity', of its realization in distinct spheres.

'(3) But this very substantiality of the state is mind knowing and willing itself *after passing through the forming processes of education*. The state, therefore, *knows* what it wills and knows it in its *universality*, i.e. as *something thought*. Hence it works and acts by reference to consciously adopted ends, known principles, and laws which are not merely *implicit* but are actually present to consciousness; and further it acts with precise knowledge of existing conditions and circumstances, inasmuch as its actions have a bearing on these.'

Let us now translate this paragraph into plain words. Thus:

(1) The *mind which knows and wills itself* is the substance of the state; (the *educated, self-conscious* mind is the subject and the foundation, the autonomous existence of the state).

(2) *The universal interest and the conservation therein of particular interests* is the general end and content of this mind, the existing substance of the state, the state-nature of the mind that wills and knows itself.

(3) The mind that wills and knows itself, the self-conscious, educated mind, achieves the *realization* of this abstract content only in the form of *distinct activities*, of *various powers*, of *organized authority*.

The following comments are relevant to Hegel's presentation:

(a) He makes *subjects* out of *abstract reality, necessity* (or the distinct spheres of substance), *substantiality*; i.e. out of *abstract logical categories*. It is true that 'abstract reality' and 'necessity' are described as '*its*', the state's, reality and necessity; however, 1. 'abstract reality' or 'substantiality' is *its* [the state's] necessity. 2. It is *this* 'abstract reality' or 'substantiality' which 'is divided into distinct spheres of its activity which correspond to the moments of its concept'. The 'distinct spheres owing to this substantiality are thus real, *fixed*' determinate characteristics, *powers*. 3. 'Substantiality' ceases to be an abstract characteristic of the state, it ceases to be '*its*' substantiality; it is converted into the subject, for in conclusion it is said that 'this very *substantiality* is mind knowing and willing itself after passing through the forming process of education'.

(b) Moreover, Hegel does not conclude that 'the educated, etc. mind is substantiality', but the opposite: 'this substantiality is the educated, etc. mind'. Thus mind becomes the predicate of its predicate.

(c) Substantiality, having been defined (1) as the universal end of the state and then (2) as its various powers, is further characterized (3) as the real mind that knows and wills itself. The true starting-point, mind knowing and willing itself, without which the 'end of the state' and the 'powers of the state' would be meaningless figments, inessential or even impossible beings, now appears only as the *final* predicate of the substantiality which had been previously defined as the *universal end* and the *various powers of the state*. If Hegel's starting-point had been *real mind*, then the 'universal end' would have been its content and the various powers would have been its mode of self-realization, its *actual* or *material* existence whose determinate characteristics would have emerged from the nature of its end. But as he begins by making the 'Idea' or 'substance' into the subject, the real essence, it is inevitable that the *real subject* should appear only as the *last predicate* of the abstract predicate.

The 'end of the state' and the 'powers of the state' are mystified because they are made to appear as 'modes of existence' of 'substance' and are thus separated from their real existence: 'mind knowing and willing itself, educated mind'.

(d) The concrete content and the real defining characteristics appear to be formal; the entire abstract, formal definition appears as the concrete content. The essence of the determining characteristics of the state is not that they define the state but that they are capable of being viewed in their most abstract form as logico-metaphysical determinations. Hegel's true interest is not the philosophy of right but logic. The task of philosophy is not to understand how thought can be embodied in political determinations but to dissolve the existing political determinations into abstract ideas. The concern of philosophy is not the logic of the subject-matter but the subject-matter of logic. Logic does not provide a proof of the state but the state provides a proof of logic.

[There are three concrete determinations:]

(1) The universal interest and therein the conservation of individual interests as the *end of the state*;

(2) the various powers as the *realization* of this end;

(3) the educated, self-conscious, willing and acting mind as the *subject* of this end and of its realization.

These concrete determinations are held to be purely external, *hors d'œuvres*; their philosophical significance is that in them the state acquires the following logical meanings:

(1) it becomes abstract reality or substantiality;

(2) its substantiality passes over into necessity, substantial reality;

(3) this substantial reality is in fact *concept, subjectivity*.

If we omit the concrete determinations, which might easily be exchanged for those of another sphere, such as physics, and which are therefore inessential, we find ourselves confronted by a *chapter of the Logic.*

The substance must be 'divided into distinct spheres of its activity which correspond to the moments of its concept, and these spheres, owing to this substantiality, are thus real, *fixed* determinate characteristics of the state'. This sentence belongs in essence to the *Logic* and exists prior to the *Philosophy of Right.* The fact that the moments of the concept are here moments of the *state*'s 'activity', and that the 'fixed determinate characteristics' are the powers of the state, constitutes a parenthesis which belongs properly to the *Philosophy of Right,* to the world of politics. Thus the entire *Philosophy of Right* is no more than a parenthesis within the *Logic.* It is self-evident that the parenthesis is but the *hors d'œuvre* to the real development. Cf. for example the Addition to §279:

'Necessity consists in this, that the whole is sundered into the differences of the concept and that this divided whole yields a fixed and permanent determinacy, though one which is not fossilized but perpetually re-creates itself in its dissolution.' Cf. also the *Logic.*

§271. 'The political constitution is, *in the first place*, the organization of the state and the *self-related* process of its organic life, a process whereby it differentiates its moments within itself and develops them to *self-subsistence.*

Secondly, the state is an individual, unique and *exclusive*, and therefore related to *others*. Thus it turns its differentiating activity *outward* and accordingly establishes within itself the ideality of its subsisting inward differentiations.'

Addition: 'The inner side of the state as such is the *civil power*, while its outward tendency is the *military power*, although this has a fixed place inside the state itself.'

1. THE CONSTITUTION (IN ITS DOMESTIC ASPECT ONLY)

§272. 'The constitution is rational in so far as the state inwardly differentiates and determines its activity *in accordance with the nature of the concept.* The result of this is that *each* of these *powers* is itself the *totality* of the constitution, because each contains the other moments and has them effective within itself, and because the moments, being expressions of the differentiation of the concept, simply abide in their ideality and constitute nothing but a *single individual* whole.'

Thus the constitution is rational in so far as its moments can be resolved into the categories of abstract logic. The state must not differentiate its activity in accordance with its own specific nature, but in accordance with the nature of the concept which is the mystified movement of abstract thought. The rationality of the constitution is therefore abstract logic and not the concept of the state. Instead of the concept of the constitution we are given the constitution of the concept. Thought is not guided by the nature of the state; the state is guided by a pre-existing system of thought.

§273. 'The state as a political entity is thus cleft' (how?) 'into three substantive divisions:

(a) the power to determine and establish the universal – the *Legislature*;

(b) the power to subsume single cases and the spheres of *particularity* under the universal – the *Executive*;

(c) the power of *subjectivity*, as the will with the power of ultimate decision – the *Crown*. In the crown, the different powers are bound into an individual unity which is thus at once the apex and basis of the whole, i.e. of *constitutional monarchy*.'

We shall return to this division once we have followed through its particular implications.

§274. '*Mind* is *real* only as that which it knows itself to be, and the state, as the mind of a nation, is both *the law permeating all relationships within the state* and also at the same time the manners and consciousness of its citizens. It follows, therefore, that the constitution of any given nation depends in general on the *character and development of its self-consciousness*. In its self-consciousness its subjective freedom is rooted and so, therefore, is the *reality of its constitution* [. . .] Hence every nation has the constitution appropriate to it and suitable for it.'

Hegel's argument only implies that a state in which the 'constitution' and 'the character and development of its self-consciousness' are in conflict is no true state. Of course, it would be petty to point out that a constitution produced by a past consciousness can become an oppressive shackle for a consciousness which has progressed. Such views would only lead to the demand for a constitution that had the property and principle of advancing in step with consciousness; i.e. advancing in step with real human beings – which is only possible when 'man' has become the principle of the constitution. Here Hegel is a *sophist*.

(a) The Crown

§275. 'The crown contains in itself the three moments of the whole (see §272), viz. (i) the *universality* of the constitution and the laws; (ii) counsel, which refers the *particular* to the universal; and (iii) the moment of ultimate *decision*, as the *self-determination* to which everything else reverts and from which everything else derives the beginning of its reality. This absolute self-determination constitutes the **distinctive principle** of the crown as such, and with this principle our exposition is to begin.'

In the first instance this paragraph means only that 'the universality of the constitution and the laws' is – the *crown*; *counsel* or the relation of the *particular* to the universal is – the *crown*. The crown does not stand outside the universality of the constitution and the laws once the crown is understood to refer to the (constitutional) monarch.

What Hegel is really after is simply that the 'universality of the constitution and the laws' is – the crown, the sovereignty of the state. But in that case it is wrong to establish the *crown* as the *subject* and to foster the illusion that, as the crown can also refer to the wearer of the crown, he, the sovereign, is the master of *this* moment, its subject. But let us first turn our attention to what Hegel pronounces '*the distinctive principle of the crown as such*', namely, 'the moment of ultimate *decision*, as the *self-determination* to which everything else reverts and from which everything else derives the beginning of its reality', 'absolute self-determination'.

Here Hegel says only that the *real*, i.e. the *individual*, *will* is the *power of the crown*. Thus in §12 we find:

'When the will gives itself the form of *individuality* . . . this constitutes the resolution of the will, and it is only in so far as it resolves that the will is a *real* will at all.'

In so far as this moment of 'ultimate decision' or 'absolute self-determination' is separated from the 'universality' of the content and the particularity of counsel, it is the *real will* in the form of *caprice*. In other words '*caprice* is the power of the crown', or 'the power of the crown is caprice'.

§276. 'The fundamental characteristic of the state as a political entity is the substantial unity, i.e. the ideality, of its moments.

(α) In this unity, the particular powers and their activities are dissolved and yet retained. They are retained, however, only in the sense that their authority is no independent one but only one of the order and breadth determined by the *Idea of the whole*; *from its might they originate*, and they are its flexible limbs while it is their single self.'

Addition. 'Much the same thing as this ideality of the moments in the state occurs with life in the physical organism.' .

It goes without saying that Hegel speaks only of the Idea of 'the particular powers and their activities . . .' Their authority may only be of the order and breadth determined by the Idea of the whole; they may only 'originate from its might'. That things *should* be so lies in the Idea of the *organism*. But in that case it would be necessary to show how all this might be achieved. For *conscious rationality* must hold sway within the state; and a *substantial* necessity which is merely internal and for that reason merely external, an adventitious [intertwining]⁶ of 'powers and their activities' cannot be passed off as true rationality.

§277. '(β) The particular activities and agencies of the state are its essential moments and therefore *proper to it*. The *individual functionaries and agents* are attached to their office not on the strength of their immediate personality, but only on the strength of their universal and objective qualities. Hence it is in an external and contingent way that these offices are linked with particular persons, and therefore the functions and powers of the state cannot be *private property*.'

It is self-evident that when *particular* activities and agencies are designated the activities and agencies of the *state*, *state activities* and *state powers*, they are not *private property* but *state property*. It is a tautology.

The activities and agencies of the state are bound to individuals (the state is effective only through individuals), but not to the individual conceived as a *physical* being, only as a being of the *state*; they are bound to the *state-like qualities* of the individual. It is therefore ridiculous for Hegel to assert that these offices 'are linked with particular persons in *an external and contingent way*'. On the contrary, they are linked to the individual by a *vinculum substantiale*,⁷ by an essential quality in him. They are the natural outcome of that essential quality. The confusion arises because Hegel regards the activities and agencies of the state abstractly, for themselves, as opposed to particular individuality; in so doing he forgets that particular individuality is a human function and that the activities and agencies of the state are likewise human functions; he forgets that the essence of the 'particular person' is not

6. Illegible in the original manuscript.   7. Essential link.

his beard and blood and abstract *Physis*,[8] but his *social quality*, and that the affairs of state are nothing but the modes of action and existence of the social qualities of men. It is self-evident, therefore, that in so far as individuals are to be regarded as the vehicles of the functions and powers of the state, it is their social and not their private capacity that should be taken into account.

§278. 'These two points (a) and (β) constitute the *sovereignty of the state*. That is to say, sovereignty depends on the fact that the particular functions and powers of the state are not self-subsistent or firmly grounded either on their own account or in the particular will of the individual functionaries, but have their roots ultimately in the *unity of the state* as their *single self*.'

[Remark] 'Despotism means any state of affairs where law has disappeared and where the particular will as such, whether of a monarch or a people, [. . .] counts as law or rather takes the place of law; while it is precisely in legal, constitutional, government that sovereignty is to be found as the moment of ideality – the ideality of the particular spheres and functions. That is to say, sovereignty brings it about that each of these spheres is not something independent, self-subsistent in its aims and modes of working, something immersed solely in itself, but that instead, even in these aims and modes of working, each is determined by and dependent on the *aim of the whole* (the aim which has been designated in general terms by the rather vague expression '*welfare of the state*').

This ideality manifests itself in a twofold way:

(i) In times of *peace*, the particular spheres and functions pursue the path of satisfying their particular aims and minding their own business, [. . .] and it is in part only by way of the unconscious *necessity* of the thing that their self-seeking is *turned into* a contribution to reciprocal support and to the support of the whole [. . .]. In part, however, it is by the *direct influence* of higher authority that they are not only continually brought back to the aims of the whole and restricted accordingly [. . .], but are also constrained to perform direct services for the support of the whole.

(ii) *In a situation of exigency*, however, whether in home or foreign affairs, the organism of which these particular spheres are members fuses into the single concept of sovereignty. The sovereign is entrusted with the salvation of the state at the cost of sacrificing these particular authorities whose powers are valid at other times, and it is then that that *ideality* comes into its *proper* reality.'

This ideality, therefore, is not developed into a known, rational system. It manifests itself in times of *peace* either as a merely

8. Nature, body, corporeality.

external compulsion exerted by the ruling power upon private life, 'by the direct influence of higher authority', or as the blind, unconscious result of self-seeking. A 'proper reality' accrues to this ideality only 'in war or a situation of exigency', so that the essence of the real existing state is seen to be 'a situation of war or exigency', while its *'peaceful'* condition consists precisely of the war and exigency of self-seeking.

Thus sovereignty, the ideality of the state, exists only as an *inner* necessity: as *Idea*. And Hegel is content with this, for the *Idea* is his only concern. Hence one aspect of sovereignty is its existence as *blind, unconscious substance*. We shall make the acquaintance of its other reality in a moment.

§279. 'Sovereignty, at first simply the *universal* thought of this ideality, *comes into existence* only as *subjectivity* sure of itself, as the will's abstract and to that extent ungrounded *self-determination* in which finality of decision is rooted. This is the strictly individual aspect of the state, and in virtue of this alone is the state *one*. The truth of subjectivity, however, is attained only in a *subject*, and the truth of personality only in a *person*; and in a constitution which has become mature as an actualization of rationality, each of the three moments of the concept has its *explicitly real* and separate formation. Hence this absolutely decisive moment of the whole is not individuality in general, but a single individual, the *monarch*.'

1. 'Sovereignty, at first simply the universal thought of this ideality, *comes into existence* only as *subjectivity sure of itself* [. . .] The truth of subjectivity is attained only in a *subject*, and the truth of *personality* only in a *person*; and in a constitution which has become mature as an actualization of rationality, each of the three moments of the concept has [. . .] explicitly real and separate formation.'

2. Sovereignty 'comes into existence only [. . .] as the will's abstract and to that extent ungrounded *self-determination* in which finality of decision is rooted. This is the strictly individual aspect of the state, and in virtue of this alone is the state *one* [. . .] (and in a constitution which has become mature as an actualization of rationality, each of the three moments of the concept has its *explicitly real* and separate formation). *Hence* this absolutely decisive moment of the whole is not individuality in general, but a single individual, the *monarch*.'

The first sentence means only that the universal thought of this ideality, whose melancholy existence we have just witnessed, must be the self-conscious creation of the subjects and must exist as such for them and in them.

If Hegel had begun by positing real subjects as the basis of the state he would not have found it necessary to subjectivize the state in a mystical way. 'The truth of subjectivity,' Hegel claims, 'is attained only in a *subject*, and the truth of personality only in a *person*.' This too is a mystification. Subjectivity is a characteristic of the subject, personality is a characteristic of the person. Instead of viewing them as the predicates of their subjects Hegel makes the predicates into autonomous beings and then causes them to become transformed into their subjects by means of a mystical process.

The existence of the predicates is the subject: thus the subject is the existence of subjectivity etc. Hegel makes the predicates, the objects, autonomous, but he does this by separating them from their real autonomy, viz. their subject. The real subject subsequently appears as a result, whereas the correct approach would be to start with the real subject and then consider its objectification. The mystical substance therefore becomes the real subject, while the actual subject appears as something else, namely as a moment of the mystical substance. Because Hegel starts not with an actual existent (ὑποκείμενον, subject) but with predicates of universal determination, and because a vehicle of these determinations must exist, the mystical Idea becomes that vehicle. Hegel's dualism manifests itself precisely in his failure to regard the universal as the real essence of the finite real, i.e. of what exists and is determined, or to regard real existent things as the *true subject* of the infinite.

Thus sovereignty, the essence of the state, is first objectified and conceived as something independent. Then, of course, this object must again become a subject. This subject, however, becomes manifest as the self-embodiment of sovereignty, whereas [in fact] sovereignty is nothing but the objectified spirit of the subjects of the state.

Passing beyond this fundamental defect in the argument, let us take another look at the first statement of this paragraph. As Hegel has formulated it, it says only that sovereignty, the ideality of the state, exists as person, as 'subject'. Evidently this means as many persons, many subjects, since no single person can encompass the entire sphere of personality, and no single subject can incorporate the entire sphere of subjectivity. For what kind of political ideality would it be which substituted for the real self-consciousness of its citizens the communal soul of the state as embodied in *one* person, *one* subject[?] Hegel did not develop this line of reasoning any further. But let us now examine the second proposition, which is intertwined with the first. Here Hegel is concerned to present the monarch as the real 'God-man', as the *real embodiment* of the Idea.

'Sovereignty [. . .] *comes into existence* only [. . .] as the will's abstract and to that extent ungrounded *self-determination* in which finality of decision is rooted. This is the strictly *individual* aspect of the state, and in virtue of this alone is the state *one* [. . .] and in a constitution which has become mature as an actualization of rationality, each of the three moments of the concept has its *explicitly real* and separate formation. *Hence* this absolutely decisive moment of the whole is not individuality in general, but a single individual, the *monarch*.'

We have already drawn attention to this sentence. The moment of resolve, of the capricious because determinate decision, is the *sovereign power* of the *will* in general. The Idea of the *sovereign power*, of the crown, as expounded by Hegel is nothing but the *Idea* of *caprice*, of the *decision* of the *will*.

Whereas Hegel has just defined sovereignty as the ideality of the state, as the real determination of the parts by the Idea of the whole, he now defines it as 'the will's *abstract* and to that extent *ungrounded* self-determination in which finality of decision is rooted. This is the strictly individual aspect of the state.' Where before he spoke of subjectivity, he now speaks of individuality: the sovereign state must be *one*, an *individual*, it must possess individuality. The state is 'not only' *one* in this, its individuality; the individuality is only the *natural* moment of its unity; the *natural determination* of the state. '*Hence* this absolutely decisive moment of the whole is not individuality in general, but a single. individual, the monarch.' Why? Because 'in a constitution, which has become mature as a realization of rationality, each of the three moments of the concept has its *explicitly real* and separate formation'. One of the moments of the concept is 'individuality' [*Einzelnheit*], but this does not yet amount to *'an individual'*. And in what sort of constitution would universality, particularity and individuality each have 'its *explicitly real* and separate formation'? Since we are not dealing with an abstraction but with the state and society, we may even adopt Hegel's own classification. What would follow from it? The citizen who determines the universal is the legislator; the citizen who decides the individual, who *really* exercises his will, is the sovereign. What can it mean to assert that *the individuality of the will of the state* is *'an individual'*? Can it mean a particular individual, different from all others? *Universality*, too, the legislature, has 'an *explicitly real* and separate formation'. Could one conclude from this that 'legislation is these particular individuals'[?]

The common man	*Hegel*
2. The monarch has sovereign power, sovereignty.	2. The *sovereignty* of the state is the monarch.
3. Sovereignty does what it wishes.	3. Sovereignty is 'the will's abstract and to that extent ungrounded *self-determination* in which finality of decision is rooted'.

Hegel converts every attribute of the constitutional monarch in contemporary Europe into the absolute self-determinations of the *will*. He does not say that the will of the monarch is the final decision, but that the final decision of the will is – the monarch. The first statement is empirical. The second twists the empirical fact into a metaphysical axiom.

Hegel conflates the two subjects, viz. sovereignty as 'subjectivity sure of itself' and sovereignty as 'the *ungrounded* self-determination of the will, as the individual will', in order to be able to prove that the 'Idea' is '*one* individual'.

It is self-evident that subjectivity sure of itself must also wish to exercise its will *in reality*, as a unity, an individual. Who has ever doubted that the state acts through individuals? If Hegel wished to demonstrate that the state must have *one* individual as the representative of its individual freedom, he did not deduce the monarch as this representative. We are thus left with a single positive result from this paragraph, that the *monarch* is the moment of *individual will* in the state, the moment of ungrounded self-determination, of caprice.

Hegel's Remark on this Paragraph is so curious that we must look at it more closely.

'The immanent development of a science, the *derivation of its entire content* from the *concept* in its simplicity [. . .] exhibits this peculiarity, that one and the same concept – the *will* in this instance – which begins by being abstract (because it is at the beginning), maintains its identity even while it consolidates its specific determinations, and that too solely by its own activity, and in this way gains a concrete content. Hence it is the basic moment of personality, abstract at the start in immediate rights, which has matured itself through its various forms of subjectivity, and now – at the stage of absolute rights, of the state, of the completely concrete objectivity of the will – has become the *personality of the state*, its *certainty of itself*. This last re-absorbs all particularity into its single self, cuts short the weighing of pros and cons between which it lets itself oscillate perpetually now this way and now that, and by saying "*I will*" *makes its decision* and so inaugurates all activity and reality.'

In the first place, it is not the 'peculiarity of a science' that the fundamental concept of its subject-matter always reappears.

Furthermore, no *progress* has taken place either. The *abstract personality* was the subject of abstract law and it has not changed: the *abstract personality* reappears intact as the *personality of the state*. Hegel should not be astonished to discover that the *real person* reappears everywhere as the essence of the state – for people make the state. He should rather have been astonished at the reverse, and even more at the fact that the person who appears in the context of his analysis of the state is the same threadbare abstraction as the person found in civil law.

Hegel here defines the monarch as the 'personality of the state, its certainty of itself'. The monarch is 'sovereignty personified', 'sovereignty in human form', the living consciousness of the state on whose account all others are excluded from this sovereignty and personality and consciousness of the state. At the same time, Hegel is unable to endow this *souveraineté personne*[9] with any other content than the idea 'I will', i.e. the moment of caprice in the exercise of the will. 'State-reason' and 'state-consciousness' is a 'single' empirical person to the exclusion of all others; but this personified rationality has no other content than the abstraction 'I will'. *L'état c'est moi.*

'*Further*, however, personality, like subjectivity in general, as infinitely self-related, has its *truth* (to be precise, its most elementary, immediate truth) only in a person, in a subject existing 'for' himself, and what exists 'for' itself is just simply a *unit*.'

9. Personified sovereignty.

It is self-evident that since personality and subjectivity are only predicates of the person and the subject they can exist only as person and subject, and the person is certainly but *one*. However, Hegel should have gone on to say that this *one* truly exists only as *many ones*. The predicate, the essence, can never exhaust the spheres of its existence in a *single one* but only in *many ones*.

Instead Hegel concludes:

'The personality of the state is real only as a *person*, the *monarch*.'

Thus because subjectivity is real only as a subject, and the subject only as one, the personality of the state can be real only as a person. A beautiful piece of logic. Hegel might argue with no less justification that because the individual man is one, the human species is only a single human being.

'Personality expresses the concept as such; but the person *also* enshrines the reality of the concept, and only when the concept is determined as person is it the *Idea* or truth.'

Now personality is undoubtedly a mere abstraction without the person, but the person is the *real Idea* of personality only in its species-existence [*Gattungsdasein*], *as persons*.

'A so-called *artificial* person',[10] be it a society, a community, or a family, however inherently concrete it may be, contains personality only abstractly, as one moment of itself. In an 'artificial person', personality has not achieved its true mode of existence. The state, however, is precisely this totality in which the moments of the concept have attained the reality correspondent to their degree of truth.'

This sentence contains a great muddle. The '*artificial* person', society etc. is called abstract, that is to say: Hegel describes as abstract the very species-forms [*Gattungsgestaltungen*] in which the *real person* realizes his content in actual existence, in which he objectifies himself and abandons the abstraction of the 'person as such'. Instead of recognizing this *realization* of the person as the most concrete of facts, the state is allegedly distinguished by the fact that in it 'the moment of the concept', 'individuality' achieves a mystical 'existence'. Thus the rational is seen to

10. Literally a 'moral person' [*moralische Person*], but Knox quotes: 'Natural persons are such as the God of nature formed us. Artificial are such as created and devised by human laws for the purpose of society and government, which are called corporations or bodies politic' (Blackstone, *Commentaries*, Vol. I, p. 123).

consist not in the realization of the reason of the real person but in the realization of the moments of the abstract concept.

'The conception of the monarch is therefore of all conceptions the hardest for ratiocination, i.e. for the method of reflection employed by the Understanding. This method refuses to move beyond isolated categories and hence here again knows only *raisonnement*, finite points of view, and *deductive* argumentation. Consequently it exhibits the dignity of the monarch as something *deduced*, not only in its form, but in its essence. The truth is, however, that to be something not deduced but *purely self-originating* is precisely the conception of monarchy. Akin, then, to this reasoning' (Of course!) 'is the idea of treating the monarch's right as grounded in the authority of God, since it is in its divinity that its unconditional character is contained.'

In a certain sense, every necessary being is 'purely self-originating'; in this respect the monarch's louse is as good as the monarch. Thus Hegel has not described anything peculiar to the monarch. And it is a real piece of folly to think that there is something specific to the monarch that is different from all the other objects of science and the *Philosophy of Right*; or rather Hegel is only right in so far as his idea of the '*single* person' is something deduced from the imagination and not from the Understanding.

'We may speak of the "*sovereignty of the people*" in the sense that any people whatever is self-subsistent *vis-à-vis* other peoples, and constitutes a state of its own . . .'

This is a triviality. If the sovereign is the 'real sovereignty of the state' then he must necessarily appear '*vis-à-vis* other peoples' as a 'self-subsistent state', even without his own people. If however he is sovereign only as the representative of the united people, then he is himself only a representative and symbol of the sovereignty of the people. The sovereignty of the people is not based on him, but he on it.

'We may also speak of *sovereignty in home affairs* residing in the people, provided that we are speaking generally about the *whole* state and meaning only what was shown above (see Paragraphs 277, 278), namely that it is to the *state* that sovereignty belongs.'

Just as if the people were not the real state. The state is an abstraction. Only the people is a concrete reality. And it is noteworthy that Hegel, who does not scruple to ascribe living qualities to the abstraction, should concede the right of the concrete reality to a living quality such as sovereignty only with reluctance and with many reservations.

'The usual sense, however, in which men have recently begun to speak of the "sovereignty of the people" is that it is something *opposed to the sovereignty existent in the monarch.* So opposed to the sovereignty of the monarch, the sovereignty of the people is one of the confused notions based on the *wild* idea of the "*people*".'

The 'confused notions' and the '*wild* idea' are to be found here solely in Hegel. It is of course true that if sovereignty *exists* in the monarch then it is foolish to speak of an opposed sovereignty in the people; for it is part of the concept of sovereignty that it cannot exist in a double form, to say nothing of an opposed, antagonistic one. But:

(1) the real question is whether the sovereignty enshrined in the monarch is not simply an illusion. Sovereignty of the monarch or of the people – that is the question.

(2) It is possible to speak of the sovereignty of the people *as opposed to the sovereignty existent in the monarch.* However, in that case we are not discussing *one and the same sovereignty* with its existence in two spheres, but two *wholly opposed conceptions of sovereignty*, of which one can come into being only in the *monarch* and the other only in the *people*. It is analogous to the question whether God or man is sovereign. One of the two must be false, even though an existing falsehood.

'Taken *without* its monarch and the *articulation* of the whole which is the indispensable and direct concomitant of monarchy, the people is a formless mass and no longer a state. It lacks *every one* of those determinate characteristics – sovereignty, government, courts, magistrates, class-divisions, etc. – which are to be found only in a whole which is *inwardly organized.* By the very emergence into a people's life of moments of this kind which have a bearing on organization, on political life, a people ceases to be that indeterminate abstraction which, when represented in a quite general way, is called the "people".'

Tautologous from beginning to end. If a people has a monarch and an articulation which is the indispensable and direct concomitant of the monarchy, i.e. if it is articulated as a monarchy, then it is obvious that once it is removed from this articulation nothing will remain but a formless mass and a general idea.

'If by "sovereignty of the people" is understood a republican form of government, or to speak more specifically [. . .] a democratic form, then [. . .] such a notion cannot be further discussed in face of the Idea of the state in its full development.'

This is perfectly correct as long as we have only 'such a notion' rather than 'a fully developed Idea' of democracy.

Democracy is the truth of monarchy; monarchy is not the truth of democracy. Monarchy is by necessity democracy in contradiction with itself; the monarchic moment is not an inconsistency within democracy. Monarchy cannot be explained in its own terms; democracy can be so explained. In democracy no moment acquires a meaning other than what is proper to it. Each is really only a moment of the *demos*[11] as a whole. In monarchy a part determines the character of the whole. The whole constitution must adapt itself to the one fixed point. Democracy is the generic constitution. Monarchy is only a variant and a bad variant at that. Democracy is both form and content. Monarchy is *supposed* to be only a form, but it falsifies the content.

In monarchy the whole, the people, is subsumed under one of its forms of existence, the political constitution; in democracy the *constitution itself* appears only as *one* determining characteristic of the people, and indeed as its self-determination. In monarchy we have the people of the constitution, in democracy the constitution of the people. Democracy is the solution to the *riddle* of every constitution. In it we find the constitution founded on its true ground: *real human beings* and the *real people*; not merely *implicitly* and in essence, but in *existence* and in reality. The constitution is thus posited as the people's *own* creation. The constitution is in appearance what it is in reality: the free creation of man. It could be argued that in certain respects this might be said also of constitutional monarchy. But the distinguishing characteristic of democracy is that in it the *constitution* is only *one* facet of the people, that the *political constitution* does not form the state for itself.

Hegel proceeds from the state and conceives of man as the subjectivized state; democracy proceeds from man and conceives of the state as objectified man. Just as religion does not make man, but rather man makes religion, so the constitution does not make the people, but the people make the constitution. In certain respects democracy is related to all other political forms in the same way as Christianity is related to all other religions. Christ-

---

11. The people.

ianity is religion κατ᾽ἐξοχήν, the *essence of religion*, deified man
as a *particular* religion. In the same way, democracy is the *essence
of all political constitutions*, socialized man as a *particular* political
constitution; it is related to other forms of constitution as a genus
to its various species, only here the genus itself comes into existence and hence manifests itself as a *particular* species in relation
to the other species whose existence does not correspond to the
generic essence. Democracy relates to all other forms of state as
its Old Testament. In democracy, man does not exist for the sake
of the law, but the law exists for the sake of man, it is *human
existence*, whereas in other political systems man is a *legal
existence*. This is the fundamental distinguishing feature of
democracy.

Every other *political formation* is a definite, determinate,
particular form of the state. In democracy the *formal* principle is
identical with the *substantive* principle. For this reason it is the
first true unity of the particular and the universal. In the monarchy,
for example, or in the republic as merely a particular form of the
state, the political man leads his particular existence alongside the
unpolitical man, the private citizen. Property, contractual agree-
ments, marriage, civil society appear in them as *particular* modes
of existence alongside the *political* aspects of the state (as Hegel
has demonstrated quite correctly in the case of *abstract* political
forms, in the mistaken belief that he was developing the Idea of
the state). Such phenomena appear as the *content* within the
framework of the political state which functions as the organized
form, as the mere Understanding devoid of any content which
defines and limits, now affirming, now negating. If in a democracy
the political state exists separately from this content and is distinguished from it, it nevertheless exists itself only as a *particular*
content, as a particular *form of existence* of the people. By contrast,
e.g. in the monarchy, this particular moment, the political constitution, assumes the significance of the *universal*, determining
and dominating all particulars. In democracy the state as particular
is *only* particular, and as universal it is really universal; i.e. it is
not something determinate set off against other contents. In
modern times the French have understood this to mean that the
political state disappears in a true democracy. This is correct in
the sense that the political state, the constitution, is no longer
equivalent to the whole.

In all forms of the state other than democracy the *state*, the *law*, the *constitution* is dominant, but without really dominating, i.e. without materially penetrating the content of all the non-political spheres. In a democracy the constitution, the law, i.e. the political state, is itself only a self-determination of the people and a determinate content of the people.

Moreover, it goes without saying that all forms of the state have democracy for their truth and that they are untrue to the extent that they are not democracy.

In former times the political state formed the content of the state to the exclusion of all other spheres; the modern state represents an accommodation between the political and the un-political state.

In a democracy the *abstract* state has ceased to be the dominant moment. The conflict between monarchy and republic still remains a conflict within the framework of the abstract state. The *political* republic is democracy within the abstract form of the state. Hence the abstract political form of democracy is the republic; here, however, it ceases to be *merely* a *political* constitution.

Property etc., in short the whole content of law and the state, is broadly the same in North America as in Prussia. Hence the *republic* in America is just as much a mere *form* of the state as the monarchy here. The content of the state lies beyond these constitutions. Hegel is therefore right when he says that the political state is the constitution, i.e. the material state is not political. Any interaction or identity established here is purely external. Of all the different expressions of the life of the people the political state, the constitution, was the hardest to evolve. When it did appear, it developed in the form of universal reason opposed to other spheres and transcending them. The task set by history was then the reclamation of universal reason, but the particular spheres do not have the feeling that their own private existence coincides with the constitution or the political state in its transcendent remoteness, or that its transcendent existence is anything but the affirmation of their own estrangement. Hitherto, the *political constitution* has always functioned as the *religious* sphere, the *religion* of the life of the people, the heaven of its universality as opposed to the *earthly existence* of its actual reality. The sphere of politics has been the only [real] state–sphere in the state, the only sphere in which both form and content was that of the species [*Gattungsinhalt*], i.e. truly universal. At the same time however, because politics was opposed to all other spheres, its content too became formal and particular. *Political life* in the modern sense is the *scholasticism* of the life of the people. The monarchy is the perfect expression of this estrangement. The *republic* is the negation of that estrangement, but within its own sphere. It is self-evident that the political constitution as such is only developed when the private spheres have achieved an independent existence. Where commerce and landed property are unfree, where they have not yet asserted their independence, there can be no political constitution. The Middle Ages were the *democracy of unfreedom*.

The abstraction of the *state as such* was not born until the modern world because the abstraction of private life was not created until modern times. The abstraction of the *political state* is a modern product.

In the Middle Ages there were serfs, feudal property, trade guilds, scholastic corporations, etc. That is to say, in the Middle Ages property, trade, society and man were *political*; the material content of the state was defined by its form; every sphere of private activity had a political character, or was a political sphere, in other words politics was characteristic of the different spheres of private life. In the Middle Ages the political constitution was the constitution of private property, but only because the constitution of private property was political. In the Middle Ages the life of the people was identical with the life of the state [i.e. political life]. Man was the real principle of the state, but man was *not free*. Hence there was a *democracy of unfreedom*, a perfected system of estrangement. The abstract reflected antithesis of this is to be found only in the modern world. The Middle Ages were an age of *real* dualism; the modern world is the age of *abstract* dualism.

'At the stage at which constitutions are divided, as above mentioned, into democracy, aristocracy and monarchy, the point of view taken is that of a *still substantial unity, abiding in itself, without having yet embarked on its infinite differentiation and the plumbing of its own depths*. At that stage, the moment of the *final self-determining decision of the will* does not come on the scene explicitly in its *own proper reality* as an organic moment *immanent* in the state.'

In the original models of monarchy, democracy and aristocracy there was at first no political constitution as distinct from the real, material state and the other aspects of the life of the people. The political state did not yet appear as the *form* of the material state.

Either the *res publica* was the real private concern of the citizens, their real content, while the private person as such was a slave – this was the case among the Greeks, where the political state as such was the only true content of their lives and their aspirations. Or else the political state was nothing but the private caprice of a single individual so that, as in Asiatic despotism, the political state was as much a slave as the material state. The modern state differs from such states with a substantive unity between people and state not in the fact that the various moments of the constitution acquire a particular reality, as Hegel asserts, but rather that the constitution itself develops a *particular* reality alongside the real life of the people and that the political state has become the *constitution* of the rest of the state.

§280. 'This ultimate self in which the will of the state is concentrated is, when thus taken in abstraction, a single self and therefore is *immediate* individuality. Hence its *natural* character is implied in its very conception. The monarch, therefore, is essentially characterized as *this* individual, in abstraction from all his other characteristics, and *this* individual is raised to the dignity of monarchy in an immediate, natural fashion, i.e. through his *birth* in the course of nature.'

We have already seen that subjectivity is the subject, and that the subject is necessarily a *single* empirical individual. We now learn that the concept of *immediate* individuality implies also *natural*, corporeal existence. Hegel has proved nothing that is not self-evident, namely that subjectivity can *exist* only as a *corporeal* individual, and of course an essential aspect of the corporeal individual is his *birth in the course of nature*.

Hegel imagines he has shown that the subjectivity of the state, sovereignty, the monarch, is 'essentially characterized as this individual, in abstraction from all his other characteristics, and *this* individual is raised to the dignity of monarchy in an immediate, natural fashion, i.e. through his *birth* in the course of nature'. Thus sovereignty, the dignity of monarchy, comes about through birth. The *body* of the monarch determines his dignity. At the apex of the state mere physicality, and not reason, is the deciding factor. Birth determines the quality of the monarch as it determines the quality of cattle.

Hegel has demonstrated that the monarch must be born, a truth no one has questioned, but he has not proved that birth makes the monarch.

It is just as difficult to erect the idea of the birth of a monarch into a metaphysical truth as the idea of the immaculate conception of the Virgin Mary. This latter notion, a fact of consciousness, can be explained, however, as the product of human illusions and circumstances; the former idea is also an empirical fact and can be explained in the same way.

We shall now look more closely at the Remark, in which Hegel indulges himself in the pleasure of demonstrating the absolute rationality of the irrational.

'This transition of the concept of pure self-determination into the immediacy of being and so into the realm of nature is of a purely speculative character, and apprehension of it therefore belongs to logic.'

This is indeed purely speculative, though not because the transition from *pure* self-determination, from an abstraction, to a *purely* natural occurrence (the accident of birth) is a leap from one extreme to the other, for extremes meet. The speculative element appears when this procedure is described as a 'transition of the concept' and an out-and-out contradiction is passed off as identity, and the greatest illogicality as logic.

The positive element in Hegel's argument is that with the substitution of the hereditary monarch for self-determining reason, abstract natural determinacy no longer appears as what it is, as natural determinacy, but as the highest determination of the state. That is to say, this is the *positive* discovery that the monarchy can no longer preserve the illusion of being the organization of rational will.

'Moreover, this transition is *on the whole the same*' (?) 'as that familiar to us in *the nature of willing*, in general, and there the process is to translate something from subjectivity (i.e. some purpose held before the mind) into existence [. . .] But the *peculiar* form of the Idea and of the transition here under consideration is the *immediate conversion* of the *pure self-determination of the will* (*i.e. of the simple concept itself*) into a *single* and natural existent without the mediation of a *particular* content (like a purpose in the case of action).'

Hegel is saying here that the *conversion* of the sovereignty of the state (a self-determination of the will) into the body of the born monarch (into a natural existent) is *on the whole* the same transition as that accomplished by the will when it *realizes* a purpose formed in the mind, translating it into existence. But Hegel says *'on the whole'*. The form peculiar to the exception he gives here is indeed so peculiar as to destroy any analogy and to replace the 'nature of willing' by *magic*.

In the first place, the *conversion* of the purpose formed in the mind into existence proceeds in an *immediate, magical* fashion. Secondly, the subject here is the *pure self-determination* of the will, the *simple concept itself*; it is the essence of the will, which functions as a mystical determining force; it is no real, individual, conscious willing, but only the abstraction of the will which is converted into natural existence, the pure Idea bodied forth as *one* individual.

Thirdly, just as the conversion of the will into natural existence takes place *immediately*, i.e. without the *means* normally required for the will to objectify itself, so too we note the complete absence of a *particular*, i.e. determinate, purpose; naturally enough, there is no 'mediation of a *particular* content, like a purpose in the case of action', because there is no *acting* subject. And if the abstraction of the pure Idea of the will is to act at all, it must act mystically. A purpose which lacks *particular* definition is no purpose at all, just as any action without aim is an aimless, senseless action. In the final analysis, the entire analogy with the teleological act of the will stands revealed as a mystification. An action of the Idea *devoid of all content*.

The means is the absolute will and the word of the philosopher; the end is once again the end of the philosophizing subject, viz. the logical construction of the *hereditary monarch* out of the pure Idea. The realization of this end is guaranteed by Hegel's simple assertion.

'In the so-called *ontological proof* of the existence of God, we have the same version of the absolute concept into existence.' (i.e. the same mystification.) 'This conversion has constituted the depth of the Idea in the modern world, although recently it has been declared *inconceivable*' (and rightly so).

'But since the idea of the monarch is regarded as being quite familiar to ordinary' (sc. Understanding) 'consciousness, the Understanding clings here all the more tenaciously to its separatism and the conclusions which its astute ratiocination deduces therefrom. As a result, it denies that the moment of ultimate decision in the state is linked *implicitly and actually* (i.e. in the rational concept) with the immediate birthright of the monarch [*literally*: with immediate natural existence].'

It is denied [by ordinary consciousness] that *ultimate decision is a birthright*, whereas Hegel maintains that the monarch is the ultimate decision in the state by right of birth. But who has ever doubted that the ultimate decision in the state is linked to real *corporeal* individuals, i.e. 'with immediate natural existence'?

§281. 'Both moments in their undivided unity – (a) the will's ultimate ungrounded self, and (b) therefore its similarly ungrounded objective existence (existence being the category which is at home in *nature*) – constitute the Idea of something against which caprice is *powerless*, the *majesty* of the monarch. In this unity lies the real unity of the state, and it is only through this, its inward and *outward immediacy*, that the unity of the state is saved from the risk of being drawn down into the sphere of particularity and its caprices, ends and opinions, and saved too from the war of factions round the throne and from the enfeeblement and overthrow of the power of the state.'

The two moments are the *accident of will*, caprice, and the *accident of Nature*, birth, and so we have *His Majesty the Accident*. Accident is accordingly the *real unity* of the state.

It is inconceivable that Hegel can believe that 'this inward and outward immediacy' [i.e. the unity of the state] can be saved from these conflicts [due to caprice, factions], as they are precisely the price of its unity.

Hegel's argument about elective monarchy applies with far greater truth to the hereditary monarchy:

'In an elective monarchy, I mean, the nature of the relation between king and people implies that the ultimate decision is left with the *particular* will, and hence the constitution becomes a *Compact* of Election, i.e. a surrender of the power of the state at the discretion of the particular will. The result of this is that the particular *offices of state turn into private property.*'

§282. 'The *right to pardon* criminals proceeds from the sovereignty of the monarch, since it is this alone which is empowered to realize mind's power of making undone what has been done and wiping out a crime by forgiving and forgetting it.'

The right to pardon is the right of *grace*. *Grace* is the highest expression of the *capricious rule of chance* and it is significant that Hegel should regard it as the authentic attribute of the monarch. In the Addition to this very paragraph Hegel locates the source of grace in the monarch's '*self-determined* [*grundlose*: groundless] *decision*'.

§283. 'The *second* moment in the power of the sovereign is the moment of *particularity*, or the moment of a determinate content and its subsumption under the universal. When this acquires a special objective existence, it becomes the supreme council and the individuals who compose it. They bring before the *monarch* for his decision the content of current affairs of state or the legal provisions required to meet existing needs, together with their *objective* aspects, i.e. the grounds on which decision is to be based, the relative laws, circumstances, etc. The *individuals* who discharge these duties are in direct contact with the person of the monarch and therefore their choice and dismissal alike rest with his *unrestricted caprice.*'

§284. 'It is only for the *objective* side of decision, i.e. for knowledge of the problem and the attendant circumstances, and for the legal and other reasons which determine its solution, that men are answerable; in other words, it is these alone which are capable of objective proof. It is for this reason that these may fall within the province of a council which is distinct from the personal will of the monarch as such. Hence it is only councils or their individual members that are *made answerable*. The personal majesty of the monarch, on the other hand, as the final *subjectivity* of decision, is above all answerability for acts of government.'

Here, Hegel gives a wholly empirical account of *ministerial* authority as it is generally defined in constitutional states. The only contribution made by philosophy is that it converts this 'empirical fact' into the existence or predicate of 'the moment of *particularity* in the power of the sovereign'.

(The ministers represent the rational, objective side of the sovereign will. For this reason it is to them that the *honour* of answerability falls, while the monarch's portion is the peculiar fiction of 'Majesty'.) Thus the contribution of speculation is very meagre. The detail of the argument is based on wholly empirical foundations, and very abstract and very unsound empirical foundations at that.

For example, the choice of ministers rests with the 'unrestricted caprice' of the monarch as 'they are in direct contact with the person of the monarch', i.e. as they are ministers. In a similar manner the 'unrestricted choice' of the monarch's valet might be deduced from the absolute Idea.

He has greater success with his argument in favour of ministerial *responsibility*, viz. 'it is only for the *objective* side of decision, i.e. for knowledge of the problem and the attendant circumstances, and for the legal and other reasons which determine its solution, that men are answerable; *in other words, it is these alone which are capable of objective proof'*. It is obvious that 'the final subjectivity of decision', pure subjectivity, pure caprice, is not objective, and therefore not capable of objective proof. As soon, therefore, as an individual becomes the *sacred, legal existence* of caprice he can no longer be deemed to be answerable. Hegel's logic is cogent if we accept the presuppositions of a constitutional state. But the fact that Hegel has *analysed* the fundamental idea of these presuppositions does not mean that he has demonstrated their validity. *It is in this confusion* that the *whole critical failure* of Hegel's *Philosophy of Right* can be discerned.

§285. 'The *third* moment in the power of the crown concerns the absolute universality which subsists subjectively in the *conscience of the monarch* and objectively in *the whole of the constitution* and the *laws*. Hence the power of the crown presupposes the other moments in the state *just as it is presupposed by each of them.*'

§286. 'The *objective* guarantee of the power of the crown, of the hereditary right of succession to the throne, and so forth, consists in the fact that just as monarchy has its own reality in *distinction* from that of the other rationally determined moments in the state, so these others possess for themselves the rights and duties appropriate to their own character. In the rational organism of the state, each member, by maintaining itself in its own position, *eo ipso* maintains the others in theirs.'

Hegel does not perceive that with this third moment of 'absolute universality', he entirely explodes the first two, or vice-versa. 'The power of the crown presupposes the other moments in the state just as it is presupposed by each of them.' If this has a real and not just a mystical meaning, it is that the power of the crown is founded not on birth, but on the other moments. It is therefore not hereditary but variable, i.e. it is a determination of the state that is distributed in turn among different individuals of the state in accordance with the organization of the other moments. A rational organism cannot have a head of iron and a body made of flesh. If the limbs are to survive they must all *be born equal*, of one flesh and blood. But the hereditary monarch is not born equal, he is of different stuff. Thus the prosaic rational will of the other members of the state is opposed by the magic of nature. Moreover, the members can only sustain each other if the whole organism 'flows' and each member is sublated [*aufgehoben*] in the flux, so that no member is, like the head of state, 'unaffected' and 'immutable'. Thus with this determination Hegel eliminates the idea of 'sovereignty by birth'.

Secondly, the question of irresponsibility. If the ruler violates 'the whole of the constitution and the laws', he ceases to be irresponsible because he has ceased to live in accordance with the constitution. But these very laws and constitution make him irresponsible. Thus they contradict themselves and this *one* paragraph undermines both constitution and law. The constitution of constitutional monarchy is *irresponsibility* itself.

However, if Hegel declares himself content with the idea that 'just as monarchy has its own reality in distinction from that of the other rationally determined moments in the state, so these others possess *for themselves* the rights and duties *appropriate* to their own character', he must logically describe the constitution of the Middle Ages as that of an organism; for he is left with a mass of particular moments which cohere only by virtue of an external necessity and it is true enough that only a monarch of flesh and blood will fit into such a framework. In a state where every determinate moment exists *for itself* the sovereignty of the state must be consolidated in a *particular* individual.

Résumé of Hegel's exposition of the Crown or the Idea of State Sovereignty

In the Remark to §279 Hegel writes:

'We may speak of the *sovereignty of the people* in the sense that any people whatever is self-subsistent *vis-à-vis* other peoples, and constitutes a state of its own, like the British people for instance. But the peoples of England, Scotland or Ireland, or the peoples of Venice, Genoa, Ceylon, etc. are not sovereign peoples at all now that they have ceased to have *rulers* or supreme governments *of their own*.'

Thus both the *sovereignty of the people* and the sovereignty of the ruler are equated with *nationality*, or better: the principle underlying the rule of a sovereign is that of *nationality*, which explicitly and exclusively constitutes the sovereignty of the people. A people whose *sovereignty* consists *solely* in nationality has a *monarch*. Different nationalities cannot be better consolidated and expressed than by different monarchs. The gulf separating one absolute individual from another is the gulf separating these nationalities.

The Greeks (and Romans) were a *nation* because and in so far as they were a *sovereign people*. The Germans are sovereign because and in so far as they are a nation.

'A so-called *artificial* [*moralisch*] *person*,' Hegel observes in the same Remark, 'be it a society, a community or a family, however inherently concrete it may be, contains personality only *abstractly, as one moment of itself*. In an "artificial person", personality has not achieved *its true mode of existence*. The state, however, is precisely this totality in which the moments of the concept have attained the reality corresponding to *their particular* degree of truth.'

The 'artificial person', i.e. society, the family etc., contains personality only abstractly; in the monarch, on the other hand, the *person* contains *the state within himself*.

The truth of the matter is that the *personality* of the *abstract person* achieves a true existence only in the 'artificial person', i.e. in society and the family etc. But Hegel regards the family, society etc. and the 'artificial person' in general not as the realization of the real, empirical person, but as the *real* person in whom, however, the moment of personality figures only abstractly. His account, therefore, does not proceed from the real person to the state, but from the state to the real person. Hence, instead of representing the state as the highest reality of the person, as the highest social reality of man, the highest reality of the state is said to be found in the empirical person, and *a single empirical* man at that. Hegel's purpose is to narrate the life-history of abstract substance, of the Idea, and in such a history human activity etc. necessarily appears as the activity and product of something other than itself; he therefore represents the essence of man as an imaginary detail instead of allowing it to function in terms of its *real human* existence. This leads him to convert the subjective into the objective and the objective into the subjective with the inevitable result that an *empirical person* is *uncritically* enthroned as the real truth of the Idea. For as Hegel's task is not to discover the truth of empirical existence but to discover the empirical existence of the truth, it is very easy to fasten on what lies nearest to hand and prove that it is an *actual* moment of the Idea. (The inevitable transformation of the empirical into the speculative and the speculative into the empirical will occupy us more later on.)

In this way Hegel is able to create the impression of *mystical profundity*. The fact that man is born is vulgar in the extreme. No less vulgar is the circumstance that an existence founded on physical birth can rise through man in society right up to the citizen of a state. Man through his birth becomes all that he can become. But it is very profound and remarkable that the Idea of the state is born without mediations and achieves empirical existence in the birth of a ruler. This profound discovery does not represent any gain in meaning, but only a change in *form* of the old meaning. It has acquired a philosophical *form*, the stamp of philosophical approval.

A further consequence of this mystical speculation is that a *particular* empirical existent, a single empirical existent distinct from all others, is deemed to be the *Idea* in empirical form. It makes a profound mystical impression to see a *particular* empirical being singled out and posited by the Idea and thus to encounter the human incarnation of God at every stage.

If, for example, the analysis of the family, civil society and the state etc. leads us to regard these modes of man's social existence as the realization and objectification of his essence, then the family etc. will appear as qualities inhering in a subject. In that event man will remain the essence of all these realities, but these realities will also appear as man's *real* universality and, therefore, as common to all men. If, on the other hand, the family, civil society and the state etc. are determinations of the Idea, of substance as subject, they must acquire an empirical reality and the mass of men in which the Idea of civil society is developed takes on the identity of citizens of civil society, while that in which the Idea of the state is developed assumes the identity of citizens of the state. As the whole point of the exercise is to create an *allegory*, to confer on some empirically existent thing or other the *significance* of the realized Idea, it is obvious that these vessels will have fulfilled their function as soon as they have become a determinate incarnation of a moment of the life of the Idea. Hence, the universal appears everywhere as a determinate particular, while the individual never achieves its true universality.

Such speculations necessarily appear at their most profound when the most abstract, socially wholly unrealized determinations, the natural bases of the state, like birth (in the case of the ruler) or private property (in the case of primogeniture), appear as the highest Ideas, the direct human incarnations of the Idea.

It is self-evident that the true way is turned upside down. The most simple thing becomes the most complicated and the most complicated becomes the most simple. What should be a starting-point becomes a mystical result and what should be a rational result becomes a mystical starting-point.

However, if the ruler is the abstract *person* who contains *the state in himself*, this means only that the essence of the state is the abstract *private person*. Only when the state blossoms forth does it reveal its secret. The ruler is the only private person in whom the relations between private persons and the state can come to fruition.

The hereditary powers of the ruler flow from the concept of the ruler. He is supposed to be specifically distinct from all other persons and from the whole species. What is the final, solid distinguishing factor between persons? The *body*. Now the highest function of the body is *sexual activity*. The highest constitutional act of the king, therefore, is his sexual activity; for by this alone does he *make* a king and so perpetuate his own body. The body of his son is the reproduction of his own body, the creation of a royal body.

(b) The Executive

§287. 'There is a distinction between the monarch's *decisions* and their *execution and application*, or in general between his decisions and the continued execution or maintenance of past decisions, existing laws, regulations, organizations for the securing of common ends, and so forth. This task of merely *subsuming* the particular under the universal is comprised in *the executive power*, which also includes the powers of the *judiciary and* the *police*. The latter have a more immediate bearing on the particular concerns of civil society and they make the universal interest authoritative over its particular aims.'

The usual explanation of the executive power. The only feature *peculiar* to Hegel is that he *brings together* the *executive*, the police and the *judiciary*, whereas it is more normal to treat the administrative and judicial arms of government as antitheses.

§288. 'Particular interests which are common to everyone fall within civil society and *lie outside the absolutely universal interest of the state proper* (see §256). The administration of these is in the hands of *corporations* (see §251), commercial and professional as well as municipal, and their officials, directors, managers and the like. It is the business of these officials to manage the *private property* and *interests* of these *particular* spheres and, from that point of view, their authority rests on the confidence of their commonalities and professional equals. On the other hand, however, these circles of particular interests must be subordinated to the higher interests of the state, and hence the filling of positions of responsibility in corporations etc. will generally be effected by a mixture of popular election by those interested with appointment and ratification by higher authority.'

A straightforward description of the empirical conditions obtaining in a number of countries.

§289. 'The *maintenance* of the state's *universal interest*, and of *legality*, in this sphere of particular rights, and the work of bringing these rights back to the universal, require to be superintended by *representatives* of the executive power, by (a) the *executive civil servants*, and (b) the higher advisory officials (who are organized into committees). These converge in their supreme heads who are in direct contact with the monarch.'

Hegel has altogether failed to provide a *logical exposition* of the *executive*. And even if we ignore that, he has still not shown that the executive is anything more than a *function*, *a determination*, of the citizen himself; he has contrived only to prove that it is a *particular*, *distinct* power by arguing that the 'particular interests of civil society lie outside the absolutely universal interest of the state proper'.

'Just as *civil society is the battlefield where everyone's individual private interest wars against everyone else's, so here we have the struggle (a) of private interests against particular matters of common concern and (b) of both of these together* against the organization of the state and its higher outlook. At the same time the corporation mind, engendered when the particular spheres gain their title to rights, is now inwardly converted into the mind of the state, since it finds in the state the means of maintaining its particular ends. This is the *secret* of the patriotism of the citizens in the sense that they know the state as their substance, *because* it is the state that maintains their particular spheres of interest together with the title, authority, and welfare of these. In the corporation mind *the rooting* of the *particular in the universal is directly entailed*, and for this reason it is in that mind that the depth and strength which the state possesses in *sentiment* is seated.'

This is remarkable:

(1) because of its definition of civil society as the *bellum omnium contra omnes*;[12]

12. War of all against all.

(2) because *private egoism* stands revealed as 'the secret of the patriotism of the citizens' and as the 'depth and strength which the state possesses in sentiment';

(3) because the 'citizen', the man with particular interests as opposed to the general interest, the member of civil society, is regarded as a 'fixed individual', while the state likewise confronts the 'citizens' as a phalanx of 'fixed individuals'.

One would have thought it necessary for Hegel to define 'civil society', the 'family' and the subsequent 'qualities of the state' as determinate characteristics of each political individual. But it is not the same individual that unfolds a new dimension of his social essence. It is the essence of the will that, so it is claimed, develops its determinations from within itself. The various, distinct, existing empirical political phenomena are regarded as the direct incarnations of one of these determinants.

As the universal is made autonomous, it is directly confounded with empirical existence and this limited existence is at once uncritically judged to be the expression of the Idea.

Hegel is inconsistent here only in his failure to regard the 'family man' as he had regarded the 'citizen', viz. as belonging to a specific race excluded from the other political characteristics.

§290. '*Division of labour* ... occurs in the *business of the executive* also. For this reason, the organization of officials has the abstract though difficult task of so arranging that (a) civil life shall be governed in a concrete manner from below where it is *concrete*, but that (b) none the less the business of government shall be divided into its *abstract* branches manned by special officials as different centres of administration, and further that (c) the operations of these various departments shall converge again when they are directed on civil life from above, in the same way as they converge into a general supervision in the supreme executive.'

We shall consider the Addition to this Paragraph later.

§291. 'The nature of the executive functions is that they are *objective* and that in their substance they have been explicitly fixed by previous decision (see §287); these functions have to be fulfilled and carried out by *individuals*. Between an individual and his office there is no immediate *natural* link. Hence individuals are not appointed to office on account of their birth or native personal gifts. The *objective* factor in their appointment is knowledge and proof of ability. Such proof guarantees that the state will get what it requires; and since it is the sole condition of appointment, it also guarantees to every citizen the *opportunity* of joining the class of civil servants' [literally: the universal class, *dem allgemeinen Stande*].

§292. 'Since the objective qualification for the civil service is not genius (as it is for work as an artist, for example), there is of necessity an *indefinite plurality* of eligible candidates whose relative excellence is not determinable with absolute precision. The selection of one of the candidates, his nomination to office, and the grant to him of full authority to transact public business – all this, as the linking of two things, a man and his office, which in relation to each other must always be fortuitous, is the *subjective* aspect of election to office, and it must lie with the crown as the power in the state which is sovereign and has the last word.'

§293. 'The particular public functions which the **monarch** entrusts to officials constitute one part of the *objective* aspect of the sovereignty residing in the crown. Their specific *discrimination* is therefore given in the nature of the thing. And while the actions of the officials are the fulfilment of their duty, their office is also a right exempt from contingency.'

Noteworthy here is only the '*objective* aspect of the sovereignty *residing* in the crown'.

§294. 'Once an individual has been appointed to his official position by the sovereign's act (see §292), the tenure of his post is conditional on his fulfilling its duties. Such fulfilment is the very essence of his appointment, and it is *only consequential* that he finds in his office his livelihood and the assured satisfaction of his particular interests (see §264), and further that his external circumstances and his official work are freed from other kinds of subjective dependence and influence.'

And in the Remark we learn:

'What the service of the state really requires [. . .] is that men shall forgo the selfish and capricious satisfaction of their subjective ends; by this very sacrifice, they acquire the right to find their satisfaction in, but only in, the dutiful discharge of their public functions. In this fact, so far as public business is concerned, there lies the link between universal and particular interests which constitutes both the concept of the state and its inner stability (see §260) ... The assured satisfaction of particular needs removes the external compulsion which may tempt a man to seek ways and means of satisfying them at the expense of his official duties. Those who are entrusted with affairs of state find in its universal power the protection they need against another subjective phenomenon, namely the personal passions of the governed, whose private interests, etc., suffer injury as the interest of the state is made to prevail against them.'

§295. 'The security of the state and its subjects against the misuse of power by ministers and their officials lies directly in their hierarchical organization and their answerability; but it lies too in the authority given to communities and corporations, because in itself this is a barrier against the intrusion of subjective caprice into the power entrusted to a civil servant, and it completes from below the state control which does not reach down as far as the conduct of individuals.'

§296. 'But the fact that a dispassionate, upright and polite demeanour becomes customary [in civil servants] is (i) partly a result of direct *education in thought and ethical conduct*. Such an education is a mental counterpoise to the mechanical and semi-mechanical activity involved in acquiring the so-called "sciences" of matters concerned with administration, in the requisite business training, in the actual work done, etc. (ii) The *size* of the state, however, is an important factor in producing this result, since it diminishes the stress of family and other personal ties, and also makes less potent and so less keen such passions as hatred, revenge, etc. In those who are busy with the important questions arising in a great state, these subjective interests automatically disappear, and the habit is generated of adopting universal interests, points of view, and activities.'

§297. 'Civil servants and the members of the executive constitute the greater part of the *middle class*, the class in which the consciousness of right and the developed intelligence of the mass of the people is found. The *sovereign* working on the middle class at the top, and *corporation-rights* working on it at the bottom, are the *institutions* which effectually prevent it from acquiring the isolated position of an aristocracy and using its education and skill as means to an arbitrary tyranny.'

Addition: 'The middle class, to which civil servants belong, is politically conscious and the one in which education is the most prominent. For this reason it is also the pillar of the state so far as honesty and intelligence are concerned [. . .] It is a prime concern of the state that a middle class should be developed, but this can be done only if the state is an organic unity like the one described here, i.e. it can be done only by giving authority to spheres of particular interests, which are relatively independent, and by appointing an *army of officials* whose personal arbitrariness is broken against such authorized bodies. Action in accordance with everyone's rights, and the habit of such action, is a consequence of the counterpoise to officialdom which independent and self-subsistent bodies create.'

Hegel's exposition of the 'executive' does not deserve the name of philosophical argument. Most of these paragraphs could be inserted word for word as they stand into the Prussian Legal Code and yet at the same time the administration is the knottiest point of the whole argument.

As Hegel has already claimed the powers of the 'police' and the 'judiciary' for the sphere of *civil society*, nothing remains for the *executive* but their administration, which he treats in terms of *bureaucracy*.

The 'self-administration' of civil society in 'corporations'[13] constitutes one premise of the bureaucracy. Hegel's only additional requirement is that their administrators and officials should be selected by a *mixed* procedure, partly by the citizens themselves, partly requiring the ratification of the actual executive power ('ratification by a *higher* authority', in Hegel's words).

Above this sphere which provides for the 'maintenance of the state's universal interest and of legality' we find the 'representatives of the executive power', the 'executive civil servants' and the 'committees of the higher advisory officials', all converging in the 'monarch'.

A 'division of labour' occurs in the 'business of the executive'. Individuals must demonstrate their capacity for the affairs of government, i.e they must pass examinations. The selection of *particular* individuals for the civil service lies with the crown. The demarcation lines between various spheres of activity are 'given in the nature of the thing'. Public office imposes duties on state officials, and constitutes their life's calling. Officials must therefore be *paid* by the state. Guarantees against the misuse of power by the bureaucracy are to be found partly in its hierarchical structure and its answerability and partly in the authority given to communities and corporations; its humanity is ensured partly by 'direct education in thought and ethical conduct', and partly by the 'size of the state'. Civil servants constitute 'the greater part of the middle class'. Protection against any threat by the middle class to develop into 'an aristocracy and arbitrary tyranny' is afforded by the 'sovereign working on the middle class at the top' and 'the corporation-rights working on it from the bottom'. The

---

13. Hegel uses the term 'corporation' for a range of organizations, similar to guilds, through which trades, professions etc. organize their activities, defend their interests *vis-à-vis* the state and make their representations to the legislative bodies of the state.

'middle class' is the 'educated' class. And there it all is. Hegel provides us with an empirical description of the bureaucracy, partly as it exists in reality and partly as it exists in its own view of itself. This concludes his treatment of the difficult problems of the 'executive'.

Hegel's starting-point is the *separation* of the 'state' from 'civil society', of 'particular interests' from 'the absolutely universal interest of the state proper', and it is perfectly true that the bureaucracy is based *on this separation*. Hegel proceeds from the presupposition of the 'corporations' and it is perfectly true that the bureaucracy does presuppose the corporations or at any rate 'the corporation mind'. Hegel does not expound the *content* of the bureaucracy, but only a number of general characteristics of its *'formal'* organization; and it is perfectly true that the bureaucracy is only a 'formal system' for a content lying outside it.

The *corporations* are the materialism of the bureaucracy, and the bureaucracy is the *spiritualism* of the corporations. The corporation is the bureaucracy of civil society; the bureaucracy is the corporation of the state. Hence, in reality, the bureaucracy is counterpoised as the 'civil society of the state' to 'the corporations, the state of civil society'. Wherever the 'bureaucracy' emerges as a new principle, wherever the universal interest of the state begins to develop into a 'separate', and therefore a 'real', interest, it comes into conflict with the corporations, just as every result comes into conflict with the existence of its own presuppositions. However, no sooner does the real state come into being and civil society, spurred on by its own impulse to rationality, emancipates itself from the corporations, than the bureaucracy attempts to restore them; for the fall of 'the state of civil society' entails the fall of 'the civil society of the state'. With the disappearance of the spiritualism, the materialism confronting it must likewise disappear. The result fights for the existence of its presuppositions as soon as a new principle attacks not just the *existence* but the *principle* of that existence. The same mentality which in society creates the corporation, in the state creates the bureaucracy. An attack on the corporation mind entails an attack on the bureaucratic mind also, and if the latter had previously attacked the corporations to create space for itself, it now attempts to ensure the survival of the corporations by force in order to preserve the corporation mind and thereby its own mind.

The 'bureaucracy' is the '*state formalism*' of civil society. It is the 'state-consciousness', the 'state will', the 'state power' in the form of a corporation, i.e. of a *particular, self-contained* society within the state. (The 'universal interest' can only maintain itself as a 'particular' opposed to other particulars, as long as the particular maintains itself as a 'universal' opposed to universals. The bureaucracy must therefore protect the *imaginary* universality of particular interests, i.e. the corporation mind, in order to protect the *imaginary* particularity of the universal interest, i.e. its own mind. The state must be a corporation as long as the corporation wishes to be a state.) However, the bureaucracy wants the corporation as an *imaginary* power. It is true that the individual corporation wants to maintain its own *particular* interest against the bureaucracy, but it also *needs* the bureaucracy against other corporations, against other particular interests. Hence, as the *perfect corporation*, the bureaucracy triumphs over the *corporation* as the imperfect bureaucracy. It therefore disparages the corporation as an appearance, or wishes to do so, but at the same time it requires this appearance to exist and to believe in its own existence. The corporation represents the attempt by civil society to become the state; but the bureaucracy is the state which has really made itself into civil society.

The 'state formalism' of the bureaucracy is the 'state as formalism', and this is how Hegel represents it. As this 'state formalism' constitutes itself as a real power and thus becomes its own material content, it follows inevitably that the 'bureaucracy' is a network of *practical* illusions or the 'illusion of the state'. The bureaucratic mind is a Jesuitic, theological mind through and through. The bureaucrats are the Jesuits and theologians of the state. The bureaucracy is the religious republic.

Since the 'state as formalism' is the *essence* of bureaucracy, it must also be its *purpose*. Accordingly, the real purpose of the state appears to the bureaucracy as a purpose *opposed* to the state. The mind of the bureaucracy is the 'formal mind of the state'. It therefore makes the 'formal mind of the state' or the *real* mindlessness of the state into a categorical imperative. The bureaucracy appears to itself as the ultimate purpose of the state. As the bureaucracy converts its 'formal' purposes into its content, it comes into conflict with 'real' purposes at every point. It is therefore compelled to pass off form as content and content as form. The purposes of the state are transformed into purposes of offices and vice-versa. The bureaucracy is a magic circle from which no one can escape. Its hierarchy is a hierarchy of knowledge. The apex entrusts insight into particulars to the lower echelons while the lower echelons credit the apex with insight into the universal, and so each deceives the other.

The bureaucracy is the imaginary state alongside the real state; it is the spiritualism of the state. Hence everything acquires a double meaning: a real meaning and a bureaucratic one; in like fashion, there is both real knowledge and bureaucratic knowledge (and the same applies to the will). Whatever is real is treated bureaucratically, in accordance with its transcendental, spiritual essence. The bureaucracy holds the state, the spiritual essence of society, in thrall, as its *private property*. The universal spirit of bureaucracy is *secrecy*, it is mystery preserved within itself by means of the hierarchical structure and appearing to the outside world as a self-contained corporation. Openly avowed political spirit, even patriotic sentiment, appears to the bureaucracy as a *betrayal* of its mystery. The principle of its knowledge is therefore *authority*, and its *patriotism* is the adulation of authority. Within itself, however, *spiritualism* degenerates into *crass materialism*, the materialism of passive obedience, the worship of authority, the *mechanism* of fixed, formal action, of rigid principles, views and traditions. As for the individual bureaucrat, the purpose of the state becomes his private purpose, *a hunt for promotion*, *careerism*. On the one hand, he regards real life as something *material* because *the spirit of that life leads its own independent existence* in the bureaucracy. The bureaucracy must therefore strive to make life as material as possible. On the other hand, real life is material for him in so far as it becomes an object of bureaucratic treatment, because his mind is prescribed for him, his purpose lies outside himself, his existence is the existence of his office. The state thus exists only as a series of fixed bureaucratic minds held together by passive obedience and their subordinate position in a hierarchy. *Real* knowledge appears lacking in content, just as real life appears dead, for this imaginary knowledge and imaginary life pass for the substance. Whether consciously or unconsciously, the bureaucrat must behave Jesuitically towards the real state. Inevitably, however, as soon as he finds himself opposed by knowledge, he must likewise become self-conscious and his Jesuitism must become deliberate.

While in one respect the bureaucracy is a crass materialism, in another respect its crass spiritualism is revealed in its wish *to do everything*. That is to say, it makes *will* the prime cause because it is nothing but active existence and receives its content from outside itself, and can therefore only prove its own existence by moulding and limiting that content. For the bureaucrat the world is no more than an object on which he acts.

When Hegel describes the executive power as the *objective* aspect of the sovereignty residing in the monarch, he is right in the same way that it was right to say that the Catholic Church represented the *actual existence* of the sovereignty, the content and the spirit of the Holy Trinity. In the bureaucracy the identity posited between the interest of the state and particular private purposes is such that the *interest of the state* becomes a *particular* private purpose opposed to the other private purposes.

The bureaucracy can be superseded [*aufgehoben*] only if the universal interest becomes a particular interest *in reality* and not merely in thought, in *abstraction*, as it does in Hegel. And this can take place only if the *particular* interest really becomes the *universal* interest. Hegel proceeds from an unreal antithesis and hence can resolve it only into an imagined identity which in reality is antagonistic. The bureaucracy is such an identity.

Let us now consider his exposition in detail.

The only philosophical category introduced by Hegel to define the *executive power* is that of the '*subsumption*' of the individual and particular under the universal etc.

Hegel rests content with this. The category of the 'subsumption' of the particular, etc., must be realized, and so he takes an empirical instance of the Prussian or modern state (just as it is — lock, stock and barrel) which can be said to realize this category among others, even though this category may fail to express its specific nature. After all, applied mathematics is also a subsumption, etc. Hegel does not inquire whether this mode of subsumption is adequate or rational. He simply holds fast to the *one* category and contents himself with searching for something corresponding to it in actual existence. Hegel thus provides his logic with a political body; he does not provide us with the logic of the body politic (§287).

With reference to the relationship of the corporations and communities to the government we learn first of all that the *administration* (i.e. appointment to the councils) 'generally' requires 'a mixture of popular election by those interested with appointment and *ratification by higher authority*'. The *mixed election* of corporation officials and parish councillors thus comprises the *first relationship* between civil society and the state or executive; it is their *first identity* (§288). Even in Hegel's own view this identity is very superficial, a *mixtum compositum*, a '*mixture*'. Remarkable as this superficial identity is, the antithesis it contains is more remarkable still. This '*mixed election*' results from the fact that 'it is the business of these officials' (i.e. of the corporations and communities) 'to manage the *private property* and *interests* of these *particular* spheres and, from that point of view, their authority rests on the confidence of their commonalities and professional equals. On the other hand, however, these circles of particular interests must be subordinated to the *higher interests of the state*.'

The administration of the corporation thus contains the following antithesis:

Private property and the interests of the particular spheres versus the higher interests of the state: the antithesis between private property and the state.

It is unnecessary to point out that the resolution of this antithesis by means of *mixed election* is a mere *accommodation*, a disquisition on and an admission of an unresolved dualism that is itself a *dualism*, a 'mixture'. Even *within their own sphere* the *particular* interests of the corporations and municipalities exhibit a dualism which similarly informs the character of their *administration*.

The most striking antithesis, however, makes its appearance in the relationship between these '*particular interests common* to everyone' which 'lie outside the absolutely universal interest of the *state* proper' and this '*absolutely universal interest of the state proper*'. And once again it appears in the same place.

'The maintenance of the state's universal interest, and of legality, in this sphere of particular rights, and the work of bringing these rights back to the universal, require *to be superintended by representatives of the executive power*, by (a) the *executive civil servants* and (b) the higher advisory officials (who are organized into *committees*). These converge in their supreme heads who are in direct contact with the monarch.' (§289)

In passing we may take note of the establishment of these executive *committees* which are unknown in France, for example. Since Hegel defines their functions as '*advisory*', it is self-evident that they should be 'organized into committees'.

Hegel causes the 'state proper', the 'executive power', to use its 'representatives' to 'superintend the state's universal interest, and legality' within civil society and according to him these 'government representatives' or 'executive civil servants' are the *true 'state representatives'* not 'of' civil society, but 'against' it. The antithesis between state and civil society is thus established; the state resides not in civil society but outside it; it comes into contact with it only through its *'representatives'* who have been entrusted with *'superintending the state's interest'* in civil society. The presence of these 'representatives' does not suffice to eliminate the antithesis; on the contrary, they only serve to 'legalize' and 'establish' it. Through its 'representatives' the 'state' intervenes as something alien and external to the *nature* of civil society. The 'police', the 'judiciary' and the 'administration' are not the representatives of a civil society which administers its *own* universal interests in them and through them; they are the representatives of the state and their task is to administer the state against civil society. Hegel explains this *antithesis* in the candid remark already commented on.[14]

'The nature of the executive functions is that they are *objective* and that [. . .] they have been explicitly fixed by previous decisions.' (§291)

Does Hegel infer from this that they may all the more easily dispense with a 'hierarchy of knowledge', that they can be carried out wholly by 'civil society itself'? By no means.

He makes the profound observation that these functions are to be carried out by 'individuals' and that 'between an individual and his office there is no immediate *natural* link'. This is an allusion to the power of the crown, which is nothing other than the *'natural power of caprice'*, to be acquired 'as a *birthright'*. The power of the crown is nothing but the representative of the natural moment in the will, of 'the rule of *physical nature in the state'*.

Accordingly, the appointment of the 'executive civil servants' to their posts is essentially different from the appointment of the 'sovereign' to his.

'The *objective factor* in their appointment is knowledge' (with which subjective caprice may dispense) 'and proof of ability. Such proof guarantees that the state will get what it requires; and since it is the

14. See above, pp. 101–2.

sole condition of appointment, it also guarantees to *every citizen the opportunity* of joining the *class of civil servants*.'

This *opportunity* to join the class of civil servants, available to every citizen, is the second bond established between civil society and the state; it is the *second identity*. It is highly superficial and dualistic in nature. Every Catholic has the opportunity of becoming a priest (i.e. of turning his back on the laity and the world). Does this mean that the priesthood ceases to be a power remote from Catholics? The fact that everyone has the opportunity of acquiring the right to *another* sphere merely proves that *his own* sphere does not embody that right in reality.

What is crucial in the true state is not the fact that every citizen has the chance to devote himself to the universal interest in the shape of a particular class, but the capacity of the universal class to be really universal, i.e. to be the class of every citizen. But Hegel starts with the assumption of a pseudo-universal, an illusory universal class,[15] of universality fixed in a particular class.

The identity he has established between civil society and the state is the identity of *two hostile armies* in which every soldier has the 'opportunity' to 'desert' and join the 'hostile' army. And it is perfectly true that in so doing Hegel has furnished us with an accurate description of the present empirical situation.

His treatment of the 'examinations' for the bureaucracy is comparable. In a rational state it would be more appropriate to ensure that a cobbler passed an examination than an executive civil servant; because shoe-making is a craft in the absence of which it is still possible to be a good citizen and a man in society. But the necessary 'knowledge of the state' is a precondition in the absence of which one lives outside the state, cut off from the air one breathes and from oneself. Thus the 'examination' is nothing but a Masonic initiation, the legal recognition of the knowledge of citizenship, the acknowledgement of a privilege.

This 'link' between the 'individual' and his 'office', this objective bond between the knowledge of civil society and the knowledge of the state, namely the *examination*, is nothing but the *bureaucratic baptism of knowledge*, the official recognition of the transubstantiation of profane knowledge into sacred knowledge (it is plain that in every examination the examiner is omniscient).

15. That is, the bureaucracy, Hegel's 'universal class' (*der allgemeine Stand*). Hegel argues that the bureaucracy is a *particular* class but that its aims are identical with the *universal* aims of the state (see below, p. 135, §303).

It is not recorded that Greek and Roman statesmen ever took examinations. But then what is a Roman statesman compared to a Prussian civil servant!

In addition to the objective bond joining the individual to his official position, i.e. in addition to the *examination*, there is a different bond – that of the *sovereign's caprice*.

'Since the objective qualification for the civil service is not genius (as it is for work as an artist, for example), there is of necessity an indefinite *plurality* of eligible candidates whose relative excellence is not determinable with absolute precision. The selection of one of the candidates, his nomination to office, and the grant to him of full authority to transact public business – all this, as the linking of two things, a man and his office, which in relation to each other must always be fortuitous, is the *subjective* aspect of election to office, and it must lie with the crown as the power in the state which is sovereign and has the last word.' [§292]

The sovereign is everywhere the representative of chance. The objective moment of a bureaucratic confession of faith (i.e. the examination) requires to be supplemented by the subjective moment of the sovereign's *grace*, without which faith would bear no fruit.

'The particular public functions which the monarch entrusts to officials constitute one part of the objective aspect of the sovereignty residing in the crown.' (Thus the monarchy distributes, entrusts the particular activities of the state as *functions* to the authorities, *it distributes the state among the bureaucrats*, just as the Holy Roman Church ordains its priests. The monarch is a system of emanations, and farms out the functions of state.) Hegel here distinguishes the *objective* side of the sovereignty residing in the crown from the *subjective* side. Previously he had conflated the two. The sovereignty residing in the crown is taken here in a wholly mystical sense, much as the theologians discover their personal God in nature. [Earlier[16]] it was argued that the monarch is the subjective side of the sovereignty residing in the *state* (§293).

In §294 Hegel derives the *payment of salaries* to officials from the Idea. Here, in the *payment of salaries* to officials, in the fact that service for the state guarantees them security in empirical existence, the *real identity* of civil society and the state is postulated. The official's *salary* is the highest identity deduced by Hegel. This identity presupposes the transformation of the *activities of*

16. German editors' addition.

state into *offices* and the separation of the state from civil society. Thus Hegel asserts:

'What the service of the state really requires [. . .] is that men shall forgo the selfish and capricious satisfaction of their subjective ends' (this is required by every service), 'and they thus acquire the right to find satisfaction in, but only in, the dutiful discharge of their public functions. In this fact, so far as public business is concerned, there lies the link between universal and particular interests which constitutes both the concept of the state and its inner stability.'

In the first place, this could be said about any servant and, in the second place, it is true that the *payment of salaries* to officials does in fact constitute the inner stability of the most modern monarchies. Only the existence of officials is *guaranteed*, as distinct from the existence of the members of civil society.

It cannot have escaped Hegel's notice that he has established the executive as an *antithesis* of civil society, and indeed as a dominant polar opposite. How then does he prove the existence of an identity?

According to §295, 'the security of the state and its subjects against the *misuse* of power by ministers and their officials' lies partly in their 'hierarchical organization'. (He could hardly be unaware that the hierarchical organization is itself the *principal abuse* and that the few personal sins of the officials are as nothing as compared to their *necessary* hierarchical sins. The hierarchy punishes the official when he sins against the hierarchy or commits a sin which is superfluous from the hierarchy's point of view, but it will come to his defence as soon as the hierarchy sins through him; moreover, it is hard to convince the hierarchy of the sinfulness of its members.) The security of the state is said to lie also 'in the authority given to communities and corporations, because in itself this is a barrier against the intrusion of subjective caprice into the power entrusted to a civil servant, and it completes from below the state control which does not reach down as far as the conduct of individuals'. (Hegel writes as if unaware that this control is directed in accordance with the views of the bureaucratic hierarchy.)

Thus the second guarantee of security against bureaucratic caprice is to be found in the privileges of the corporation.

If we ask Hegel what protection civil society has against the bureaucracy, he replies:

(1) The bureaucratic '*hierarchy*'. *Control*. The fact that the opponent is himself tied hand and foot, and if he acts as hammer on what is under him, he serves as anvil to what is above him. But what protection is there against the 'hierarchy'? The lesser evil is certainly eliminated by the greater in the sense that its impact is minimal by comparison.

(2) *Conflict*, the unresolved conflict between the bureaucracy and the corporations. *Struggle* and the *possibility* of struggle is security against defeat. Later (in §297) Hegel adds 'the sovereign working . . . at the top' as a further guarantee, but this is simply a further reference to the hierarchy.

However, Hegel mentions two additional factors (§296).

In the official himself – and this is supposed to humanize him and make a 'dispassionate, upright and polite demeanour . . . customary' – 'direct education in thought and ethical conduct' is supposed to act as 'a mental counterpoise' to the *mechanical* nature of his knowledge and his 'actual work'. But is it not rather that the 'mechanical' nature of his 'bureaucratic' knowledge and his 'actual work' act as a counterpoise to his 'education in thought and ethical conduct'? Will not his real mind and his real work as substance inevitably triumph over his accidental personal gifts? His 'office' is his 'substantive' being and his 'daily bread'. It is charming of Hegel to oppose 'direct education in thought and ethical conduct' to the 'mechanical' nature of bureaucratic knowledge and work! The human being in the official is supposed to save the official from himself. But what a unity! *Mental counterpoise* indeed. What a dualistic category that turns out to be!

Hegel further adduces the 'size of the state', although this has not been successful in providing security against the caprice of the 'executive civil servant' in Russia, and it is in any event a circumstance '*external*' to the '*nature*' of bureaucracy.

Hegel has expounded the 'executive' in terms of the 'state bureaucracy'.

Here in the sphere of 'the absolutely universal interest of the state proper' we discover nothing but unresolved conflicts. The officials' *examinations* and *daily bread* are the final syntheses.

The final consecration of the bureaucracy is found by Hegel to lie in its very impotence, in its conflict with the corporations.

An identity is posited in §297 with the statement that 'civil servants and the members of the executive constitute the greater part of the middle class'. In the Addition to this paragraph Hegel extols this 'middle class' as the 'pillar' of the state 'so far as honesty and intelligence are concerned'.

'It is a prime concern of the state that a middle class should be developed, but this can be done only if the state is an organic unity like the one described here, i.e. it can be done only by giving authority to spheres of particular interests, which are relatively independent, and by appointing an *army of officials* whose personal arbitrariness is broken against such authorized bodies.'

It is true enough that the people can appear as one class, the *middle class*, only in an organic unity of this kind, but can such an organic unity survive by maintaining a balance between opposing privileges? Of all the various powers the executive is the hardest to analyse. To a much greater degree than the legislature it is the property of the whole people.

Later on (in the Remark to §308) Hegel describes the authentic spirit of the bureaucracy much more accurately when he talks of 'mere business routine' and 'the horizon of a restricted sphere'.

(c) The Legislature

§298. 'The *legislature* is concerned (a) with the laws as such in so far as they require fresh and extended determination; and (b) with the content of *home* affairs affecting *entirely general* problems' (an entirely general expression). 'The legislature is itself *a part of the constitution* which is presupposed by it and to that extent lies absolutely outside the sphere directly determined by it; none the less, the constitution becomes progressively more mature in the course of the further elaboration of the laws and the advancing character of the universal business of government.'

It is very striking that Hegel should emphasize that 'the legislature is itself a part of the constitution which is presupposed by it and to that extent lies absolutely outside the sphere directly determined by it'; for he had not made this comment in the case of either the sovereign or the executive powers, where it is no less apposite. But then Hegel is actually engaged in constructing the constitution in its entirety and for that reason cannot presuppose it; however, his profundity always shows itself in the way in which he proceeds from and emphasizes the antagonistic character of the determinations (as they apply in our states).

The 'legislature is itself a part of the constitution' which 'lies absolutely outside the sphere directly determined by it'. But the constitution did not create itself. The laws which 'require fresh and extended determination' must surely have been somehow established. A legislature must exist or have existed *before* the constitution, or *apart from* the constitution. There must be a legislature apart from the real, *empirical* legislature already *posited*. But, Hegel will retort, we are presupposing an *existing* state. However, Hegel is a philosopher of right and is engaged in an analysis of the generic nature of the state. He may not measure the Idea by what exists, he must rather measure what exists in accordance with the Idea.

The contradiction is simple. The *legislature* is the power to organize the universal. It is the power of the constitution. It extends beyond the constitution.

On the other hand, the legislature is a constitutional power. It is, therefore, subsumed under the constitution. The constitution is *law* for the legislature. It *has* given laws to the legislature in the past and constantly gives it laws. The legislature only has legislative power within the constitution, and the constitution would fall outside the law if it were to exceed the limits set by the legislature. And there is the conflict! There has been much nibbling away at the problem in recent French history.[17]

How does Hegel resolve this contradiction?

He states firstly that the *constitution* is '*presupposed* by' the legislature; 'and *to that extent* lies absolutely *outside* the sphere directly determined by it'.

'*None the less*' – none the less, 'in the course of the further elaboration of the laws and the advancing character of the universal business of government', it 'becomes progressively more mature'.

This means then that *directly* the constitution lies outside the sphere of the legislature; but *indirectly* the legislature modifies the constitution. It thus does circuitously what it may not do straightforwardly. It pulls it apart retail because it cannot modify it wholesale. By the nature of things and circumstances it achieves what, according to the nature of the constitution, it ought not to achieve at all. The things it may not do *formally, legally* and constitutionally it does *materially* and *in fact*.

Hegel has not eliminated the contradiction, he has only ex-

17. See below, pp. 119–20.

changed it for another one. He has placed the *activity* of the legislature, its *constitutional* activity, in contradiction to its constitutional *determination*. The antithesis between the *constitution* and the *legislature* remains as before. Hegel has built into his definition a contradiction between the *actual* and the *legal* activity of the legislature, i.e. a contradiction between what the legislature should be and what it really is, between what it means to do and what it really does.

How can Hegel present this contradiction as the truth? 'The advancing character of the universal business of government' explains little because it is precisely this advancing character that requires an explanation.

In the Addition to this Paragraph Hegel adds nothing that might help to resolve these difficulties. But he does succeed in stating them more clearly.

'The constitution must in and by itself be the fixed and recognized ground on which the legislature stands, and for this reason it must not first be constructed. Thus the constitution *is*, but just as essentially it *becomes*, i.e. it advances and matures. This advance is an *alteration* which is *imperceptible* and which lacks the *form of alteration*.'

This means that the constitution *is* according to law (in illusion), but that it *becomes* according to reality (in truth). By definition it is immutable, but in reality it changes; however, it only changes unconsciously, lacking the form of change. Its *appearance* contradicts its *essence*. The appearance is the *conscious* law of the constitution, while the essence is its *unconscious* law, in conflict with the conscious one. The law does not reflect the true state of affairs, but rather the contrary.

Is it now the case that the dominant moment – in the state which according to Hegel is the highest incarnation of *freedom*, the incarnation of self-conscious reason – is not the law, the incarnation of reason, but the blind necessity of nature? And if now the actual laws are seen to contradict the legal definitions, then why not recognize the actual laws, namely the laws of reason, as the law of the state? How can the dualism be retained once it has become conscious? Hegel always attempts to represent the state as the realization of the free spirit, but in reality he solves all serious contradictions by appealing to a natural necessity antithetical to freedom. Thus the transition from the particular interest to the universal interest is not achieved by a conscious law of the state, but is mediated by chance and *against* consciousness. And yet Hegel aims to show the realization of free will throughout the state! (In this we see Hegel's *substantive* point of view.)

The examples cited by Hegel in support of his view of the *gradual* modification of the constitution are badly chosen. Thus he points out that the private property of the German rulers and their families was converted into the public domain, and that the custom whereby the German Emperor used to dispense justice personally was superseded by the appointment of judges on his behalf. But in the first case, for example, the change was brought about in such a way that all state property was really transformed into the private property of the princes.

Moreover all such changes are merely individual. Whole constitutions have in fact been transformed by the gradual growth of new needs and the collapse of the old, etc., but *new* constitutions have always depended on an actual revolution for their introduction.

Hegel concludes:

'Hence the advance from one state of affairs to another is tranquil *in appearance* and unnoticed. In this way a constitution changes over a long period of time into something quite different from what it was originally.'

The category of *gradual* transition is firstly historically false and, secondly, it explains nothing.

If the constitution is not merely to be subject to change, if this illusory appearance is not merely to be shattered by force, if man is to perform consciously what otherwise he would be compelled by the force of circumstance to perform unconsciously, it is necessary for the movement of the constitution, its *progress*, to be made into *its principle*. And this means that the real incarnation of the constitution, namely the people, would become the principle of the constitution. Progress itself would then be the constitution.

Does this mean that the 'constitution' should be thought of as belonging to the sphere of the 'legislature'? The question makes sense only if (1) the political state exists purely as the formal shell of the real state, if the political state is a separate realm, if it exists as the 'constitution'; and (2) if the legislature has a different origin than the executive, etc.

The legislature made the French Revolution; in fact, wherever it has emerged as the dominant factor it has brought forth great, organic, universal revolutions. It has not attacked the constitution as such but only a particular antiquated constitution; this is because the legislature acted as the representative of the people, of the species-will [*Gattungswillen*]. In contrast to this, the executive has made all the petty revolutions, the retrograde revolutions, the reactions. Its revolutions were not fought against an old institution and on behalf of a new one; they were fought against the constitution itself, simply because the executive was the representative of the particular will, subjective caprice, the magical aspect of the will.

If the question is to make any sense at all, it can only mean: does the people have the right to make a new constitution? And this question can only be answered unreservedly in the affirmative, for a constitution that has ceased to be the real expression of the will of the people has become a practical illusion.

The contradiction between the constitution and the legislature is nothing but the *conflict within the constitution itself*, a contradiction in the concept of the constitution.

The constitution is nothing but an accommodation between the political and the unpolitical state; inevitably, therefore, it is itself a synthesis of essentially heterogeneous powers. Hence it is impossible for the law to proclaim that one of these powers, a part of the constitution, should have the right to modify the whole, the constitution itself.

If the constitution is at all to be considered as a particular, it must be thought of as part of a whole.

If by the constitution we mean the universal, fundamental determinants of the rational will, it follows that every people (state) must have this as its premise and that this premise must constitute its political credo. This is actually a matter of knowledge rather than will. The will of a people may not transcend the laws of reason any more than the will of an individual. In the case of an irrational people we cannot speak of the rational organization of the state. Moreover, in the *Philosophy of Right* our concern must be with the species-will.

The legislature does not make the law, it only discovers and formulates it.[18]

Attempts have been made to solve this contradiction by dis-

18. Marx crossed out the following: '. . . so that in democracy, accordingly, the legislature does not decide the organization of the whole . . .' [*Note by* MEGA *editor*]

tinguishing between '*assemblée constituante*' and '*assemblée constituée*'.[19]

§299. 'Legislative business is more precisely determined, in relation to private individuals, under these two heads: (α) provision by the state for their well-being and happiness, and (β) the exaction of services from them. The former comprises the laws dealing with all sorts of private rights, the rights of communities, corporations and organizations affecting the entire state, and further it indirectly (see Paragraph 298) comprises the whole of the constitution. As for the services to be exacted, it is only if these are reduced to terms of *money*, the really existent and universal *value* of both things and services, that they can be fixed justly and at the same time in such a way that any *particular* tasks and services which an individual may perform come to be mediated through his own arbitrary will.'

In the Remark on this Paragraph Hegel himself comments on this definition of the business of the legislature:

'The proper object of universal legislation may be distinguished in a general way from the proper function of administrative officials or of some kind of state regulation, in that the content of the former is *wholly universal*, i.e. determinate laws, while it is what is *particular* in content which falls to the latter, together with ways and means of *enforcing* the law. This distinction, however, is not a hard and fast one, because a law, by being a law, is *ab initio* something more than a mere command in general terms (such as 'Thou shalt not kill' [. . .]). A law must in itself be something *determinate*, but the more determinate it is, the more readily are its terms capable of being carried out as they stand. At the same time, however, to give to laws such a fully detailed determinacy would give them empirical features subject inevitably to alteration in the course of their being actually carried out, and this would contravene their character as laws. *The organic unity* of the powers of the state itself implies that it is one single mind which both firmly establishes the universal and also brings it into its determinate reality and carries it out.'

However, it is precisely this *organic* unity which Hegel has failed to justify logically. The different powers each have a different principle. Each moreover is a definite reality. To flee from the genuine conflict between them by taking refuge in an *imaginary* 'organic unity', instead of proving them to be the various moments of an organic unity, is therefore an empty, mystical evasion.

19. Constituent assembly and constituted assembly.

The first unsolved contradiction was the conflict between the *legislature* and the *constitution as a whole*. The second is the conflict between the *legislature* and the *executive*, between the law and its implementation.

The second provision of this *Paragraph* is that *money* is the only service exacted from individuals by the state.

Hegel adduces these reasons in support of this claim:

(1) Money is the really existent and universal *value* of both things and services.

(2) It is only by this reduction that the services required can be determined in a *just* manner.

(3) Only in this way can the *particular* tasks and services which an individual may perform come to be mediated through his own arbitrary will.

In the Remark Hegel argues:

ad 1. 'In the state it may come as a surprise at first that the numerous aptitudes, possessions, pursuits and talents of its members, together with the infinitely varied richness of life intrinsic to these – all of which are at the same time linked with their owner's mentality – are not subject to direct levy by the state. It lays claim only to *a single* form of riches, namely *money*. – Services requisitioned for the defence of the state in war arise for the first time in connection with the duty considered in the next subdivision of this book.' (We shall postpone until later discussion of the personal liability to military service, not because of the next subdivision, but for other reasons.)

'In fact, however, money is not one particular type of wealth among others, but the universal form of all types so far as they are expressed in an external embodiment and so can be taken as "*things*".' 'In our day,' he continues in the Addition, 'the state *purchases* what it requires.'

ad 2. 'Only by being translated into terms of this extreme culmination of externality' (sc. in which the various talents are expressed in an external embodiment and so can be taken as '*things*') 'can services exacted by the state be fixed *quantitatively* and so justly and *equitably*.' And in the Addition we find: 'By means of money, however, the *justice of equality* can be achieved much more efficiently. Otherwise, if assessment depended on concrete ability, a talented man would be more heavily taxed than an untalented one.'

ad 3. 'In Plato's *Republic*, the Guardians are left to allot individuals to their particular classes and impose on them their *particular* tasks [. . .] Under the feudal monarchies the services required from vassals were equally indeterminate, but they had also to serve in their *particular* capacity, e.g. as judges. The same particular character pertains to tasks imposed in the East and in Egypt in connection with colossal architectural undertakings, and so forth. In these circumstances the principle of *subjective freedom* is lacking, i.e. the principle that the individual's substantive activity – which in any case becomes something particular in content in services like those mentioned – shall be mediated through his *particular volition*. This is a right which can be secured only when the demand for service takes the form of a demand for something of universal value, and it is this right which has brought with it this conversion of the state's demands into demands for cash.'

And in the Addition, he remarks:

'In our day, the state *purchases* what it requires. This may at first sight seem an abstract, heartless, and dead state of affairs, and for the state to be satisfied with abstract services may also look like decadence in the state. But the principle of the modern state requires that the whole of an individual's activity shall be mediated through his will [. . .] But nowadays *respect* for subjective freedom is publicly recognized precisely in the fact that the state lays hold of a man only by that which is capable of being held.'

Do what you wish. Pay what you must.

In the opening words of the Addition Hegel states:

'The two sides of the constitution bear respectively on the rights and services of individuals. Services are now almost entirely reduced to money payments, and military service is now almost the only personal one exacted.'

§300. 'In the legislature *as a whole* the other powers are the first two moments which are effective, (i) the *monarchy* as that to which ultimate decisions belong; (ii) the *executive* as the advisory body since it is the moment possessed of (*a*) a concrete knowledge and oversight of the whole state in its numerous facets and the real principles *firmly established* within it, and (*β*) a knowledge in particular of what the state's power needs. The last moment in the legislature is the *Estates*.'

The monarchy and the executive are . . . the legislature. If, however, the legislature is the *whole*, then the monarchy and the executive must surely be the moments of the legislature. The additional element of the *Estates* is thus *only* the legislature or it is the legislature *as distinct from* the monarchy and the executive.

§301. 'The *Estates* have the function of bringing matters of universal concern into existence not only *implicitly* [*an sich*], but also *explicitly* [*für sich*], i.e. of bringing into existence the moment of subjective *formal freedom*, the public consciousness as an *empirical universal*, of which the thoughts and opinions of the *Many* are particulars.'

The Estates[20] are a deputation of civil society to the state, with which, as the 'Many', they are contrasted. The Many are supposed for a moment *consciously* to treat matters of universal concern as if they were their own, as matters concerning the *public consciousness*, which according to Hegel is nothing but the '*empirical universal* of which the thoughts and opinions of the *Many* are particulars' (and this is in fact the case in modern monarchies, even constitutional ones). It is significant that Hegel should have such great respect for the state-mind – the ethical mind, state-consciousness – but when it actually and empirically appears before his very eyes he should regard it with such undiluted contempt.

And this is the key to the entire riddle of his mysticism. The same fantastic abstraction according to which *state-consciousness* is to be discovered in the inappropriate form of the *bureaucracy* with its hierarchy of knowledge, and which then uncritically accepts this inappropriate form as a *fully adequate* reality, this same fantastic abstraction does not hesitate to declare that the real, *empirical* state-mind, *public consciousness*, is a mere hotch-potch made up of 'the thoughts and opinions of the Many'. Just as this abstraction credits the bureaucracy with an essence alien to it, so it also attributes to the true essence the inappropriate form of mere appearance. Hegel idealizes the bureaucracy and empiricizes public consciousness. Hegel can treat real public consciousness very marginally because he treats the marginal consciousness as the true public one. He may all the more readily ignore the real existence of the state-mind because he thinks that he has realized it sufficiently in its supposedly existent forms. As long as the state-mind mystically haunted the antechambers it was treated with obsequious courtesy. Here, where we meet it in person, it is scarcely heeded.

'The Estates have the function of bringing matters of universal concern into existence not only *implicitly*, but also *explicitly*.' Moreover, they bring them explicitly into existence as the 'public consciousness', as 'the *empirical universal* of which the thoughts and opinions of the Many are particulars'.

The development of 'matters of universal concern' into the

20. An 'estate' (*Stand*) is an order or class of men in civil society which is distinguished by trade, profession, status, etc. In the sphere of political society 'Estates' (*Stände*) is a term used to designate that body which in the field of legislation represents the various particular interests of civil society.

subject, and thus into independent existence, is represented here as a moment in the life-process of these 'matters of universal concern'. Rather than make the subjects objectify themselves in 'matters of universal concern', Hegel causes the 'matters of universal concern' to extend into the 'subject'. The 'subjects' do not require 'matters of universal concern' for their own true concern, but matters of universal concern stand in need of the subjects for their *formal* existence. It is a matter of concern to the 'matters of universal concern' that they should also exist as subjects.

Above all, we must take a closer look at the distinction between the *implicit* and the *explicit* existence of matters of universal concern [between their '*Ansichsein*' and '*Fürsichsein*'].

'*Matters of universal concern*' already exist '*implicitly*', in themselves, as the business of the executive, etc.; they exist without *really* being matters of *universal* concern; they are in fact anything but that for they are of no concern to '*civil society*'. They have already achieved their *essential*, implicit existence. If they now really enter 'public consciousness' and achieve 'empirical universality', this is purely formal and amounts to no more than a *symbolic* achievement of reality. The 'formal' or 'empirical' existence of matters of universal concern is separate from their *substantive existence*. The truth of the matter is that the *implicit* 'matters of universal concern' are not *really universal*, and the real, *empirical* matters of universal concern are purely *formal*.

Hegel thus separates *content* and *form*, *implicit* and *explicit* existence, and admits the latter only *formally* and externally. The content is fully developed and assumes many forms which are not the forms of that content, and it clearly follows from this that the form which should be the real form of the content does not in fact have this content as its own.

The *matters of universal concern* are now complete without having become the real concern of the people. The real affairs of the people have sprung into being without the interference of the people. The Estates are the illusory existence of state affairs conceived as the affairs of the people. They are the illusion that *matters of universal concern* are really matters of universal, public concern or the *illusion* that the affairs of the people are matters of universal concern. Things have come to such a pass both in our states and in Hegel's *Philosophy of Right* that the tautology that 'matters of universal concern are matters of universal concern' can only make its appearance as an *illusion of the practical consciousness*. The *Estates* are the *political illusion of civil society*. *Subjective* freedom is purely *formal* for Hegel because he refuses to regard objective freedom as the realization, the activation of subjective freedom (although it is of course important that a free action should be performed freely, that freedom should not rule as an unconscious natural instinct of society). Because he has endowed the presumed or real content of freedom with a mystical persona, it is inevitable that the real subject of freedom should be assigned a purely formal significance.

The separation of *implicit* from *explicit* existence, of substance from subject, is a piece of abstract mysticism.

In the Remark Hegel expounds the Estates very much in terms of a 'formal', 'illusory' phenomenon.

Both the *knowledge* and the *volition* of the 'Estates' are either unimportant or suspect; i.e. the Estates are not *a meaningful predicate*.

1. 'The idea uppermost in men's minds when they speak about the necessity or the expediency of "summoning the Estates" is generally something of this sort: (i) The deputies of the people, or even the people themselves, *must know best* what is in their best interest, and (ii) their will for its promotion is undoubtedly the most disinterested. So far as the first of these points is concerned, however, the truth is that if "people" means a particular section of the citizens, then it means precisely that section, which does *not* know what it wills. To know what one wills, and still more to know what the absolute will, Reason, wills, is the fruit of profound knowledge and insight' (so common in bureaucrats), 'precisely the things which are *not* popular.'

Further on he says of the Estates themselves:

'The highest civil servants necessarily have a deeper and more comprehensive insight into the nature of the state's organization and requirements. They are also more habituated to the business of government and have greater skill in it, so that even without the Estates they are *able* to do what is best, just as they also continually *have* to do while the Estates are in session.'

And of course this is a completely true picture of the organization described by Hegel.

2. 'As for the conspicuously *good will* for the general welfare which the Estates are supposed to possess, it has been pointed out already

[. . .] that to regard the will of the executive as bad or as less good [than that of the ruled][21] is a presupposition characteristic of the rabble or of the negative outlook generally. This presupposition might at once be answered on its own ground by the counter-charge that the Estates start from isolated individuals, from a private point of view, from particular interests, and so are inclined to devote their activities to these at the expense of the general interests, while *per contra* the other moments in the power of the state explicitly take up the standpoint of the state from the start and devote themselves to the universal end.'

The *knowledge* and *good will* of the Estates are, therefore, partly superfluous and partly suspect. The people does not know what it wants. The Estates do not possess the same degree of knowledge of state affairs as the civil servants who have a monopoly of it. In the task of dealing with 'matters of universal concern' the Estates are quite superfluous. The civil servants *are able* to do what is best without the Estates, and indeed they *must* do what is best despite the Estates. Viewed substantively, then, the Estates are a pure luxury. Their existence is a mere *form* in the most literal sense of the word.

The *good will* of the Estates, moreover, is suspect because their actions are rooted in their private standpoint and their private interests. The truth of the matter is that private interests are their universal concern, and not that universal concerns are their private interest. But how curious that the 'universal interest' should acquire the *form* of the universal interest in a will which does not know what it wants, which does not possess any special knowledge of universal interest and whose actual content is an interest opposed to itself.

In the modern state, as in Hegel's *Philosophy of Right*, the *conscious, true reality of the universal interest is merely formal*, in other words, only *what is formal constitutes the real, universal interest*.

Hegel should not be blamed for describing the essence of the modern state as it is, but for identifying what is with the *essence of the state*. That the rational is real is *contradicted* by *the irrational reality* which at every point shows itself to be the opposite of what it asserts, and to assert the opposite of what it is.

Instead of showing how 'universal concern' acquires 'subjective and therefore real universality' and how it acquires the form of the universal concern, Hegel shows only that *formlessness* is its

21. Knox's addition.

subjectivity, and a form without content must be formless. The form acquired by matters of universal concern in a state which is not the state of such universal concerns can only be a non-form, a self-deceiving, self-contradictory form, a *pseudo-form* whose illusory nature will show itself for what it is.

Hegel only needs the luxury of the Estates for the sake of logic. The *being-for-itself* [*Fürsichsein*] of the universal interest stands in need of an actual empirical existence. Hegel does not look for an adequate realization of the 'being-for-itself' of the universal concern'; he is content to find an empirical existent which can be resolved into this logical category. This turns out to be the Estates, and he even points out himself what a wretched, self-contradictory existence it is. And to cap it all, he rebukes ordinary consciousness because it does not rest content with this satisfaction of logic, because it refuses to dissolve reality into logic by means of *arbitrary* abstraction, but would rather see logic translated into truly objective reality.

I say '*arbitrary* abstraction'. For, since the executive wills, knows and realizes the *universal concern*, since it emerges from the people and is itself an empirical manifold (Hegel himself informs us that it is not the totality), why should not the executive be defined as the 'being-for-itself of the universal concern'? And why should the Estates not be regarded as its *being-in-itself* [*Ansichsein*], in view of the fact that matters of universal concern acquire light and definition and implementation and independence only in and through the executive?

But the true antithesis is this: 'the universal concern' must be *represented* somewhere in the state as 'real', i.e. as an 'empirical universal concern'; it must become manifest somewhere or other wearing the crown and the robes of the universal – whereupon it automatically becomes a mere role, an illusion.

The antithesis is between the 'universal' as '*form*', in the 'form of universality', and the 'universal as content'.

In science, for example, an 'individual' can perform the tasks required by the universal concern and in fact these tasks are always performed by individuals. But science becomes truly universal only when it is no longer an individual affair but becomes a social one. This changes its content as well as its form. However, we are discussing the state and here the people is itself the universal concern; we are thus concerned with a will which can achieve its true existence as species-will only in the self-conscious will of the people. We are concerned, moreover, with the Idea of the state.

In the modern state the 'universal concern' and anything to do with it is a monopoly, and, conversely, the monopolies are the real universal concerns: this modern state has formed the strange idea of taking possession of the 'universal concern' as a *mere form*. (The truth of the matter is that only the *form* is a universal concern.) It has thereby discovered the form most appropriate to its content which is only the semblance of the real universal concern.

The constitutional state is that form of the state in which the state-interest, i.e. the real interest of the people, is present only *formally*, though as a definite form alongside the real state; the state-interest has here again *formally* acquired reality as the interest of the people, but this reality is destined to remain *formal*. It has become a *formality*, the spice of popular existence, a *ceremony*. The *Estates* are the lie, *legally sanctioned* in constitutional states, that the *state* is the *interest of the people* or that the *people* is the *interest of the state*. The lie will be revealed in the *content*. It established itself in the legislature because the content of the legislature is the universal and, more a business of knowledge than volition, it is the *metaphysical* state power. Had the same lie assumed the form of the executive either it would break down at once or it would transform itself into a truth. The metaphysical state power was the most suitable repository for the metaphysical universal state-illusion.

[Remark to §301] 'The Estates are a guarantee of the general welfare and public freedom. A little reflection will show that this guarantee does not lie in their particular power of insight [. . .] No, the guarantee lies on the contrary, (α) in the *additional insight*' [!!] 'of the deputies, insight in the first place into the activity of such officials as are not immediately under the eye of the higher functionaries of state, and in particular into the more pressing and more specialized needs and deficiencies which are directly in their view; (β) in the fact that the anticipation of criticism from the Many, particularly of public criticism, has the effect of inducing officials to devote their best attention beforehand to their duties and the schemes under consideration, and to deal with these only in accordance with the purest motives. This same compulsion is effective also on the members of the Estates themselves.

'As for the general guarantee which is supposed to lie peculiarly in the Estates, *each of the other political institutions* shares with the Estates in being a guarantee of public welfare and rational freedom, and some of these institutions, as for instance the sovereignty of the monarch, hereditary succession to the throne, the judicial system, etc., guarantee these things far more effectively than the Estates can. Hence the *specific* function which the concept assigns to the Estates is to be sought in the fact that in them the subjective moment in universal freedom – the private judgement and private will of the sphere called "civil society" in this book – *comes into existence integrally related to the state.* This moment is a determination of the Idea once the Idea has developed to totality, a moment arising as a result of an inner necessity not to be confused with *external necessities* and *expediencies.* The proof of this follows, like all the rest of our account of the state, from adopting the philosophical point of view.'

Universal, public freedom is ostensibly guaranteed in the other political institutions: the Estates are its ostensible self-guarantee. The fact is that the people attaches greater significance to the Estates, in which it believes it can secure its freedom, than to institutions which claim to secure it without its own participation; which confirm its freedom without activating it. Hegel's attempt to assimilate the Estates to other institutions conflicts with their essence.

Hegel solves the riddle when he discovers the 'specific function which the concept assigns to the Estates' in the fact that in them 'the private judgement and the private will of civil society *comes into existence integrally related to the state*'. It is the *reflection of civil society upon the state.* Just as the bureaucrats are *deputies from the state* to civil society, so too the Estates are *deputies from civil society* to the state. What we have, in short, are the *transactions of two antithetical wills.*

In the Addition to this Paragraph he asserts:

'The attitude of the executive to the Estates should not be *essentially* hostile, and a belief in the necessity of such hostility is a sad mistake.'

... a sad truth.

'The executive is not a party standing over against another party.'

The opposite is true.

'The taxes voted by the Estates are not to be regarded as a *present* given to the state. On the contrary they are voted in the best interests of the voters themselves.'

According to widespread *opinion* the voting of taxes in a constitutional state is necessarily a present.

'The real significance of the Estates lies in the fact that it is through them that *the state enters the subjective consciousness of the people* and that the people begins to participate in the state.'

This latter is perfectly correct. Through the Estates the people *begins* to participate in the state. Similarly, the state as a transcendental being enters its subjective consciousness. But how can Hegel bring himself to welcome this *beginning* as the full *reality*?

§302. 'Regarded as a *mediating* organ, the Estates stand between the government in general on the one hand and the nation broken up into particulars (people and associations) on the other. Their function requires them to possess a *political* and *administrative sense* and *temper*, no less than a sense for the *interests* of *individuals* and *particular groups*. At the same time the significance of their position is that, in common with the organized[22] executive, they are a middle term preventing both the *extreme isolation* of the power of the crown, which otherwise might seem a mere arbitrary tyranny, and also the isolation of the particular interests of persons, communities, and corporations. Further, and more important, they prevent individuals from having the appearance of a mass or an *aggregate* and so from acquiring an unorganized opinion and volition and from crystallizing into a powerful mass in opposition to the organic state.'

The state and the government are consistently placed on one side as identical and the people broken up into associations and individuals are placed on the other. The Estates stand as a *mediating* organ between the two. The Estates are the meeting-point where the 'political and administrative sense and temper' and the sense and temper of 'individuals and particular groups' come together and merge. The identity of these two opposed senses and tempers ought properly to constitute the state but in Hegel's account it merely achieves *symbolic* representation in the *Estates*. Transaction between the state and civil society becomes manifest as a *particular* sphere. The Estates are the *synthesis of the state and civil society*. There is no indication as to how the Estates should go about reconciling the two opposed tempers. The *Estates* are the incarnation of *contradiction* between the state and civil society within the state. At the same time they symbolize the *demand* that this contradiction be *resolved*.

'At the same time the significance of their position is that in common with the *organized*[23] executive, they are a middle term, etc.'

22. Marx has 'organic' here.   23. Marx again has 'organic' here.

The *Estates* do not merely mediate between people and government. They prevent the 'extreme isolation' of the 'power of the crown' which would manifest itself as 'mere arbitrary tyranny'; the same applies to the 'isolation' of 'particular interests etc.' and the 'appearance of individuals as a *mass* or an aggregate'. This mediating function is common to both the Estates and the organized executive. A state in which the 'position' of the 'Estates' prevents 'individuals from having the appearance of a *mass* or an *aggregate* and so from acquiring an unorganized opinion and volition and from crystallizing into a powerful mass in opposition to the organic state', is one in which the '*organic* state' exists apart from the 'mass' and the 'aggregate'. Or alternatively, the 'mass' and the 'aggregate' are an integral part of the organization of the state; but in that case their 'unorganized opinion and volition' should not be allowed to become 'opinion and volition in opposition to the state' because such a *definite trend* would constitute an 'organized opinion and volition'. Similarly, the 'powerful mass' should remain no more than a 'mass' uninformed by reason and unable to set itself in motion, but instead only be set in motion by the monopolists of the 'organic state' and exploited by them. Wherever we find not 'the isolation of the particular interests of persons, communities and corporations' from the state, but instead 'individuals who assume the appearance of a mass or aggregate and thus acquire an unorganized opinion and volition, crystallizing into a powerful mass in opposition to the organized state', it turns out that the state is not in fact contradicted by 'particular interests'; it is rather the case that the 'real organic universal idea of the mass and the aggregate' is not the 'idea of the organic state', i.e. that it cannot be realized in it. In what way, then, can the Estates appear as mediating against this extreme? Only because of 'the isolation of the particular interests of persons, communities and corporations', or because these isolated interests *use the Estates as an agency whereby to come to terms with the state*. Equally, because 'the unorganized mass and aggregate' occupies its *volition* (activity) in creating the Estates and its *opinion* in judging their activities, and thus enjoys the illusion of its own objectification. The *Estates*, in short, preserve the state from the disorganized mass only by disorganizing the mass.

Furthermore, the mediation of the *Estates* is supposed to prevent the 'isolation' of 'the particular interests of persons, communities and corporations'. They achieve this (i) by entering into relations with the 'interest of the state', and (ii) because they are themselves the '*political* isolation' of these particular interests; they embody this *isolation as a political act* inasmuch as through them these 'isolated interests' acquire the rank of 'universal interests'.

Finally, the Estates prevent the '*extreme isolation*' of the power of the crown (which 'otherwise *might seem* a mere arbitrary *tyranny*'). This is correct in the sense that the *principle* of the *power of the crown* (caprice) is limited, or at best can only move in chains, and also in that they become the partners and accomplices of the crown.

In consequence, either the power of the crown really ceases to be extreme (and as it does not represent an organic principle it can exist only as an extreme, as something one-sided). It thus becomes an *illusory power*, a symbol. Alternatively, it loses only the *semblance* of arbitrary tyranny. The Estates prevent the 'isolation' of special interests by representing this isolation as a *political* act. Their *mediation* against the extreme isolation of the power of the crown is achieved partly by their becoming part of the power of the crown and partly by making the executive into an extreme.

In the 'Estates' all the contradictions of the organization of the modern state are to be found united. They 'mediate' in every direction because they are themselves in every sense something intermediate.

It should be noted that Hegel is less concerned with the content of the Estates' activity, i.e. their legislative power, than with their *position*, their political rank.

It should further be noted that Hegel begins by stating that the Estates 'stand between the *government in general* on the one hand and the nation broken up into particulars (people and associations) on the other'. However, as we have seen, they are then defined as 'a middle term, *in common with* the organized executive'.

The first of these positions implies that the Estates are the people against the government, not the people as a whole but the people *en miniature*. This is their oppositional function.

The second implies that they are the government against the people, but the government amplified. This is their conservative function. They form a part of the executive against the people; at the same time, however, their apparent significance as the people against the government is retained.

Earlier (in §300) Hegel had referred to the 'legislature as a whole'. The *Estates* are really this *whole*, they are the state within the state; but it is precisely the Estates which *make it appear* as if the state were not a whole, a totality, but a dualism. The Estates represent the state in a society which is *no state*. The state is a *mere representation*.

In the Remark, Hegel observes:

'It is one of the most important discoveries of logic that a specific moment which by standing in an opposition, has the position of an extreme, ceases to be such and is a moment in an *organic* whole by being at the same time a *mean*.'

(The Estates, then, are (i) the extreme pole of the people as opposed to the government, and (ii) a mean between people and government, or alternatively, an opposition *within the people* itself. The opposition between government and people is mediated by the opposition between the *Estates* and the *people*. *Vis-à-vis* the government the Estates are in the position of the people, but *vis-à-vis* the people they are in the position of the government. Because the people appear as *idea*, fantasy, illusion, *representation* – the Estates, or the *represented* people, existing as a *particular power* apart from the real people – the real opposition between people and government is abolished. The people thus appear trussed and dressed and devoid of any recognizable character, as they must be if they are to be integrated into the organic state.)

'In connection with our present topic it is all the more important to emphasize this aspect of the matter because of the popular, but most dangerous, prejudice which regards the Estates principally from the point of view of their opposition to the executive, as if that were their essential attitude. If the Estates become an organ in the whole by being taken up into the state, they evince themselves *solely through their mediating function*. In this way their *opposition* to the executive is reduced to a show. There may indeed be an *appearance* of opposition between them, but if they were *opposed*, not merely superficially, but *in reality and in substance*, then the state would be in the throes of destruction. That the clash is not of this kind is evident in the nature of the thing, because the Estates have to deal, not with the essential elements in the organism of the state, but only with rather specialized and trifling matters, while the passion which even these arouse spends itself in party cravings in connection with purely subjective interests such as appointments to the higher offices of state.'

And in the *Addition* we find:

'*The constitution is essentially a system of mediation.*'

§303. 'The *universal* class, or more precisely, the class of *civil servants*, must, purely in virtue of its character as universal, have the universal as the end of its essential activity. In the *Estates*, as an element in the legislative power, the *class of private citizens* acquires its *political significance* and efficacy; it appears, therefore, in the Estates neither as a mere indiscriminate multitude nor as an aggregate dispersed into its atoms, but as *what it already is*, namely a class subdivided into two, one sub-class [the agricultural class] being based on a tie of substance between its members, and the other [the business class][24] on particular needs and the work whereby these are met [. . .] It is only in this way that there is a genuine link between the *particular* which is effective *in* the state and the universal.'

Here we have the solution to the puzzle. 'In the Estates, as an element in the legislative power, the *class of private citizens* acquires its *political significance*.' It is self-evident that the *class of private citizens* acquires this significance in terms of what it is, i.e. in terms of its *articulation in civil society* (Hegel has already defined the universal class as the class of civil servants; the universal class is therefore represented in the legislature by the executive).

The Estates are the *political significance of the class of private citizens*, of the unpolitical class – a contradiction in terms. Or, in the Estates as defined by Hegel the *class of private citizens* (and in general the distinctions within it) acquires *political* significance. The *class of private citizens* is an integral part of the essence and the politics of this state. The state therefore confers upon it a *political significance*, i.e. a significance other than its real significance.

In the Remark, Hegel states:

'This runs counter to another prevalent idea, the idea that since it is in the legislature that the class of private citizens rises to the level of *participating* in matters of state, it must appear there in the form of *individuals*, whether individuals are to choose representatives for this purpose, or whether every single individual is to have a vote in the legislature himself. This atomistic and abstract point of view vanishes at the stage of the family, as well as that of civil society where the individual is in evidence only as a member of a general group. The

24. Knox's additions.

state, however, is essentially an organization each of whose members
is a *group for itself*, and hence no one of its moments should appear as
an unorganized aggregate. The *Many*, as units – a congenial interpretation of "people", are of course *something connected*, but they are
connected only as an *aggregate*, a formless mass whose commotion
and activity could therefore only be elementary, irrational, barbarous,
and frightful.

'The circles of association in civil society are already communities.
To picture these communities as once more breaking up into a mere
conglomeration of individuals as soon as they enter the field of politics,
i.e. the field of the *highest concrete universality*, is *eo ipso* to hold *civil
and political life apart from one another* and as it were to hang the latter
in the air, because its basis could then only be the abstract individuality
of caprice and opinion, and hence it would be grounded on chance and
not on what is absolutely *stable* and *justified*.

'So-called theories of this kind involve the idea that the *classes of
civil society* and the Estates, which are the *classes given a political
significance*, stand wide apart from each other. But the *German
language*, by calling them both *Stände*, has still maintained the unity
which in any case they actually *possessed in former times*.

'The *universal* class, or more precisely, the class of civil servants.'

Hegel proceeds from the assumption that the *universal* class is
the class of civil servants. He assumes that the universal intelligence is a permanent function of a class.

'In the *Estates* etc.' The 'political significance and efficacy' of
the *class of private citizens* is here a *particular* significance and
efficacy. The *class of private citizens* does not transform itself into
a *political* class but enters into its political significance and
efficacy as the class of private citizens. It does not simply have a
right to political significance and efficacy. Its political significance
and efficacy is the *political significance and efficacy of the class of
private citizens as the class of private citizens*. This class can therefore enter the sphere of politics only in accordance with the *class
distinctions of civil society*. The *class distinctions* of civil society
thus become established as political distinctions.

The German language itself, Hegel observes, by referring to
both as *Stände*, expresses the identity of the *classes of civil society*
and the *Estates which are the classes given a political significance*,
a 'unity which in any case they actually *possessed* in *former* times'
– from which it would appear to follow that they no longer possess
it today.

Hegel states that 'there is a genuine link between the *particular* which is effective *in* the state and the universal'. *He thus hopes to heal the split between 'civil and political life' and to establish their identity.*

Hegel bases his argument on this consideration:

'The circles of association' (family and civil society) 'are already *communities.*' How could anyone wish 'to break them up into a mere conglomeration of individuals as soon as they enter the field of politics, i.e. the field of the *highest concrete universality*'?

It is important to pursue the thread of this argument in detail.

As Hegel himself admits, the identity he is seeking was most perfectly fulfilled in the *Middle Ages.* At that time there really was an identity between the *classes of civil society* and the *Estates,* i.e. *the classes given a political significance.* The spirit of the Middle Ages may be summed up in this way: the classes of civil society were identical with the Estates in the political sense, because civil society was political society: because the organic principle of civil society was the principle of the state.

However, Hegel proceeds from the assumption that '*civil society*' is *separate* from the '*political state*', that they are two fixed antitheses, two really different spheres. To be sure, this separation really does exist in the *modern* state. The identity of the civil and political classes in the Middle Ages was the *expression* of the *identity* of civil and political society. This identity has disappeared. Hegel presupposes its disappearance. If the 'identity of the civil and political classes' still expressed any truth at all, it could now only be that of the *separation* of civil society from political society! Or rather, only the separation of the civil and the political classes can express the *true* relationship of the civil and the political in *modern* society.

Secondly, when Hegel speaks of the political classes he means something quite different from the Estates of the Middle Ages whose identity *with the classes of civil society* he affirms.

Their whole existence was political; their existence was the existence of the state. Their *legislative activity, their voting of taxes for the Empire* was only a *particular* emanation of their general political importance and activity. Their class was their state [*Ihr Stand war ihr Staat*]. The relationship of the various states to the Empire was one of transactions at the level of *nationality*; for the political state, as distinct from civil society, was nothing but the *representation of nationality.* Nationality was the point of honour, the κατ'ἐξοχὴν[25] political meaning of these various bodies, and taxes etc. were raised only with nationality in view. This was the relationship of the legislative Estates to the Empire. A similar situation obtained *within the particular principalities*. *Principality* or *sovereignty* functioned as a *particular* Estate which enjoyed certain privileges but was equally impeded by the privileges of other Estates. (In Greece civil society was the *slave* of political society.) The fact that the classes of civil society had general *legislative functions* did not mean that the *class of private citizens* had acquired political significance and efficacy; these functions were merely an emanation of their real and universal political significance and efficacy. Their appearance as a legislative power was simply the complement of their sovereign, governmental (executive) power; or rather it signified that they treated matters of universal concern as *private matters*, they treated the sovereign power as though it were a *private class*. In the Middle Ages, the classes of civil society were as such an integral part of the legislature, because they were *not* classes of private citizens, or, because the *classes of private citizens* were political classes. Their political function added nothing new to the classes of the Middle Ages. They did not become political Estates because they played a role in the legislature; on the contrary, they played a role in the legislature because they were already political. Now what has this in common with Hegel's *class of private citizens* which as part of the *legislature* achieves a piece of political bravura, an ecstatic condition, an exceptional, eccentric and extraordinary political significance and efficacy?

In this argument we discover all the contradictions of Hegel's presentation.

(1) He has based his argument on the assumption of the *separation* of civil society and the political state (a modern phenomenon) and has gone on to show it to be a *necessary moment of the Idea*, the absolute truth of Reason. He has depicted the political state in its *modern* form, i.e. with the *separation* of the different powers of the state. He has made the bureaucracy into the actual body of the real, *acting* state and installed it as the omniscient mind enthroned above the materialism of civil society. He has opposed the absolutely universal interest of the state to the particular interests and needs of civil society. In a word: at every point he draws attention to the *conflict* between the state and civil society.

25. Principal.

(2) Hegel defines civil society as a *class of private citizens* as opposed to the political state.

(3) He characterizes the legislative function of the *Estates* merely as the *political formalism* of civil society. He characterizes them as the *reflection of civil society upon the state*, a relationship that does not modify the *essence* of the state. A relationship of reflection is also the highest identity between essentially different things.

On the other hand, Hegel maintains:

(1) that when civil society constitutes itself into a legislature it does so neither as a mere undifferentiated mass, nor as an aggregate dispersed into its atoms. He aims at *no* separation of *civil and political life.*

(2) He forgets that he is dealing with a relationship of reflection and makes the civil classes into political Estates; but once again, only with reference to the legislative power, so that their very efficacy is proof of their separation.

He makes the *Estates* into the expression of the *separation* [of civil and political life], but simultaneously they are supposed to represent an identity – one which does not exist. Hegel knows of the separation of civil society and the political state but he wishes to see their unity expressed within the state. He hopes to achieve this by showing that the classes of civil society as such constitute the *Estates* in the legislature (cf. XIV, X).[26]

§304. 'The Estates as an element in political life, still retain in their own function the class distinctions already present in the lower spheres of civil life. The position of the classes is abstract to begin with, i.e. in contrast with the whole principle of the *monarchy* or the *crown*, their position is that of an *extreme – empirical universality*. This extreme opposition implies the *possibility*, though no more, of *harmonization*, and the equally likely *possibility* of set hostility. This abstract position changes into a rational relation (into a syllogism, see Remark to §302) only if the *middle term* between the opposites comes into existence. From the point of view of the crown, the executive already has this character (see §300). So, from the point of view of the classes, one moment in them must be adapted to the task of existing as in essence the moment of mediation.'

§305. 'The principle of one of the classes of civil society is in itself capable of adaptation to this political position. The class in question is the one whose ethical life is natural, whose basis is family life, and,

26. Marx refers here to sheets of his manuscript. Here, pp. 88–91 and 105–9.

so far as its livelihood is concerned, the possession of land. Its particular members attain their possession by birth, just as the monarch does, and, in common with him, they possess a will which rests on itself alone.'

§306. 'This class is more particularly fitted for political position and significance in that its capital is independent alike of the state's capital, the uncertainty of business, the quest for profit, and any sort of fluctuation in possessions. It is likewise independent of favour, whether from the executive or the mob. It is even fortified *against its own wilfulness*, because those members of this class who are called to political life are not entitled, as other citizens are, either to dispose of their entire property at will, or to the assurance that it will pass to their children, whom they love equally, in similarly equal divisions. Hence their wealth becomes *inalienable*, *entailed*, and burdened by primogeniture.'

Addition. 'This class has a volition of a more independent character. On the whole, the class of landed-property owners is divided into an educated section and a section of farmers. But over against both of these sorts of people there stands the business class, which is dependent on needs and concentrated on their satisfaction, and the civil servant class, which is essentially dependent on the state. The security and stability of the agricultural class may be still further increased by the institution of primogeniture, though this institution is desirable only from the point of view of politics, since it entails a sacrifice for the political end of giving the eldest son a life of independence. Primogeniture is grounded on the fact that the state should be able to reckon not on the bare possibility of political institutions, but on something necessary. Now an inclination for politics is of course not bound up with wealth, but there is a relatively necessary connection between the two, because a man with independent means is not hemmed in by external circumstances and so there is nothing to prevent him from entering politics and working for the state. Where political institutions are lacking, however, the foundation and encouragement of primogeniture is nothing but a chain on the freedom of private rights, and either political meaning must be given to it, or else it will in due course disappear.'

§307. 'The right of this section of the agricultural class is thus based in a way on the **natural principle of the family**. But this principle is at the same time reversed owing to hard sacrifices made for *political* ends, and thereby the activity of this class is essentially directed to those ends. As a consequence of this, this class is summoned and *entitled* to its political vocation by *birth* without the hazards of election. It therefore has the fixed, substantive position between the subjective wilfulness or contingency of both extremes; and while it mirrors in itself [. . .] the moment of the monarchical power, it also shares in other respects the needs and rights of the other extreme [i.e. civil society][27] and hence it becomes a support at once of the throne and of society.'

Hegel has accomplished the feat of deducing the hereditary peerage, landed estates etc. etc., these 'supports of the throne and society', from the absolute Idea.

The deeper truth is that Hegel experiences the separation of the state from civil society as a *contradiction*. The mistake he makes is to rest content with the semblance of a resolution which he declares to be the real thing. By contrast, he treats with contempt the '*so-called theories*' which call for the '*separation*' of the classes and Estates. These theories, however, are right in that they express a *consequence* of modern society, for here the Estates are nothing more than the factual expression of the real relationship between the state and civil society, namely one of *separation*.

Hegel does not give the problem its familiar name. It is in fact the dispute between the *representative* constitutions and the constitution based on Estates. The representative constitution is a great advance because it is the *open*, *logical* and *undistorted* expression of the *situation of the modern state*. It is an *undisguised contradiction*.

Before coming to the problem itself let us take another look at Hegel's presentation of it.

'In the *Estates*, as an element in the legislative power, the *class of private citizens* acquires its *political* significance.'

Earlier on (in the Remark to §301) he had said:

'Hence the *specific* function which the concept assigns to the *Estates* is to be sought in the fact that . . . the private judgement and private will of the sphere called "*civil society*" in this book *comes into existence integrally related to the state*.'

Summarizing this definition we find that '*civil society* is the *class of private citizens*', in other words the *class of private citizens* is the immediate, essential, concrete class of civil society. Only in the Estates as an element in the legislative power does it acquire 'political significance and efficacy'. The new attribute thus acquired is a *particular* function; for its very character as a class of private citizens indicates its *antithesis* to political significance and efficacy, its absence of a political character: it expresses the idea that civil society is in and for itself *without* any political significance and

27. Knox's addition.

efficacy. The *class of private citizens* is the class of civil society, or, civil society is the *class of private citizens*. Consistently with this Hegel excludes the 'universal class' from the 'Estates as an element in the legislative power'.

'The *universal* class, or, more precisely, the class of *civil servants*, must, purely in virtue of its character as universal, have the universal as the end of its essential activity.'

The universal forms no part of the character of civil society or the class of private citizens; its essential activity does not have the universal as its end, alternatively, its essential activity is not determined by the universal, it is *not a universal* determination. The class of private citizens is the class of civil society *against* the state. The class of civil society is *not* a political class.

By defining civil society as a private class, Hegel has arrived at a position in which he must declare that the class distinctions of civil society are *non*-political and that civil and political life are heterogeneous and even *antithetical*. How does he continue?

'[The class of private citizens][28] appears, therefore, in the Estates neither as a mere indiscriminate multitude nor as an aggregate dispersed into its atoms, but as *what it already is*, namely a class subdivided into two, one sub-class [the agricultural class][29] being based on a tie of substance between its members, and the other [the business class][29] on particular needs and the work whereby they are met (see §201 ff.). It is only in this way that there is a genuine link between the *particular* which is effective *in* the state and the universal.'

[§303.]
It is true enough that civil society (*the class of private citizens*) cannot appear in the Estates as 'a mere indiscriminate multitude', and this is because the 'mere indiscriminate multitude' exists only in the 'imagination', in 'fantasy', and not in *reality*. In reality there are only multitudes of varying sizes, according to chance (cities, market towns, etc.). This multitude or multitudes not only *appear* but *are* in reality 'an aggregate dispersed into its atoms' and they *must* enter upon their *political* functions in the Estates in this atomized state. The *class of private citizens*, civil society, cannot appear there as '*what it already is*'. For what is it? A *private* class, i.e. the antithesis of the state and in separation from it. In order to 'acquire political significance and efficacy' it must

28. Translator's addition.   29. Knox's additions.

rather abandon what it is, viz. its *private* status. Only by this sacrifice can it acquire its '*political* significance and efficacy'. This political act entails a thoroughgoing transubstantiation. Civil society must completely renounce itself as civil society, as a *private class*, and must instead assert the validity of a part of its being which not only has nothing in common with, but is directly opposed to, its real civil existence.

What we see here in the individual case is in fact the *general rule*. Civil society is separated from the state. It follows, therefore, that the citizen of the state is separated from the citizen as a member of civil society. He must therefore *divide up his own essence*. As a *real citizen* he finds himself in a double organization. On the one hand, he is part of the *bureaucratic* order; this is an outward, formal determination of the state, the executive in its remoteness, and does not affect him and his independent reality. On the other hand, he is part of the *social* order, the order of civil society. But here he exists as a *private citizen* outside the state; the political state as such remains unaffected by the social order. The first [the bureaucratic] is an organization of the state for which he furnishes the *material*. The second [the social] is a *civil organization* whose material is not the state. In the first case, the state stands in formal opposition to him, in the second case he stands in material opposition to the state. If he is to become effective as a real *citizen of the state*, if he is to acquire true political significance and efficacy, he must abandon his civil reality, abstract from it and withdraw from the whole organization into his individuality. The only form in which he can exist as a citizen is the form of pure, unadorned *individuality*. For the existence of the state is complete without him and his existence in civil society is complete without the state. He can advance to the status of *citizen of the state* only as an *individual*, i.e. in contradiction with the *only available forms of community*. His existence as a citizen of the state is one which lies beyond the scope of his existence in any *community*, i.e. it is entirely *individual*. Only by becoming part of the 'legislature', as a 'power', is he *supposed* to become part of an *organization*, a *communal body*. *Prior* to joining the 'legislature' civil society, the class of private citizens, *does not* exist as an *organization of the state* and in order to acquire such an existence its *real organization*, real civil life, must be assumed to be *non-existent*, because the assumption of its *non-existence* is a part of the definition of the Estates as an element in the legislative power. The separation of

civil and political society appears *necessarily* as the separation of
the *political* citizen, the citizen of the state, from civil society and
from his own real empirical reality; for as an ideal political entity
[*Staatsidealist*] he is a *quite different being*, wholly distinct from
and opposed to his actual reality. Civil society thus manufactures
within itself the same relation between state and civil society that
we have already found in the *bureaucracy*. In the Estates the
universal really becomes *explicitly* [*für sich*] what it is *implicitly*
[*an sich*], namely the *antithesis of particular* interests. If the
citizen is to acquire political significance and efficacy, he must
discard his class, civil society, the *class of private citizens*; for it is
precisely this *class* that stands between the *individual* and the
political state.

Now if Hegel counterposes the whole of civil society as a
private class to the political state, it inevitably follows that all
distinctions *within* the private class, i.e. the various classes of
citizens, have only a private significance in respect to the state and
no political status at all. For the various classes of citizens are
merely the realized existence of the *principle* of the private class
as the principle of civil society. If, however, this principle is to be
abandoned, it follows inevitably that the divisions *within* the
principle will not exist for the political state.

'It is only in this way,' Hegel concludes, 'that there is a genuine link
between the *particular* which is effective *in* the state and the
universal.'

Hegel here confuses the state as the existence of a people as a
whole with the political state. The particular he refers to is not the
'*particular in* the state' but the particular '*outside* it', i.e. outside
the political state. Not only is it not 'the particular which is
effective [*wirkliche*] in the state', it is in fact the '*unreality*
[*Unwirklichkeit*] of the state'. Hegel wishes to demonstrate that
the classes of civil society are the political Estates and to achieve
this he suggests that the classes of civil society are the 'particular
moments of the political state', i.e. that civil society is identical
with political society. The expression 'the particular *in* the state'
can only have the meaning of 'the particular moments of the
state'. Hegel's bad conscience leads him to give preference to the
vague expression. He himself has not only argued the opposite
case, he even confirms it in this paragraph by referring to civil
society as 'the class of private citizens'. No less cautious is his

statement that there is a '*link*' between the particular and the universal. It is possible to 'link' the most heterogeneous objects. But here we are confronted not with a gradual *transition* but with a *transubstantiation* and it is of no use to pretend that the gulf does not exist when we prove the contrary by the very act of leaping over it.

In the Remark [to §303] Hegel says:

'This runs counter to another prevalent idea' etc. We have already shown that this prevalent idea is logically and necessarily 'a necessary idea at the present stage of the development of the people' and that Hegel's idea is mistaken notwithstanding its prevalence in certain circles. Returning to this prevalent idea, Hegel observes:

'This atomistic and abstract point of view vanishes at the stage of the family' etc. 'The state, however, is' etc. etc. This point of view is certainly abstract, but the 'abstraction' is that of the political state as Hegel has presented it. It is also atomistic, but its atomism is that of society itself. The 'point of view' cannot be concrete when its *object* is 'abstract'. The atomism into which civil society is plunged by its *political* actions is a necessary consequence of the fact that the community, the communistic entity [*das Gemeinwesen, das kommunistische Wesen*] in which the individual exists, civil society, is separated from the state, or in other words: the *political state is an abstraction* from civil society.

Even though this atomistic point of view vanishes in the family and perhaps (??) also in civil society, it returns in the political state just because the latter is an abstraction from the family and civil society. The converse is equally true. However, the mere fact that Hegel draws attention to the *strangeness* of this situation does not imply that he has eliminated the *estrangement* it entails.

'The circles of association in civil society,' he continues, '*are already communities*. To picture these communities as once more breaking up into a mere conglomeration of individuals as soon as they enter the field of politics, i.e. the field of the *highest concrete universality*, is *eo ipso* to *hold* civil and political life apart from one another and as it were to hang the latter in the air, because its basis could then only be the abstract individuality of caprice and opinion, and hence it would be grounded on chance and not on what is absolutely *stable* and *justified*.' [§303, Remark]

This idea [of these communities breaking up] does not *hold* political and civil life apart; it is just the idea of a *separation that actually exists.*

Nor does this idea hang political life in the air; it is rather that political life is the *airy life*, the aethereal region of civil society.

Let us now consider the *Estate* and *representative* systems.

It was a definite advance in history when the *Estates* were transformed into social classes so that, just as the Christians are equal in heaven though unequal on earth, the individual members of the people became *equal* in the heaven of their political world, though unequal in their earthly existence in *society*. The actual transformation of the Estates into *classes* took place under the *absolute monarchy*. Thanks to the bureaucracy the idea of unity was made to prevail over the various states within the state. Nevertheless, alongside the bureaucracy of the absolutist government, the *social distinctions* between the classes remained political and this *political difference* persisted *within* and alongside the bureaucracy of the absolute government. Not until the French Revolution was the process completed in which the *Estates* were transformed into *social* classes, i.e. the *class distinctions* in civil society became merely *social* differences in private life of no significance in political life. This accomplished the separation of political life and civil society.

This was accompanied by a comparable transformation of the classes of civil society: with its separation from the political state, civil society also changed. The medieval 'Estate' survived only in the bureaucracy, in which civil and political position are immediately identical. In contrast to this, civil society exists as the *class of private citizens*. Class distinction here is no longer a distinction between autonomous groups distinguished by their *needs* and their *work*. The only universal distinction to survive is the superficial and formal one of the difference between town and country. Within society itself, however, distinctions are variable and fluid and their principle is that of *arbitrariness*. The chief criteria are those of *money* and *education*. However, this is a matter to be dealt with in our critique of Hegel's analysis of civil society. Enough. The principle underlying civil society is neither need, a natural moment, nor politics. It is a fluid division of masses whose various formations are arbitrary and *without* organization.

The only noteworthy feature is that the *absence of property* and the *class of immediate labour*, of concrete labour, do not so much constitute a class of civil society as provide the ground on which the circles of civil society move and have their being.[30] The only class in which civil and political positions coincide is that of the *members of the executive*. The present state of society is distinguished from that which preceded it by the fact that civil society does not sustain the individual as a member of a community, as a communal being [*Gemeinwesen*]. On the contrary, whether an individual remains in a class or not depends partly on his work, partly on chance. The *class* itself is now no more than a *superficial* determination of the individual, for it is neither implicit in his work, nor does it present itself to him as an objective community, organized according to established laws and standing in a fixed relationship to him. It is rather the case that he has no real relation to his substantive activity, to his *real* class. The doctors do not constitute a special class in civil society. One businessman belongs to a different class from another and has a different *social position*. Just as civil society has split off from the political state, so too civil society has divided within itself into *class* and *social position*, even though the two are linked by numerous relations. The principle of the civil class or civil society is *enjoyment* and the *capacity to enjoy*. In his political role, the member of civil society breaks away from his class, his real private position; only then does he come into his own as a *human being*, only then does his determination as the member of a state, as a social being, appear as his human determination. For all of his other determinations in civil society *appear* as *inessential* to the man, to the individual, as *external* determinations, necessary to his existence within the whole, i.e. forming a bond with the whole, but a bond which he can just as easily cast away. (The civil society of the present is the principle of *individualism* carried to its logical conclusion. Individual existence is the ultimate goal; activity, work, content, etc., are *only* means.)

The *constitution based on the Estates*, when not a tradition of the Middle Ages, is the attempt, partly within the political sphere itself, to plunge man back into the limitations of his private sphere, to make his particular concerns into his substantive consciousness and to use the existence of political class distinctions to re-introduce corresponding distinctions of social class.

30. The term 'proletariat' does not yet figure in the *Critique*, but this passage foreshadows Marx's imminent discovery in the *Introduction* of the proletariat as 'universal class' (see below, pp. 255–7).

The *real human being* is the *private human being* of the present political constitution.

In general, *Estate* means that *distinction* and *separation* constitute the *existence* of the individual. Instead of his mode of life, his activity etc., making him a member, a function of society, they turn him into an *exception*, they are his privilege. This *distinguishing* characteristic is not merely *individual*, but establishes itself as a *community*, Estate or corporation, a fact which, far from eliminating its exclusive nature, is in reality its expression. Instead of the individual function being the function of society, the individual function is made into a society for itself.

Estate is based on the supreme law of the *division* of society, but, in addition, it separates man from his universal essence, it transforms him into an animal that is identical with its own immediate determinate nature. The Middle Ages is the *animal history* of mankind, its zoology.

The modern age, *civilization*, commits the opposite mistake. It isolates the *objective* essence of man, treating it as something purely *external* and material. It does not treat the content of man as his true reality.

This is a matter to be dealt with more thoroughly in the section on 'Civil Society'. We come, therefore, to

§304. 'The Estates, as an element in political life, still retain in their *own* function the class distinctions already present in the lower spheres of civil life.'

We have already shown that 'the class distinctions already present in the lower spheres of civil life' have no significance for the political sphere, or at best the significance of private, i.e. nonpolitical, distinctions. However, according to Hegel, class does not retain the significance 'already present' (i.e. present in civil society), but instead, when the 'Estates' incorporate it into themselves, they affirm its essence and, for its part, once a class has immersed itself in the sphere of politics it acquires its 'own' significance, i.e. one proper *not to itself but to the world of politics*.

At a time when the structure of civil society was political and when the political state was civil society, this *separation* and *duplication* of the significance of the classes did not exist. They did not mean *one* thing in civil society and *another* in the world of politics. They did not take on new *meaning* in the world of politics, they *retained what meaning they had*. The dualism of civil society and the political state which the constitution based on Estates imagines that it can overcome with the aid of a *reminiscence*, appears in the fact that class distinctions (i.e. the distinctions within civil society) mean one thing in the political sphere and another in civil life. There is here an apparent identity, *the same subject*, but it has *essentially different* determinations, i.e. in reality there is a *double* subject. (That this identity is illusory is evident, despite the fact that the *real subject*, man, remains the same and does not forfeit his identity in the various determinations of his being. For here the subject is not man, but rather man is identified with a predicate – class – and at the same time it is maintained that he has both this definite determinacy and another determinacy and that in the latter he is different from the limited, exclusive being that he is in the former.) This illusory identity is artificially upheld by the supposition that, on the one hand, the class distinctions in civil society are defined by criteria rooted in the political sphere and, conversely, the class distinctions in the political sphere are defined by criteria rooted not in itself but in civil society. In order to represent the limited subject, the determinate class (class distinction) as the essential subject, or, in other words, in order to demonstrate the identity of the two predicates, they are both mystified and expounded in an illusory and vague duplicated form.

The same subject is given different *meanings*, but the meaning is not that of self-determination, but of an *allegory* foisted on to it. The same meaning could be given to a different subject, the same subject could be given a different meaning. The meaning of civil class distinctions in the political sphere is not their own meaning, but one derived from the political sphere itself; and moreover, they might easily have quite a different meaning, as was historically the case. The converse is equally true. This is the *uncritical, mystical* way in which to *interpret* an *old view of the world* in terms of a new one; the consequence must inevitably be a wretched hybrid in which the form falsifies the meaning and the meaning falsifies the form, and neither the form nor the meaning can ever become real form and real meaning. This *uncritical mysticism* is the key both to the riddle of modern constitutions (especially constitutions based on Estates) and also to the mystery of the Hegelian philosophy, above all the *Philosophy of Right* and the *Philosophy of Religion*.

We may best free ourselves from this illusion if we take the meaning to be what it is, viz. the *authentic determination*, turn it into the subject and then decide whether the subject *allegedly* belonging to it is its *real predicate*, and whether it represents its essence and true realization.

'The position' (of the Estates) 'is abstract to begin with, i.e. in contrast with the whole principle of *monarchy* or the *crown*, their position is that of an extreme – *empirical universality*. This extreme opposition implies the possibility, though no more, of *harmonization*, and the equally likely *possibility of set hostility*. This abstract position changes into a rational relation (into a *syllogism*, see Remark to §302) only if the *middle term* between the opposites comes into existence.'

We have already seen that the Estates in common with the executive form the middle term between the monarchical principle and the people, between the state-will expressed as *one* empirical will and as *many* empirical wills, between *empirical individuality* and *empirical universality*. Since he defined the will of civil society as *empirical universality*, Hegel had to define the will of the monarch as *empirical individuality*; but he does not allow the *antithesis* to emerge in all its clarity.

Hegel continues:

'From the point of view of the crown, the executive already has this character (see §300). So, from the point of view of the Estates, one moment in them must be adapted to the task of existing as in essence the moment of mediation.'

But the true antitheses are the sovereign and civil society. And we have already seen the parallel between the meaning of the executive *vis-à-vis* the sovereign and the meaning of the Estates *vis-à-vis* the people. Just as the executive *expands* into a complex orbit, so the people are *condensed* into a miniature edition, for the constitutional monarch is compatible only with the *people en miniature*. The Estates are precisely *the same abstraction* of the political state *vis-à-vis* civil society as the executive is *vis-à-vis* the sovereign. The process of mediation seems therefore to have been fully achieved. Both extremes have relaxed their rigidity, have exchanged the spirit of their particular essence, and the *legislature*, which is made up of both the executive and the Estates, appears to be the middle term incarnate rather than the agent which brings the middle term into existence. Moreover, Hegel has already designated the Estates in common with the executive as the middle term between the people and the monarch (and likewise as the middle term between civil society and the executive, etc.). The rational relation, the *syllogism*, thus appears to be complete. The *legislature*, the middle term, is a hotch-potch of the two extremes of the monarchical principle and civil society, of empirical individuality and empirical universality, of subject and predicate. And in general Hegel regards the *syllogism* as a middle term, as a hotch-potch. We may say that in his exposition of this deductive process the whole transcendental and mystical dualism of his system becomes manifest. The middle term is the wooden sword, the concealed antithesis between the particular and the universal.

As a general comment on the whole argument we may point out that the 'mediation' that Hegel wishes to bring about here is not something that he derives from the *essential nature* of the *legislature* from its own determinate character. On the contrary, he derives it in *deference* to an *existent being* unconnected with the essential being of the legislature. It is a *construction based on deference*. The logical structure of the legislature is developed chiefly in deference to a third thing. For this reason, it is the *construction of its formal existence* that occupies the forefront of our attention. The legislature is construed very *diplomatically*. This follows from the *false*, illusory, pre-eminently political role of the legislature in the modern state (whose interpreter Hegel is). It follows inevitably that this is no *true* state, because its determinations (of which the legislature is one) have no theoretical standing in and for themselves, but must be regarded from a practical point of view; they are not autonomous powers but rather powers involving an antithesis, their laws are not defined according to the nature of the case but according to conventional rules.

In theory the Estates ought 'in common with the executive' to form the middle term between the will of empirical individuality, the sovereign, and the will of empirical universality, civil society. But in *reality* '*their* position' is 'abstract to begin with; i.e. in contrast with the whole *principle of monarchy or the crown*, their position is that of an *extreme – empirical universality*. This extreme opposition implies the *possibility*, though no more, of *harmonization*, and the equally likely *possibility of set opposition*.' – An 'abstract position', as Hegel rightly observes.

Now it may appear at first as if there were no opposition between '*the extreme of empirical universality*' and the 'principle of monarchy or the crown', the extreme of empirical individuality. For the Estates *deputize* for civil society, just as the executive *deputizes* for the monarch. In its deputy the executive, the monarchical principle ceases to be the extreme of empirical individuality, it forsakes its '*groundless*' will and condescends to the level of '*finite*' knowledge, responsibility and thought. Similarly, in the Estates, civil society seems to cease to be empirical universality and becomes instead a very definite whole which 'possesses a political and administrative sense and temper, no less than a sense for the interests of individuals and particular groups' (§302). In its miniature edition as the Estates civil society has ceased to be 'empirical universality'. It has instead sunk to the level of a committee, a very definite number, and if the monarch has achieved empirical universality through the executive, civil society has achieved empirical individuality or particularity through the Estates. Both have become particular institutions.

The only antithesis that can still survive in this situation appears to be that between the two representatives of the two wills of the state, between the two emanations, between the *executive* and the *Estates* as a part of the legislature, and this appears as an *antithesis within the legislature* itself. These 'common' middle terms seem destined to be at loggerheads. In the executive part of the legislature, the inaccessible, empirical individuality of the sovereign has *come down to earth* and assumed the shape of a number of limited, tangible, responsible persons. In the Estates, civil society has *ascended to Heaven* in the shape of a number of political persons. Both sides have lost their definability. The crown, the inaccessible, exclusive, *empirical One*, loses its rigidity, and civil society, the inaccessible, amorphous, *empirical All*, loses its fluidity. With the Estates and the executive supplying the middle term between the sovereign and civil society we find for the first time all the prerequisites for an *antithesis* in which the two sides are not only drawn up ready for battle, but have also reached the point of *irreconcilable conflict*.

Thus this '*middle term*' stands in great need of 'coming into existence', as Hegel so rightly infers. Far from accomplishing a mediation, it is the embodiment of contradiction.

Hegel seems to claim without offering any proof that this mediation is brought about by the Estates. He says:

'From the point of view of the crown, the executive already has this character (see §300). So, from the point of view of the Estates, one moment in them must be adapted to the task of existing as in essence the moment of mediation.'

However, we have already seen how Hegel arbitrarily and illogically represents the crown and the Estates as opposed extremes. Just as the executive has the character of a middle term from the point of view of the crown, so have the Estates from the point of view of civil society. The Estates not only stand together with the executive between the crown and civil society; they also stand between the government as a whole and the people (§302). They have to do more in the way of mediation for civil society than the executive does for the crown, for the executive itself stands in opposition to the people. Their cup of mediation runneth over. Why burden the asses with even more sacks? Why should the Estates everywhere act as the asses' bridge, even between themselves and their enemy? Why are they always so self-sacrificing? Why should they cut off *one* of their own hands when both are needed to repulse their opponents, the executive part of the legislature?

A further difficulty is that Hegel first derived the Estates from the corporations, class distinctions, etc., in order that they should be no 'mere empirical universality'; whereas now he reduces them to a 'mere empirical universality' in order to derive the class distinctions from them! Just as the monarch uses the executive to mediate as Christ between himself and civil society, so civil society uses the Estates to mediate as priests between itself and the monarch.

But it now appears as if the extremes of the crown (empirical individuality) and civil society (empirical universality) have to assume the role of mediators 'between their middle terms'. All the more so since 'it is one of the most important discoveries of logic that a specific moment which, by standing in an opposition, has the position of an extreme, ceases to be such and is a moment in an *organic* whole by being at the same time a *mean*' (Remark to §302). Civil society appears to be unable to assume this role since it has no place in the 'legislature' as *itself*, as an extreme. Since the other extreme, the crown, has a place in the legislature *in its own right*, it seems right that it should act as mediator between the Estates and the executive. Moreover, it seems well qualified for the task. On the one hand, the whole of the state, inclusive of civil society, is represented in the crown and, in particular, the crown has one thing in common with the Estates, namely 'empirical individuality' of the will – for empirical universality is only real in the form of empirical individuality. Furthermore, the crown, unlike the executive, does not confront civil society simply as a formula, as a state *consciousness*. The crown *is* itself the state, and has the material, natural moment in common with civil society. On the other hand, the sovereign is the apex and the representative of the executive. (Hegel, who turns everything back to front, converts the executive into the representative, the emanation of the sovereign. When he deals with the idea which is to acquire reality in the sovereign, he does not have in mind the real idea of the executive, the executive conceived as an idea; he thinks instead of the subject of the absolute Idea which exists *bodily* in the sovereign. In consequence the executive becomes a *mystical continuation of the soul existing in his body, the sovereign body*.)

In the legislature, therefore, the sovereign has to form the middle term between the executive and the Estates. However, the executive already forms the middle term between the sovereign and the Estates, and the Estates mediate between him and civil society. How, then, can he mediate between things which he needs as a means to avoid being a one-sided extreme? We see here the confusion that results from the definition of extremes which assume the roles both of extremes and of mediating factors. They are Janus-heads facing both ways, with one character from the front and another from behind. What at first appeared as middle term between two extremes, now appears as an extreme in its own right, and one of the two extremes that had formerly been mediated by it now reappears as an extreme[31] (because *distinct* from the other extreme) between its extreme and its middle term. There is a mutual exchange of compliments. It is like one man intervening between two men fighting, whereupon one of the disputants intervenes between his opponent and the mediator. It is the old story of the quarrel between a man and his wife. When the doctor attempts to intervene the man has to mediate between the doctor and his wife and the wife has to mediate between the doctor and her husband. It is like the lion in *A Midsummer Night's Dream* who proclaims both that he is the lion and that 'I one Snug the joiner am, No lion fell'.[32] At one moment an extreme is the lion of opposition, at another moment

31. Following the Lieber and Furth edition (Stuttgart, 1962). *MEW* has 'middle term' (*Mitte*) in place of 'extreme'.

32. Marx quotes the German translation, which re-translated reads: 'I am the lion, and am not the lion, but Snug'.

it is the Snug of mediation. Once one extreme has called out: 'Now I am in the middle!', the other two may not touch each other but must attack him. It is evident that the company as a whole like a fight but are too afraid of getting bruised to take things too far. So the two who wish to fight arrange matters so that the third man who intervenes will bear the brunt of the blows. But then one of the original two becomes the third and altogether they are so cautious that they never reach a decision. This system of mediation can also arise when a man wishes to thrash his opponent but must at the same time protect him against other enemies so that his dual role prevents him from carrying out his original intention. It is remarkable that Hegel could have reduced this absurd process of mediation to its abstract, logical and hence ultimate undistorted form, while at the same time enthroning it as the *speculative mystery* of logic, as the scheme of reason, the rational mode of deduction *par excellence*. Real extremes cannot be mediated precisely because they are real extremes. Nor do they require mediation, for their natures are wholly opposed. They have nothing in common with one another, they have no need for one another, they do not complement one another. The one does not bear within its womb a longing, a need, an anticipation of the other. (However, when Hegel treats universality and individuality, the abstract moments of the logical inference, as real antitheses, he reveals the fundamental dualism of his logic. This point needs to be developed further in a critique of Hegel's *Logic*.)

This appears to be refuted by the dictum that 'extremes meet'. The North and South Poles mutually attract each other; male and female likewise attract one another and human beings can arise only from the union of these two extremes.

And on the other hand: every extreme *is* its opposite. Abstract *spiritualism* is *abstract materialism*; *abstract materialism* is the *abstract spiritualism* of matter.

To the first point we may reply that both the North and South Poles are *poles*; they are identical in *essence*. Similarly, both the *male* and *female* sex belong to one *species* and have one *essence*, the essence of man. North and South are the opposite determinations of a *single* essence; the distinct sides of one *essence* at the *highest point of its development*. They are the essence in a state of *differentiation*. They are what they are *only* as a *distinct* determination, and moreover as *this* distinct determination of an essence. The true, real extremes would be a pole as opposed to a non-pole, a human as opposed to a *non*-human sex. The differentiation in this case [i.e. '*extremes meet*'] is *one of existence*, in the former situation ['the true real extremes'] it is *one of essence, of two essences*.

On the second point, we may remark that the issue turns on the fact that a *concept* (existence, etc.) is viewed *abstractly*, that it is not treated as something autonomous but as an *abstraction* from something else and that only this *abstraction* has meaning; thus, for example, mind is only an *abstraction* from matter. It is then self-evident that, precisely because this form constitutes its content, the concept is in fact the *abstract opposite*, while the object from which it abstracts (in this case abstract materialism) is in its abstract state its real essence. If it had been possible to avoid confusing the *distinctions* within one essence partly with autonomous *abstractions* (of course, not abstractions from something else, but, ultimately, self-abstractions), and partly with the *real* antitheses between mutually exclusive essences, it would also have been possible to avoid three pitfalls. (1) The first fallacy is to infer that, because only the extreme is true, it must follow that every abstraction and one-sidedness is true. This leads to a situation in which a principle does not appear as a totality in itself, but only as an abstraction from something else. (2) The second mistake occurs when the *sharp definition of real antitheses*, their assumption of extreme forms, is held to be something pernicious which has to be prevented, whereas this is nothing but the process of self-knowledge and the preliminaries necessary to resolving the conflict between them. (3) The final error is to attempt to mediate between them. For however much it may appear as if both extremes were equally real and extreme it nevertheless remains true that only one is an extreme by *nature*, while the extremity of the other does not have the significance of *true reality*. The one affects the other, but their positions are not identical. For example, Christianity or religion in general is an extreme opposite of philosophy. But in reality there is no *true* antithesis between religion and philosophy. For philosophy comprehends *religion* in its *illusory* reality. In the eyes of philosophy, religion – inasmuch as it wishes to become a reality – must necessarily disintegrate. There is no real dualism of *essence*. More about this later.

We may ask why Hegel arrives at the necessity for a new *mediation* on the Estates' side? Does he share the 'popular, but most dangerous, prejudice which regards the Estates principally

from the point of view of their *opposition* to the executive, as if
that were their essential attitude'? (Remark to §302.)

The position is simply this. On the one hand, we have seen that
in the 'legislature' civil society in the form of the 'Estates' has
for the first time come into immediate, real, practical conflict
with the crown in the form of the 'executive'.

On the other hand, the legislature is the totality. It contains
(1) the monarchical principle as represented by the 'executive';
(2) the representatives of civil society, i.e. the 'Estates'; but in
addition we find also (3) one *extreme as such*, viz. the monarchical
principle, while the other extreme, civil society, is excluded as
such. This means that whereas civil society ought to form the
opposite extreme to the 'monarchical' principle, the 'Estates' do
so in fact. We recollect that civil society comes into *political*
existence only with the 'Estates'. The 'Estates' are its *political*
existence, its *transubstantiation* into the political state. Therefore,
as we have seen, it is only with the 'legislature' that we arrive at
the *political* state in its totality. Thus we have (1) the monarchical
principle, (2) the executive and (3) civil society. The 'Estates' are
'*the civil society of the political state*', of the 'legislature'. Therefore, the extreme that civil society is supposed to form in opposition to the monarchical principle is the '*Estates*'. (Because civil
society represents the unreality of its political existence, the
political existence of civil society represents its own disintegration,
its separation from itself.) In similar fashion it forms an antithesis
to the executive.

Hence Hegel refers to the 'Estates' as the 'extreme position of
empirical universality', which actually applies properly to civil
society itself. (Hence it was pointless for Hegel to cause the
political Estates to arise out of the corporations and the different
classes. This would only have been meaningful if the different
classes as such were the Estates and if the determination of civil
life were in reality identical with that of political life. In that case
we would not have a *legislature* of the state as a whole, but a
legislature of the different Estates, corporations and classes over
the state as a whole. In that event the classes of civil society
would not receive their political determination from elsewhere, but
instead they would determine the political state. They would turn
their *particularity* into the power determining the whole. They
would represent the power of the particular over the universal.
We would not have a single legislature but a plurality of legisla-

tive powers which would come to an understanding among themselves and with the executive. But what Hegel has in mind here is the modern significance of the Estates, viz. the realization of statecitizenship, of the bourgeois. He wants the 'absolute universal', the political state, to determine civil society instead of being determined by it. He resuscitates the form of the medieval Estates but reverses their meaning by causing them to be determined by the political state. But in that case the Estates which represented the corporations, etc. would not be 'empirical universality' but 'empirical particularity', the 'particularity of empirical reality'!) The 'legislature' therefore requires *mediation* within itself, i.e. the concealment of its internal antagonisms. This mediation must proceed from the Estates because within the legislature the latter cease to represent civil society and so become a *primary* moment, i.e. they become the civil society of the legislature. The 'legislature' is the totality of the political state and precisely for that reason *forcibly brings out its contradictions*. To that extent it is its *established* disintegration. Widely differing principles come into conflict within it. *This becomes manifest*, of course, as a conflict between the monarchical principle and the principle of the Estates, etc. But *in reality* it is the antinomy of the *political state* and *civil society*, the *contradiction of the abstract political state* with itself. The legislature is the political state as revolt. [*Die gesetzgebende Gewalt ist die gesetzte Revolte*.]

(Hegel's chief error is that he regards *contradiction in the phenomenal world as unity in its essence, in the Idea*. There is however a profounder reality involved, namely an *essential contradiction*, e.g. in this case the contradiction in the legislature is itself only the self-contradiction of the political state, and hence of civil society.

Vulgar criticism falls into the opposite *dogmatic* error. Thus it criticizes the constitution. It points to the existence of antagonistic powers, etc. It discovers contradictions everywhere. A criticism that still *struggles* with its object remains dogmatic. For example, it was dogmatic to attack the dogma of the Holy Trinity by pointing out the contradiction of the three that were one. True criticism shows the inner genesis of the Holy Trinity in the brain of man. It describes its birth. Similarly, a truly philosophical criticism of the present constitution does not content itself with showing that it contains contradictions: it *explains* them, comprehends their genesis, their necessity. It grasps their *particular* significance. This act of comprehension does not however consist, as Hegel thinks, in discovering the determinations of the concepts of logic at every point; it consists in the discovery of the particular logic of the particular object.)

Hegel expresses this by saying that the opposition of the political Estates to the monarch 'implies the *possibility*, though no more, of *harmonization*, and the equally likely *possibility of set hostility*'.

The possibility of hostility is to be found everywhere where *different* wills come into contact. Hegel himself states that the 'possibility of harmonization' is the 'possibility of hostility'. He must therefore attempt to construct an element that would guarantee the '*impossibility of hostility*' and the '*reality* of harmonization'. Such an element would be the freedom of thought and decision *vis-à-vis* the will of the monarch and the executive. This would no longer be a part of the 'Estates'. It would rather be an element of the will of the monarch and of the executive and would thus find itself in the same conflict with the *real* classes as does the executive.

This requirement is considerably toned down in the conclusion to this Paragraph:

'From the point of view of the crown, the executive already has this character (see §300). So, from the point of view of the Estates, one moment in them must be adapted to the task of existing as *in essence the moment of mediation*.'

The moment emerging from the Estates must have the opposite meaning to that which the executive has in relation to the sovereign, because sovereign and Estates stand at opposing extremes. Just as the monarch democratizes himself in the executive, so the Estates *monarchize* themselves in the power that is to deputize for them. What Hegel requires, then, is a sovereign-moment *arising from the Estates*. Just as the executive represents an Estate-moment on the side of the sovereign, so there must also be a sovereign-moment on the side of the Estates.

The 'reality of harmonization' and the 'impossibility of hostility' thus become translated into the following postulate: 'So, from the point of view of the Estates, one moment in them must be adapted to the *task* of existing as *in essence the moment of mediation*.' Adapted to the *task*! According to §302 this is the general task of the Estates. What is required here is not a '*task*', but something more *specific*.

And what sort of a task is it that requires one to 'exist as in essence the moment of mediation'? It is the task of being 'in essence' Buridan's ass.[33]

The position is simply this:

The Estates are supposed to 'mediate' between the sovereign and the executive on the one hand, and the people on the other; but they do not do this. Instead they are the organized *political* antagonism of civil society. The 'legislature' itself stands in need of *mediation*. This mediation, moreover, should proceed from the Estates. It does not suffice to posit a *moral* harmony between the two sides, between the political will in the form of the will of the sovereign and the political will in the form of the will of civil society. It is true that it is only with the legislature that we find the organized, *total* political state, but it is precisely here at the apex of the system that we also find the self-contradictions of the *political state* revealed in all their starkness. Hence there is a need to establish the *appearance* of a *real identity* between the will of the sovereign and the will of the Estates. *The Estates must be established as the will of the sovereign, or the will of the sovereign must be established as the Estates.* The Estates must establish themselves as the reality of a will which is not their own. The *unity* which cannot be found in the *essence* of the situation (for otherwise it would have to prove itself in terms of the *efficacy* of the Estates, and not their *mode of existence*) must at least be present in its *existence*, in other words, an actually *existing* element of the legislature (of the Estates) has the *task* of representing the *unity of the disunited*. This moment of the Estates, the chamber of peers or upper house, etc., is the highest *synthesis* of the political state in the organization under consideration. It does not, it is true, achieve Hegel's aim of the 'reality of harmonization' and the 'impossibility of hostility'. On the contrary, it does not advance beyond the 'possibility of harmonization'. Nevertheless, it *establishes the illusion of the unity of the political state in itself* (i.e. the unity of wills of the sovereign and the Estates, and unity of the principle of the political state with that of civil society); moreover, this *unity* is a *material* principle, i.e. it is not merely the case that two opposed principles are reconciled, but that their unity exists in *nature*, in actual existence. This moment of the Estates is, then, the *romanticism* of the political state, it contains its dreams of its

33. The ass in question is said to have been unable to choose between two bundles of hay and so starved to death.

essential unity, its harmony with itself. It is an *allegorical* existence.

Whether this *illusion* is efficacious or whether it is a *conscious self-deception* depends on the real *status quo* of the relationship between the Estates and the crown. As long as Estates and crown have an actual understanding and are in actual harmony, the *illusion* of their *essential* unity is a *real* and hence *efficacious* illusion. Where this is not the case it becomes *conscious untruth* and farce as soon as it has to prove itself.

§305. 'The principle of one of the *classes of civil society* is in itself capable of adaptation to this *political* position. The class in question is the one whose ethical life is natural, whose basis is family life, and so far as its livelihood is concerned, the possession of land. Its particular members attain their position by birth, just as the monarch does, and, in common with him, they possess a will which rests on itself alone.'

We have already exposed the fallacies of Hegel's argument here. (1) After he has argued that the Estates develop from the corporations he goes on to confound this with the Estates in their *modern* abstraction from civil society. (2) After he has defined the Estates as such as the 'extreme of empirical universality', he goes on to define them in terms of the *class distinctions of civil society*.

Logic would not require him to consider the *Estates* as a new element in their own right and then to deduce from them the mediation he postulated in §304.

But let us see how Hegel re-introduces civil class distinctions while at the same time creating the impression that the legislature as the *highest political sphere*, is not determined by the *reality*, the *particular* nature of civil class distinctions, but that, on the contrary, this reality, this particular nature of class distinctions, sinks to the level of *material* that is shaped by the political sphere in accordance with *its own* self-generated needs.

'The *principle* of one of the classes of civil society is in itself capable of *adaptation to this political position*. The class in question is the one whose *ethical life is natural* . . .' (i.e. the agricultural class).

But what is the nature of the *principled ability* of the agricultural class, what is the *capability of its principle*? It has 'its *basis* in *family life*, and, so far as its livelihood is concerned, *the possession of land*. Its particular members attain their *position by birth*, just as the *monarch* does, and, in common with him, they possess a will which rests *on itself alone*.'

The 'will which rests on itself alone' is treated here in the context of the livelihood afforded by the 'possession of land', while the fact that like the monarch one owes one's position to one's birth is based on 'family life'.

The livelihood based on 'the possession of land' and 'a will which rests on itself alone' are two quite separate things. Hegel should speak rather of 'a will which *rests* on the possession of land'. Even more properly he should speak of a will resting 'on political principles', i.e. not a will which rests *on itself*, but one which rests *within society as a whole*.

The place of 'principles', of the 'possession of political mind', is taken by the 'possession of *land*'.

Furthermore, as for the basis in '*family life*', the 'social' ethical life of civil society seems to be superior to this 'natural' ethical life. Moreover, 'family life' is the '*natural ethical life*' of the *other classes*, i.e. of the citizens in civil society, as much as it is of the agricultural class. But if among the agricultural class 'family life' supplies not only the principle of the family but also the foundation of social life as such, this would seem to debar it from the highest political tasks because it involves the attempt to apply patriarchal laws to an unpatriarchal situation and to treat the *political* state and *state-citizenship* in terms of father and child, master and servant.

As to the statement that the *monarch* owes his *position to his birth*, it should be pointed out that Hegel has expounded the theory not of a patriarchal monarch but of the *modern constitutional* king. The fact of his birth ensures that he is the *physical representative* of the state and is born to kingship, in other words that the kingdom is his *family* inheritance. But what has this to do with family life as the basis of the agricultural class, what has natural ethical life in common with the fact that one owes one's position to one's birth? The king has this much in common with a horse, that just as the latter is born a horse, so the king is born a king.

Once Hegel had turned his own class distinctions as such into political distinctions, the agricultural class as such became an independent part of the Estates; but if as such it is already a moment of mediation with the crown, why did Hegel need to construct a *new* mediation? And why was it necessary to isolate this class from the actual moment of the Estates when it is only this isolation that brings it into its 'abstract' relation to the crown? And having once shown that the Estates have a proper identity, involving the *transubstantiation of the class of private citizens into citizens of the state*, and having argued further that they therefore stand in need of mediation, how can Hegel go on to dissolve this organism back into the distinct private classes and then hope to derive the middle term in the political state from them?

And in general is it not anomalous that the highest *synthesis* of the political state should be none other than the synthesis of family life and landownership!

In a word:

If the civil classes as such are political classes there is no need for any mediation, and, if there is a need for mediation, then the civil classes cannot be political and hence cannot provide that mediation. The farmer is then a part of the Estates as a citizen and not as a farmer and, conversely (where it is as a *farmer* that he is a citizen, or is a farmer in his capacity as citizen), his citizenship is his *membership of the agricultural class* and it is not as a farmer that he is a citizen but as a citizen that he is a farmer!

We are confronted here with an inconsistency *within Hegel's own* analysis and such an inconsistency is part of a *compromise*. The Estates in their modern sense, i.e. in the sense given to them by Hegel, *postulate a complete separation of civil society from the class of private citizens and its components*. How can Hegel put forward the class of private citizens as a *solution* to the internal contradictions of the legislature? Hegel would like to retain the medieval system of Estates but in the form of the modern legislature, and he would like to retain the modern legislature but in the shape of the medieval system of Estates! It is syncretism of the very worst sort.

§304 begins with the words:

'The Estates, as an element in political life, still retain in their own function the class distinctions already present in the lower spheres of civil life.'

But in their *own* function the Estates only retain these distinctions by annulling them, by destroying them and *abstracting from them*.

If the agricultural class or, as we shall learn later on, the *potentiated* agricultural class, namely the landed gentry, is converted in the way already described into the mediating factor of the total *political* state, of the legislature, this will undoubtedly lead to mediation between the Estates and the crown in the sense that the Estates will cease to function as a real political element. The operative factor in *restoring the unity of the political state* is not the agricultural class but *class*, the *class of private citizens*, the *analysis* (reduction) of the Estates into a private class. (Not the agricultural class as such, but rather its separation from the political Estates in its quality as private, civil class, is the mediating factor here; it is the fact that its private status gives it a special position in the Estates and this ensures that the other portion of the Estates acquires the position of a *particular* private class and thus *ceases* to represent the citizens of civil society.) Thus we are no longer confronted with the *political* state in the form of *two opposed wills* but, on the one hand, with the political state (government and monarch) and, on the other, with civil society as distinct from the political state (i.e. the different classes). This completes the destruction of the political state as a totality.

The most obvious meaning of the internal duplication of the Estates as a means of mediation with the crown is that this *separation*, this internal contradiction in the Estates represents the restored unity with the crown. The fundamental dualism between crown and Estates within the legislature is *neutralized* by the internal dualism in the Estates. In Hegel this neutralization is achieved by separating the Estates from their political dimension.

We shall return later to the question of the correspondence of landed property as a means of livelihood with the *sovereign* will, the *sovereignty of the crown* and *family life* as the basis of the agricultural class – something which corresponds to the *natural birthright* of the monarch. Here in §305 Hegel expounds the '*principle*' of the agricultural class as something 'capable of adaptation to this political position'.

In §306 the process of 'adaptation to this political position and significance' is elaborated. It reduces itself to the statement that 'their wealth becomes *inalienable*, *entailed* and burdened by *primogeniture*'.[34] 'Primogeniture' is thus seen as the institution by which the landowning class is 'fitted' for politics.

34. Primogeniture is that system whereby a noble family's first-born inherits intact the family's entire landed property. Hegel considered that primogeniture stabilized wealth, protecting it from the fluctuations of the business world. It therefore worked in the interests of social and political unity by giving members of the landowning class independence from government and people, and protection from personal extravagance. The members of this class were hence, according to Hegel, public-spirited and politically disinterested.

'Primogeniture is grounded on the fact that the state should be able to reckon not on the *bare possibility* of political inclinations, but on something *necessary*. Now an inclination for politics is of course not bound up with wealth, but there is a *relatively necessary* connection between the two, because a man with independent means is not hemmed in by external circumstances and so there is *nothing to prevent him* from entering politics and working for the state.' [Addition to §306]

·*First statement*. The state cannot remain content with '*the bare possibility of political inclinations*', it must be able to reckon on something '*necessary*'.

Second statement. 'An inclination for politics is not bound up with wealth', i.e. the political inclinations bound up with wealth remain a '*bare possibility*'.

Third statement. But there is a '*relatively necessary connection*' and this lies in the circumstance that 'there is *nothing to prevent* a man with independent means, etc. from working for the state', i.e. *wealth* provides the '*possibility*' of political inclinations, but according to the first statement 'possibility' does not suffice.

Furthermore, Hegel has not shown that *landed property* is the only form of 'independent means'.

The fact that the wealth of the agricultural class is *so constituted as to be independent* is what fits this class 'for political position and significance'. Or, in other words, the 'independence' of its 'means' *is* its 'political position and significance'.

Hegel elaborates on this independence as follows:

The '*means*' of the agricultural class are '*independent* of the *state's capital*'. By the state's capital he evidently means the *government treasury*. In this respect a contrast is intended with 'the *universal* class' which is 'essentially dependent on the state'. Thus in the Preface [to the *Philosophy of Right*] Hegel writes:

'Apart from anything else, *philosophy* with us is not as it was with the Greeks for instance, pursued in private like an art, but has an existence in the open, in contact with the public, and especially, or even *only*, in the *service of the state*.'

Thus even philosophy is '*essentially*' dependent on the government treasury.

The *wealth* of the agricultural class is independent 'of the uncertainty of business, the quest for profit, and any sort of fluctuation in possessions'. In this respect it is to be contrasted with the 'business class' which is based 'on particular needs and the work whereby these are met'.

This wealth is likewise 'independent of *favour*, whether from the *executive* or the *mob*'.

Finally, it is even fortified *against its own wilfulness* because 'those members of this class who are called to political life are not entitled, as other citizens are, either to dispose of their entire property at will, or to the assurance that it will pass to their children, whom they love equally, in similarly equal divisions'.

The antagonisms have now assumed a wholly novel and very material shape – something that we had hardly expected to find in the heaven of the political state.

Expressed in all its starkness, the antagonism Hegel has uncovered is the conflict between *wealth* and *private property*.

Landed property is the pre-eminent form of *private property*, it is *private property par excellence*. The exact nature of its privacy emerges in that (1) in its '*independence of the state's capital*', of the 'favour of the executive', of property existing as the 'universal property of the political state', it emerges as one *particular form of wealth* among other forms, in accordance with the structure of the political state. It appears (2) as 'independent of the needs' of society or 'social wealth' or the 'favour of the mob'. (The fact that a share in the state's capital should be regarded as a '*favour of the executive*' is just as significant as that a share in the wealth of society should appear as the 'favour of the mob'.) The wealth of the 'universal class' and of the 'business class' is *no true private property* because in the first case *directly* and in the second case *indirectly* it is conditioned by its connections with the wealth of the whole society, with property conceived as social property. There is no doubt that a *share* in this property is indeed mediated on both sides by 'favour', i.e. by 'accident of will'. In contrast with this *landed property* is sovereign *private property* which has not yet acquired the form of wealth, i.e. has not yet become property as established by the *will of society*.

The political constitution at its highest point is thus the *constitution of private property*. The loftiest *political principles* are the *principles of private property*. Primogeniture is merely the *external* manifestation of the *inner* nature of landed property. Because such property is *inalienable*, the nerves connecting it to *society* are severed and its *isolation from civil society* is assured. Because it may not even pass to equally loved children in similarly equal divisions, it is even compelled to renounce the smaller natural society of the family with its will and its laws. It thus even preserves the *harsh* nature of *private property* from passing over into *family wealth*.

In §305 Hegel judged the class of landed property to be capable of adaptation to 'political position' because of its 'basis in family life'. He has himself declared that 'love' is the basis, the principle and the *spirit* informing family life. We now see that the class which is based on family life is deprived of the *basis of family life*, it is deprived of love as the real, and thus effective and determining, principle. It is the *illusion* of family life, family life in its most soulless form. At the point of its highest development the principle of private property *contradicts* the principle of family life. Family life therefore comes into its own as the life of the family, the *life of love*, only in civil society, and not in the class 'whose ethical life is natural', i.e. the class of family life. This latter represents the *barbarism* of private property as opposed to family life.

This then is *private property, landed property* in all its *sovereign glory*; it is this that has been the occasion of so much sentimentality in recent years, it is for this that so many colourful crocodile tears have been shed.

It is of no avail for Hegel to argue that *primogeniture* is merely *an exigency of politics* and so must be judged according to its *political* significance. It is of no avail for him to assert that 'the security and stability of the landowning class may be still further increased by the institution of primogeniture, though this institution is desirable *only from the point of view of politics*, since it entails a sacrifice for the *political end* of giving the eldest son *a life of independence*.' Hegel is not without a certain decency, the *decency of the understanding*. He does not wish to retain primogeniture in and for itself, but only in reference to something else, as something determined rather than self-determining, not as an end but as a *means* to justify and construct an end. In reality primogeniture is a consequence of private property in the *strict* sense, private property petrified, private property (*quand même*) at the point of its greatest autonomy and sharpest definition. What Hegel asserts to be the end, the determining factor, the *prime cause* of primogeniture is in fact an effect of it, a consequence. Whereas according to Hegel primogeniture represents the *power of the political state over private property*, it is in fact the *power of abstract private property over the political state*. He makes the cause into the effect and the effect into the cause, the determining factor into the determined and vice-versa.

But what is the *content* of its political function, of its political purpose, what is the purpose of this purpose? What is its substance? *Primogeniture, the superlative form of private property, private property supreme.* What power does the political state exercise over private property through primogeniture? It *isolates* it from society and the family by bringing it to a peak of *abstract independence.* What then is the power of the political state over private property? It is the power of private property itself, its essence brought into existence. What remains to the state as opposed to this essence? The *illusion* that it determines where it is in fact determined. No doubt it breaks the *will of the family and society,* but only to make way for the *will of a private property purified of family and society* and to acknowledge the existence of this private property as the highest reality of the political state, as the highest *ethical* reality.

Let us consider the different component parts of the *legislature,* of the total state, the real, consequential and conscious state, the *real* political state, let us see how they behave and let us view them in the light of their *ideal* of what ought to be, and of their *logical* form and determination.

(Primogeniture is not as Hegel claims 'a chain on the freedom of private rights', it is rather 'the freedom of private rights that has liberated itself from all social and ethical chains'.) ('The highest political construction is the construction of abstract private property.')

Before entering into this comparison let us first take a closer look at one assertion contained in this paragraph [§306], viz. the statement that thanks to primogeniture the wealth of the agricultural class, landed property, private property 'is even fortified *against its own wilfulness,* because those members of this class who are called to political life are not entitled, as other citizens are, to dispose of their entire property at will'.

We have already emphasized how the social nerves of private property were severed by the 'inalienability' of landed property. Private property (landed property) is fortified against the *wilfulness* of its owner in consequence of the conversion of his universally human wilfulness into the *specific wilfulness of private property*; that is to say, private property has become the *subject* of will; the will survives only as the *predicate* of private property. Private property is no longer a *determined* object of wilfulness, but instead wilfulness is the *determined* predicate of private property. But let us compare what Hegel has said himself in the context of civil law:

§65. 'The reason I can *alienate* my property is that it is mine only in so far as I put my will into it [. . .] provided always that the thing in question is a thing *external by nature*.'

§66. 'Therefore those goods, or rather substantive characteristics, which constitute my private personality and the universal essence of my self-consciousness are *inalienable* and my right to them *cannot lapse*. Such characteristics are my personality as such, my universal freedom of will, my ethical life, my religion.'

In the institution of primogeniture, then, landed property, private property in the strict sense, becomes *inalienable*, and thus a *substantive characteristic* which constitutes the 'private personality and the universal essence of the self-consciousness' of the class of noble entailed estates, 'its personality as such, its universal freedom of will, its ethical life, its religion'. It is perfectly logical that where private property, landed property, is *inalienable*, 'the universal freedom of will' (of which the right to dispose freely of an external object, such as landed property, is an essential part) is alienable. The same thing holds good for *ethical life* (which includes *love* as the moving spirit and the real law governing the family). The *'inalienability' of private property implies the 'alienability' of the universal freedom of the will and of ethical life.* Property is no longer mine in so far as 'I put my will into it'; it is truer to say that my will only exists 'in so far as it exists in the property'. My will does not possess, it is possessed. What makes the glories of primogeniture appear in such a *romantic* light is that private property, i.e. private wilfulness in its most abstract form, *utterly philistinic*, unethical and barbaric wilfulness, is made to appear as the highest synthesis of the political state, the loftiest elimination of wilfulness and the bitterest, most self-denying struggle with *human frailty*. For the *humanization* of private property appears to be nothing more than a piece of *human* frailty. Primogeniture is private property *enchanted* by its own independence and splendour, and wholly immersed in itself; it is private property elevated to the status of a *religion*. By analogy with its protection against direct alienation, private property is similarly excluded from *contract*. Hegel presents the transition from property to contract in the following manner:

§71. 'Existence as determinate being is in essence being for another [. . .] One aspect of property is that it is an existent as an external thing, and in this respect property exists for other external things, and is connected with their necessity and contingency. But it is also an existent as an embodiment of the *will*, and from this point of view the "other" for which it exists can *only be the will* of another person. This relation of will to will is the true and proper ground in which freedom is *existent*. – The sphere of *contract* is made up of this mediation whereby I hold *property* not merely by *means of a thing and my subjective will*, but by means of another person's will as well and so hold it in virtue of my participation in a *common* will.'

(In primogeniture the fact that property is held not in virtue of *participation in a common will*, but only 'by means of a *thing* and a *subjective will*' is made an integral part of the law of the land.) Whereas in *civil law* Hegel confers the status of *true idealism* upon the *alienability* of private property and its dependence on a *common* will, in constitutional law he extols the imaginary virtues of independent property in contrast with 'the uncertainty of business, the quest for profit, the fluctuations of possessions and dependence upon the government treasury'. What sort of a state is it that cannot even tolerate the idealism of its own civil law? What sort of a philosophy of right is it that assigns one meaning to independent private property in civil law and another in constitutional law?

As contrasted with the *barbaric stupidity* of independent private property, the uncertainty of business is pure elegy, the quest for profit has a moving solemnity (drama), the fluctuations of possessions have a grim inevitability (tragedy), the dependence upon the government treasury has a high ethical content. In a word, in all these relations the *human heart* can be heard throbbing behind the façade of property, in all of them we witness man's dependence upon man. Whatever the nature of this dependence it is *human*, unlike the situation of these slaves who, because they are bound not to society but to the *soil*, imagine themselves free; freedom of will in these circumstances amounts simply to the *absence* of any content but that of *private property*.

To define such monstrosities as primogeniture as a determination of private property by the state is the kind of unavoidable error that arises when an old world-view is seen in terms of a new one, when an institution like private property is given two contrary meanings, one in the courtroom of abstract law, the other in the heaven of the political state.

Let us turn now to the comparison foreshadowed above [p. 144].

In §257 we find:

'The state is the reality of the ethical Idea. It is ethical mind *qua* the substantial will *manifest* and revealed to itself [. . .] The state exists immediately in *custom*, mediately in individual *self-consciousness* [. . .] while self-consciousness in virtue of its sentiment towards the state finds in the state, as its essence and the end and product of its activity, its *substantive freedom*.'

In §268:

'The political *sentiment, patriotism* pure and simple, is assured conviction with *truth* as its basis [. . .] and a volition that has become *habitual*. In this sense it is simply a product of the institutions subsisting in the state, since rationality is *really* present in the state, while action in conformity with these institutions gives rationality its practical proof. This sentiment is, in general, *trust* (which may pass over into a greater or lesser degree of educated insight), or the consciousness that my interest, both substantive and particular, is contained and preserved in another's (i.e. the state's) interest and end, i.e. in the other's relation to me as an individual. In this way, this very other is immediately not an other in my eyes, and in being conscious of this fact, I am free.'

The *reality* of the ethical idea becomes manifest here as the *religion of private property*. (Because primogeniture is the religious form of private property we find that in our modern age religion has generally become an integral part of landed property and all writings on the subject of primogeniture are imbued with religious unction. Religion is the highest conceptual form of this brutality.) The 'substantial will *manifest* and revealed to itself' becomes transformed into a mysterious will broken on the soil, a will intoxicated by the very opacity of the element to which it is attached. The 'assured conviction with truth as its basis' which is Hegel's description of 'political sentiment' is a conviction based (literally) 'on its own ground'. The political 'volition that has become habitual' is no longer 'simply a product' etc., but an institution subsisting outside the state. Political sentiment is no longer '*trust*' [*Zutrauen*] but rather 'the confidence [*Vertrauen*], the consciousness that my interest as an individual, both substantive and particular, is *independent* of another's (i.e. the state's) interest and end'. This is the nature of my consciousness of my *freedom from the state*.

'The maintenance of the state's universal interest', etc., was the task assigned to the 'executive' (§289). The latter was the repository of 'the consciousness of right and the developed intelligence of the mass of the people' (§297). It actually renders 'the Estates unnecessary' because [the higher civil servants] 'even without the Estates are *able* to do what is best, just as they also continually *have* to do while the Estates are in session' (Remark to §301). 'The universal class, or, more precisely, the class of civil servants, must, purely in virtue of its character as universal, have the universal as the end of its essential activity' (§303).

And how does the universal class, the executive, appear now? 'As essentially dependent upon the executive', as 'wealth, *dependent upon the favour of the executive*'. Civil society underwent a similar transformation. At first it had achieved an ethical existence in the corporation; later it was found to be dependent upon 'the uncertainty of business' etc. and 'the favour of the mob'.

What then does Hegel see as the specific quality of the owner of an entailed estate? And what could the *ethical* value of *inalienable wealth* possibly consist in? In its *incorruptibility. Incorruptibility* thus becomes the *highest* political virtue, an abstract virtue. At the same time in Hegel's construction of the state, incorruptibility is held to be something so very special as to require a *special* political institution and it becomes conscious precisely because it is not the spirit informing the political state, not the rule, but an *exception*, and it is in fact constructed as such an exception. In order to preserve the owners of entailed estates from bribery, they are bribed by their independent property. In theory dependence upon the state and the feeling of this dependence represent the pinnacle of political freedom, because it is the feeling experienced by the private person as an abstract, dependent person who feels and should feel himself to be free only in his capacity as a citizen. Here, by contrast, Hegel develops the idea of the *independent private person*. 'Their capital is independent alike of the state's capital as of the uncertainty of business' etc. It is thus contrasted with the business class which is based on particular needs and the work whereby these are met, and the universal class with its essential dependence upon the state. Thus *independence* of the state and civil society, and this abstract embodiment of both (which in reality represents the most primitive dependence upon the soil), come to form the mediating synthesis of both the state

and civil society in the legislature. *Independent private capital*, i.e.
abstract private property and the *private person* corresponding to
it, are the logical apex of the political state. Political 'independence'
is interpreted to mean 'independent private property' and the
'person corresponding to that independent private property'.
We shall soon see the true nature of this 'independence' and
'incorruptibility' and the political sentiment they engender.

It is self-evident that an *entailed estate* is acquired through
inheritance. The fact that it falls to the *first-born* (as Hegel points
out in the *Addition*) is an accident of history.

§307. 'The right of this section of the landowning class is thus based
in a way on the natural principle of the family. But this principle is at
the same time reversed owing to *hard sacrifices* made for *political ends*,
and *thereby* the activity of this class is essentially directed to those ends.
As a consequence of this, this class is summoned and *entitled* to its
political vocation by *birth* without the hazards of election.'

Hegel has failed to prove that the right of this landowning class
is based on the *natural principle* of the family unless by this he
means landed property is acquired by *inheritance*. But this does
not establish the entitlement of this class to any political rights
but only the right of the landowner to inherit his land. 'But this'
– i.e. the natural principle of the family – 'is at the same time
reversed owing to hard sacrifices made for political ends.' We have
indeed seen how 'the natural principle of the family is reversed',
not so much 'owing to hard sacrifices made for political ends' but
in order to *give concrete reality to the abstraction of private
property*. On the contrary, this *reversal of the natural principle of
the family* leads naturally to the reversal of the political end,
'*whereby*' – by the fact of the emancipation of private property?
– 'the activity of this class is essentially directed to those ends. As
a consequence of this, this class is summoned and *entitled* to its
political vocation by *birth* without the hazards of election.'

Participation in the legislature is then an *innate right of man*.
Here we have *born legislators*, the *born mediation of the political
state with itself*. Many people and especially the owners of entailed estates have made fun of the *innate rights of man*. Is it not
even funnier that a particular race of men should have a natural
right to the highest dignity of government? Nothing could be more
ridiculous than for Hegel to oppose the selection by birth of
legislators, of representatives of the body politic, to their selection

by 'the hazards of election'. Can he be unaware that *elections*, the conscious product of the trust of the citizenry, stand in quite a different necessary connection to the political end than does the physical accident of birth? At every point Hegel's political spiritualism can be seen to degenerate into the crassest *materialism*. At the apex of the political state birth is the decisive factor that makes particular individuals into the incarnations of the highest political office. At the highest level political office coincides with a man's birth in just the same way that the situation of an animal, his character and mode of life, etc., are the direct consequence of its birth. The highest offices of the state thus acquire an *animal* reality. Nature takes revenge on Hegel for the contempt he has shown her. If matter is to be shorn of its reality in favour of human will then here human will is left with no reality but that of matter.

The *false* identity, the fragmentary, intermittent identity of nature and spirit, body and soul, becomes manifest here as *embodiment, incorporation*. Birth only provides a man with his *individual* existence and constitutes him in the first instance only as a *natural* individual, while political determinations such as the legislature etc. are *social products*, born of society and not of the natural individual. Hence what is striking and even *miraculous* is to conceive of an immediate identity, an immediate coincidence, between the *birth of an individual* and the individual conceived as the *individual embodiment of a particular social position or function*. In this system nature *creates* kings and *peers* directly just as it creates eyes and noses. What is striking is to discover the product of a self-conscious species represented as the product of a physical species. I am a man simply by my birth without the agreement of society; a particular birth can become the birth of a peer or a king only by virtue of general agreement. Only this agreement can convert the birth of a man into the birth of a king: hence kings are made not by birth but by agreement. If it is true that a man can owe his position directly to his birth, as distinct from other determinations, then it must be by virtue of *his body* that he can fulfil *this particular* social function. His body is his *social* prerogative. According to this system the *physical dignity of man* or the *dignity of the human body* (or we might go further and say: the dignity of the natural physical element of the state) is made manifest in such a way that definite social positions, indeed the highest ones, are in fact the *dignity of specific bodies predestined by birth*. Hence, the nobility takes a natural pride in its blood, its extraction, in short the whole *life-history of its body*: this is its natural, *zoological* way of thinking and *heraldry* is the science appropriate to it. Thus zoology is the secret of the nobility.

Two aspects of the institution of primogeniture are particularly worthy of note:

(1) What is lasting is the *hereditary landed property*. It is the permanent element in the situation – the *substance*. The hereditary proprietor, the owner, is in reality only an *accident*. Landed property thus anthropomorphizes itself in the various generations. One might say that the *estate* always *inherits* the first-born of the family as an attribute bound to itself. Every first-born in the series of landowners is the *inheritance*, the *property of the inalienable estate*, the *predestined substance of its will and activity*. The subject is the thing and the predicate is the human being. The will becomes the property of property.

(2) The *political qualifications* of the hereditary landowner are the political qualifications of his estate, qualifications inherent in the estate itself. Thus political qualifications appear here as the *property of landed property*, as something directly arising from the *purely physical earth* (nature).

The first point implies that the hereditary landowner is a *serf* attached to the estate and that the *serfs* subject to him are no more than the *practical* consequence of the *theoretical* relationship binding him to the estate. The profundity of Germanic subjectivity becomes manifest everywhere as the barbarism of mindless objectivity.

We have here to analyse (1) the relation between *private property* and *inheritance*, (2) between *private property*, inheritance and the resulting prerogative of certain families to a share in the sovereign power of the state, and (3) the *real historical situation*, i.e. the *Germanic* situation.

As we have seen, primogeniture is an abstraction of '*independent private property*'. This has yet another implication. *Independence, autonomy* within the political state whose structure we have been considering, is embodied in *private property* which appears in its highest form in *inalienable landed property*. Thus political independence does not proceed from the nature of the political state, it is not the gift of the political state to its members, it is not the spirit that breathes life into the state. On the contrary, the members of the political state receive their independence from a

being other than that of the state, from a being belonging to
abstract civil law, from abstract *private property*. Political independence is an accident of private property, not the substance
of the political state. As we have seen, the political state, and in it
the legislature, is the revealed mystery of the *true value and
essence* of the moments of the state. The meaning that *private
property* acquires in the political state is its *essential, true* meaning;
the meaning acquired by *class distinctions* in the political state is
their *essential* meaning. In the same way, the *essential* meaning of
the crown and the executive becomes manifest in the 'legislature'.
It is here, in the sphere of the political state, that the individual
moments of the state achieve the *essential reality* of their *species*,
their '*species-being*'. And this is because the political state is the
sphere of their universal meaning, their *religious* sphere. The
political state is the *mirror of truth* which reflects the disparate
moments of the *concrete* state.

Therefore, if 'independent private property' acquires in the
political state and in the legislature the meaning of political
independence, then it *is* the political independence of the state. In
that case 'independent private property' or '*real* private property'
is not only the 'pillar of the constitution' but also the '*constitution
itself*'. And indeed what is the pillar of the constitution if not the
constitution of constitutions, i.e. the primary, the real constitution?

In his analysis of the hereditary monarch, Hegel, who seems
himself to be somewhat astonished about 'the immanent development of a science, the *derivation of its entire content* from the
concept in its simplicity' (Remark to §279), makes the following
observation:

'Hence it is the basic moment of *personality, abstract* at the start in
immediate rights, which has matured itself through its various forms
of subjectivity, and now – at the stage of absolute rights, of the state,
of the completely concrete objectivity of the will – has become the
personality of the state, its certainty of itself.'

That is to say, what becomes *manifest* in the political state is that
'*abstract personality*' is the *highest political* personality, the
political basis of the state as a whole. Similarly, in primogeniture
the right of this abstract personality, its *objectivity*, 'abstract
private property', comes into existence as the highest objectivity
of the state, its *highest expression of right*.

The statement that the state is the hereditary monarchy, abstract personality, means no more than that the personality of the state is abstract, or that it is the state of abstract personality, in the same way that the Romans placed the prerogatives of the monarch within the sphere of civil law or viewed civil law as the highest development of constitutional law.

The *Romans* are the rationalists of sovereign private property, the Germans its *mystics*.

Hegel describes civil law as the *law of abstract personality*, as *abstract law*. And in fact it must be represented as the *abstraction* of law and hence as the *illusory law of abstract personality*, just as he previously represented morality as the *illusory existence of abstract subjectivity*. Hegel shows both civil law and morality to be such abstractions, but he does not proceed to infer from this that the state whose ethical life is based on these presuppositions can only be the society (the social life) of these illusions. On the contrary, he concludes that they are subordinate aspects of this ethical existence. But what is civil law if not the law relating to the subjects of the state, and what is morality if not their morality? In other words the juridical person of civil law and the subject of morality are the *person* and the *subject* of the state. Hegel has often been attacked for his theory of morality. But he has done no more than describe the morality of the modern state and modern civil law. Others have wished to separate morality further from the state and emancipate it. But what does this prove? That the divorce of the contemporary state from morality is moral, that morality is remote from the state and the state is immoral. It should rather be seen as a great achievement on Hegel's part to have provided a true assessment of modern morality, even though in one sense he did so unconsciously (viz. in the sense that Hegel holds the state based on such a morality to be the actual incarnation of the ethical Idea).

In the constitution guaranteed by *primogeniture, private property* is the guarantee of the political constitution. In primogeniture this guarantee appears to be provided by a *particular* form of private property. Primogeniture is merely the particular form of the general relationship obtaining between *private property* and the *political state*. Primogeniture is the *political* meaning of private property, private property in its political significance, i.e. in its universal significance. Here then, the constitution is the *constitution of private property*.

When we meet primogeniture in its *classical* form, i.e. among the Germanic peoples, we also encounter the constitution of *private property*. *Private property* is the universal category, the universal bond of the state. Even the general functions appear to be privately owned, the property of either a corporation or a class.

The various forms of trade and business are here the private property of particular corporations. Offices at court, powers of jurisdiction, etc., are the private property of particular classes. The different provinces are the private property of particular princes, etc. Service for one's country is the private property of the ruler. Spirit is the private property of the clergy. Any activities I carry out in the course of my duty are the private property of someone else, just as my rights are the private property of someone else. Sovereignty, in this case *nationality*, is the private property of the Emperor.

It has often been claimed that in the Middle Ages every form of law, freedom or social existence appeared as a *privilege*, an *exception* from the rule. The empirical evidence that all of these privileges appeared in the form of *private property* could not be ignored. What is the general reason for this coincidence? *Private property* was the *generic form* of *privilege*, of law as an *exception*.

Where, as in France, the rulers attacked the *independence* of private property they directed their assault at the property of the *corporations*, before impugning that belonging to *individuals*. But by attacking the private property of the corporations they attacked private property as corporation, as *social* bond.

Under the *feudal system* even the power of the sovereign looked as if it were the power of private property and the *power of the sovereign* thus became the repository of the secret of *universal power*, the *power of all the elements in the state*.

(As the representative of the state power, the monarch expresses what is powerful in the state. Hence the constitutional monarch expresses the idea of the constitutional state in its most abstract form. On the one hand he is the Idea of the state, the sacred majesty of the state, in the shape of one particular person. But at the same time he is a *mere figment* of the imagination, and neither as person nor as monarch does he possess real power or a real function. Here the separation of the political person from the real one, the formal from the material, the universal from the particular, of man from social man, is expressed in its most contradictory form.)

Private property is the child of *Roman* reason and *Germanic* sentiment. It will be instructive here to compare these two extreme versions of the same phenomenon. Such a comparison will aid us in finding a solution to the political problem we have been discussing.

The Romans were the first to develop the *law of private property*, abstract law, civil law, the law relating to the abstract person. *Roman civil law* is the *classical form of civil law*. But the Romans never mystified the law of private property as the Germans have done. They never developed it into *constitutional law*.

The law of private property was the *jus utendi et abutendi*,[35] the law enabling one to dispose of things *as one wished*. The chief preoccupation of the Romans was to develop and determine the *abstract relations* pertaining to private property. The actual foundation of private property, *ownership*, was a *fact*, an *inexplicable fact* with *no basis in law*. It only assumed the character of rightful ownership, of *private property*, by virtue of the legal determinations which society bestowed upon the mere fact of possession.

On the subject of the relationship between private property and the political constitution in Rome, we find the following situation:

(1) *Man* (appears as a *slave*). He is an article of private property, as was generally the case among the ancients.

There is nothing specific to the Romans here.

(2) Conquered countries are treated as private property, the *jus utendi et abutendi* is applied in them.

(3) Their history itself exhibits the struggle between the rich and the poor (patricians and plebeians).

Apart from this, private property as a whole asserts itself as *public* property, as with all the ancient classical peoples, either (in times of prosperity) in the form of grand display on the part of the republic, or else as *luxurious forms of general welfare* for the benefit of the mob (public baths, etc.).

Slavery is explained in terms of the rights of war, of conquest: men become slaves because their political existence has been destroyed.

Their practice differs from that of the Germans chiefly in two respects.

(1) The Imperial power was not the power of private property,

---

35. Right to use and abuse.

but the sovereignty of the empirical will as such. Far from regarding private property as the bond joining him to his subjects, the Emperor could dispose freely of private property as of all other social goods. In consequence the Imperial power was only *hereditary as a matter of fact*. It is true that private property and civil law experienced their greatest development under the Empire but this was nevertheless more an effect of political degeneration, rather than political degeneration being an effect of private property. Moreover, by the time civil law had become fully developed in Rome, constitutional law was in the process of dissolution, whereas in Germany the opposite was true.

(2) The dignities of state were never hereditary in Rome, i.e. private property was not the dominant political category.

(3) In contrast to the Germanic system of primogeniture, the result of private property in Rome was the *arbitrary practice of testamentary inheritance*. This distinction illuminates the entire difference between the Roman and Germanic conceptions of private property.

(In primogeniture it appears that private property is the relationship to the state which makes the state into an inherent characteristic or an accident of *immediate* private property, of *landed property*. Thus at the highest levels the state appears as private property, whereas private property should really appear as the property of the state. Instead of making private property into an attribute of the body politic, Hegel transforms the body politic, political existence and political sentiment into an attribute of private property.)

§308. 'The second section of the Estates comprises the *fluctuating element in civil society*. This element can enter politics only through its *deputies*; the multiplicity of its members is an external reason for this, but the essential reason is the specific character of this element and its activity. Since these deputies are the deputies of civil society, it follows as a direct consequence that their appointment is made by the *society as a society*. That is to say, in making the appointment, society is not dispersed into atomic units, collected to perform only a single and temporary act, and kept together for a moment and no longer. On the contrary, it makes the appointment as a society, articulated into associations, communities and corporations, which although constituted already for other purposes, acquire in this way a connection with politics. The existence of the Estates and their assembly finds a constitutional guarantee of its own in the fact that this class is *entitled* to send deputies at the summons of the crown, while members of the former class are entitled to present themselves in person in the Estates (see §307).'

Here we come to a further antithesis within civil society and the Estates: Hegel distinguishes between the fluctuating, *mobile* element and an *immobile* element (viz. landed property). This antithesis has also been represented as the antithesis of time and *space*, conservative and progressive. On this point see the foregoing paragraphs. Incidentally by bringing in the corporations Hegel has introduced an element of stability into the fluctuating part of society.

The second antithesis arises from the fact that the first element in the Estates expounded above, the *landed gentry*, are legislators in their own right; the legislature is an attribute of their empirical person; they are there not as *deputies* but in *their own right*. By contrast, *election* and *representations* are characteristic of the second Estate.

Hegel gives two reasons to explain why this *fluctuating* part of civil society may enter the political state, the legislature, only by means of *deputies*. The first is the *multiplicity of its members*, but as he himself admits that this is an *external* reason we do not need to rebut it.

The *essential* reason, however, 'is the specific character of this element and its activity'. 'Political activities' and 'preoccupations' are alien to 'the specific character of this element and its activity'.

Hegel then resumes his old song to the effect that these Estates are the '*deputies* of civil society'. They are appointed 'by the *society as a society*'. On the contrary, they are appointed by the society acting as what it is *not*, for society is *unpolitical*, and here it is supposed to perform a *political* act as an act *essential* to itself and proceeding from itself. Thus society *is* 'dispersed into atomic units, collected to perform only a single and temporary act and kept together for a moment and no longer'. In the first place, its *political* act is *single* and *temporary* and must therefore appear as such in the moment of its realization. It is a sensational act, it is political society at a moment of *ecstasy* and it can only *appear* as such. In the second place, Hegel raised no objection, in fact he presented it as necessary, that civil society should *materially* divorce itself from its civil reality (emerge as a *second society deputizing for the first*) and posit itself as that which it is *not*. How then can he now reject this formally?

Hegel believes that because society is represented through its corporations, etc., these 'although constituted already for other purposes, acquire in this way a *political* connection'. However, this means either that they acquire a significance which is *not* their own, or that their connection *is* political in itself and does not need to '*acquire*' the political complexion proposed above, as 'politics' rather derives its meaning from its connection with them. By describing only this section of the Estates as 'representative' Hegel unconsciously summed up the essential nature of the two chambers (at the very point where they really have the relation to each other that he claims for them). The chamber of deputies and the chamber of peers (or whatever else they are called) are not different manifestations of the same principle. Instead they spring from *two* essentially different principles and social conditions. The chamber of deputies is the *political constitution* of civil society in the modern sense, while the chamber of peers belongs to a constitution in the sense of the old Estates. In the antithesis between the chambers of peers and of deputies we are confronted by the opposed principles of the *hierarchical* and *political* representation of civil society. The first is the existing hierarchical principle of civil society, the second is the realization of its abstract political existence. It is obvious that the latter *cannot* act as the representative of Estates, corporations, etc., because it represents not the Estates element but the political existence of civil society. It is no less obvious that only the hierarchical section of civil society, only the 'sovereign landowners', the hereditary nobility, can have a seat in the first chamber. For the nobility is not *one* class among others, but on the contrary it would be more accurate to say that the hierarchical principle, the principle of the Estates, survives as a really social and hence political principle only in this one class. It is *the* Estate. Thus in the chamber of the Estates civil society has the representative of its medieval existence, in the chamber of deputies it has the representative of its *political* (modern) existence. The only advance here over the Middle Ages lies in the fact that the *Estates* have been reduced to a particular political existence alongside the *citizens*. England, the *empirical* instance of this political system which Hegel has in mind here, has therefore quite a different significance from the one he imputes to it.

In this respect the French constitution also shows an advance. It has indeed reduced the chamber of peers to an *empty formality*, but *within the framework* of a constitutional monarchy as ostensibly set out by Hegel it can be nothing but an empty formality, representing the *fictitious* harmony between the monarch and civil society, the fictitious or internal harmony of the *legislature* and the *political state* as embodied in a particular and hence *contradictory* institution.

The French have retained *life peers* as an expression of their independence of election either by the government or the people. But they have abolished the medieval concept of the *hereditary* peerage. The advance here is that the chamber of peers now no longer grows naturally out of *civil society as it really is*, but is an *abstract* creation. Elevation to the peerage is the prerogative of the *actual* political state, the *monarch*, who is not bound by any other factor in civil society. In this constitution the peerage really represents a purely political *class in civil society*, an abstract creation of the *political state*. However, it is much closer to being a *political decoration* than a real class equipped with particular rights. The chamber of peers during the Restoration was a reminiscence. The chamber of peers resulting from the July revolution is the *authentic* creation of the constitutional monarchy.

Since in the modern world the idea of the state can appear only in the abstraction of the '*merely* political state', or the *abstraction of civil society from itself*, from its own real situation, the French deserve the credit for having produced and held onto this abstract reality and hence for having produced the *political* principle itself. The accusation of abstraction so often levelled at them misses the point, for what is called abstract is the authentic logical product of the *rediscovery of political sentiment*; admittedly this is rediscovered in an antithesis, but it is a necessary antithesis. Thus the achievement of the French is to have established the chamber of peers as a product *peculiar* to the political state, in other words, to have made the political principle *as such* into the effective determining principle.

Hegel also observes that in the system of representation as he has presented it, in 'the entitlement of the corporations etc. to send deputies', 'the *existence* of the Estates and their assembly finds a constitutional guarantee of its own'. Thus what *guarantees the existence*, the true, *primitive* existence, of the Estates and their assembly is the *privilege* of the corporations, etc. Such views show that Hegel has regressed entirely to the standpoint of the Middle Ages and has wholly abandoned his 'abstraction of the state as the sphere of the state as itself, as the actual and explicit universal'.

To a modern view the existence of the assembly of the Estates is the political existence of civil society and its true *guarantee*. To question the existence of the assembly of the Estates is to question the existence of the state. Just as Hegel had previously located the guarantee of 'political sentiment', the essence of the legislature, in 'independent private property', so here he discovers the guarantee of the existence of the legislature in the 'privileges of the corporations'.

However, one of the elements of the Estates is itself the *political privilege* of civil society, its *privilege* of being *political*. Therefore it can never be the privilege of a particular, civil mode of the existence of civil society, even less can it discover its own guarantee in it. On the contrary, the Estates themselves are *supposed* to constitute the universal guarantee.

Thus Hegel constantly retreats from the view of the 'political state' as the highest actual and explicit reality of society, and assigns to it instead a precarious reality, *dependent upon other factors*: instead of regarding the state as the *true reality* of the other spheres of society, he forces the state to discover its reality in these other spheres. The state constantly requires the guarantee of spheres external to itself. It is not realized power. It is *supported* impotence; it represents not power over these supports but the power of these supports. The power lies in the supports.

What sort of sublime existence is it that stands in need of a guarantee outside itself, especially when it is supposed to be the *universal* embodiment of that guarantee, i.e. the real guarantee of the guarantee? In his analysis of the legislature, Hegel continually regresses from the philosophical point of view to the other standpoint which refuses to see a thing *in relation to itself*.

If the Estates stand in need of a guarantee of their existence, then they are not a *real* but only a *fictitious form of the state*. In constitutional states it is the law that provides the Estates with this guarantee. Thus their existence is *legal*, it is dependent not on the power or impotence of particular corporations and associations but on the universal essence of the state; their existence is the reality of the *state as an association*. (It is precisely here, in the Estates, that the corporations, etc., the particular spheres of civil society, were supposed to come into their own universal existence; but now Hegel *changes his tack* and conceives of this universal existence as a privilege, as the existence of these particular spheres.)

If political rights are the rights of corporations, etc., this contradicts the idea of political rights as something *political*, as the right of the state, of citizenship. For the whole point is that these rights should not be the rights of a particular existent being, not right, law, as a particular existence.

Before we move on to consider the concept of *election* as the political act whereby civil society separates out into a political committee, let us first examine some of the comments from the Remark to this Paragraph.

'To hold that *all, as individuals,* should share in deliberating and deciding on political matters of general concern on the ground that *all* individuals are members of the state, that its concerns are their concerns, and that it is their *right* that what is done should be done with their knowledge and volition, is tantamount to a proposal to put the *democratic* element *without any rational form* into the organism of the state, although it is only in virtue of the possession of such a form that the state is an organism at all. This idea comes readily to mind because it does not go beyond the abstraction of "being a member of a state", and it is superficial thinking which clings to abstractions.' [§308]

In the first place Hegel describes 'being a member of a state' as an abstraction, although even according to the *Idea*, and thus the *tendency* of his own theory, it is the highest, *most concrete* social determination of the legal person, of the member of a state. To arrive at the definition of 'a member of a state' and to see it as the attribute of the individual does not appear to be an instance of the 'superficial thinking which clings to abstractions'. But if 'being a member of a state' is an '*abstraction*' this is not the fault of thought but of Hegel's theory and the realities of the modern world, in which the separation of real life from political life is presupposed and political attributes are held to be 'abstract' determinations of the real member of the state.

The direct participation of *all* individuals in deliberating and deciding on political matters of general concern is, according to Hegel, 'tantamount to a proposal to put the *democratic* element *without any rational form* into the organism of the state, although it is only in virtue of the possession of such a form that the state is an organism at all'. This is to say that where the state organism is purely formal, the democratic element can enter into it only as a *formal* element. However, the democratic element should rather be the real element which confers a *rational form* on the organism of the state as a *whole*. If on the other hand it enters the organism or formalism of the state as a 'particular' element, its 'rational form' will be nothing more than an emasculation, an accommodation, denying its own particular nature, i.e. it will function purely as a *formal* principle.

We have already hinted that Hegel has developed only a *political formalism*. His authentic *material* principle is the *Idea*, the abstract mental *form* of the state as a subject, the absolute Idea innocent of any passive, *material* elements. Confronted with the abstraction of this Idea the determinations of the real, empirical formalism of the state appear as *content*, while the *real* content appears as formless, inorganic matter (in this case, real human beings, real society, etc.).

Hegel has already defined the essence of the Estates by the fact that in them the 'empirical universal' becomes the subject of the actually and explicitly existing universal. Can this have any other meaning than that the concerns of the state 'are the concerns of *all*, and that it is their *right* that what is done should be done with their knowledge and volition'? Who if not the Estates can be the embodiment of that right? And is it really so strange that 'all' should wish to possess this right in 'reality'?

'*All*, as individuals, should share in deliberating and deciding on political matters of general concern.'

In a really rational state one could reply: 'Not *all*, *as individuals* should share in deliberating and deciding on political matters of general concern', for 'individuals' do share in deliberating and deciding on *matters of general concern* as 'all', i.e. within society and as the members of society. Not all as individuals, but the individuals as all.

Hegel poses the dilemma himself. Either civil society (the Many, the mass) shares in deliberating and deciding on political matters of general concern through its deputies, or *all people* do so as *individuals*. There is no *essential* contradiction here, as Hegel later attempts to show, but only an *actual* one, a contradiction of the most *external* sort moreover, namely a *numerical* one. And it turns out that the objection that Hegel himself had dismissed as '*external*', i.e. the *mass of individuals*, is still the best argument against the direct participation of all. The *problem* whether civil society should participate in the legislature through *deputies* or in such a way that 'all' act directly as 'individuals' is itself a problem arising in the *abstraction of the political state*, or in the *abstract political state*; it is an *abstract* political problem.

On Hegel's own showing, either solution reveals the political significance of the 'empirical universal'.

The true formulation of the antithesis is as follows: either *all the individuals act*, or *a few, i.e. not all the individuals act*. In either case 'all' refers only to an *external* multiplicity or totality of the individuals. 'Allness', the aggregate, is not an essential, mental, real attribute of the individual. An aggregate is not acquired at the cost of one's abstract individuality. Instead, the aggregate is only the complete *sum* of *individuality*. *One* individual, *many* individuals, *all* individuals. One, many, all – none of these determinations affects the *essence* of the subject, of the individual.

'All' should 'as individuals share in deliberating and deciding on political matters of general concern'; i.e. *all* people should play their part, not as all but as 'individuals'.

The problem seems to contain a twofold contradiction.

The general concerns of the state are political concerns, the state as a *real concern*. Deliberation and decision are the means by which the state becomes *effective* as a real concern. It therefore appears to be self-evident that all the members of the state have a *relation* to the state: it is a matter of *real concern* to them. The very concept '*member of the state*' implies that they are a *part* of the state, that the state regards them as a part of itself. However, if they are a *part* of the state, it is obvious that their very *social existence* already constitutes their *real participation* in it. Not only do they share in the state, but the state is *their* share. To be a conscious part of a thing means to take part of it and to take part in it consciously. Without this consciousness the member of the state would be an animal.

When people speak of the 'general concerns of the state', the impression is given that the 'general concerns' are one thing and the 'state' is another. However, the *state* is the 'matter of general concern', and in reality by 'matters of general concern' we mean the state.

Thus to take part in the general concern of the state is identical with taking part in the state. It is therefore a *tautology* to assert that a member, a part of the state takes part in the state, that this participation can only take some such form as deliberation and decision, and to say at the same time that every member of the state takes part in deliberating and deciding on general matters of concern to the state (always assuming these functions to involve *real* participation in the state). So that when we are speaking of *real* members of the state we cannot assert that they *ought* to participate in the affairs of the state. For in that event we would be talking about those subjects who *want* and *ought* to be members of the state, but *are not* in reality.

On the other hand, when we speak of *specific* affairs of state, of a single political act, it is again obvious that it cannot be performed by *all people individually*. If this were not so it would mean that the individual was himself the *true* society and thus would make society superfluous. The individual would have to do everything all at once, whereas in fact society has him act for the others, just as it has them act for him.

The question whether *all people individually* 'should take part in deliberating and deciding on political matters of general concern' is a problem that arises from the separation of the political state from civil society.

As we have seen, the state exists *only* as a political state. The totality of the political state is the legislature. To take part in the legislature, therefore, is to take part in the political state, it is to prove and realize one's *existence* as a *member of the political state*, as a *member of the state*. The fact that *all as individuals* should wish to share in the legislature only proves that it is the will of *all* to be real (active) members of the state, or to acquire a political existence, or to prove and give reality to their existence as something *political*. We have also seen that the Estates constitute *civil society* as a legislature: they are its *political existence*. Hence if civil society forces its way into the *legislature en masse*, or even *in toto*, if the real civil society wishes to substitute itself for the *fictitious* civil society of the legislature, then all that is nothing but the striving of civil society to create a *political* existence for itself, or to make its real existence into a *political* one. The efforts of *civil society* to transform itself into a political society, or to make the *political* society into the *real* one, manifest themselves in the attempt to achieve as general a participation as possible in the *legislature*.

The question of *quantity* is not without importance here. If an increase in the *Estates* involves a physical and intellectual increase in the forces of the enemy – and we have seen that the various elements in the legislature exist in a state of mutual hostility –

then the problem of whether all are individually members of the legislature or whether they are represented there by deputies implies the questioning of the principle of *representation* from within itself, within the fundamental idea of the political state as found in a constitutional monarchy.

(1) The abstract view of the political state is that the *legislature* is the *totality* of the political state. Because this *single* activity [of legislation] is the only *political* activity of civil society, *everyone* both wishes and ought to share in it at once.

(2) *All people* as *individuals*. In the *Estates* the act of legislation is not regarded as *social*, as a function of *societal existence*, but rather as the activity by virtue of which individuals first begin to perform *social*, i.e. political, functions really and *consciously*. Thus in this view the legislature is not a function of society, not something that grows out of it, but only its *formation*. The formation of civil society into a legislature requires *all* the members of society to see themselves as *individuals*, and stand opposed to each other as *individuals*. To define them as 'members of the state' is to define them 'abstractly', a definition which is not realized in their actual lives.

There are two possibilities here: (1) Either the political state is separated from civil society; in that event it is not possible for *all as individuals* to take part in the legislature. The political state leads an existence *divorced* from civil society. For its part, civil society would cease to exist if everyone became a legislator. On the other hand, it is opposed by a political state which can only tolerate a civil society that conforms to its own *standards*. In other words, the fact that civil society takes part in the political state through its *deputies* is the expression of the separation and of the merely dualistic unity.

(2) Alternatively, civil society is the *real* political society. If so, it is senseless to insist on a requirement which stems from the conception of the political state as something existing apart from civil society, and which has its roots only in the *theological* conception of the political state. On this assumption the *legislature* entirely ceases to be important as a *representative* body. The legislature is representative only in the sense that *every* function is representative. For example, a cobbler is my representative in so far as he satisfies a social need, just as every definite form of social activity, because it is a species activity, represents only the species. That is to say, it represents a determination of my own being just

as every man is representative of other men. In this sense he is a representative not by virtue of another thing which he represents but by virtue of what he *is* and *does*.

'Legislative power' is not sought for its *content* but for the sake of its *formal* political significance. Intrinsically *executive* power, for example, is a much more appropriate goal for the people's wishes than the legislature, the *metaphysical* function of the state. The *legislature* embodies the energy of the will in its theoretical and not in its practical form. The point here is not to substitute the *will* for the *law*, but to *discover* and *formulate* the real law.

This division of the legislature into its real *legislative* function and its *representative*, *abstract political* function gives rise to a peculiarity which is particularly evident in France, the land of political culture.

(The *executive* always contains *two* things: a real activity and the reason given by the state for this activity. This latter exists as another real consciousness which in its total organization constitutes the bureaucracy.)

The real content of the legislature is always treated very marginally, as something of secondary importance (unless dominant special *interests* come into a significant conflict with the object in question). A question really attracts attention only when it becomes *political*, and for this to happen either it must be linked with a ministerial issue, i.e. the problem of the power of the legislature over the executive, or else it must involve rights which themselves implicate the political formalism. What is the source of this phenomenon? It arises because the legislative power also represents the political form of civil society; because the fact that a question is political means that it exists in relation to the different powers of the political state; and because the legislature represents political consciousness and this can show itself to be *political* only through a conflict with the executive. It is an essential requirement that every social need, law, etc., should be investigated *politically*, i.e. as determined by the *totality of the state*, in its *social* meaning, but in the abstract political state this requirement is given a *formal* meaning over against another power (content) lying outside its real content. This is no mere abstraction on the part of the French but a necessary logical consequence of the fact that the real state exists only in the shape of the *political state-formalism* we have been examining. The *opposition* within the representative power is the pre-eminently *political* form of the representative power. However, within this representative constitution the problem we are investigating takes a form different from the one it assumes for Hegel. The question is not whether civil society should exercise legislative power through deputies or through all people as individuals. What is crucial is the extension and the greatest possible *universalization* of the *vote*, i.e. of both *active* and *passive* suffrage. This is the real point of conflict on the issue of political *reform* both in France and in England.

To consider the *vote* in its relation to the power of the *crown* or the *executive* is to fail to look at it philosophically, i.e. to grasp its particular nature. The vote expresses the *real relation of real civil* society to the *civil society of the legislature*, to the *representative* body. Or, in other words, the *vote* is the *immediate, direct, not merely representative but actually existing* relation of civil society to the political state. It is therefore self-evident that the vote must constitute the chief political interest of real civil society. Only when civil society has achieved *unrestricted* active and passive *suffrage* has it *really* raised itself to the point of abstraction from itself, to the *political* existence which constitutes its true, universal, essential existence. But the perfection of this abstraction is also its transcendence [*Aufhebung*]. By really establishing its *political* existence as its authentic existence, civil society ensures that its civil existence, in so far as it is distinct from its political existence, is *inessential*. And with the demise of the one, the other, its opposite, collapses also. Therefore, *electoral reform* in the *abstract political state* is the equivalent to a demand for its *dissolution* [*Auflösung*] and this in turn implies the *dissolution of civil society*.

We shall encounter the problem of electoral reform later on in another guise, namely in the context of specific *interests*. We shall likewise have occasion to discuss the other conflicts that arise out of the twofold determination of the *legislature* (viz. on the one hand the *deputies* with a mandate from civil society, and on the other hand the *specific political* existence of civil society itself within the political state-formalism).

For the moment let us return to the Remark to this Paragraph.

'The rational consideration of a topic, the consciousness of the Idea, is *concrete*, and to that extent coincides with a genuine *practical* sense. Such a sense is itself nothing but the sense of rationality of the Idea.' . . . 'The *concrete* state is the *whole, articulated into its particular groups*. The member of a state is a *member* of such a group, i.e. of a *social class*, and it is only as characterized in this objective way that he comes under consideration when we are dealing with the state.' (§308)

We have already made the necessary comments on this passage.

'His' (the member of the state's) 'mere character as universal implies that he is at one and the same time both a *private person* and also a *thinking* consciousness, a will which wills the *universal*. This consciousness and will, however, lose their emptiness and acquire a *content* and a *living* reality only when they are filled with particularity, and particularity means determinacy as particular and a particular class-status; or, to put the matter otherwise, abstract individuality is a *generic* essence, but has its *immanent* universal *reality* as the generic essence *next higher* in the scale.'

All that Hegel says here is correct with the reservation (1) that he equates *determinacy* and *particular class position*, and (2) that this determinacy, this species, this generic essence next higher in the scale should have been *really* established, not merely *in itself* but also *for itself*, as the species belonging to the *universal generic essence*, as *its* particularity. However, Hegel is content to show that in the state, which he has defined as the self-conscious existence of the ethical mind, this ethical mind only becomes a *determining* thing *in itself*, in accordance with the universal Idea. He does not allow society to become a truly determining thing because this would require a *real* subject while he has nothing more than an abstract one, a figment of the *imagination*.

§309. 'Since deputies are elected to deliberate and decide on political matters of general concern, the point about their election is that it is a choice of individuals on the strength of confidence felt in them, i.e. a choice of such individuals as have a better understanding of these affairs than their electors have and such also as essentially vindicate the universal interest, not the particular interest of a community or corporation in preference to that interest. Hence their relation to their electors is not that of agents with a commission or specific instructions. A further bar to their being so is the fact that their assembly is meant to be a living body in which all members deliberate in common and reciprocally instruct and convince each other.'

(1) The deputies are not supposed to be 'agents with a commission or specific instructions', because 'they essentially vindicate the universal interest, not the particular interest of a community or corporation in preference to that interest'. Hegel began by regarding the representatives as representing the corporations,

etc., but then introduces the further political determination to the effect that they should not vindicate the *particular interest* of the corporation, etc. He thereby nullifies his own definition, for he draws a dividing line between their *essential* determination as representatives and their *existence as part of a corporation*. Furthermore, he also cuts the corporation off from itself, from its own real content, for the corporation is supposed to elect deputies not from *its own point of view* but from the *point of view of the state*, i.e. it votes in its *non-existence as corporation*. Hegel thus acknowledges in the *material* determination what he denied *formally*, namely that civil society abstracts from itself at the moment of its political activity, and that its *political existence* is nothing but *this abstraction*. Hegel explains this by saying that the deputies are elected precisely in order that they may take part in 'public affairs'; but the corporations are not instances of public affairs.

(2) 'The point about the election of deputies' is that 'it is a choice of individuals on the strength of confidence felt in them, i.e. a choice of such individuals as have a better understanding of these affairs than their electors have.' This too should lead us to the conclusion that the deputies are not agents with a mandate.

The fact that they do not 'simply' understand, but have a 'better' understanding can only be proved by a piece of sophistry. This would only follow if the electors had the choice *either* to deliberate and decide on public affairs *for themselves or* to delegate specific individuals to perform these tasks on their behalf. That is to say, it would follow only if *delegation* or *representation* were not an essential part of the *legislative power* of civil society. But, as we have seen, it is just this that constitutes the *specific* essence of the state as expounded by Hegel.

This example illustrates very well how Hegel half intentionally abandons the crux of the matter and imputes to it in its narrow form a significance the very opposite of narrow.

Only at the end does Hegel reveal the true explanation. The deputies of civil society are constituted into an 'assembly' and only in this assembly does the *political existence and will* of civil society become *real*. The separation of the political state from civil society takes the form of a separation of the deputies from their electors. Society simply deputes elements of itself to become its political existence.

There is a twofold contradiction:

(1) A *formal* contradiction. The deputies of civil society are a society which is not connected to its electors by any 'instruction' or commission. They have a formal authorization but as soon as this becomes *real* they *cease* to be *authorized*. They should be *deputies* but they are *not*.

(2) A *material* contradiction. In respect to actual interests. More on this later. Here we find the converse. They have authority as the representatives of *public* affairs, whereas in reality they represent *particular* interests.

It is significant that Hegel singles out trust as the substance of delegation, as the crux of the relation between elector and deputy. *Trust* is a personal relation. In the Addition, Hegel has this to say about it:

'Representation is grounded on trust, but trusting another is something different from giving my vote myself in my own personal capacity. Hence majority voting runs counter to the principle that I should be personally present in anything which is to be obligatory on me. We have confidence in a man when we take him to be a man of discretion who will manage our affairs conscientiously and to the best of his knowledge, just as if they were his own.'

§310. 'The *guarantee* that deputies will have the qualifications and disposition that accord with this end – since independent means attains its right in the first section of the Estates – is to be found so far as the second section is concerned – the section drawn from the fluctuating and changeable element in civil society – above all in the knowledge (of the organization and interests of the state and civil society), the temperament, and the skill which a deputy acquires as a result of the *actual* transaction of business in *managerial* or *official* positions, and then evinces in his actions. As a result he also acquires and develops a *managerial and political sense*, tested by his experience, and this is a further guarantee of his suitability as a deputy.'

Hegel first constructed the upper chamber, the *chamber of independent private property*, as a *guarantee* for the crown and the executive against the sentiments of the lower chamber as the *political existence* of empirical universality. Now, however, he demands a *new guarantee*, one which will guarantee the sentiments, etc., of the lower chamber itself.

Previously, trust – the guarantee of the electors – had also been the guarantee of the deputies. Now, however, this trust itself stands in need of a further guarantee of its value.

Hegel would not be averse to making the lower chamber into

the chamber of *pensioned-off* civil servants. He calls not only for 'political sense' but also for 'managerial', bureaucratic sense.

What he really wants is for the legislature to be the *real governing power*. He expresses this by making a *double* demand on the bureaucracy, on the one hand as the representative of the crown, and on the other as the representative of the people.

If in constitutional states it is permissible for civil servants to become deputies this is possible only because *class, civil status* is set aside and abstract *state citizenship* is the decisive factor.

But Hegel forgets that he had based representation on the corporations and that these stand directly opposed to the executive. His forgetfulness – which recurs in the very next paragraph – goes so far that he even creates an *essential* distinction between the deputies of the corporations and the deputies of the classes.

In the Remark to this Paragraph he states:

'Subjective opinion, naturally enough, finds superfluous and even perhaps offensive the demand for such guarantees, if the demand is made with reference to what is called the "people". The state, however, is characterized by objectivity, not by a subjective opinion and its *self-confidence*. Hence it can recognize in individuals only their objectively recognizable and tested character, and it must be all the more careful on this point in connection with the second section of the Estates, since this section is rooted in interests and activities directed towards the particular, i.e. in the sphere where chance, mutability and caprice enjoy their right of free play.'

Hegel's mindless illogicality and '*managerial*' sense are really nauseating here. The conclusion to the Addition to the preceding paragraph [§309] reads as follows:

'*The electors* require a guarantee that their deputy will further and secure this general interest.'

Imperceptibly this guarantee required *by the electors* has been transformed into a *guarantee against* the electors, against their '*self-confidence*'. In the Estates the 'empirical universal' was supposed to embody the 'moment of subjective formal freedom'. 'Public consciousness' was supposed to come into existence in the Estates as 'an empirical universal, of which the thoughts and opinions of the Many are particulars'. (§301.)

Now, however, these 'thoughts and opinions' must first prove to the executive that they are '*its*' thoughts and opinions. For, stupidly enough, Hegel speaks of the state here as if it were a *finished* existence even though he is actually engaged in finishing it with his construction of the Estates. He speaks of the state as a concrete subject which 'does not take offence at subjective opinion and its self-confidence' and for which individuals have first made themselves 'recognizable' and have 'proved' themselves. The only thing Hegel omits is to require the *Estates* to submit to an *examination* at the hands of the gracious executive. His attitude here borders on servility. He has evidently been thoroughly contaminated by the wretched arrogance of *Prussian* officialdom which, full of its own bureaucratic narrow-mindedness, regards with disdain the 'self-confidence' of the 'subjective opinion of the people'. At every point Hegel consistently equates the 'state' with the 'executive'.

To be sure, a real state cannot rest content with 'mere trust' and 'subjective opinion'. But in the state constructed by Hegel the *political* convictions of civil society are mere *opinion* just because its political existence is an *abstraction* from its real existence; just because the state in its totality is not the objectification of those political convictions. If Hegel had wished to be consistent he would have had to do all in his power to show that according to their *essential determination* (§301) the Estates were the being-for-itself of public affairs in the thoughts, etc., of the *Many*, and thus that they were independent of the other premises of the political state.

Earlier on Hegel said that to assume the executive to be actuated by bad will was characteristic of the rabble. It is just as true if not truer that the assumption that the people is actuated by bad will is the view of the rabble. Hegel has no right to find it either 'superfluous' or 'insulting' when the theoreticians he despises require guarantees in respect to the *so-called* state, the *soi-disant* state, the executive, viz. guarantees that the sentiments of the bureaucracy should be patriotic sentiments.

§311. 'A *further* point about the election of deputies is that, since civil society is the electorate, the deputies should themselves be conversant with and participate in its special needs, difficulties, and particular interests. Owing to the nature of civil society, its deputies are the deputies of the various corporations (see §308), and this simple mode of appointment obviates any confusion due to conceiving the electorate abstractly and as an agglomeration of atoms. Hence the deputies *eo ipso* adopt the point of view of society, and their actual election is therefore either something wholly superfluous or else reduced to a trivial play of opinion and caprice.'

Firstly, with the simple word 'further', Hegel conflates the definition of deputation as 'legislature' (§309, 310) with its definition as 'arising from civil society', i.e. as representation. The tremendous contradictions implicit in this 'further' are then spelled out just as thoughtlessly.

According to §309 the deputies should '*essentially* vindicate the universal interest, not the particular interest of a community or a corporation in preference to that interest'.

According to §371 the deputies are drawn from the corporations, they represent these *particular* interests and needs and do not allow themselves to be distracted by 'abstractions', as if the 'universal interest' were not just such an abstraction, namely an abstraction from *their* corporate and similar interests.

According to §310 the deputies have to 'acquire and develop a managerial and political sense as a result of the actual transaction of business, etc.'. In §311 they are required to have corporate and civic sense.

In the Addition to §309 it is stated that 'representation is grounded on *trust*'. According to §311 'election', the realization of trust, its activation and manifestation 'is either something wholly superfluous or else reduced to a trivial play of opinion and caprice'.

The basis of representation, its essence, turns out to be 'something wholly superfluous, etc.' for representation. With one and the same breath Hegel puts forward absolutely contradictory statements: representation is grounded on trust, on the confidence placed by one man in another, and, at the same time, it is not grounded on trust. It is rather a merely formal game.

The object of representation is not the particular interest but man and his citizenship of the state, the universal interest. On the other hand, the particular interest is the material of representation, and the spirit of this interest is the spirit of the representative.

In the Remark on this Paragraph, which we shall now consider, these contradictions become even more glaring. At one moment representation is the representation of the man, at another of the particular interest, the particular matter.

'It is obviously of advantage that the deputies should include representatives of each particular main branch of society (e.g. trade, manufactures, etc.) – representatives who are thoroughly conversant with it and who themselves belong to it. The idea of free unrestricted election leaves this important consideration entirely at the mercy of chance. All such branches of society, however, have equal rights of representation. Deputies are sometimes regarded as "representatives"; but they are representatives in an organic, rational sense only if they are *representatives* not of *individuals* or a conglomeration of them, but of one of the essential *spheres* of society and its large-scale interests. Hence representation cannot now be taken to mean simply the *substitution of one man for another*; the point is rather that the interest itself is *really present* in its representative, while he himself is there to represent the objective element of his own being.

'As for popular suffrage, it may be further remarked that especially in large states it leads inevitably to electoral *indifference*, since the casting of a single vote is of no significance where there is a multitude of electors. Even if a voting qualification is highly valued and esteemed by those who are entitled to it, they still do not enter the polling booth. Thus the result of an institution of this kind is more likely to be the opposite of what was intended; election actually falls into the power of a few, of a caucus, and so of the particular and contingent interest which is precisely what was to have been neutralized.' [Remark to §311]

The substance of the two Paragraphs 312 and 313 has already been dealt with and requires no special discussion. We simply cite them as they stand:

§312. 'Each class in the Estates (see §§305–8) contributes something particularly its own to the work of deliberation. Further, one moment in the class-element has in the sphere of politics the special function of mediation, mediation between two existing things. Hence this moment must likewise acquire a separate existence of its own. For this reason the assembly of the Estates is divided into *two houses*.'

God help us all!

§313. 'This division, by providing chambers of the first and second *instance*, is a surer guarantee for ripeness of decision and it obviates the accidental character which a snap division has and which a numerical majority may acquire. But the principal advantage of this arrangement is that there is less chance of the Estates being in direct opposition to the executive; or that, if the mediating element is at the same time on the side of the lower house, the weight of the lower house's opinion is all the stronger, because it appears less partisan and its opposition appears neutralized.'[36]

36. The manuscript ends here on page 4 of the printer's sheet numbered xl by Marx. At the top of the first page of the following sheet, which is otherwise empty, Marx wrote:

Table of Contents
Concerning Hegel's Transition and Explication

Letters from the *Franco–German Yearbooks*

[*The Letters were written in the course of 1843. In them Marx criticizes the actual world, which he sees as 'perverted'. In particular he criticizes political society, that is the Prussian state, as a despotism whose principle is the dehumanization of man. The sole political person, he finds, is the monarch, who rules through caprice. Marx counterposes to this the notion of the liberation of a 'thinking mankind' and the formation of a 'community of men that can fulfil their highest needs, a democratic state'. In a passage which accurately predicts the events of the coming years Marx says that the basis for the imminent revolt against the existing order is the 'system of industry and commerce, the exploitation of man'. Criticism of the sort that Marx has in mind should involve the critic in* practical *political struggle ('hitherto the philosophers have left the key to all riddles lying in their desks').*]

Marx to Ruge

From a barge on the way to D., March 1843

I am now travelling in Holland. From both the French papers and the local ones I see that Germany has ridden deeply into the mire and will sink into it even further. I assure you that even if one can feel no national pride one does feel national shame, even in Holland. In comparison with the greatest Germans even the least Dutchman is still a citizen. And the opinions of foreigners about the Prussian government! There is a frightening agreement, no one is deceived any longer about the system and its simple nature. So the new school has been of some use after all. The glorious robes of liberalism have fallen away and the most repulsive despotism stands revealed for all the world to see.

This too is a revelation, albeit a negative one. It is a truth which at the very least teaches us to see the hollowness of our patriotism, the perverted nature of our state and to hide our faces in shame. I can see you smile and say: what good will that do? Revolutions are not made by shame. And my answer is that shame is a revolution in itself; it really is the victory of the French Revolution over that German patriotism which defeated it in 1813. Shame is a kind of anger turned in on itself. And if a whole nation were to feel ashamed it would be like a lion recoiling in order to spring. I admit that even this shame is not yet to be found in Germany; on the contrary the wretches are still patriots. But if the ridiculous system of our new knight[1] does not disabuse them of their patriotism, then what will? The comedy of despotism in which we are being forced to act is as dangerous for him as tragedy was once for the Stuarts and the Bourbons. And even if the comedy will not be seen in its true light for a long time yet it will still be a revolution.

The state is too serious a business to be subjected to such buffoonery. A Ship of Fools can perhaps be allowed to drift before the wind for a good while; but it will still drift to its doom precisely because the fools refuse to believe it possible. This doom is the approaching revolution.

[*In his reply Ruge, in a mood of deep despair, tells Marx that there is no chance of a political revolution. He argues that the Germans are by nature a docile people: 'our nation has no future, so what is the point in our appealing to it?'*]

Marx to Ruge

Cologne, May 1843

Your letter, my friend, is a fine elegy, a breath-taking funeral dirge; but it is utterly unpolitical. No people despairs and if stupidity induces it to live on hopes for many years a sudden burst of cleverness will eventually enable it to fulfil its dearest wishes.

However, you have stimulated me. Your theme is by no means exhausted. I am tempted to add a finale and when all is at an end give me your hand and we can start all over again. Let the dead bury the dead and mourn them. In contrast, it is enviable to be the first to enter upon a new life: this shall be our lot.

It is true that the old world belongs to the philistines. But we must not treat them as bogeymen and shrink from them in terror.

1. Frederick William IV of Prussia came to the throne in 1840.

On the contrary, we must take a closer look at them. It is rewarding to study these lords of the world.

Of course, they are lords of the world only in the sense that they fill it with their presence, as worms fill a corpse. They require nothing more than a number of slaves to complete their society and slave-owners do not need to be free. If their ownership of land and people entitles them to be called lords and master *par excellence* this does not make them any less philistine than their servants.

Human beings – that means men of intellect, free men – that means republicans. The philistines wish to be neither. What is left for them to be and to wish?

What they wish is to live and to procreate (and Goethe says that no one achieves more). And this they have in common with animals. The only thing a German politician might wish to add is that man *knows* this is what he wants and that the Germans are determined to want nothing more.

Man's self-esteem, his sense of freedom, must be re-awakened in the breast of these people. This sense vanished from the world with the Greeks, and with Christianity it took up residence in the blue mists of heaven, but only with its aid can society ever again become a community of men that can fulfil their highest needs, a democratic state.

By contrast, men who do not feel themselves to be men accumulate for their masters like a breed of slaves or a stud of horses. The hereditary masters are the aim and goal of the entire society. The world belongs to them. They take possession of it as it is and feels itself to be. They accept themselves as they are and place their feet where they naturally belong, viz. on the necks of these political animals who have no other vocation than to be their 'loyal, attentive subjects'.

The philistine world is the *animal kingdom of politics* and if we must needs acknowledge its existence we have no choice but to accept the *status quo*. Centuries of barbarism have produced it and given it shape, and now it stands before us as a complete system based on the principle of the *dehumanized world*. Our Germany, the philistine world at its most perfect, must necessarily lag far behind the French Revolution which restored man to his estate. A German Aristotle who wished to construct his *Politics* on the basis of our society would begin by writing 'Man is a social but wholly unpolitical animal'. And as for the state, he would not be able to better the definition provided by Herr Zöpfl, the author of *Constitutional Law in Germany*. According to him the state is an 'association of families' which, we may continue, is the hereditary property of a family higher than all others and called the dynasty. The more fertile the families, the happier the people, the greater the state, the more powerful the dynasty, for which reason a premium of 50 Talers is placed on the seventh-born son in the normal despotism of Prussia.

The Germans are such prudent realists that not one of their wishes and their wildest fancies ever extends beyond the bare actualities of life. And this reality, no more no less, is accepted by those who rule over them. They too are realists, they are utterly removed from all thought and human greatness, they are ordinary officers and provincial Junkers, but they are not mistaken, they are right: just as they are, they are perfectly adequate to the task of exploiting and ruling over this animal kingdom – for here as everywhere rule and exploitation are *identical* concepts. When they make people pay them homage, when they gaze out over the teeming throng of brainless creatures, what comes into their minds but the thought that occurred to Napoleon on the Berezina. It is said that he pointed to the mass of drowning men and declared to his entourage: Voyez ces crapauds![2] The story is probably invented, but it is true nevertheless. Despotism's only thought is disdain for mankind, dehumanized man; and it is a thought superior to many others in that it is also a fact. In the eyes of the despot men are always debased. They drown before his eyes and on his behalf in the mire of common life from which, like toads, they always rise up again. If even men capable of great vision, like Napoleon before he succumbed to his dynastic madness, are overwhelmed by this insight, how should a quite ordinary king be an idealist in the midst of such a reality?

The principle on which monarchy in general is based is that of man as despised and despicable, of *dehumanized man*; and when Montesquieu declares that its principle is honour he is quite in error. He attempts to make this plausible by distinguishing between monarchy, despotism and tyranny. But these names refer to a *single* concept denoting at best different modes of the same principle. Where the monarchical principle is in the majority, human beings are in the minority; where it is not called in question,

2. Look at those toads!

human beings do not even exist. Now, when a man like the King of Prussia has no proof that he is problematic, why should he not simply follow the dictates of his own fancy? And when he does so, what is the result? Contradictory intentions? Very well, so they all lead to nothing. Impotent policies? They are still the only political reality. Scandals and embarrassments? There is only *one* scandal, and *one* source of embarrassment: abdication. As long as caprice remains in its place it is in the right. It may be as fickle, inane and contemptible as it pleases; it is still adequate to the task of governing a people which has never known any law but the arbitrary will of its kings. I do not claim that an inane system and the loss of respect both at home and abroad can remain without consequence; I am certainly not prepared to underwrite the Ship of Fools. But I do maintain that as long as the topsy-turvy world is the real world the King of Prussia will remain a man of his time.

As you know, he is a man I have been much interested in. Even when his only mouthpiece was the *Berlin Political Weekly* I could see his worth and his vocation clearly. As early as the act of homage in Königsberg he confirmed my suspicion that all issues would now become purely personal. He proclaimed that henceforth his own heart and feelings would constitute the basic law of the Prussian domains, of *his* state; and in Prussia the King really is the system. He is the only political person. His personality determines the nature of the system. Whatever he does or is made to do, whatever he thinks or is put into his mouth, constitutes the thought and action of the Prussian state. It is therefore a positive good that the present King has admitted this so frankly.

The only mistake was to attribute any significance, as people did for a while, to the wishes and ideas actually produced by the King.[3] But these could not affect the situation since the philistine is the material of the monarchy and the monarch is no more than the King of the philistines. As long as both remain themselves he can turn neither himself nor them into real, free human beings.

The King of Prussia tried to change the system with the help of a theory such as his father did not possess. The fate of this attempt is well known: it failed utterly, naturally enough. For once you

---

3. Frederick William IV of Prussia was influenced by the Romantic movement. It was his intention to revive an imaginary concept of the Middle Ages, with Estates of the Realm as his answers to the calls, which he opposed, for a Constitution.

have arrived at the animal kingdom of politics there is no reaction that can go further back and no way of progressing beyond it without abandoning its basis and effecting the transition to the human world of democracy.

The old King had no extravagant aims, he was a philistine and made no claims to intelligence. He knew that the servile state and his own possession of it stood in need of nothing more than a tranquil, prosaic existence. The young King was more lively and quick-witted; he had a much more grandiose idea of the omnipotent monarch limited only by his own heart and understanding. He felt only repugnance for the old, ossified state of slaves and servants. He desired to infuse new life into it and imbue it with his own wishes, thoughts and feelings; and this, if anything, he could demand in *his own* state. Hence his liberal speeches and effusions. Not the dead letter of the law, but the living heart of the King would govern all his subjects. He wished to set all hearts and minds in motion to fulfil his heart's desires and his long-meditated plans. And people were set in motion, but their hearts did not beat at one with his and the governed could not open their mouths without demanding the abolition of the old form of authority. The idealists who are impertinent enough to want human beings to be human spoke up and while the King gave vent to his Old German fantasies, they imagined that they could begin to philosophize in New German. This had never happened before in Prussia. For a moment it looked as if the old order had been turned upside down; things began to be transformed into people and some of these people even had names, although the naming of names is not permitted in the Provincial Diets. But the servants of the old despotism soon put a stop to these un-German activities. It was not difficult to bring about a palpable conflict between the wishes of the King who dreamed of a great past epoch full of priests, knights and bondsmen, and the intentions of the idealists who simply aspired to realize the aims of the French Revolution, i.e. who in the last analysis wanted a republic and an order of free men instead of an order of dead things. When this conflict had become sufficiently acute and uncomfortable, and the irascible King was in a state of great excitement, his servants, who had formerly managed affairs with such ease, now came to him and announced that the King would be unwise to encourage his subjects in their idle talk, they would not be able to control a race of people who talked. Moreover, the lord of all posterior Russians [*Hinterrussen*] was disturbed by all the activity going on in the heads of the anterior Russians [*Vorderrussen*][4] and demanded the restoration of the old peaceful state of affairs. This led to a new edition of the old proscription of all the wishes and ideas men have cherished concerning human rights and duties, that is, it meant a return to the old ossified, servile state in which the slave serves in silence and the owner of land and people rules as silently as possible over well-trained, docile servants. Neither can say what he wishes, the one that he wishes to be human, the other that he has no use for human beings on his territory. Silence is therefore the only means of communication. *Muta pecora, prona et ventri oboedientia.*[5]

This then is the abortive attempt to transform the philistine state on the basis of itself; its only result was that it revealed for all the world to see that for a despotism brutality is necessary and humanity impossible. A brutal state of affairs can only be maintained by means of brutality. And this brings me to the end of our common task of analysing the philistine and the philistine state. You will hardly suggest that my opinion of the present is too exalted and if I do not despair about it this is only because its desperate position fills me with hope. I will say nothing of the incapacity of the masters and the indolence of their servants and subjects who allow everything to proceed as God would have it; and yet taken together both would certainly suffice to bring about a catastrophe. I would only point out that the enemies of philistinism, i.e. all thinking and suffering people, have arrived at an understanding for which formerly they lacked the means and that even the passive system of procreation characteristic of the old subjects now daily wins new recruits to serve the new race of men. However, the system of industry and commerce, of property and the exploitation of man, will lead much faster than the increase in the population to a rupture within existing society which the old system cannot heal because, far from healing and creating, it knows only how to exist and enjoy. The existence of a suffering mankind which thinks and of a thinking mankind which is suppressed must inevitably become unpalatable and indigestible

4. Marx ironically calls the Prussians (Latin: *Borussi*) '*Vorderrussen*' (anterior Russians) in order to associate them with the '*Hinterrussen*' (Posterior Russians) of Emperor Nicholas I of Russia (1825–55). Nicholas I's hatred and fear of revolution was one of the main considerations of his foreign policy.

5. The herd is silent, docile and obeys its stomach.

for the animal kingdom of the philistines wallowing in their passive and thoughtless existence.

For our part it is our task to drag the old world into the full light of day and to give positive shape to the new one. The more time history allows thinking mankind to reflect and suffering mankind to collect its strength the more perfect will be the fruit which the present now bears within its womb.

[*Bakunin and Feuerbach contribute letters to the correspondence in which they both reject Ruge's pessimism. Feuerbach, agreeing that the situation in Germany is intolerable, calls for 'united forces' to rebuild everything by means of united 'praxis'. He considers a new journal to be a vital element in that praxis. Ruge, in a final letter to Marx, announces his conversion to atheism and his support for the 'new philosophers'. He now sees the* Yearbooks *as a means by which to 'criticize ourselves and all Germany'. It is in this context that Marx stresses the idea that criticism must involve itself in actual political struggle.*]

Marx to Ruge

Kreuznach, September 1843

I am very pleased to find you so resolute and to see your thoughts turning away from the past and towards a new enterprise. In Paris, then, the ancient bastion of philosophy – *absit omen!*[6] – and the modern capital of the modern world. Whatever is necessary adapts itself. Although I do not underestimate the obstacles, therefore, I have no doubt that they can be overcome.

Our enterprise may or may not come about, but in any event I shall be in Paris by the end of the month as the very air here turns one into a serf and I can see no opening for free activity in Germany.

In Germany everything is suppressed by force, a veritable anarchy of the spirit, a reign of stupidity itself has come upon us and Zurich obeys orders from Berlin. It is becoming clearer every day that independent, thinking people must seek out a new centre. I am convinced that our plan would satisfy a real need and real needs must be satisfied in reality. I shall have no doubts once we begin in earnest.

In fact the internal obstacles seem almost greater than the

6. May there be no ill omen.

external difficulties. For even though the question 'where from?' presents no problems, the question 'where to?' is a rich source of confusion. Not only has universal anarchy broken out among the reformers but also every individual must admit to himself that he has no precise idea about what ought to happen. However, this very defect turns to the advantage of the new movement, for it means that we do not anticipate the world with our dogmas but instead attempt to discover the new world through the critique of the old. Hitherto philosophers have left the keys to all riddles lying in their desks, and the stupid, uninitiated world had only to wait around for the roasted pigeons of absolute science to fly into its open mouth. Philosophy has now become secularized and the most striking proof of this can be seen in the way that philosophical consciousness has joined battle not only outwardly, but inwardly too. If we have no business with the construction of the future or with organizing it for all time there can still be no doubt about the task confronting us at present: the *ruthless criticism of the existing order*, ruthless in that it will shrink neither from its own discoveries nor from conflict with the powers that be.

I am therefore not in favour of our hoisting a dogmatic banner. Quite the reverse. We must try to help the dogmatists to clarify their ideas. In particular, *communism* is a dogmatic abstraction and by communism I do not refer to some imagined, possible communism, but to communism as it actually exists in the teachings of Cabet, Dézamy and Weitling, etc. This communism is itself only a particular manifestation of the humanistic principle and is infected by its opposite, private property. The abolition of private property is therefore by no means identical with communism and communism has seen other socialist theories, such as those of Fourier and Proudhon, rising up in opposition to it, not fortuitously but necessarily, because it is only a particular, one-sided realization of the principle of socialism.

And by the same token the whole principle of socialism is concerned only with one side, namely the *reality* of the true existence of man. We have also to concern ourselves with the other side, i.e. with man's theoretical existence, and make his religion and science, etc., into the object of our criticism. Furthermore, we wish to influence our contemporaries, our German contemporaries above all. The problem is how best to achieve this. In this context there are two incontestable facts. Both religion and politics are matters of the very first importance in contemporary Germany.

Our task must be to latch onto these as they are and not to oppose them with any ready-made system such as the *Voyage en Icarie*.[7]

Reason has always existed, but not always in a rational form. Hence the critic can take his cue from every existing form of theoretical and practical consciousness and from this ideal and final goal implicit in the *actual* forms of existing reality he can deduce a true reality. Now as far as real life is concerned, it is precisely the *political* state which contains the postulates of reason in all its *modern* forms, even where it has not been the conscious repository of socialist requirements. But it does not stop there. It consistently assumes that reason has been realized and just as consistently it becomes embroiled at every point in a conflict between its ideal vocation and its actually existing premises.

This internecine conflict within the political state enables us to infer the social truth. Just as religion is the table of contents of the theoretical struggles of mankind, so the *political state* enumerates its practical struggles. Thus the particular form and nature of the political state contains all social struggles, needs and truths within itself. It is therefore anything but beneath its dignity to make even the most specialized political problem – such as the distinction between the representative system and the Estates system – into an object of its criticism. For this problem only expresses at the *political* level the distinction between the rule of man and the rule of private property. Hence the critic not only can but must concern himself with these political questions (which the crude socialists find entirely beneath their dignity). By demonstrating the superiority of the representative system over the Estates system he will *interest* a great party in *practice*. By raising the representative system from its political form to a general one and by demonstrating the true significance underlying it he will force this party to transcend itself – for its victory is also its defeat.

Nothing prevents us, therefore, from lining our criticism with a criticism of politics, from taking sides in politics, i.e. from entering into real struggles and identifying ourselves with them. This does not mean that we shall confront the world with new doctrinaire principles and proclaim: Here is the truth, on your knees before it! It means that we shall develop for the world new principles from the existing principles of the world. We shall not say: Abandon your struggles, they are mere folly; let us provide

7. Étienne Cabet, *Voyage en Icarie*, Paris, 1842. This book is a description of a communist utopia.

you with the true campaign-slogans. Instead we shall simply show the world why it is struggling, and consciousness of this is a thing it *must* acquire whether it wishes or not.

The reform of consciousness consists *entirely* in making the world aware of its own consciousness, in arousing it from its dream of itself, in *explaining* its own actions to it. Like Feuerbach's critique of religion, our whole aim can only be to translate religious and political problems into their self-conscious human form.

Our programme must be: the reform of consciousness not through dogmas but by analysing mystical consciousness obscure to itself, whether it appear in religious or political form. It will then become plain that the world has long since dreamed of something of which it needs only to become conscious for it to possess it in reality. It will then become plain that our task is not to draw a sharp mental line between past and future but to *complete* the thought of the past. Lastly, it will become plain that mankind will not begin any *new* work, but will consciously bring about the completion of its old work.

We are therefore in a position to sum up the credo of our journal in a *single word*: the self-clarification (critical philosophy) of the struggles and wishes of the age. This is a task for the world and for us. It can succeed only as the product of united efforts. What is needed above all is a *confession*, and nothing more than that. To obtain forgiveness for its sins mankind needs only to declare them for what they are.

On the Jewish Question

[*This article was written towards the end of 1843 and first published in the* Yearbooks. *In it Marx criticizes the ideas of Bruno Bauer, who had argued against a campaign for religious freedom for Jews. Religious equality for Jews, Bauer said, would be nothing more than equality with slaves, for the Germans were the slaves of the Christian state. Why should freedom-loving Germans help Jews in the struggle for civil rights, he asks, if Jews are not ready to join in the general struggle for a 'totally free state'?*

Marx replies that it is possible to be emancipated politically without being emancipated from religion. He cites the cases of America and France, where religion is no longer the concern of the state but the private concern of each individual. Bauer, Marx continues, cannot see that religious ideas are not the product of the 'Christian state' (which he reviles) but of the 'free state' (which he glorifies). Once again Marx cites America to establish his case. The citizen of the 'free state', he says, leads a double life. In his real *life in civil society, i.e. economic society, he is isolated and at war with everyone else in defence of his private interests. And in his* imaginary *life as a citizen of the state, he is integrated into and at one with the world in theory but not in practice. It is this situation which gives rise to religious feelings. Religion is the heart's cry of alienated, atomized man, who overcomes the separation he experiences in everyday life, but only on the level of fantasy. Religious ideas will finally evaporate only when we have put an end to the atomism of society and chased away the fear and anxiety caused by the rule of money.*

The 'Jewish spirit' (that is, commerce) is merely a reflection of the life of civil society. The Jew engaged in commerce is realizing the essence of civil society: the pursuit of money and self-interest. The Jew will not be socially emancipated until society is emancipated from the rule of money, and man achieves in reality *(that is, in civil society) the integration and unity which in a 'free state' he experiences only in* appearance.]

I

Bruno Bauer, *The Jewish Question*, Brunswick, 1843

The German Jews want emancipation. What sort of emancipation do they want? *Civil, political* emancipation.

Bruno Bauer answers them: No one in Germany is politically emancipated. We ourselves are not free. How are we to liberate you? You Jews are *egoists* if you demand a special emancipation for yourselves as Jews. You should work as Germans for the political emancipation of Germany and as men for the emancipation of mankind, and you should look upon the particular form of oppression and shame which you experience not as an exception to the rule but rather as a confirmation of it.

Or do the Jews want to be put on an equal footing with *Christian subjects*? If so, they are recognizing the *Christian state* as legitimate, they are recognizing the regime of general enslavement. Why should their particular yoke not please them when they are pleased to accept the general yoke? Why should the German be interested in the liberation of the Jew when the Jew is not interested in the liberation of the German?

The *Christian* state only knows *privileges*. In it the Jew has the privilege of being a Jew. As a Jew he has rights which the Christian does not have. Why does he want rights he does not have and which Christians enjoy?

If the Jew wants to be emancipated from the Christian state, then he is demanding that the Christian state give up its *religious* prejudice. But does the Jew give up *his* religious prejudice? Does he have the right, then, to demand of someone else that he renounce his religion?

The Christian state is by its very *nature* incapable of emancipating the Jew; but, Bauer adds, the Jew by his very nature cannot be emancipated. As long as the state is Christian and the Jew Jewish, they are both equally incapable of either giving or receiving emancipation.

The Christian state can behave towards the Jew only in the manner of the Christian state, that is, by granting him as a privilege the right to separate himself off from the other subjects but subjecting him to the pressure of the other separate spheres. He experiences this pressure all the more intensely since as a Jew he is in *religious* opposition to the dominant religion. But the Jew himself can behave only like a Jew towards the state, i.e. treat it as something foreign, for he opposes his chimerical nationality to actual nationality, his illusory law to actual law, he considers himself entitled to separate himself from humanity, he refuses on principle to take any part in the movement of history, he looks forward to a future which has nothing in common with the future of mankind as a whole and he sees himself as a member of the Jewish people and the Jewish people as the chosen people.

On what grounds, then, do you Jews want emancipation? On account of your religion? It is the deadly enemy of the religion of the state. As citizens? There are no citizens in Germany. As men? You are not men, any more than those to whom you appeal.

After criticizing previous positions and solutions, Bauer poses the question of Jewish emancipation in a new way. What, he asks, is the *nature* of the Jew who is to be emancipated and the Christian state which is to emancipate him? He answers with a critique of the Jewish religion, he analyses the *religious* opposition between Judaism and Christianity and he explains the essence of the Christian state, all this with dash, perception, wit and thoroughness in a style as precise as it is pithy and trenchant.

How then does Bauer solve the Jewish question? What is the result? To formulate a question is to answer it. To make a critique of the Jewish question is to answer the Jewish question. We shall therefore sum up as follows:

We must emancipate ourselves before we can emancipate others.

The most rigid form of opposition between Jew and Christian is the *religious* opposition. How does one resolve an opposition? By making it impossible. How does one make a *religious* opposition impossible? By *abolishing religion*. Once Jew and Christian recognize their respective religions as nothing more than *different stages in the development of the human spirit*, as snake-skins cast off by *history*, and *man* as the snake which wore them, they will no longer be in religious opposition, but in a purely critical and *scientific*, a human relationship. *Science* will then be their unity. But oppositions in science are resolved by science itself.

The *German* Jew in particular suffers from the general lack of political emancipation and the pronounced Christianity of the state. For Bauer, however, the Jewish question has a universal significance which is independent of the specific German conditions. It is the question of the relationship of religion and state, of the *contradiction between religious prejudice and political emancipation*. Emancipation from religion is presented as a condition both for the Jew who wants to be politically emancipated and for the state which is to emancipate him and itself be emancipated.

'Very well,' you say, and the Jew himself says it, 'the Jew should not be emancipated because he is a Jew, because he has such an admirable code of universally human ethical principles. Rather, the *Jew* will recede behind the *citizen* and be a *citizen*, in spite of the fact that he is a Jew and is to remain a Jew; i.e., he is and remains a *Jew* in spite of the fact that he is a *citizen* and lives in universal human conditions: his Jewish and restricted nature always triumphs in the long run over his human and political obligations. The *prejudice* remains, even though it is overtaken by *universal* principles. But if it remains, it is more likely to overtake everything else.' 'The Jew could only remain a Jew in political life in a sophistical sense, in appearance; if he wanted to remain a Jew, the mere appearance would therefore be the essential and would triumph, i.e. his *life in the state* would be nothing more than an appearance or a momentary exception to the essential nature of things and to the rule.'[1]

Now let us see how Bauer formulates the role of the state.

'France,' he says, 'recently[2] provided us, in connection with the Jewish question (as she constantly does in all other *political* questions), with the glimpse of a life which is free but which revokes its freedom by law, thus declaring it to be a mere appearance, and on the other hand denies its free law through its actions.'[3]

'Universal freedom is not yet law in France and the *Jewish question* is *not* yet settled because legal freedom – the equality of all citizens – is restricted in actual life, which continues to be dominated and fragmented by religious privileges, and because the lack of freedom in actual life reacts on the law and forces it to

---

1. Bruno Bauer, 'The Capacity of Present-day Jews and Christians to Become Free', *Einundzwanzig Bogen aus der Schweiz*, Zürich 1843, p. 57.
2. *Proceedings of the Chamber of Deputies*, 26 December 1840.
3. Bauer, *The Jewish Question*, p. 64.

sanction the division of what are intrinsically free citizens into oppressed and oppressors.'[4]

So when would the Jewish question be settled in France?

'The Jew, for example, would have stopped being a Jew if he did not allow his [religious] laws to prevent him from fulfilling his duties to the state and to his fellow citizens, for example, if he went to the Chamber of Deputies on the Sabbath and took part in the public proceedings. All *religious privileges*, including the monopoly of a privileged church, would have to be abolished and if some or many or *even the overwhelming majority still considered themselves obliged to fulfil their religious duties*, then this should be *left to them* as a *purely private affair.*'[5] 'There is no longer any religion when there is no longer any privileged religion. Deprive religion of its powers of excommunication and it ceases to exist.'[6] 'Just as M. Martin du Nord saw the proposal to omit all mention of Sunday in the law as a declaration that Christianity has ceased to exist, with the same right (and this right is well founded) the declaration that the law of the Sabbath is no longer binding on the Jew would be a proclamation of the dissolution of Judaism.'[7]

So Bauer demands on the one hand that the Jew give up Judaism and that man in general give up religion in order to be emancipated as a *citizen*. On the other hand, it logically follows that for him the *political* abolition of religion amounts to the abolition of religion as a whole. The state which presupposes religion is not yet a true, a real state.

'Admittedly the idea of religion gives the state some guarantees. But what state? *What sort of state*?'[8]

It is at this point that the *one-sidedness* of Bauer's treatment of the Jewish question emerges.

It was in no way sufficient to ask who should emancipate and who be emancipated. It was necessary for the critique to ask a third question: *What kind of emancipation* is involved? What are the essential conditions of the emancipation which is required? Only the critique of *political emancipation* itself would constitute a definitive critique of the Jewish question itself and its true resolution into the 'general question of the age'.

Because Bauer fails to raise the question to this level, he falls into contradictions. He poses conditions which are not essential to *political* emancipation itself. He raises questions which are not

4. ibid., p. 65.   5. ibid.   6. ibid., p. 66.   7. ibid., p. 71.
8. ibid., p. 97.

contained within the problem and he solves problems which leave his question unanswered. When Bauer says of the opponents of Jewish emancipation: 'Their only mistake was to presuppose that the Christian state was the only true one and not to subject it to the same criticism as Judaism,' his own mistake lies clearly in the fact that he subjects only the 'Christian state' to criticism, and not the 'state as such', that he fails to examine *the relationship between political emancipation and human emancipation* and that he therefore poses conditions which can be explained only by his uncritical confusion of political emancipation and universally human emancipation. Bauer asks the Jews: Do you from your standpoint have the right to demand *political emancipation*? We pose the question the other way round: Does the standpoint of *political* emancipation have the right to demand from the Jews the abolition of Judaism and from man the abolition of religion?

The form in which the Jewish question is posed differs according to the state in which the Jew finds himself. In Germany, where there is no political state, no state as such, the Jewish question is a purely *theological question*. The Jew is in *religious* opposition to the state, which acknowledges Christianity as its foundation. This state is a theologian *ex professo*. Criticism is here criticism of theology, double-edged criticism, criticism of Christian and of Jewish theology. But we are still moving in the province of theology, however *critically* we may be moving in it.

In France, in the *constitutional* state, the Jewish question is a question of constitutionalism, a question of the *incompleteness of political emancipation*. Since the *appearance* of a state religion is preserved here in the formula – albeit an insignificant and self-contradictory one – of a *religion of the majority*, the relationship of the Jew to the state also retains the *appearance* of a religious, theological opposition.

Only in the free states of North America – or at least in some of them – does the Jewish question lose its *theological* significance and become a truly *secular* question. Only where the political state exists in its fully developed form can the relationship of the Jew and of religious man in general to the political state, i.e., the relationship of religion and state, appear in its characteristic and pure form. The criticism of this relationship ceases to be a theological criticism as soon as the state ceases to relate itself in a *theological* way to religion, as soon as the state relates to religion as a state, i.e., *politically*. Criticism then becomes *criticism of the political state*. At this point, where the question ceases to be *theological*, Bauer's criticism ceases to be critical.

'In the United States there is neither a state religion nor an officially proclaimed religion of the majority, nor the predominance of one faith over another. The state is foreign to all faiths.'[9] There are even some states in North America where 'the constitution does not impose religious beliefs or practice as a condition of political privileges'.[10] Nevertheless, 'people in the United States do not believe that a man without religion can be an honest man'.[11]

And yet North America is the land of religiosity *par excellence*, as Beaumont, Tocqueville and the Englishman Hamilton all assure us. However, we are using the North American states only as an example. The question is: What is the relationship between *complete* political emancipation and religion? If in the land of complete political emancipation we find not only that religion *exists* but that it exists in a *fresh* and *vigorous* form, that proves that the existence of religion does not contradict the perfection of the state. But since the existence of religion is the existence of a defect, the source of this defect must be looked for in the *nature* of the state itself. We no longer see religion as the *basis* but simply as a *phenomenon* of secular narrowness. We therefore explain the religious restriction on the free citizens from the secular restriction they experience. We do not mean to say that they must do away with their religious restriction in order to transcend their secular limitations. We do not turn secular questions into theological questions. We turn theological questions into secular questions. History has been resolved into superstition for long enough. We are now resolving superstition into history. The question of the *relationship of political emancipation to religion* becomes for us the question of the *relationship of political emancipation to human emancipation*. We criticize the religious weakness of the political state by criticizing the political state in its *secular* construction, *regardless* of its religious weaknesses. We humanize the contradiction between the state and a *particular religion*, for example Judaism, by resolving it into the contradiction between the state and *particular secular* elements, and we humanize the contradiction between the state and *religion in*

9. Gustave de Beaumont, *Marie ou l'esclavage aux États-Unis*, Paris, 1835, p. 214.

10. ibid., p. 225.   11. ibid., p. 224.

general by resolving it into the contradiction between the state
and its own general *presuppositions.*

The *political* emancipation of the Jew, the Christian, the
religious man in general, is the *emancipation of the state* from
Judaism, from Christianity, from *religion* in general. The state
emancipates itself from religion in a form and manner peculiar to
its nature as *state* by emancipating itself from the *state religion,*
i.e., by acknowledging no religion, by instead acknowledging itself
as state. *Political* emancipation from religion is not complete and
consistent emancipation from religion, because political emancipation is not the complete and consistent form of *human* emancipation.

The limitations of political emancipation are immediately
apparent from the fact that the *state* can liberate itself from a
restriction without man himself being *truly* free of it, that a state
can be a *free state* without man himself being *a free man.* Bauer
himself tacitly admits this when he poses the following condition
for political emancipation:

'All religious privileges, including the monopoly of a privileged
church, would have to be abolished and if some or many or even
the *overwhelming majority still considered themselves obliged to
fulfil their religious duties,* then this should be left to them as a
purely private affair.'

Therefore the *state* can have emancipated itself from religion
even if the *overwhelming majority* is still religious. And the
overwhelming majority does not cease to be religious by being
religious *in private.*

But the attitude of the state, especially *the free state,* to religion
is still only the attitude to religion of the *men* who make up the
state. It therefore follows that man liberates himself from a
restriction through the *medium of the state,* in a *political* way, by
transcending this restriction in an *abstract* and *restricted* manner,
in a partial manner, in contradiction with himself. It also follows
that when man liberates himself *politically* he does so in a *devious
way,* through a *medium,* even though the medium is a *necessary*
one. Finally it follows that even when man proclaims himself an
atheist through the mediation of the state, i.e., when he proclaims
the state an atheist, he still remains under the constraints of
religion because he acknowledges his atheism only deviously,
through a medium. Religion is precisely that: the devious acknowledgement of man, through an intermediary. The state is the

intermediary between man and man's freedom. Just as Christ is the intermediary to whom man attributes all his divinity, all his *religious constraints*, so the state is the intermediary to which man transfers all his non-divinity, all his *human unconstraint*.

The *political* elevation of man above religion shares all the shortcomings and all the advantages of political elevation in general. For example, the state as state annuls *private property*, man declares in a *political* way that private property is *abolished*, immediately the *property qualification* is abolished for active and passive election rights, as has happened in many North American states. *Hamilton* interprets this fact quite correctly from the political standpoint: '*The masses have gained a victory over the property owners and financial wealth.*'[12] Is not private property abolished in an ideal sense when the propertyless come to legislate for the propertied? The *property qualification* is the last *political* form to recognize private property.

And yet the political annulment of private property does not mean the abolition of private property; on the contrary, it even presupposes it. The state in its own way abolishes distinctions based on *birth, rank, education* and *occupation* when it declares birth, rank, education and occupation to be *non-political* distinctions, when it proclaims that every member of the people is an equal participant in popular sovereignty regardless of these distinctions, when it treats all those elements which go to make up the actual life of the people from the standpoint of the state. Nevertheless the state allows private property, education and occupation to *act* and assert their *particular* nature in *their* own way, i.e., as private property, as education and as occupation. Far from abolishing these *factual* distinctions, the state presupposes them in order to exist, it only experiences itself as *political state* and asserts its *universality* in opposition to these elements. *Hegel* therefore defines the relationship of the political state to religion quite correctly when he says:

In order for the state to come into existence as the *self-knowing* ethical actuality of spirit, it is essential that it should be distinct from the form of authority and of faith. But this distinction emerges only in so far as divisions occur in the ecclesiastical sphere itself. It is only in this

12. Thomas Hamilton, *Men and Manners in America*, 2 vols., Edinburgh, 1833. Marx is quoting from the German translation, *Die Menschen und die Sitten in den Vereinigten Staaten von Nordamerika*, Mannheim, 1834, Vol. 1, p. 146.

way that the state, above the *particular* churches, has attained to the universality of thought – its formal principle – and is bringing this universality into existence.[13]

Of course! It is only in this way, *above* the *particular* elements, that the state constitutes itself as universality.

The perfected political state is by its nature the *species-life* of man in *opposition* to his material life. All the presuppositions of this egoistic life continue to exist *outside* the sphere of the state in *civil* society, but as qualities of civil society. Where the political state has attained its full degree of development man leads a double life, a life in heaven and a life on earth, not only in his mind, in his consciousness, but in *reality*. He lives in the *political community*, where he regards himself as a *communal being*, and in *civil society*, where he is active as a *private individual*, regards other men as means, debases himself to a means and becomes a plaything of alien powers. The relationship of the political state to civil society is just as spiritual as the relationship of heaven to earth. The state stands in the same opposition to civil society and overcomes it in the same way as religion overcomes the restrictions of the profane world, i.e. it has to acknowledge it again, reinstate it and allow itself to be dominated by it. Man in his *immediate* reality, in civil society, is a profane being. Here, where he regards himself and is regarded by others as a real individual, he is an illusory phenomenon. In the state, on the other hand, where he is considered to be a species-being, he is the imaginary member of a fictitious sovereignty, he is divested of his real individual life and filled with an unreal universality.

The conflict in which the individual believer in a *particular* religion finds himself with his own citizenship and with other men as members of the community is reduced to the *secular* division between the *political* state and civil society. For man as *bourgeois*[14] 'life in the state is nothing more than an appearance or a momentary exception to the essential nature of things and to the rule'. Of course the *bourgeois*, like the Jew, only takes part in the life of the state in a sophistical way, just as the *citoyen* only remains a Jew or a bourgeois in a sophistical way; but this sophistry is not personal. It is the *sophistry of the political state* itself. The difference between the religious man and the citizen is the difference

---

13. Hegel, *The Philosophy of Right*, tr. T. M. Knox, London, 1942, p. 173.
14. *Bourgeois* in this sense means a member of civil society.

between the tradesman and the citizen, between the day-labourer and the citizen, between the landowner and the citizen, between the *living individual* and the *citizen*. The contradiction which exists between religious man and political man is the same as exists between the *bourgeois* and the *citoyen*, between the member of civil society and his *political lion's skin*.

This secular conflict to which the Jewish question ultimately reduces itself – the relationship of the political state to its presuppositions, whether they be material elements, like private property, etc., or spiritual ones, like education, religion, the conflict between the *general interest* and the *private interest*, the split between the *political state* and *civil society* – these secular oppositions Bauer does not touch, but polemicizes instead against their *religious* expression.

It is precisely its foundation – the need that assures *civil society* its existence and *guarantees its necessity* – that exposes it to constant dangers, maintains an element of uncertainty in it and brings forth that restless alternation of wealth and poverty, need and prosperity which constitutes change in general.[15]

Compare the whole section 'Civil Society',[16] which broadly follows the main features of Hegel's Philosophy of Right. Civil society in its opposition to the political state is recognized as necessary because the political state is recognized as necessary.

Political emancipation is certainly a big step forward. It may not be the last form of general human emancipation, but it is the last form of human emancipation *within* the prevailing scheme of things. Needless to say, we are here speaking of real, practical emancipation.

Man emancipates himself *politically* from religion by banishing it from the province of public law to that of private law. It is no longer the spirit of the *state* where man behaves – although in a limited way, in a particular form and a particular sphere – as a species-being, in community with other men. It has become the spirit of *civil society*, the sphere of egoism and of the *bellum omnium contra omnes*. It is no longer the essence of *community* but the essence of *difference*. It has become the expression of the *separation* of man from his *community*, from himself and from other men, which is what it was *originally*. It is now only the abstract confession of an individual oddity, of a *private whim*, a caprice. The

15. Bauer, *The Jewish Question*, p. 8.   16. ibid., pp. 8–9.

continual splintering of religion in North America, for example, already gives it the *external* form of a purely individual affair. It has been relegated to the level of a private interest and exiled from the real community. But it is important to understand where the limit of political emancipation lies. The splitting of man into his *public* and his *private* self and the *displacement* of religion from the state to civil society is not one step in the process of political emancipation but its *completion*. Hence political emancipation neither abolishes nor tries to abolish man's *real* religiosity.

The *dissolution* of man into Jew and citizen, Protestant and citizen, religious man and citizen, is not a denial of citizenship or an avoidance of political emancipation: it *is political emancipation itself*, it is the *political* way of emancipating oneself from religion. Of course, in periods when the political state as political state comes violently into being out of civil society and when human self-liberation attempts to realize itself in the form of political self-liberation, the state can and must proceed to the *abolition of religion*, to the *destruction* of religion; but only in the same way as it proceeds to the abolition of private property (by imposing a maximum, by confiscation, by progressive taxation) and the abolition of life (by the *guillotine*). At those times when it is particularly self-confident, political life attempts to suppress its presupposition, civil society and its elements, and to constitute itself as the real, harmonious species-life of man. But it only manages to do this in *violent* contradiction to the conditions of its own existence, by declaring the revolution *permanent*, and for that reason the political drama necessarily ends up with the restoration of religion, private property and all the elements of civil society, just as war ends with peace.

Indeed, the perfected Christian state is not the so-called *Christian* state which recognizes Christianity as its foundation, as the state religion, and which therefore excludes other religions. The perfected Christian state is rather the *atheist* state, the *democratic* state, the state which relegates religion to the level of the other elements of civil society. The state which is still theological, which still officially professes the Christian faith, which still does not dare to declare itself a *state*, has not yet succeeded in expressing in *secular, human* form, in its *reality* as state, the *human* basis of which Christianity is the exaggerated expression. The so-called Christian state is simply the *non-state*, since it is only the *human basis* of the Christian religion, and not Christianity as a religion, which can realize itself in real human creations.

The so-called Christian state is the Christian negation of the state, but is certainly not the political realization of Christianity. The state which still professes Christianity in the form of religion does not yet profess it in a political form, for it still behaves towards religion in a religious manner, i.e. it is not the *true realization* of the human foundation of religion because it continues to accept the *unreality* and the *imaginary* form of this human core. The so-called Christian state is the *imperfect* state and Christianity serves as *supplement* and *sanctification* of this imperfection. Therefore religion necessarily becomes a *means* for the state, which is a *hypocritical* state. A *perfected* state which counts religion as one of its presuppositions on account of the deficiency which exists in the general *nature* of the state is not at all the same thing as an *imperfect* state which declares religion its *foundation* on account of the deficiency which lies in its *particular existence* as a deficient state. In the latter case religion becomes *imperfect politics*. In the former, the imperfection even of perfected *politics* manifests itself in religion. The so-called Christian state needs the Christian religion to complete itself as a *state*. The democratic state, the true state, does not need religion for its political completion. On the contrary, it can discard religion, because in it the human foundation of religion is realized in a secular way. The so-called Christian state, on the other hand, behaves in a political way towards religion and in a religious way towards politics. In the same way as it demeans political forms to mere appearances, it demeans religion to a mere appearance.

In order to make this opposition clearer let us consider Bauer's construction of the Christian state, a construction which derives from his study of the Christian–Germanic state.

Bauer says:

In order to prove the *impossibility* or the *non-existence* of the Christian state, people have recently been making frequent references to those passages in the Gospel which the [present] state *not only* does *not* observe but also *cannot observe unless it wishes to dissolve itself entirely* [as a state].

But the matter is not settled so easily. What do those passages in the Gospel demand? Supernatural self-denial, submission to the authority of revelation, turning away from the state and the abolition of secular relationships. But the Christian state demands and accomplishes all these things. It has made the *spirit of the Gospel* its own, and if it does not reproduce it in the same words that the Gospel uses, this is because it is expressing that spirit in political forms, that is, in forms which are borrowed from the political system of this world but are reduced to mere appearances in the religious rebirth they are forced to undergo. This turning away from the state realizes itself through political forms.[17]

Bauer goes on to show how the people in a Christian state are in fact a non-people with no will of their own and how their true existence resides in the ruler to whom they are subjected and who is, by origin and by nature, alien to them, i.e. given to them by God without their agreement. He also shows how the laws of this people are not their own creation but actual revelations; how the supreme ruler needs privileged intermediaries in his relations with the real people, with the masses; how the masses themselves disintegrate into a multitude of distinct spheres formed and determined by chance, differentiated by their interests, their particular passions and prejudices, and allowed as a privilege to seclude themselves from one another, etc.[18]

But Bauer himself says:

Politics, if it is to be nothing more than religion, can no longer be called politics, just as washing dishes, if it is to take on a religious significance, can no longer be called housework.[19]

But in the Christian–Germanic state religion is an 'economic matter' just as 'economic matters' are religion. In the Christian–Germanic state the dominance of religion is the religion of dominance.

The separation of the 'spirit of the Gospel' from the 'letter of the Gospel' is an irreligious act. The state which allows the Gospel to speak in the language of politics or in any other language than the language of the Holy Ghost commits a sacrilegious act, if not in human eyes, then at least in its own religious eyes. The state which acknowledges Christianity as its supreme law and the *Bible* as its *charter* must be measured against the *words* of the Holy Scripture, for the Scripture is holy even in its words. This state, like the *human debris* upon which it is based, becomes involved in a painful contradiction, a contradiction which from the standpoint of religious consciousness is insuperable, when we refer it to those passages in the Gospel which it 'not only does not observe but *also cannot observe unless it wishes to dissolve itself*

17. Bauer, *The Jewish Question*, p. 55.   18. ibid., p. 56.
19. ibid., p. 108.

entirely as a state'. And why does it not want to dissolve itself entirely? It is not capable of answering either others or itself on this point. In its *own consciousness* the official Christian state is an *ought* whose realization is impossible; it cannot convince itself of the *reality* of its own existence except through lies and therefore remains in its own eyes a perpetual object of doubt, an unreliable and problematic object. Criticism therefore has every justification in forcing the state which bases itself on the Bible into intellectual disarray in which it no longer knows whether it is *illusion* or *reality* and in which the infamy of its *secular* ends – for which religion serves as a cover – comes into irreconcilable conflict with the integrity of its *religious* consciousness, which sees religion as the aim of the world. This state can free itself from its inner torment only by becoming the *bailiff* of the Catholic Church. In the face of this Church, which declares the secular power to be its servant, the state – the *secular* power which claims to rule over the religious spirit – is powerless.

In the so-called Christian state it is *estrangement* [*Entfremdung*] which carries weight, and not *man himself*. The only man who carries weight, the *king*, is specifically distinct from other men: he is still religious and is in direct communion with Heaven, with God. The relationships which prevail here are still relationships of *faith*. This means that the religious spirit is not yet truly secularized.

But the religious spirit can never be *truly* secularized, for what is it but the *unsecular* form of a stage in the development of the human spirit? The religious spirit can be realized only in so far as that stage in the development of the human spirit of which it is the religious expression emerges and constitutes itself in its *secular* form. This happens in the democratic state. Not Christianity but the human foundation of Christianity is the foundation of this state. Religion remains the ideal, unsecular consciousness of its members because it is the ideal form of the *stage of human development* which has been reached in this state.

The members of the political state are religious because of the dualism between individual life and species-life, between the life of civil society and political life. They are religious inasmuch as man considers political life, which is far removed from his actual individuality, to be his true life and inasmuch as religion is here the spirit of civil society and the expression of the separation and distance of man from man. Political democracy is Christian inasmuch as it regards man – not just one man but all men – as a *sovereign* and supreme being; but man in his uncultivated, unsocial aspect, man in his contingent existence, man just as he is, man as he has been corrupted, lost to himself, sold, and exposed to the rule of inhuman conditions and elements by the entire organization of our society – in a word, man who is not yet a *true* species-being. The sovereignty of man – but of man as an alien being distinct from actual man – is the fantasy, the dream, the postulate of Christianity, whereas in democracy it is a present and material reality, a secular maxim.

In a perfected democracy the religious and theological consciousness regards itself as all the more religious and all the more theological since it is apparently without any political significance or earthly aims, an unworldly and spiritual affair, an expression of the inadequacy of reason, the product of caprice and fantasy, an actualization of the life to come. Christianity here achieves the *practical* expression of its universal religious significance in that the most disparate outlooks come together in one group in the form of Christianity. Moreover, it demands of no one that he accept Christianity, but simply that he accept religion in general, any religion (cf. the book we mentioned earlier by Beaumont[20]). The religious consciousness revels in a wealth of religious opposition and religious diversity.

We have therefore shown that political emancipation from religion allows religion – but not privileged religion – to continue in existence. The contradiction in which the adherent of a particular religion finds himself in relation to his citizenship is only *one aspect* of the general *secular contradiction between the political state and civil society*. The final form of the Christian state is one which recognizes itself as state and disregards the religion of its members. The emancipation of the state from religion is not the emancipation of actual man from religion.

Therefore we do not tell the Jews that they cannot be emancipated politically without radically emancipating themselves from Judaism, which is what Bauer tells them. We say instead: the fact that you can be politically emancipated without completely and absolutely renouncing Judaism shows that *political emancipation* by itself is not *human* emancipation. If you Jews want to be politically emancipated without emancipating yourselves as humans, the incompleteness and the contradiction lies not only in you but in the *nature* and the *category* of political emancipation.

20. See above, p. 217.

If you are ensnared within this category, then your experience is a universal one. In the same way as the state *evangelizes* when, although a state, it adopts the attitude of a Christian towards the Jew, the Jew *acts politically* when, although a Jew, he demands civil rights.

But if man, although a Jew, can be politically emancipated and acquire civil rights, can he claim and acquire the *rights of man*? In Bauer's view he cannot.

The question is whether the Jew as such, i.e. the Jew who himself admits that he is compelled by his true nature to live in eternal separation from others, is capable of acquiring and granting to others the *universal rights of man*.

The idea of the rights of man was not discovered in the Christian world until the last century. It is not innate in man. On the contrary, it can only be won in a struggle against the historical traditions in which man has up to now been educated. Therefore the rights of man are not a gift of nature or a legacy of previous history, but the prize of the struggle against the accident of birth and the privileges which history has handed down from generation to generation. They are the product of culture, and only he can possess them who has earned them and deserved them.

But can the Jew really take possession of them? As long as he is a Jew the restricted nature that makes him a Jew will inevitably gain the ascendancy over the human nature which should join him as a man to other men; the effect will be to separate him from non-Jews. He declares through this separation that the particular nature which makes him a Jew is his true and highest nature in the face of which human nature is forced to yield.

In the same way the Christian as Christian cannot grant the rights of man.[21]

According to Bauer man must sacrifice the '*privilege of faith*' in order to be in a position to receive the universal rights of man. Let us consider for one moment these so-called rights of man. Let us consider them in their most authentic form – the form they have among those who *discovered* them, the North Americans and the French! These rights of man are partly *political* rights, rights which are only exercised in community with others. What constitutes their content is *participation* in the *community*, in the *political* community or *state*. They come under the category of *political freedom*, of *civil rights*, which as we have seen by no means presupposes the consistent and positive abolition of

21. Bauer, *The Jewish Question*, pp. 19–20.

religion and therefore of Judaism. It remains for us to consider the other aspect, the *droits de l'homme*[22] as distinct from the *droits du citoyen*.[23]

Among them we find freedom of conscience, the right to practise one's chosen religion. The *privilege of faith* is expressly recognized, either as one of the *rights of man* or as a consequence of one of these rights, namely freedom.

Declaration of the Rights of Man and of the Citizen, 1791, Article 10: 'No one is to be molested on account of his convictions, even his religious convictions.' In Title 1 of the Constitution of 1791 the following is guaranteed as one of the rights of man: 'the liberty of every man to practise the religion he professes'.

The Declaration of the Rights of Man etc., 1793, counts among the rights of man, Article 7: 'Liberty of worship'. What is more, it even says, in connection with the right to publish views and opinions, to assemble and to practise religion, that 'the need to enunciate these rights supposes either the presence or the recent memory of despotism'. Compare the Constitution of 1795, Title XIV, Article 354.

Constitution of Pennsylvania, Article 9, §3: 'All men have received from nature the imprescriptible *right* to worship the Almighty according to the dictates of their consciences and no one can of right be compelled to follow, to institute or to support against his will any religion or religious ministry. No human authority can under any circumstances whatsoever intervene in questions of conscience and control the powers of the soul.'

Constitution of New Hampshire, Articles 5 and 6: 'Among the natural rights, some are by their very nature inalienable because they cannot be replaced by anything equivalent. The *rights* of conscience are of this sort.'[24]

The incompatibility of religion with the rights of man is so alien to the concept of the rights of man that the *right to be religious* – to be religious in whatever way one chooses and to practise one's chosen religion – is expressly enumerated among the rights of man. The *privilege of faith* is a *universal right of man*.

The rights of man as *such* are distinguished from the rights of the citizen. Who is this man who is distinct from the citizen? None other than the *member of civil society*. Why is the member of civil society simply called 'man' and why are his rights called

22. Rights of man.　　　23. Rights of the citizen.
24. Beaumont, op. cit., pp. 213–14.

the rights of man? How can we explain this fact? By the relationship of the political state to civil society, by the nature of political emancipation.

The first point we should note is that the so-called *rights of man*, as distinct from the *rights of the citizen*, are quite simply the rights of the *member of civil society*, i.e. of egoistic man, of man separated from other men and from the community. Consider the most radical constitution, the Constitution of 1793:

Declaration of the Rights of Man and of the Citizen.

Article 2. 'These rights, etc. (the natural and imprescriptible rights) are: equality, liberty, security, property.'

What is liberty?

Article 6. 'Liberty is the power which belongs to man to do anything that does not harm the rights of others', or according to the Declaration of the Rights of Man of 1791: 'Liberty consists in being able to do anything which does not harm others.'

Liberty is therefore the right to do and perform everything which does not harm others. The limits within which each individual can move *without* harming others are determined by law, just as the boundary between two fields is determined by a stake. The liberty we are here dealing with is that of man as an isolated monad who is withdrawn into himself. Why does Bauer say that the Jew is incapable of acquiring the rights of man?

'As long as he is a Jew the restricted nature which makes him a Jew will inevitably gain the ascendancy over the human nature which should join him as a man to other men; the effect will be to separate him from non-Jews.'

But the right of man to freedom is not based on the association of man with man but rather on the separation of man from man. It is the *right* of this separation, the right of the *restricted* individual, restricted to himself.

The practical application of the right of man to freedom is the right of man to *private property*.

What is the right of man to private property?

Article 16 (Constitution of 1793): 'The right of *property* is that right which belongs to each citizen to enjoy and dispose *at will* of his goods, his revenues and the fruit of his work and industry.'

The right to private property is therefore the right to enjoy and dispose of one's resources as one wills, without regard for other men and independently of society: the right of self-interest. The individual freedom mentioned above, together with this application of it, forms the foundation of civil society. It leads each man to see in other men not the *realization* but the *limitation* of his own freedom. But above all it proclaims the right of man 'to enjoy and dispose *at will* of his goods, his revenues and the fruit of his work and industry'.

There remain the other rights of man, equality and security.

Equality, here in its non-political sense, simply means equal access to liberty as described above, namely that each man is equally considered to be a self-sufficient monad. The Constitution of 1795 defines the concept of this equality, in keeping with this meaning, as follows:

Article 3 (Constitution of 1795): 'Equality consists in the fact that the law is the same for everyone, whether it protects or whether it punishes.'

And security?

Article 8 (Constitution of 1793): 'Security consists in the protection accorded by society to each of its members for the conservation of his person, his rights and his property.'

Security is the supreme social concept of civil society, the concept of *police*, the concept that the whole of society is there only to guarantee each of its members the conservation of his person, his rights and his property. In this sense Hegel calls civil society 'the state of need and of reason'.

The concept of security does not enable civil society to rise above its egoism. On the contrary, security is the *guarantee* of its egoism.

Therefore not one of the so-called rights of man goes beyond egoistic man, man as a member of civil society, namely an individual withdrawn into himself, his private interest and his private desires and separated from the community. In the rights of man it is not man who appears as a species-being; on the contrary, species-life itself, society, appears as a framework extraneous to the individuals, as a limitation of their original independence. The only bond which holds them together is natural necessity, need and private interest, the conservation of their property and their egoistic persons.

It is a curious thing that a people which is just beginning to free itself, to tear down all the barriers between the different sections of the people and to found a political community, that such a people should solemnly proclaim the rights of egoistic man, separated from his fellow men and from the community (Declara-

tion of 1791), and even repeat this proclamation at a time when
only the most heroic devotion can save the nation and is for that
reason pressingly required, at a time when the sacrifice of all the
interests of civil society becomes the order of the day and egoism
must be punished as a crime. (*Declaration of the Rights of Man*,
etc., 1793.) This fact appears even more curious when we observe
that citizenship, the *political community*, is reduced by the
political emancipators to a mere *means* for the conservation of
these so-called rights of man and that the citizen is therefore
proclaimed the servant of egoistic man; that the sphere in which
man behaves as a communal being [*Gemeinwesen*] is degraded to
a level below the sphere in which he behaves as a partial being,
and finally that it is man as *bourgeois*, i.e. as a member of civil
society, and not man as citizen who is taken as the *real* and
authentic man.

'The *goal* of all *political association* is the *conservation* of the
natural and imprescriptible rights of man' (*Declaration of the
Rights of Man* etc., 1791, Article 2). '*Government* is instituted in
order to guarantee man the enjoyment of his natural and imprescriptible rights' (*Declaration* etc., 1793, Article 1).

Thus even during the ardour of its youth, urged on to new
heights by the pressure of circumstances, political life declares
itself to be a mere *means* whose goal is the life of civil society.
True, revolutionary practice is in flagrant contradiction with its
theory. While, for example, security is declared to be one of the
rights of man, the violation of the privacy of letters openly becomes
the order of the day. While the '*unlimited* freedom of the press'
(Constitution of 1793, Article 122) is guaranteed as a consequence
of the right to individual freedom, the freedom of the press is
completely destroyed, for 'the freedom of the press should not be
permitted when it compromises public freedom'.[25] This therefore
means that the right to freedom ceases to be a right as soon as it
comes into conflict with *political* life, whereas in theory political
life is simply the guarantee of the rights of man, the rights of
individual man, and should be abandoned as soon as it contradicts
its *goal*, these rights of man. But practice is only the exception
and theory is the rule. Even if we were to assume that the relationship is properly expressed in revolutionary practice, the problem
still remains to be solved as to why the relationship is set upon its

25. 'Robespierre Jeune', *Histoire parlementaire de la révolution française*
by Buchez and Roux, Vol. 28, p. 159.

head in the minds of the political emancipators so that the end appears as the means and the means as the end. This optical illusion present in their minds would continue to pose the same problem, though in a psychological and theoretical form.

But there is a straightforward solution.

Political emancipation is at the same time the *dissolution* of the old society on which there rested the power of the sovereign, the political system [*Staatswesen*] as estranged from the people. The political revolution is the revolution of civil society. What was the character of the old society? It can be characterized in one word: *feudalism*. The old civil society had a *directly political* character, i.e. the elements of civil life such as property, family and the mode and manner of work were elevated in the form of seignory, estate and guild to the level of elements of political life. In this form they defined the relationship of the single individual to the *state as a whole*, i.e. his *political* relationship, his relationship of separation and exclusion from the other components of society. For the feudal organization of the life of the people did not elevate property or labour to the level of social elements but rather completed their *separation* from the state as a whole and constituted them as *separate* societies within society. But the functions and conditions of life in civil society were still political, even though political in the feudal sense, i.e. they excluded the individual from the state as a whole, they transformed the *particular* relationship of his guild to the whole state into his own general relationship to the life of the people, just as they transformed his specific civil activity and situation into his general activity and situation. As a consequence of this organization, the unity of the state, together with the consciousness, the will and the activity of the unity of the state, the universal political power, likewise inevitably appears as the *special* concern of a ruler and his servants, separated from the people.

The political revolution which overthrew this rule and turned the affairs of the state into the affairs of the people, which constituted the political state as a concern of the whole people, i.e. as a real state, inevitably destroyed all the estates, corporations, guilds and privileges which expressed the separation of the people from its community. The political revolution thereby *abolished* the *political character of civil society*. It shattered civil society into its simple components – on the one hand *individuals* and on the other the *material* and *spiritual elements* which constitute the vital content and civil situation of these individuals. It unleashed the political spirit which had, as it were, been dissolved, dissected and dispersed in the various cul-de-sacs of feudal society; it gathered together this spirit from its state of dispersion, liberated it from the adulteration of civil life and constituted it as the sphere of the community, the *universal* concern of the people ideally independent of those *particular* elements of civil life. A person's *particular* activity and situation in life sank to the level of a purely individual significance. They no longer constituted the relationship of the individual to the state as a whole. Public affairs as such became the universal affair of each individual and the political function his universal function.

But the perfection of the idealism of the state was at the same time the perfection of the materialism of civil society. The shaking-off of the political yoke was at the same time the shaking-off of the bonds which had held in check the egoistic spirit of civil society. Political emancipation was at the same time the emancipation of civil society from politics, from even the *appearance* of a universal content.

Feudal society was dissolved into its foundation [*Grund*], into *man*. But into man as he really was its foundation – into *egoistic* man.

This *man*, the member of civil society, is now the foundation, the presupposition of the *political* state. In the rights of man the state acknowledges him as such.

But the freedom of egoistic man and the acknowledgement of this freedom is rather the acknowledgement of the *unbridled* movement of the spiritual and material elements which form the content of his life.

Hence man was not freed from religion – he received the freedom of religion. He was not freed from property – he received the freedom of property. He was not freed from the egoism of trade – he received the freedom to engage in trade.

The *constitution* of the *political state* and the dissolution of civil society into independent *individuals* – who are related by *law* just as men in the estates and guilds were related by *privilege* – are achieved in *one and the same act*. But man, as member of civil society, inevitably appears as *unpolitical* man, as *natural* man. The rights of man appear as natural rights, for *self-conscious activity* is concentrated upon the *political act*. Egoistic man is the *passive* and merely *given* result of the society which has been dissolved, an object of *immediate certainty*, and for that reason a *natural* object. The *political revolution* dissolves civil society into its component parts without *revolutionizing* these parts and subjecting them to criticism. It regards civil society, the world of needs, of labour, of private interests and of civil law, as the *foundation of its existence*, as a *presupposition* which needs no further grounding, and therefore as its *natural basis*. Finally, man as he is a member of civil society is taken to be the *real* man, *man* as distinct from *citizen*, since he is man in his sensuous, individual and *immediate* existence, whereas *political* man is simply abstract, artificial man, man as an *allegorical*, *moral* person. Actual man is acknowledged only in the form of the *egoistic* individual and *true* man only in the form of the *abstract citizen*.

Rousseau's description of the abstraction of the political man is a good one:

> Whoever dares to undertake the founding of a people's institutions must feel himself capable of *changing*, so to speak, *human nature*, of *transforming* each individual, who in himself is a complete and solitary whole, into a *part* of a greater whole from which he somehow receives his life and his being, of substituting a *partial* and *moral existence* for physical and independent existence. He must take *man's own powers away from him* and substitute for them alien ones which he can only use with the assistance of others.[26]

All emancipation is *reduction* of the human world and of relationships to *man himself*.

Political emancipation is the reduction of man on the one hand to the member of civil society, the *egoistic*, *independent* individual, and on the other to the *citizen*, the moral person.

Only when real, individual man resumes the abstract citizen into himself and as an individual man has become a *species-being* in his empirical life, his individual work and his individual relationships, only when man has recognized and organized his *forces propres*[27] as *social forces* so that social force is no longer separated from him in the form of *political* force, only then will human emancipation be completed.

26. J.-J. Rousseau, *Du contrat social*, Book II, London, 1782, p. 67.
27. Own forces.

II

Bruno Bauer, 'The Capacity of Present-day Jews and Christians to Become Free', *Einundzwanzig Bogen aus der Schweiz*, pp. 56–71.

Bauer deals in this form with the relation between the *Jewish and Christian religions*, as well as their relation to criticism. Their relation to criticism is their relation 'to the capacity to become free'.

His conclusion is:

The Christian has only one hurdle to overcome, namely, his religion, in order to dispense with religion altogether, and hence to become free. The Jew, on the other hand, does not only have to break with his Jewish nature; he also has to break with the development towards the completion of his religion, a development which has remained alien to him.[28]

Thus Bauer here transforms the question of Jewish emancipation into a purely religious question. The theological problem as to who has the better chance of gaining salvation – Jew or Christian – is here repeated in a more enlightened form: who is the more *capable of emancipation?* The question is no longer: which gives freedom, Judaism or Christianity? Rather it is the reverse: which gives more freedom, the negation of Judaism or the negation of Christianity?

If they wish to become free, the Jews should not embrace Christianity but Christianity in dissolution and more generally religion in dissolution, i.e. enlightenment, criticism and its product – free humanity.[29]

It is still a matter of *embracing a religion* for the Jew. It is no longer a question of Christianity, but of Christianity in dissolution.

Bauer demands of the Jew that he break with the essence of the Christian religion – a demand which, as he himself says, does not proceed from the development of the Jewish nature.

Since Bauer, at the end of his *Jewish Question*, represented Judaism as nothing more than a crude religious criticism of Christianity, and therefore gave it 'only' a religious significance, it was clear in advance that he would also transform the emancipation of the Jews into a philosophico-theological act.

28. Bauer, 'The Capacity . . .', *Einundzwanzig Bogen aus der Schweiz*, p. 71.
29. ibid., p. 70.

Bauer sees the *ideal* and abstract essence of the Jew, his *religion*, as his *whole* essence. He is therefore right to conclude: 'The Jew gives nothing to humanity when he lays aside his limited law,' when he abolishes all his Judaism.[30]

According to this the relationship of Jews and Christians is as follows: the only interest Christians have in the emancipation of the Jews is a general human and *theoretical* interest. Judaism is an offensive fact for the religious eye of the Christian. As soon as his eye ceases to be religious, this fact ceases to be offensive. The emancipation of the Jews is in and for itself not the task of the Christian.

However, if the Jew wants to liberate himself, he has to complete not only his own task but also the task of the Christian – the *Critique of the Evangelical History of the Synoptics* and the *Life of Jesus*, etc.[31]

'They must see to it themselves: they will determine their own destiny; but history does not allow itself to be mocked.'[32]

We will try to avoid looking at the problem in a theological way. For us the question of the Jews' capacity for emancipation is transformed into the question: what specific *social* element must be overcome in order to abolish Judaism? For the capacity of the present-day Jew for emancipation is the relation of Judaism to the emancipation of the present-day world. This relation flows inevitably from the special position of Judaism in the enslaved world of today.

Let us consider the real secular Jew – not the *sabbath Jew*, as Bauer does, but the *everyday Jew*.

Let us not look for the Jew's secret in his religion: rather let us look for the secret of religion in the real Jew.

What is the secular basis of Judaism? *Practical* need, self-interest.

What is the secular cult of the Jew? *Haggling*. What is his secular God? *Money*.

Well then! Emancipation from *haggling* and from *money*, i.e. from practical, real Judaism, would be the same as the self-emancipation of our age.

An organization of society that abolished the basis upon which

30. ibid., p. 65.
31. These two books are by Bruno Bauer (Brunswick, 1842) and David Friedrich Strauss (Tübingen, 1835–6) respectively.
32. Bauer, 'The Capacity . . .', p. 71.

haggling exists, i.e. the possibility of haggling, would have made the Jew impossible. His religious consciousness would vanish like an insipid haze in the vital air of society. On the other hand, when the Jew recognizes this his *practical* nature as null and works to abolish it, he is working outwards from his previous course of development in the direction of general *human emancipation* and turning against the *supreme practical* expression of human self-estrangement.

We therefore recognize in Judaism the presence of a universal and *contemporary anti-social* element whose historical evolution – eagerly nurtured by the Jews in its harmful aspects – has arrived at its present peak, a peak at which it will inevitably disintegrate.

The *emancipation of the Jews* is, in the last analysis, the emancipation of mankind from *Judaism*.

The Jew has already emancipated himself in a Jewish way.

The Jew, who is merely tolerated in Vienna, for example, determines the fate of the whole empire through the financial power he possesses. The Jew, who can be without rights in the smallest of the German states, decides the fate of Europe. While the corporations and the guilds exclude him or are not yet willing to look upon him with favour, the audacity of his industry mocks the obstinacy of medieval institutions.[33]

This is not an isolated fact. The Jew has emancipated himself in a Jewish way not only by acquiring financial power but also because through him and apart from him *money* has become a world power and the practical Jewish spirit has become the practical spirit of the Christian peoples. The Jews have emancipated themselves in so far as the Christians have become Jews.

For example, Captain Hamilton informs us[34] that the pious and politically free inhabitant of New England is a kind of Laocoön who does not make even the slightest effort to free himself from the snakes that are choking him. *Mammon* is his idol and he prays to him not only with his lips but with all the power of his body and his soul. For him the world is nothing but a Stock Exchange and he is convinced that his sole vocation here on earth is to get richer than his neighbours. He is possessed by the spirit of bargaining and the only way he can relax is by exchanging objects. When he travels it is as if he carried his shop and office on his

33. Bauer, *The Jewish Question*, p. 114.
34. In the work quoted above, p. 219.

back and spoke of nothing but interest and profit. If he takes his eyes off his own business for a moment, it is simply so that he can poke his nose into someone else's.

Indeed, the practical domination of Judaism over the Christian world is expressed in such an unambiguous and natural fashion in North America that the very *proclamation of the Gospel*, Christian teaching, has become a commercial object and the bankrupt businessman is just as likely to go into evangelizing as the successful evangelist into business.

'The man you see at the head of a respectable congregation started out as a businessman; his business failed so he became a minister; the other started out as a priest, but as soon as he had saved some money he left the pulpit for business. In many people's eyes the religious ministry is a veritable industrial career.'[35]

In Bauer's view it is 'a dishonest state of affairs when in theory the Jew is deprived of political rights while in practice he possesses enormous power and exercises a political influence in the larger sphere that is denied him as an individual'.[36]

The contradiction between the practical political power of the Jew and his political rights is the contradiction between politics and financial power in general. Ideally speaking the former is superior to the latter, but in actual fact it is in thrall to it.

Judaism has kept going *alongside* Christianity not simply as a religious critique of Christianity and an embodiment of doubts about the religious origins of Christianity but also because the practical Jewish spirit, Judaism, has managed to survive in Christian society and has even reached its highest level of development there.[37] The Jew, who is a particular member of civil society, is only the particular manifestation of the Judaism of civil society.

Judaism has managed to survive not despite history but through it.

Civil society ceaselessly begets the Jew from its own entrails.

What was the essential basis of the Jewish religion? Practical need, egoism.

The monotheism of the Jew is therefore in reality the polytheism of the many needs, a polytheism that makes even the

35. Beaumont, op. cit., pp. 185–6.
36. Bauer, *The Jewish Question*, p. 114.
37. The German word *Judentum* – 'Judaism' – could also be used to mean 'commerce'. Marx plays on this double meaning of the word.

lavatory an object of divine law. *Practical need, egoism,* is the principle of *civil society* and appears as such in all its purity as soon as civil society has fully brought forth the political state. The god of *practical need and self-interest* is *money.*

Money is the jealous god of Israel before whom no other god may stand. Money debases all the gods of mankind and turns them into commodities. Money is the universal and self-constituted *value* of all things. It has therefore deprived the entire world – both the world of man and of nature – of its specific value. Money is the estranged essence of man's work and existence; this alien essence dominates him and he worships it.

The god of the Jews has been secularized and become the god of the world. Exchange is the true god of the Jew. His god is nothing more than illusory exchange.

The view of nature which has grown up under the regime of private property and of money is an actual contempt for and practical degradation of nature which does exist in the Jewish religion but only in an imaginary form.

In this sense Thomas Münzer declares it intolerable that 'all creatures have been made into property, the fish in the water, the birds in the air, the plants on the earth – all living things must also become free'.[38]

What is present in an abstract form in the Jewish religion – contempt for theory, for art, for history, for man as an end in himself – is the *actual* and *conscious* standpoint, the virtue, of the man of money. The species-relation itself, the relation between man and woman, etc., becomes a commercial object! Woman is put on the market.

The *chimerical* nationality of the Jew is the nationality of the merchant, of the man of money in general.

The ungrounded and unfounded law of the Jew is only the religious caricature of ungrounded and unfounded morality and law in general, of the purely *formal* rites with which the world of self-interest surrounds itself.

Here too the supreme relation of man is the *legal* relation, the relation to laws which apply to him not because they are the laws of his own will and nature but because they *dominate* him and because breaches of them would be *avenged.*

38. From the pamphlet issued by Münzer in 1524 and entitled *Hoch verursachte Schutzrede und Antwort wider das geistlose, sanftlebende Fleisch zu Witterberg.*

Jewish Jesuitry, the same practical Jesuitry that Bauer finds in the Talmud, is the relationship of the world of self-interest to the laws that dominate it; the wily circumvention of those laws constitutes the principal skill of that world.

Indeed, the motion of that world within its laws is necessarily a continual supersession [*Aufhebung*] of the law.

Judaism could not develop further as a *religion*, could not develop further theoretically, because the world-view of practical need is by nature narrow-minded and rapidly exhausted.

The religion of practical need could not by its very nature find its completion in theory but only in *practice*, precisely because its truth is practice.

Judaism could not create a new world; it could only draw the new creations and conditions of the world into the province of its own activity, since practical need, whose understanding is only at the level of self-interest, is passive and incapable of extending itself in directions of its own choosing; instead, it *finds* itself extended in line with the development of social conditions themselves.

Judaism reaches its peak with the completion of civil society; but civil society first reaches its completion in the *Christian* world. Only under the rule of Christianity, which makes *all* national, natural, moral and theoretical relationships *external* to man, could civil society separate itself completely from political life, tear apart all the species-bonds of man, substitute egoism and selfish need for those bonds and dissolve the human world into a world of atomistic individuals confronting each other in enmity.

Christianity sprang from Judaism. It has now dissolved back into Judaism.

The Christian was from the very beginning the theorizing Jew. The Jew is therefore the practical Christian and the practical Christian has once again become a Jew.

Christianity overcame real Judaism only in appearance. It was too *refined*, too spiritual, to do away with the crudeness of practical need except by raising it into celestial space.

Christianity is the sublime thought of Judaism and Judaism is the vulgar application of Christianity. But this application could not become universal until Christianity as perfected religion had *theoretically* completed the self-estrangement of man from himself and from nature.

Only then could Judaism attain universal domination and turn alienated man and alienated nature into *alienable*, saleable objects subject to the slavery of egoistic need and to the market.

Selling is the practice of alienation [*Die Veräusserung ist die Praxis der Entäusserung*]. As long as man is restrained by religion he can objectify his essence only by making it into an *alien*, fantastic being. In the same way, when under the sway of egoistic need he can act practically and practically produce objects only by making his products and his activity subordinate to an alien substance and giving them the significance of an alien substance – money.

Translated into practice, the Christian egoism of eternal happiness inevitably becomes the material egoism of the Jew, celestial need becomes terrestrial need and subjectivism becomes self-interest. We can explain the tenacity of the Jew not from his religion but from the human foundation of his religion, from practical need and egoism.

Since the real essence of the Jew is universally realized and secularized in civil society, civil society could not convince the Jew of the *unreality* of his *religious* essence, which is nothing more than the ideal expression of practical need. Therefore not only in the Pentateuch and the Talmud but also in present-day society we find the essence of the modern Jew not in an abstract but in a supremely empirical form, not only as the narrowness of the Jew but as the Jewish narrowness of society.

As soon as society succeeds in abolishing the *empirical* essence of Judaism – the market and the conditions which give rise to it – the Jew will have become *impossible*, for his consciousness will no longer have an object, the subjective basis of Judaism – practical need – will have become humanized and the conflict between man's individual sensuous existence and his species-existence will have been superseded.

The *social* emancipation of the Jew is the *emancipation of society from Judaism*.

A Contribution to the Critique of Hegel's Philosophy of Right. Introduction

[This article was written between the end of 1843 and the beginning of 1844. It was published in the Deutsch–Französische Jahrbücher. *In it Marx is concerned with redefining the object of philosophy. Philosophy must criticize not religion (as Feuerbach and others would have it) but the real world, of which religion is merely the 'halo'. Not critical thought but the revolutionary transformation of society will emancipate mankind.*

Marx develops his reformulation of the relation between theory and practice when for the first time he identifies the proletariat as that force which is capable of realizing philosophy in practice and thereby abolishing it as a separate sphere. But the proletariat's liberation coincides with the liberation of all mankind. Unlike other classes, the proletariat claims no special *rights for itself because the nature of its deprivation is universal. It is in fact the* actually *universal class which Hegel imagined to have found in the bureaucracy.*

Germany, which compared to England and France is very backward, is only now seeing the maturation of a proletariat. Because of its backwardness, Germany has lived in thought *the history which more advanced nations have lived in* reality. *German history, broken off in reality, has continued to develop in philosophy.]*

For Germany, the *criticism of religion* has been essentially completed, and the criticism of religion is the prerequisite of all criticism.

The *profane* existence of error is compromised as soon as its *heavenly oratio pro aris et focis*[1] has been refuted. Man, who has found only the *reflection* of himself in the fantastic reality of heaven, where he sought a superman, will no longer feel disposed

1. Plea on behalf of hearth and home.

to find the mere *appearance* of himself, the non-man, where he seeks and must seek his true reality.

The foundation of irreligious criticism is: *Man makes religion, religion does not make man.* Religion is indeed the self-consciousness and self-esteem of man who has either not yet won through to himself or has already lost himself again. But *man* is no abstract being squatting outside the world. Man is *the world of man,* state, society. This state and this society produce religion, which is an *inverted consciousness of the world,* because they are an *inverted world.* Religion is the general theory of this world, its encyclopedic compendium, its logic in popular form, its spiritual *point d'honneur,* its enthusiasm, its moral sanction, its solemn complement and its universal basis of consolation and justification. It is the *fantastic realization* of the human essence since the human essence has not acquired any true reality. The struggle against religion is therefore indirectly the struggle against *that world* whose spiritual *aroma* is religion.

Religious suffering is at one and the same time the *expression* of real suffering and a protest against real suffering. Religion is the sigh of the oppressed creature, the heart of a heartless world and the soul of soulless conditions. It is the *opium* of the people.

The abolition of religion as the *illusory* happiness of the people is the demand for their *real* happiness. To call on them to give up their illusions about their condition is to *call on them to give up a condition that requires illusions.* The criticism of religion is therefore in *embryo* the *criticism of that vale of tears* of which religion is the *halo.*

Criticism has plucked the imaginary flowers on the chain not in order that man shall continue to bear that chain without fantasy or consolation but so that he shall throw off the chain and pluck the living flower. The criticism of religion disillusions man, so that he will think, act and fashion his reality like a man who has discarded his illusions and regained his senses, so that he will move around himself as his own true sun. Religion is only the illusory sun which revolves around man as long as he does not revolve around himself.

It is therefore the *task of history,* once the *other-world of truth* has vanished, to establish the *truth of this world.* It is the immediate *task of philosophy,* which is in the service of history, to unmask self-estrangement in its *unholy forms* once the *holy form* of human self-estrangement has been unmasked. Thus the criticism of heaven turns into the criticism of earth, the *criticism of religion* into the *criticism of law* and the *criticism of theology* into the *criticism of politics.*

The following exposition[2] – a contribution to this undertaking – concerns itself not directly with the original but with a copy, with the German *philosophy* of the state and of law. The only reason for this is that it is concerned with *Germany.*

If we were to begin with the German *status quo* itself, the result – even if we were to do it in the only appropriate way, i.e. negatively – would still be an *anachronism.* Even the negation of our present political situation is a dusty fact in the historical junk room of modern nations. If I negate powdered wigs, I am still left with unpowdered wigs. If I negate the situation in Germany in 1843, then according to the French calendar I have barely reached 1789, much less the vital centre of our present age.

Indeed, German history prides itself on having travelled a road which no other nation in the whole of history has ever travelled before, or ever will again. We have shared the restorations of modern nations without ever having shared their revolutions. We have been restored firstly because other nations dared to make revolutions and secondly because other nations suffered counter-revolutions: on the one hand, because our masters were afraid, and on the other, because they were not afraid. With our shepherds to the fore, we only once kept company with freedom, on the *day of its interment.*

One school of thought that legitimizes the infamy of today with the infamy of yesterday, a school that stigmatizes every cry of the serf against the knout as mere rebelliousness once the knout has aged a little and acquired a hereditary significance and a history, a school to which history shows nothing but its *a posteriori,* as did the God of Israel to his servant Moses,[3] the *historical school of law* – this school would have invented German history were it not itself an invention of that history. A Shylock, but a cringing Shylock, that swears by its bond, its historical bond, its Christian–Germanic bond, for every pound of flesh cut from the heart of the people.

2. This article was intended to be an introduction to a full-scale critical study of Hegel's *Philosophy of Right.* The *Critique of Hegel's Doctrine of the State* (pp. 57–198 above) is one part of this projected study.
3. 'And I will take away mine hand, and thou shalt see my back parts; but my face shall not be seen' (Exodus 33:23).

On the other hand, good-natured enthusiasts, German chauvinists by temperament and free-thinking liberals by reflection, seek the history of our freedom beyond our history, in the primeval Teutonic forests. But how does the history of our freedom differ from that of the wild boar, if it is only to be found in the forests? And besides, everyone knows that what is shouted into a forest is echoed back again. So peace to the primeval Teutonic forests!

But *war* on conditions in Germany! By all means! They are *below the level of history*, they are *beneath all criticism*, but they remain an object of criticism, in the same way as the criminal who is beneath the level of humanity remains an object for the *executioner*. In its struggle against them criticism is not a passion of the head but the head of passion. It is not a scalpel but a weapon. Its object is its *enemy*, which it aims not to refute but to *destroy*. For the spirit of these conditions is already refuted. In themselves they are not *worthy of thought*: rather, they are *existences* as despicable as they are despised. Criticism itself does not require any further understanding of this object, for it is already clear about it. Criticism is no longer an *end in itself*, but simply a *means*. The essential force that moves it is *indignation* and its essential task is *denunciation*.

It must set out to depict the stifling pressure which all the different spheres of society exercise on one another, the universal but apathetic ill-feeling and the narrowness of vision that both acknowledges and misconstrues itself – all this contained within the framework of a system of government which lives by conserving all this wretchedness and is itself nothing but *wretchedness in government*.

What a spectacle! A society infinitely divided into the most diverse races which confront one another with their petty antipathies, their bad consciences and their brutal mediocrity and which, precisely because of their ambivalent and suspicious attitude towards one another, are dealt with by their *masters* without distinction, although with different formalities, as if their *existence* had been granted to them on *licence*. And they are even forced to recognize and acknowledge the fact that they are *dominated, ruled* and *possessed* as a *privilege from heaven*! On the other hand there are the rulers themselves, whose greatness is in inverse proportion to their numbers!

The criticism which deals with these facts is involved in a

hand-to-hand fight, and in such fights it does not matter what the opponent's rank is, or whether he is noble or *interesting*: what matters is to *hit* him. The important thing is not to permit the German a single moment of self-deception or resignation. The actual burden must be made even more burdensome by creating an awareness of it. The humiliation must be increased by making it public. Each sphere of German society must be depicted as the *partie honteuse* of that society and these petrified conditions must be made to dance by having their own tune sung to them! The people must be put in *terror* of themselves in order to give them *courage*. In this way a pressing need of the German nation will be fulfilled, and the needs of nations are themselves the ultimate causes of their satisfaction.

And even for *modern* nations this struggle against the restricted nature of the German *status quo* is not without interest, for the German *status quo* is the *undisguised consummation of the ancien régime* and the *ancien régime* is the *hidden defect of the modern state*. The struggle against the German political present is the struggle against the past of modern nations, which continue to be harassed by reminiscences of this past. It is instructive for them to see the *ancien régime*, which in their countries has experienced its *tragedy*, play its *comic* role as a German phantom. Its history was *tragic* as long as it was the pre-existing power in the world and freedom a personal whim – in a word, as long as it believed, and had to believe, in its own privileges. As long as the *ancien régime*, as an established world order, was struggling against a world that was only just emerging, there was a world-historical error on its side but not a personal one. Its downfall was therefore tragic.

The present German regime, on the other hand – an anachronism, a flagrant contradiction of universally accepted axioms, the futility of the *ancien régime* displayed for all the world to see – only imagines that it still believes in itself and asks the world to share in its fantasy. If it believed in its own *nature*, would it try to hide that nature under the *appearance* of an alien nature and seek its salvation in hypocrisy and sophism? The modern *ancien régime* is merely the *clown* of a world order whose *real heroes* are dead. History is thorough and passes through many stages while bearing an ancient form to its grave. The last stage of a world-historical form is its *comedy*. The Greek gods, who already died once of their wounds in Aeschylus's tragedy *Prometheus Bound*, were forced to die a second death – this time a comic one – in Lucian's dialogues. Why does history take this course? So that mankind may part *happily* from its past. We lay claim to this *happy* historical destiny for the political powers of Germany.

But as soon as *modern* socio-political reality itself is subjected to criticism, i.e. as soon as criticism begins to deal with truly human problems, it finds itself outside the German *status quo*, or it would grasp its object at a level *below* its object. For example: the relationship of industry and the world of wealth in general to the political world is one of the main problems of the modern age. In which form does this problem begin to preoccupy the Germans? In the form of *protective tariffs*, of a *system of prohibitions* of *national economy*.[4] German chauvinism has made the passage from men to matter, and one fine morning our cotton barons and iron heroes woke to find themselves transformed into patriots. In Germany, therefore, we are beginning to recognize the sovereignty of monopoly within our borders by granting it *sovereignty without them*. In Germany, therefore, we are about to begin at the point where France and England are about to conclude. The old and rotten order against which these countries are theoretically up in arms, and which they continue to bear only as one would bear chains, is greeted in Germany as the dawn of a beautiful future – a future which scarcely dares to make the transition from *cunning*[5] theory to pitiless practice. In France and England the alternatives are posed: *political economy* or the *rule of society over wealth*, whereas in Germany they are posed: *national economy* or the *rule of private property over nationality*. In France and England, therefore, it is a question of abolishing monopoly, which has progressed to its final consequences; in Germany it is a question of progressing to the final consequences of monopoly. There it is a question of the solution; here it is only a question of the collision. This is a good example of the *German* form of modern problems, an example of how our history, like some raw recruit, has up to now been restricted to repeating hackneyed routines that belong to the past of other nations.

So if Germany's development as a *whole* were not at a more advanced stage than Germany's *political* development, a German

4. *Nationalökonomie*. This word is usually rendered as 'political economy'; here, exceptionally, the context requires 'national economy'.

5. In German, *listig* – a pun on the name of the economist Friedrich List (1789–1846), a supporter of protectionism.

would not be able to participate in contemporary problems any more than can a *Russian*. But if the individual is not confined within the bounds of the nation, still less is the nation as a whole liberated through the liberation of an individual. The Scythians did not advance one step towards Greek culture because the Greeks numbered a Scythian[6] among their philosophers.

Fortunately we Germans are not Scythians.

Just as ancient peoples lived their previous history in the imagination, in *mythology*, so we Germans have lived our future history in thought, in *philosophy*. We are the *philosophical* contemporaries of the present without being its *historical* contemporaries. German philosophy is the *ideal prolongation* of German history. Therefore when we criticize the *œuvres posthumes* of our ideal history, i.e. philosophy, instead of the *œuvres incomplètes* of our real history, our criticism stands at the centre of those problems of which the present age says: *That is the question*. What for advanced nations is a *practical* quarrel with modern political conditions is for Germany, where such conditions do not yet exist, a *critical* quarrel with their reflection in philosophy.

The *German philosophy of law and of the state* is the only *German history* which stands on an equal footing with the *official* modern present. The German nation must therefore link its dream history to its present conditions and subject not only these conditions but also their abstract continuation to criticism. Its future cannot be *restricted* either to the direct negation of its real political and juridical conditions or to the direct realization of its ideal political and juridical conditions, for the direct negation of its real conditions is already present in its ideal conditions and it has almost *outlived* the direct realization of its ideal conditions by watching developments in neighbouring nations. The *practical* political party in Germany is therefore right to demand the *negation of philosophy*. Where it goes wrong is in limiting itself to a demand which it does not and cannot achieve. It believes that it can carry out this negation by turning its back on philosophy and mumbling a few irritable and banal phrases over its shoulder at it. Its approach is so restricted that it does not even look upon philosophy as a part of *German* reality, or it regards it as *beneath* German practice and its associated theories. You demand that we make the *real seeds of life* our point of departure, but you forget that the real seed of life of the German people has up to

6. Anarcharsis.

now only flourished inside its cranium. In a word: *You cannot transcend [aufheben] philosophy without realizing [verwirklichen] it.*

The same mistake, but with the factors reversed, was committed by the *theoretical* political party, which has its origins in philosophy.

This party saw in the present struggle *only* the *critical struggle of philosophy with the German world* and failed to realize that *previous philosophy* itself belongs to this world and is its *complement*, even though an ideal complement. It was critical towards its counterpart, but not towards itself, for it took the *presuppositions* of philosophy as its point of departure and either took for granted the conclusions of that philosophy or passed off demands and conclusions drawn from other quarters as direct philosophical demands and conclusions. But this is to ignore the fact that such demands and conclusions – assuming that they are legitimate – can be achieved only through the *negation of previous philosophy*, i.e. of philosophy as philosophy. We shall save for later a more detailed account of this party. Its basic defect can be summed up as follows: *It believed that it could realize philosophy without transcending it.*

The criticism of the *German philosophy of the state and of law*, which received its most consistent, thorough and complete formulation from *Hegel*, is both these things: it is at once a critical analysis of the modern state and of the reality connected with it and a decisive negation of all previous *forms* of *political and juridical consciousness in Germany*, whose most refined and universal expression, elevated to the level of a *science*, is precisely the *speculative philosophy of law*. Only Germany could develop the speculative philosophy of law, this abstract and high-flown *thought* of the modern state, the reality of which remains part of another world (even if this other world is only the other side of the Rhine). Conversely, the *German* conception of the modern state, which abstracts from *real man*, was only possible because and in so far as the modern state itself abstracts from *real man* or satisfies the *whole* man in a purely imaginary way. The Germans have *thought* in politics what other nations have *done*. Germany has been their *theoretical conscience*. The abstraction and arrogance of Germany's thought always kept pace with the one-sided and stunted character of their reality. So if the *status quo* of the *German political system* is an expression of the *consummation of the ancien régime*, the completion of the thorn in the flesh of the modern state, then the *status quo* of *German political thought* is an expression of the *imperfection of the modern state*, the damaged condition of the flesh itself.

As the determined opponent of the previous form of *German* political consciousness, the criticism of the speculative philosophy of law finds its progression not within itself but in *tasks* which can only be solved in one way – through *practice* [*Praxis*].

We must then ask ourselves: can Germany attain a practice *à la hauteur des principes*, that is to say, a revolution that raises it not only to the *official level* of modern nations but to the *human level* that will be their immediate future?

Clearly the weapon of criticism cannot replace the criticism of weapons, and material force must be overthrown by material force. But theory also becomes a material force once it has gripped the masses. Theory is capable of gripping the masses when it demonstrates *ad hominem*, and it demonstrates *ad hominem* as soon as it becomes radical. To be radical is to grasp things by the root. But for man the root is man himself. Clear proof of the radicalism of German theory and its practical energy is the fact that it takes as its point of departure a decisive and *positive* transcendence of religion. The criticism of religion ends with the doctrine that *for man the supreme being is man*, and thus with the *categorical imperative to overthrow all conditions* in which man is a debased, enslaved, neglected and contemptible being – conditions that are best described in the exclamation of a Frenchman on the occasion of a proposed tax on dogs: Poor dogs! They want to treat you like human beings!

For Germany, theoretical emancipation has a specific practical significance even from a historical point of view. For Germany's *revolutionary* past, in the form of the *Reformation*, is also theoretical. Just as it was then the *monk*, so it is now the *philosopher* in whose brain the revolution begins.

Luther certainly conquered servitude based on *devotion*, but only by replacing it with servitude based on *conviction*. He destroyed faith in authority, but only by restoring the authority of faith. He transformed the priests into laymen, but only by transforming the laymen into priests. He freed mankind from external religiosity, but only by making religiosity the inner man. He freed the body from its chains, but only by putting the heart in chains.

But even if Protestantism was not the true solution, it did pose the problem correctly. It was now no longer a question of the struggle of the layman with the *priest outside himself*, but rather of his struggle with his *own inner priest*, with his *priestly nature*. And if the Protestant transformation of the German laymen into priests emancipated the lay priests – the *princes* together with their clergy, the privileged and the philistines – the philosophical transformation of the priestly Germans into men will emancipate the *people*. But just as emancipation did not stop with the princes, so will secularization of property not stop with the *dispossession of the churches*, which was set going above all by hypocritical Prussia. At that time the Peasants' War, the most radical episode in German history, suffered defeat because of theology. Today, when theology itself has failed, the most unfree episode in German history, our *status quo*, will founder on philosophy. On the eve of the Reformation official Germany was Rome's most unquestioning vassal. On the eve of its revolution Germany is the unquestioning vassal of lesser powers than Rome – of Prussia and Austria, of clod-hopping squires and philistines.

But a major difficulty appears to stand in the way of a *radical* German revolution.

The point is that revolutions need a *passive* element, a *material* basis. Theory is realized in a people only in so far as it is a realization of the people's needs. But will the enormous gap that exists between the demands of German thought and the responses of German reality now correspond to the same gap both between civil society and the state and civil society and itself? Will the theoretical needs be directly practical needs? It is not enough that thought should strive to realize itself; reality must itself strive towards thought.

But Germany did not pass through the intermediate stages of political emancipation at the same time as modern nations. Even the stages that it has left behind in theory it has not yet reached in practice. How is Germany, in one *salto mortale*, to override not only its own limitations but also those of the modern nations, to override limitations which in point of fact it ought to experience and strive for as liberation from its real limitations? A radical revolution can only be the revolution of radical needs, but the preconditions and seedbeds for such needs appear to be lacking.

Yet, even if Germany has only kept company with the development of the modern nations through the abstract activity of thought, without taking an active part in the real struggles of this development, it has nevertheless shared in the *sufferings* of this development without sharing in its pleasures and its partial satisfaction. Abstract activity on the one hand corresponds to abstract suffering on the other. Germany will therefore one day find itself at the level of European decadence before it has ever reached the level of European emancipation. It will be like a fetish-worshipper suffering from the diseases of Christianity.

If we examine the *German governments*, we find that as a result of the circumstances of the time, the situation in Germany, the standpoint of German education and finally their own happy instincts they are driven to combine the *civilized defects* of the *modern political world*, whose advantages we lack, with the *barbaric defects* of the *ancien régime*, of which we have our full measure. In this way Germany must participate more and more, if not in the reason then at least in the unreason even of those state forms which have progressed beyond its own *status quo*. For example, is there any country in the world which shares as naïvely as so-called constitutional Germany all the illusions of the constitutional state without sharing any of the realities? Or was it just an accident that the idea of combining the torments of censorship with the torments of the French September laws,[7] which presuppose freedom of the press, was the invention of a German government? Just as the *gods* of all nations could be found in the Roman Pantheon, so the *sins* of all state forms will be found in the Holy Roman German Empire. That this eclecticism will take on unheard-of proportions is assured in particular by the *politico-aesthetic gourmandise* of a German king,[8] who proposes to play all the roles of royalty – feudal and bureaucratic, absolute and constitutional, autocratic and democratic – if not in the person of the people then at least in his *own* person, and if not for the people, then at least for *himself. Germany, as a world of its own embodying all the deficiencies of the present political age*, will not be able to overcome the specifically German limitations without overcoming the universal limitation of the present political age.

It is not *radical* revolution or *universal human* emancipation which is a utopian dream for Germany; it is the partial, *merely* political revolution, the revolution which leaves the pillars of the building standing. What is the basis of a partial and merely

7. The September laws of 1835 limited the activity of juries and the press. Harsh penalties were introduced for those people who agitated against private property and the existing state order.
8. Frederick William IV.

political revolution? Its basis is the fact that one *part of civil society* emancipates itself and attains *universal* domination, that one particular class undertakes from its *particular situation* the universal emancipation of society. This class liberates the whole of society, but only on condition that the whole of society finds itself in the same situation as this class, e.g. possesses or can easily acquire money and education.

No class of civil society can play this role without awakening a moment of enthusiasm in itself and in the masses; a moment in which this class fraternizes and fuses with society in general, becomes identified with it and is experienced and acknowledged as its *universal representative*; a moment in which its claims and rights are truly the rights and claims of society itself and in which it is in reality the heart and head of society. Only in the name of the universal rights of society can a particular class lay claim to universal domination. Revolutionary energy and spiritual self-confidence are not enough to storm this position of liberator and to ensure thereby the political exploitation of all the other spheres of society in the interests of one's own sphere. If the *revolution of a people* and the *emancipation of a particular class* [*Klasse*] of civil society are to coincide, if *one* class is to stand for the whole of society, then all the deficiences of society must be concentrated in another class [*Stand*], one particular class must be the class which gives universal offence, the embodiment of a general limitation; one particular sphere of society must appear as the *notorious crime* of the whole of society, so that the liberation of this sphere appears as universal self-liberation. If one class [*Stand*] is to be the class of liberation *par excellence*, then another class must be the class of overt oppression. The negative general significance of the French nobility and the French clergy determined the positive general significance of the class which stood nearest to and opposed to them – the *bourgeoisie*.

But in Germany every particular class lacks not only the consistency, acuteness, courage and ruthlessness which would stamp it as the negative representative of society; equally, all classes lack that breadth of spirit which identifies itself, if only for a moment, with the spirit of the people, that genius which can raise material force to the level of political power, that revolutionary boldness which flings into the face of its adversary the defiant words: *I am nothing and I should be everything*. The main feature of German morality and honour, not only in individuals but in classes, is that *modest egoism* which asserts its narrowness and allows that narrowness to be used against it. The relationship of the different spheres of German society is therefore epic rather than dramatic. Each begins to experience itself and to set up camp alongside the others with its own particular claims, not as soon as it is oppressed but as soon as circumstances, without any contribution from the sphere concerned, create an inferior social stratum which it in its turn can oppress. Even the *moral self-confidence of the German middle class* is based simply on an awareness of being the general representative of the philistine mediocrity of all the other classes. It is therefore not only the German kings who mount the throne *mal-à-propos*, but every sphere of civil society which experiences defeat before it celebrates victory, develops its own limitations before it overcomes the limitations confronting it, and asserts its narrow-mindedness before it has had a chance to assert its generosity. As a result, even the opportunity of playing a great role has always passed by before it was ever really available and every class, as soon as it takes up the struggle against the class above it, is involved in a struggle with the class beneath it. Thus princes struggle against kings, bureaucrats against aristocrats, and the bourgeoisie against all of these, while the proletariat is already beginning to struggle against the bourgeoisie. The middle class scarcely dares to conceive of the idea of emancipation from its own point of view, and already the development of social conditions and the progress of political theory have demonstrated this point of view to be antiquated or at least problematical.

In France it is enough to be something for one to want to be everything. In Germany no one may be anything unless he renounces everything. In France partial emancipation is the basis of universal emancipation. In Germany universal emancipation is the *conditio sine qua non* of any partial emancipation. In France it is the reality, in Germany the impossibility, of emancipation in stages that must give birth to complete freedom. In France each class of the people is a *political idealist* and experiences itself first and foremost not as a particular class but as the representative of social needs in general. The role of *emancipator* therefore passes in a dramatic movement from one class of the French people to the next, until it finally reaches that class which no longer realizes social freedom by assuming certain conditions external to man and yet created by human society, but rather by organizing all the conditions of human existence on the basis of social freedom. In Germany, however, where practical life is as devoid of intellect as intellectual life is of practical activity, no class of civil society has the need and the capacity for universal emancipation unless under the compulsion of its *immediate* situation, of *material* necessity and of its *chains themselves.*

So where is the *positive* possibility of German emancipation?

This is our answer. In the formation of a class with *radical chains,* a class of civil society which is not a class of civil society, a class [*Stand*] which is the dissolution of all classes, a sphere which has a universal character because of its universal suffering and which lays claim to no *particular right* because the wrong it suffers is not a *particular wrong* but *wrong in general*; a sphere of society which can no longer lay claim to a *historical* title, but merely to a *human* one, which does not stand in one-sided opposition to the consequences but in all-sided opposition to the premises of the German political system; and finally a sphere which cannot emancipate itself without emancipating itself from – and thereby emancipating – all the other spheres of society, which is, in a word, the *total loss* of humanity and which can therefore redeem itself only through the *total redemption of humanity.* This dissolution of society as a particular class is the *proletariat.*

The proletariat is only beginning to appear in Germany as a result of the emergent *industrial* movement. For the proletariat is not formed by *natural* poverty but by *artificially produced* poverty; it is formed not from the mass of people mechanically oppressed by the weight of society but from the mass of people issuing from society's *acute disintegration* and in particular from the dissolution of the middle class. (Clearly, however, the ranks of the proletariat are also gradually swelled by natural poverty and Christian–Germanic serfdom.)

When the proletariat proclaims the *dissolution of the existing world order,* it is only declaring the secret of its own existence, for it *is* the *actual* dissolution of that order. When the proletariat demands the *negation of private property,* it is only elevating to a *principle for society* what society has already made a principle *for the proletariat,* what is embodied in the proletariat, without its consent, as the negative result of society. The proletarian then finds that he has the same right, in relation to the world which is coming into being, as the *German King* in relation to the world as it is at present when he calls the people *his* people just as he calls his horse *his* horse. By calling the people his private property, the king is merely declaring that the owner of private property is king.

Just as philosophy finds its *material* weapons in the proletariat, so the proletariat finds its *intellectual* weapons in philosophy; and once the lightning of thought has struck deeply into this virgin soil of the people, emancipation will transform the *Germans* into *men*.

Let us sum up the result:

The only liberation of Germany which is *practically* possible is liberation from the point of view of *that* theory which declares man to be the supreme being for man. Germany can emancipate itself from the *Middle Ages* only if it emancipates itself at the same time from the *partial* victories over the Middle Ages. In Germany *no* form of bondage can be broken without breaking *all* forms of bondage. Germany, which is renowned for its *thoroughness*, cannot make a revolution unless it is a *thorough* one. The *emancipation of the German* is the *emancipation of man*. The *head* of this emancipation is *philosophy*, its *heart* the *proletariat*. Philosophy cannot realize itself without the transcendence [*Aufhebung*] of the proletariat, and the proletariat cannot transcend itself without the realization [*Verwirklichung*] of philosophy.

When all the inner conditions are met, the *day of the German resurrection* will be heralded by the *crowing of the Gallic cock*.

Excerpts from James Mill's *Elements of Political Economy*

[*Marx wrote the* Excerpts *during the spring and summer of 1844. In them he writes that money, wage-labour, credit and banking are all forms of human alienation. They transform man from a real, living individual into an abstract caricature of his true self. The system of exchange is social intercourse not between men but between men as things of value, that is, an alienated form of social intercourse. Finally, Marx expounds his positive ideas on labour as the free expression of human nature, based on love and mutual affirmation.*

*

Marx's manuscript begins with eighty-four quotations of varying length from James Mill's book. Following the procedure of the editors of the Werke *from which this translation was made, these quotations have been omitted. It may be helpful to point out, however, that the two quotations immediately preceding the text deal with the determination of the value of money by the value of metal and of the value of metal by the costs of production. As in the* Werke, *the quotations before the section on exchange on the basis of private property have been retained. Marx's quotations were partly a summary, partly a translation from the French version of Mill's book. The original text as found in the edition of 1826 has been restored. The Roman numerals refer to the pagination of the manuscript. It will be observed that pp.* XXV *and* XXXIII *occur twice.*]

[XXV] Both on the question of the relations of money to the value of metal and in his demonstration that the cost of production is the sole factor in the determination of value Mill succumbs to the error, made by the entire Ricardo school, of defining an *abstract law* without mentioning the fluctuations or the continual suspension through which it comes into being. If e.g. it is an *invariable* law that in the last analysis – or rather in the sporadic (accidental)[1] coincidence of supply and demand – the cost of production determines price (value),[2] then it is no less an *invariable law* that these relations do not obtain, i.e. that value and the cost of production do not stand in any necessary relation. Indeed, supply and demand only ever coincide momentarily thanks to a previous fluctuation in supply and demand, to the disparity between the cost of production and the exchange value. And in like fashion, the momentary coincidence is succeeded by the same fluctuations and the same disparity. This is the *real* movement, then, and the above-mentioned law is no more than an abstract, contingent and one-sided moment in it. Yet recent economists dismiss it as accident, as inessential. Why? Because if the economists were to attempt to fix this movement in the sharp and precise terms to which they reduce the whole of economics this would produce the following basic formula: laws in economics are determined by their opposite, lawlessness. The true law of economics is *chance*, and we learned people arbitrarily seize on a few moments and establish them as laws.

Mill aptly sums up the whole essence of the matter in a single concept when he describes *money* as the *medium* of exchange. The nature of money is not, in the first instance, that property is externalized within it, but that the *mediating function* or movement, human, social activity, by means of which the products of man mutually complement each other, is *estranged* and becomes the property of a *material thing* external to man, viz. money. If a man himself alienates this mediating function he remains active only as a lost, dehumanized creature. The *relation* between things, human dealings with them, become the operations of a being beyond and above man. Through this *alien mediator* man gazes at his will, his activity, his relation to others as at a power independent of them and of himself – instead of man himself being the mediator for man. His slavery thus reaches a climax. It is obvious that this *mediator* must become a *veritable God* since the mediator is the *real* power over that with which he mediates me. His cult becomes an end in itself. Separated from this mediator, objects lose their worth. Thus they have value only in so far as they *represent* him,

---

1. In the manuscript 'accidental' has been written above 'sporadic'.
2. In the manuscript 'value' has been written above 'price'.

whereas it appeared at first that he had value only to the extent to which *he* represented *them*. This reversal of the original relationship is necessary. Hence this *mediator* is the lost, estranged *essence* of private property, private property *alienated* and external to itself; it is the *alienated mediation* of human production with human production, the *alienated* species-activity of man. All the qualities proper to the generation of this activity are transferred to the mediator. Thus man separated from this mediator becomes poorer as man in proportion as the mediator becomes *richer*.

Christ originally represents (1) man before God, (2) God for man and (3) man for man.

In the same way *money* originally represents (1) private property for private property; (2) society for private property; (3) private property for society.

But Christ is God *alienated* and *man* alienated. God continues to have value only in so far as he represents Christ, man continues to have value only in so far as he represents Christ. Likewise with money.

Why must private property finish up in money? Because as a social animal man must finish up in exchange [xxv] and exchange – given the premise of private property – must finish up in *value*. For the mediating movement of man engaged in exchange is not a social, human movement, it is no *human relationship*: it is the *abstract relation* of private property to private property, and this abstract relation is the *value* which acquires a real existence as value only in the form of *money*. Since in the process of exchange men do not relate to each other as men, *things* lose the meaning of personal, human property. The social relationship of private property to private property is already one in which private property is estranged from itself. Hence, money, the existence-for-itself of this relationship, represents the alienation of private property, an abstraction from its *specific* personal nature.

For all its ingenuity, then, the hostility of modern economics to the money system, *système monétaire*, cannot lead to a decisive victory. For the primitive economic superstitions of people and governments cling to tangible, palpable and visible bags of money and hold that the sole reality of wealth lies in the absolute value of the precious metals and in the possession of them. Of course, the enlightened, worldly-wise economist comes along and proves to them that money is a commodity like any other and its value, like that of any other commodity, depends on the relations between the costs of production and supply and demand (competition),[3] between the costs and the quantity of competition of other commodities. However, such an economist will be confounded by the observation that the *real* value of things is their exchange value and that in the last analysis this resides in money, which resides in its turn in the precious metals and that consequently money is the *true* value of things and the most desirable thing of all. The economist's theories in fact amount to the same thing except that his powers of abstraction enable him to perceive the existence of money behind all the commodity forms and destroy his faith in the exclusive value of its official metal existence. The existence of money in metal is only the official, visible expression of the money-soul which has percolated all the productions and movements of civil society.

The opposition of the modern economists to the money system does not go beyond the fact that they view *money* in its abstract and general form. They have seen through the *sensuous* superstition which believes that this essence exists exclusively in precious metals. They replace this crude superstition with a sophisticated one. But since both have their roots in the same idea the enlightened form of the superstition cannot finally do away with its crude sensuous counterpart, because it does not attack its essence but only a specific form of that essence. – The more abstract money is, the less natural its relationship to other commodities, the more it appears to be the product and yet also not the product of man, the less *organic* its mode of existence and the more it appears as the artifact of man, or, in economic terms, the greater the *inverse* ratio of its *value as money* to the exchange value or money value of the material in which it exists, the closer to the essence of money is the *personal* existence of money as money – and not only as the inner, implicit, concealed conversational relationships or *relationship of rank* between commodities. For this reason, *paper money* and the numerous *paper representatives of money* (such as bills of exchange, authorizations, I.O.U.s, etc.) are the *more perfect* forms of *money as money* and a necessary stage in the progress of the money system. In the *credit system*, of which *banking* is the most complete expression, the illusion is created that the might of the alien, material power has been broken, the state of self-estrangement abolished and man rein-

3. In the manuscript 'competition' has been written above 'demand'.

stated in his human relationship to man. Led astray by this *illusion,* the *Saint Simonians* regarded the development of money, bills of exchange, paper money, paper representatives of money, *credit, banking,* as a progressive abolition of the separation of man from things, of capital from labour, of private property from money and money from man, of the separation of man from man. Their ideal was, therefore, the organized *banking system.* But this abolition of estrangement [xxvi], this *return* of man to himself and thus to other men, is only an *illusion.* It is a *self-estrangement,* dehumanization, all the more *infamous* and *extreme* because its element is no longer a commodity, metal or paper, but the *moral* existence, the *social* existence, the very heart of man, and because under the appearance of mutual *trust* between men it is really the greatest *distrust* and a total estrangement. What constitutes the essence of credit? We disregard here the *content* of credit which is once again money. We disregard then the content of this trust according to which a man accords *recognition* to another man by advancing money to him and – at best, i.e. when he does not call in the securities, that is to say, if he is no usurer – expresses his confidence that his fellow human being is a 'good' man and not a scoundrel. By a 'good' man the creditor, like Shylock, means a 'sufficient' man. – Credit is conceivable in two situations and on two conditions. The two situations are: (1) a rich man extends credit to a poor man whom he regards as industrious and orderly. This kind of credit belongs to the romantic, sentimental side of economics, to its aberrations, excesses, *exceptions,* not to the rule. But even assuming that it is exceptional, even granting this romantic possibility it remains true that the poor man's life, his talent and his labours serve the rich man as a *guarantee* that the money he has lent will be returned. This means, then, that the totality of the poor man's social virtues, the content of his life's activity, his very existence, represent for the rich man the repayment of his capital together with the usual interest. For the creditor the death of the poor man is the very worst thing that can happen. It means the death of his capital together with the interest. We should reflect on the immorality implicit in the *evaluation* of a man in terms of *money,* such as we find in the credit system. It is self-evident that over and above these moral guarantees the creditor also has the guarantee provided by the force of law and varying degrees of other *real* guarantees at his disposal. If (2) the borrower is himself not without means, then *credit* merely facilitates ex-

change, i.e. it is money raised to a completely *ideal* form. Credit is
the *economic* judgement on the *morality* of a man. In the credit
system *man* replaces metal or paper as the mediator of exchange.
However, he does this not as a man but as the *incarnation of
capital and interest*. Thus although it is true that the medium of
exchange has migrated from its material form and returned to man
it has done so only because man has been exiled from himself and
transformed into material form. Money has not been transcended
in man within the credit system, but man is himself transformed
into *money*, or, in other words, money is *incarnate* in him. Human
individuality, human *morality*, have become both articles of commerce and the *material* which money inhabits. The substance, the
body clothing the *spirit of money* is not money, paper, but instead
it is my personal existence, my flesh and blood, my social worth
and status. Credit no longer actualizes money-values in actual
money but in human flesh and human hearts. Thus all the advances and illogicalities within a false system turn out to be the
greatest imaginable regression and at the same time they can be
seen as perfidy taken to its logical conclusion. – Within the credit
system credit, estranged from men, functions with all the appearance of the greatest possible recognition of man's worth by
economics. It works in the following ways: (1) The opposition
between capitalist and worker, large and small capitalist, becomes
even greater since credit is given only to him that hath and only
the rich man can take advantage of it as a new opportunity for
accumulation. Moreover, since the *entire* existence of the poor
man depends on the chance whim and opinion of the rich his life
hangs entirely on this chance. (2) Mutual dissimulation, hypocrisy and cant reach a climax since the man in need of credit is not
only defined simply by his poverty but also has to put up with the
demoralizing judgement that he does not inspire confidence, that
he is unworthy of recognition, that he is, in short, a social pariah
and a bad man. So that in addition to his actual deprivation he has
to endure this ignominy and the humiliation of having to *ask* the
rich man for credit. [XXVII] (3) This wholly *ideal* existence of
money means then that the *counterfeiting* of man must be carried
out on man himself rather than on any other material, i.e. he
must make counterfeit coin of himself, obtain credit by lies and
underhand means, etc. Thus the credit relationship – both from
the point of view of the man who needs credit and of him who
gives it – becomes an object of commerce, an object of mutual

deception and exploitation. This brilliantly illustrates the fact that the basis of trust in economics is mistrust: the mistrustful reflection about whether to extend credit or not; the spying-out of the secrets in the private life of the borrower; the revelation of temporary difficulties so as to embarrass a competitor by undermining his credit, etc. The whole system of bankruptcy, fictitious enterprises, etc. . . . In *state credit systems* the state is in the same position as the individual as described above . . . The games played with state loans show to what extent it has become a toy in the hands of businessmen, etc.

(4) The *credit system* achieves its consummation in *banking*. The creation of the bankers, the state-dominance of the bank, the concentration of wealth in these hands, this economic Areopagus of the nation, is the worthy climax of the money system. When, in the credit system, the granting of *moral recognition to a man*, like the placing of *confidence in the state*, takes the form of *credit*, then the mystery implicit in the lie of moral recognition, the sheer depravity of this morality, no less than the hypocrisy and egoism contained in that confidence in the state, emerges clearly and shows its true colours.

The process of *exchange* both of human activities in the course of production and of *human products* is equal to the species-activity and the species-spirit whose real, conscious and authentic existence consists in *social* activity and *social* enjoyment. Since the essence of *man* is the *true community* of man, men, by activating their own essence, produce, create this human community, this social being which is no abstract, universal power standing over against the solitary individual, but is the essence of every individual, his own activity, his own life, his own spirit, his own wealth. Therefore, this *true community* does not come into being as the product of reflection but it arises out of the *need* and the *egoism* of individuals, i.e. it arises directly from their own activity. The existence or non-existence of this community does not depend on man; but as long as man does not recognize himself as man, and hence give the world a human organization, this *community* appears in the guise of estrangement. For its *subject*, man, is a being estranged from himself. Men, not as abstractions, but as real, living, particular individuals *are* this community. *As* they are, so it is too. To say therefore that *man* is estranged from himself is identical with the statement that the *society* of this estranged man is the caricature of a *true community*, of his true species-existence, that therefore his activity is a torment to him, his own creation confronts him as an alien power, his wealth appears as poverty, the essential bond joining him to other men appears inessential, in fact separation from other men appears to be his true existence, his life appears as the sacrifice of his life, the realization of his essence appears as the de-realization of his life, his production is the production of nothing, his power over objects appears as the power of objects over him; in short, he, the lord of his creation, appears as the servant of that creation.

Now economics conceives of the *community of man*, or the self-activating essence of man, man's attainment of a species-life, a truly human existence through the mutuality of men, in terms of *exchange* and *trade*. *Society*, according to Destutt de Tracy, is a *series of reciprocal exchanges*.[4] It is just this process of reciprocal integration. *Society*, according to Adam Smith, is a *commercial society*. Each of its members is a *merchant*.[5]

We see then how economics *establishes* the *estranged* form of social commerce as the *essential* and *fundamental* form appropriate to the vocation of man.

[XXVIII] Economics – like the process of reality itself – begins with the *relations between men* as relations between *private property owners*. If we proceed from the premise that man is a private property owner, i.e. an exclusive owner whose exclusive ownership permits him both to preserve his personality and to distinguish himself from other men, as well as relate to them, if we assume that private property is man's personal, *distinguishing* and hence essential existence – then it follows that the loss or sacrifice of that private property signifies the *alienation of the man* as much as of the *property* itself. We are concerned here only with the latter determination. If I cede my private property to another it ceases to be mine; it becomes independent of me, something outside my domain, something *external* [*äusserlich*] to me. I thus externalize, alienate [*entäussern*] my private property. I define it as *alienated* private property so far as I myself am concerned. But I only define it as something *alienated* in general; I renounce only

4. See Destutt de Tracy, *Éléments d'idéologie. IVe et V^e parties. Traité de la volonté et de ses effets*, Paris, 1826, p. 68; '... society is purely and solely a series of reciprocal exchanges'.

5. See Adam Smith, *The Wealth of Nations*, Book 1, Ch. 4: 'Every man thus lives by exchanging, or becomes, in some measure, a merchant, and the society itself grows to what is properly a commercial society.'

my *personal* connection with it, I return it to the *elemental* powers of nature when I alienate it only from myself. It becomes estranged *private property* only when it ceases to be *my* private property, without at the same time ceasing to be *private property*, i.e. when it enters into the same relationship with *another* which it formerly had with *me*, in a word, when it becomes *someone else's private property*. Setting aside cases where *force* is used, how do I ever come to alienate *my* private property to another? Economics provides the correct answer: from *necessity*, from *need*. The other man is also the owner of private property, but of *another* thing which I lack but which I neither can nor will dispense with, which I *need* to complete my own existence and to realize my own essence.

The bond which unites the two owners is the *specific nature of the object* which constitutes their private property. The longing for these two objects, i.e. the need for them, shows each owner, makes him conscious of the fact, that he stands in another *essential* relation to the objects than that of private property, that he is not the particular being as he imagines, but a *total* being and as a *total* being his needs stand in an *inner* relation to the products of the labour of others – for the felt need for a thing is the most obvious, irrefutable proof that that thing is part of *my* essence, that its being is for me and that its *property* is the property, the particular quality peculiar to my essence. Thus both owners are impelled to give up their private property. But in so doing they yet confirm private property: they give up private property within the context of private property. Thus each alienates a portion of his private property for the benefit of the other.

Hence the social nexus or social relationship between the two owners is that of *mutual alienation*, the relationship of *alienation* transposed to both sides, or alienation is the relationship of the two owners, whereas in simple private property *alienation* only takes place in relation to oneself, unilaterally.

Thus *exchange* or *barter* is the social species-activity, the community, social commerce and integration of man within *private* property, and for that reason it is the external, *alienated* species-activity. It appears as *barter* just because of this. By the same token it is the very antithesis of a *social* relationship.

Through the mutual alienation or estrangement of private property, *private property* itself comes into the category of *alienated* private property. For (1) it has ceased to be the produce of the labour and the exclusive, distinguishing personality of its owner, for the latter has alienated it, it has parted from its owner whose product it was and has acquired a personal significance for the new owner who has *not* produced it. It has lost its personal significance for its [former] owner. (2) It has been related to and equated with other private property. Its place has been taken by private property of a *different* nature, just as it has replaced private property of a *different* nature. On both sides, then, private property appears as the representative of a different kind of private property, as the *equivalent* of a *different* kind of product. Thus from both sides the relationship is such that each embodies the existence of the *other*, each exists as his own *surrogate* and as the surrogate of the other. Thus private property as such is a *surrogate*, an *equivalent*. Its immediate identity with itself has given way to a relation to *another*. As an *equivalent* its existence is no longer peculiar to it. It thus becomes a *value*, in fact an immediate *exchange value*. Its existence as *value* is a determination *of itself* diverging from its immediate nature, external to it, alienated from it, a merely *relative* existence. [xxix]

The problem of defining this *value* more precisely, as well as showing how it becomes *price*, must be dealt with elsewhere.

In a situation based on *exchange*, labour immediately becomes *wage-labour*. Two factors are crucial in bringing about the supremacy of estranged labour. (1) *Wage-labour* and the product of the worker does not stand in any *direct* relation to his wants and to his vocation, but in both respects is determined by social configurations alien to the worker. (2) The man who *purchases* the product does not himself produce but only exchanges the produce of others. In *barter*, the primitive form of *alienated* private property, each of the owners has produced whatever his immediate needs, his bent and the available resources dictated. Hence each offers for barter only his surplus produce. Labour was indeed the immediate *source of subsistence* but at the same time it meant the activation of his *individual* existence. With the advent of barter his labour became in part a *source of income*. Its purpose and existence have become different. As *value, exchange value, equivalent,* the product is no longer produced on account of its direct personal connection with the producer. The more production is diversified, i.e. the more needs become diversified and the more the activity of the producer becomes one-sided, the more completely work falls into the category of *wage-labour* until, finally, no other meaning is left to it. It thus becomes wholly *accidental* and *unimportant* whether the relationship between producer and product is governed by immediate enjoyment and personal needs and whether the *activity*, the act of working, involves the fulfilment of his personality, the realization of his natural talents and spiritual goals.

Wage-labour consists of the following elements: (1) the estrangement of labour from its subject, the labourer, and its arbitrariness from his point of view; (2) the estrangement of labour from its object, its arbitrariness *vis-à-vis* the object; (3) the determination of the labourer by social needs alien to him and which act upon him with compulsive force. He must submit to this force from egoistic need, from necessity; for him the needs of society mean only the satisfaction of his personal wants while for society he is only the slave that satisfies its needs; (4) the labourer regards the maintenance of his individual existence as the *aim* of his activity; his actual labours serve only as a means to this end. He thus activates his life to acquire the means of *life*.

Thus the more developed and important is the power of society within private property, the more man is *egoistic*, un-social and estranged from his own essence.

Just as the reciprocal exchange of the produce of *human activity* appears as *barter*, *horse-trading*, so the reciprocal complementing and exchange of human activity itself appears in the form of: the *division of labour*. This makes man, as far as is possible, an abstract being, a lathe, etc., and transforms him into a spiritual and physical abortion.

The very *unity* of human labour is regarded only in terms of *division* because man's social nature is realized only as its antithesis, as estrangement. With civilization the *division of labour* is intensified.

Within the context of the division of labour, the product, the material of private property, increasingly acquires the meaning of an *equivalent*. The individual no longer exchanges his surplus, so the object of his production becomes a matter of complete *indifference* to him. Hence he no longer exchanges his own product for something he *needs*. His equivalent now acquires its own existence as *money*, which now becomes both the immediate result of labour and the *mediator* of exchange. (See above.)

Money represents a total indifference both to the nature of the material, to the specific nature of private property and the personality of the owner of private property. In money the un-fettered dominion of the estranged thing *over* man becomes manifest. The rule of the person over the person now becomes the universal rule of the *thing* over the *person*, the product over the producer. Just as the *equivalent*, value, contained the determina-tion of the alienation of private property, so now we see that *money* is the sensuous, corporeal existence of that *alienation*.

[xxx] It goes without saying that economics understands this whole development only as a fact, as the deformed product of accidental needs.

The separation of labour from itself = the separation of the labourer from the capitalist = the separation of labour and capital, which in its original form is divided into *landed property* and *movable* property . . . The original determination of private property is monopoly. Hence as soon as a political constitution is formed it becomes the constitution of monopoly. The perfected form of monopoly is competition. The economist sees *production* and *consumption* as separate and sees *exchange* or *distribution* as *mediating* between them. The separation of production and con-sumption, of activity and mind among different individuals and within the same individual is the *separation of labour* from its *object* and from itself as one mind. *Distribution* is the self-activat-ing power of private property. The mutual separation of labour, capital and landed property, i.e. of labour from labour, capital from capital and landed property from landed property, and finally the separation of labour from wages, of capital from profits, of profits from interest, and finally of landed property from ground rent, ensures that self-estrangement becomes manifest both as self-estrangement and mutual estrangement.

'We have next to examine the effects which take place by the attempts of government to control the increase or diminution of money, and to fix the quantity as it pleases. When it endeavours to keep the quantity of money less than it would be, if things were left in freedom, it raises the value of the metal in the coin, and renders it the interest of every-body, who can, to convert his bullion into money . . . He must, there-fore, have recourse to private coining. This the government must, if it perseveres, prevent by punishment. On the other hand, were it the object of government to keep the quantity of money *greater* than it would be, if left in freedom, it would reduce the value of the metal in money, below its value in bullion, and make it the interest of every-body to melt the coins. This, also, the government would have only one expedient for preventing, namely, punishment. But the prospect of punishment will prevail over the prospect of profit, only if the profit is small.' (pp. 138–9)

§9. '. . . if there were two individuals, one of whom owed to the other £100, and the other to him £100, instead of the first man's taking the trouble to count down £100 to the second, and the second man's taking the same trouble to count down £100 to the first, all they had to do was to exchange their mutual obligations. The case was the same between England and Holland . . . Hence the invention of *bills of exchange* . . . The use of them was recommended by a still stronger necessity, at the period of invention, because the coarse policy of those times prohibited the *exportation* of the precious metals, and punished with the greatest severity any infringement of that barbarous law.' (pp. 146–8)

§10. 'The advantage of paper money in saving on *unproductive* consumption.' (pp. 150–51)

§11. 'The inconveniences of paper money are: (1) The *failure* (sin)[6] of the parties, by whom the notes are issued, to fulfil their engagements. (2) Forgery. (3) The alteration of the value of the currency.' (p. 152)

§12. 'Precious metals . . . are commodities. Those commodities alone can be exported, which are cheaper in the country from which, than in the country to which, they are sent; . . . those commodities alone can be imported, that are dearer in the country to which, than in the country from which, they are sent . . . Whether the precious metals should be exported or imported, depends, therefore, on their value in a particular country.' (p. 171)

§13. 'When we speak of the value of the precious metal, we mean the quantity of other things for which it will exchange. But it is well known that money . . . goes further in the purchase of commodities, not only in one country than another, but in one part than another of the same country . . . In common language, we say, that living is more cheap; in other words, commodities may be purchased with a smaller quantity of money.' (p. 174)

§14. 'The relationship between countries is like that between merchants . . . if left to themselves, they will always buy in the cheapest market, and sell in the dearest.' (p. 200)

CHAPTER IV. CONSUMPTION

'*Production, distribution* [and] *exchange* . . . are means. They are intermediary operations. The end is *consumption*.' (p. 219)

6. In the manuscript 'sin' has been written above 'failure'.

§1. 'Consumption is 1. *productive*. That production should take place, a certain expenditure is required. This includes the necessaries of the labourer ... machinery, including tools of all sorts, the buildings necessary for the productive operations, and even the cattle. Lastly, the materials of which the commodity to be produced must be formed, or from which it must be derived ... Of these three classes of things, it is only the second [the machinery, etc.] the consumption of which is not completed in the course of the productive operations.' (pp. 220–21)

§2. *Unproductive* consumption. 'The wages given to a groom, ... all consumption which does not take place to the end that an income or revenue may be derived from it, is unproductive consumption.' (pp. 221–2) 'Productive consumption is itself a *means*; it is a means to production. Unproductive consumption, on the other hand, is not a means. This species of consumption is the end. This, or the *enjoyment* that is involved in it, is the good which constituted the *motive* to all the operations by which it was preceded.' (p. 222) 'By productive consumption nothing is lost ... [whereas] whatever is unproductively consumed, is lost ... That which is *productively* consumed is always *capital*. This is a property of productive consumption, which deserves to be particularly remarked ... It thus appears, that the whole of every capital *undergoes* the productive consumption. It is equally obvious that whatever is consumed productively becomes capital ... The whole of what the productive powers of the country have brought into existence, in the course of a year, is called the gross annual produce. Of this the greater part is required to replace the capital which has been consumed ... What remains of the gross produce, after replacing the capital which has been consumed, is called the net produce; and is always distributed, either as profits of stock, or as rent ... This net produce is the fund, from which all addition to the national capital is commonly made ... The two species of labour, *productive* and *unproductive*, may be said to correspond to the two species of consumption, *productive* and *unproductive*.' (pp. 222–4)

§2. 'That which is annually produced is annually consumed', productively or unproductively. (p. 226)

§3. 'Consumption is co-extensive with production ... A man produces only because he *wishes to possess*. If the commodity, which he produces, is the commodity which he desires to possess, he stops when he has produced as much as he desires ... When a man produces a greater quantity of any commodity than he desires for himself, it can only be on one account: namely, that he desires some other commodity which he can obtain in exchange for the surplus of what he himself has produced ... If he desires one thing and produces another, it is only because the thing which he desires can be obtained by means of the thing which he produces, and better obtained, than if he had endeavoured to produce it himself. After labour has been divided and distributed . . . each producer confines himself to some one commodity or part of a commodity, a small portion only of what he produces is used for his own consumption. The remainder he destines for the purpose of supplying him with all the other commodities which he desires; and when each man confines himself to one commodity and exchanges what he produces for what is produced by other people, it is found that each obtains more of the several things, which he desires, than he would have obtained, had he endeavoured to produce them all for himself. [xxxi] . . . In the case of the man who produces for himself, there is no *exchange*. He neither offers to buy any thing, nor to sell any thing. He has the property; he has produced it; and does not mean to part with it. If we apply, by a sort of metaphor, the terms "demand" and "supply" to this case, it is implied . . . that the demand and supply are exactly proportioned to one another. As far then as regards the demand and supply of the market, we may leave that portion of the annual produce, which each of the owners consumes in the shape in which he produces or receives it, altogether out of the question.' (pp. 228–30)

'In speaking here of demand and supply, it is evident that we speak of aggregates. When we say of any particular nation, at any particular time, that its supply is equal to its demand, we do not mean in any one commodity, or any two commodities. We mean, that the amount of its demand, in all commodities taken together, is equal to the amount of its supply in all commodities taken together. It may very well happen, notwithstanding this equality in the general sum of demands and supplies, that some one commodity or commodities may have been produced in a quantity either above or below the demand for those particular commodities.

'Two things are necessary to constitute a *demand*. These are (1) a wish for the commodity; (2) an equivalent to give for it. A demand means the *will* to purchase, and the *means* of purchasing. If either is wanting, the purchase does not take place. An equivalent is the necessary foundation of all demand. It is in vain that a man wishes for commodities, if he has nothing to give for them. The equivalent which a man brings is the *instrument* of demand. The extent of his demand is measured by the extent of his equivalent. The demand and the equivalent are convertible terms, and *the one may be substituted for the other*.

'We have already seen that every man who produces has a wish for other commodities, than those which he has produced, to the extent of all that he brings to market. And it is evident, that whatever a man has produced, and does not wish to keep for his own consumption, is a stock which he may give in exchange for other commodities. *His will*, therefore, *to purchase*, and *his means of purchasing*, in other words, his demand, is exactly equal to the amount of what he has produced and does not mean to consume.' (pp. 230–31)

With his wonted cynical sharpness and insight Mill here analyses exchange based on private property.

Man – this is the fundamental premise of private property – *produces* only in order to *have*. *Having* is the aim of production. Furthermore, production not only has such a *useful* aim; it has a *selfish* aim. Man produces only to *have* something for himself. The object of his production is the objectification of his own *immediate* selfish *needs*. Man, for himself – in a state of savage barbarism – confines his production to the *limits* of his immediate needs, the content of which is the *immediate* object he produces.

Thus in that state man produces *no more* than his immediate needs. *The limit of his needs is the limit of his production.* Hence supply and demand coincide exactly. His production is *measured* by his need. In this situation no exchange takes place or else, exchange reduces itself to the exchange of his labour for the produce of his labour. Such exchange is the latent form (the embryo)[7] of real exchange.

As soon as exchange takes place there is a surplus production beyond the bounds of immediate possessions. This surplus production does not mean, however, any advance beyond selfish needs. It is rather a form of *mediation* by means of which it becomes possible to satisfy a need which does not find its objectification directly in *one's own* production, but in the production of another. Production thus becomes a *source of acquisition*, it becomes wage-labour. Whereas in the first stage need had been the measure of production, in the second stage production, or rather the *possession of produce*, became the measure of the extent to which one might satisfy one's needs.

I have produced for myself and not for you, just as you have produced for yourself and not for me. In itself the result of my production has just as little direct relation to you as the result of your production has to me. That is to say, our production is not man's production for man as man, i.e. it is not *social* production. As men none of us has a claim to enjoy the product of another. As men we do not exist as far as our mutual productions are con-

7. In the manuscript 'embryo' has been written above 'form'.

cerned. Hence our exchange cannot be the mediating movement which confirms that my product is for you [xxxii] because it is an *objectification* of your own nature, of your need. For our products are not united for each other by the bond of *human nature*. Exchange can only set in *motion*, it can do no more than confirm the *character* each of us bears in relation to his own product and hence to the product of the other. Each of us sees in his product only his *own* objectified self-interest, hence in the product of others the objectification of a *different*, alien self-interest, independent of oneself.

Naturally, as a human being you have a human relation to my product: you have *need* of my product. It exists for you, therefore, as an object of your desire and your will. But your need, your desire and your will are impotent as far as my product is concerned. That is to say, although your human nature necessarily implies an intimate relationship with my human production, it gives you no *power*, no rights of *possession*, over that production, since in my production the *specific character* and the *power* of human nature are not recognized. The latter are rather the *bond* which makes you dependent upon me because they place you in a position of dependence on my product. Far from their being the *means* giving you *power* over my production, they are rather the *means* whereby I acquire power over you.

When I produce *more* of a thing than I can use myself, then my surplus production is *calculated* and adapted to your *need*. I produce a surplus of the object only in *appearance*. In reality I produce a *different* object, the object of your production which I intend to exchange for your surplus, an exchange which I have already accomplished in my mind. Thus the social relation I bear to you, the labour I perform to satisfy your need, is likewise merely an *appearance* and our mutual supplementing of each other is equally but an *appearance*, based on our mutual plundering of each other. The intention to *plunder*, to *deceive*, inevitably lurks in the background, for, since our exchange is self-interested on your side as well as on mine, and since every self-interested person seeks to outdo the other, we must necessarily strive to deceive each other. Of course, in order for the power which I confer upon my own possession at the expense of yours to become a real power, it must be *acknowledged* by you. But our mutual recognition of the mutual power of our possessions is a struggle and the victory in the struggle goes to the man who has the greater energy, strength, insight or agility. If my physical strength is great enough, I will plunder you directly. If the realm of physical force has been neutralized then we each attempt to delude the other and the shrewdest will get the better of the bargain. Which of the two gets the better bargain is a matter of indifference as far as the total relationship is concerned. On both sides we see the *ideal*, *intended* superiority, i.e. in his own judgement each has got the better of the other.

On both sides, then, the exchange is mediated necessarily by the *objects* of mutual production and mutual possession. It is true of course that the ideal relation to the mutual objects of our production should be given by our mutual needs. But in practice the *actual real* and *true* relation is the mutually *exclusive possession* of our mutual production. The thing that gives your need for my possessions a *value*, a *worth* and an *effect* in my eyes is simply and solely your *possession*, the *equivalent* of my possession. Our mutual product, therefore, is the *means*, the *mediator*, the. *instrument*, the *acknowledged power*, of our mutual needs over each other. Your *demand* and your equivalent possessions are synonymous, convertible terms for me, and your demand has an effective *meaning* only if it has a meaning and an effect upon me. In the absence of this, you are merely a human being and your demand is no more than an ungratified desire on your part, a non-existent idea as far as I am concerned. As a human being, then, you have no relation to my product because *I myself* have no human relation to it. But the *means* is the *true power* over an object and hence we each regard our own products as the *power* each has over the other and over himself, i.e. our own product has stood up on its hind legs against us: it had seemed to be our property, but in reality we are its property. We find ourselves excluded from *true* property because our *property* excludes other human beings.

The only comprehensible language we have is the language our possessions use together. We would not understand a human language and it would remain ineffectual. From the one side, such a language would be felt to be begging, imploring and hence *humiliating*. [XXXIII] It could be used only with feelings of shame or debasement. From the other side, it would be received as *impertinence* or *insanity* and so rejected. We are so estranged from our human essence that the direct language of man strikes us as an *offence against the dignity of man*, whereas the estranged language of objective values appears as the justified, self-confident and self-acknowledged dignity of man incarnate.

Of course, in your eyes your product is an *instrument*, a *means* whereby to obtain possession of my product and hence to gratify your needs. But in my eyes it is the *end* of our exchange. It is you who serve as the means, the instrument, in the production of this object which is my goal, just as in this relation to my object you are the reverse of my goal. But (1) each of us really *does* act out the role in which the other casts him. You really have turned yourself into the means, the instrument, the producer of *your* own object so as to gain possession of mine. (2) Your own object is merely the *sensuous husk*, the *hidden form* of my object. For its production *signifies expressly*: the *acquisition* of my object. Thus you have really become a *means*, an *instrument* of your object even for yourself; your desire is its slave and you have performed menial tasks so that the object need never again become the fulfilment of your desire. If our mutual servitude to the object really appears at the beginning of the development as the relation of *dominance* and *slavery* this is no more than the *brutal* and *frank* expression of our essential relationship.

Our mutual value, then, is the *value* of our mutual objects. For us, therefore, man himself is *worthless*.

Let us suppose that we had produced as human beings. In that event each of us would have *doubly affirmed* himself and his neighbour in his production. (1) In my *production* I would have objectified the *specific character* of my *individuality* and for that reason I would both have enjoyed the *expression* of my own individual *life* during my activity and also, in contemplating the object, I would experience an individual pleasure, I would experience my personality as an *objective sensuously perceptible* power *beyond all shadow of doubt*. (2) In your use or enjoyment of my product I would have the *immediate* satisfaction and knowledge that in my labour I had gratified a *human* need, i.e. that I had objectified *human nature* and hence had procured an object corresponding to the needs of another *human being*. (3) I would have acted for you as the *mediator* between you and the species, thus I would be acknowledged by you as the complement of your own being, as an essential part of yourself. I would thus know myself to be confirmed both in your thoughts and your love. (4) In the individual expression of my own life I would have brought about the immediate expression of your life, and so in my individual activity I would have directly *confirmed* and *realized* my authentic nature, my *human, communal* nature.

Our productions would be as many mirrors from which our natures would shine forth.

This relation would be mutual: what applies to me would also apply to you:

My labour would be the *free expression* and hence the *enjoyment of life*. In the framework of private property it is the *alienation of life* since I work *in order to live*, in order to procure for myself the *means* of life. My labour is *not* life.

Moreover, in my labour the *specific character* of my individuality would be affirmed because it would be my *individual* life. Labour would be *authentic, active, property*. In the framework of private property my individuality has been alienated to the point where I loathe this activity, it is torture for me. It is in fact no more than the *appearance* of activity and for that reason it is only a *forced* labour imposed on me *not* through an *inner necessity* but through an *external* arbitrary need.

In the object I produce my labour can only become manifest as what it is. It cannot appear to be what it is *not*. It therefore becomes manifest only as the objective, sensuous, perceived and hence quite indubitable expression of my *self-loss* and my *impotence*. [XXXIII]

Economic and Philosophical Manuscripts

[The Manuscripts *were written during the months April to August 1844. They were not intended for publication. In them Marx transforms his earlier criticism of politics into a criticism of economics. He approves of the idea, which he found in the writings of the political economists, of labour as the source of all wealth. He contrasts this to the 'fetishistic' idea of the Physiocrats who considered land the source of wealth. But he criticizes the political economists for taking the existence of private property for granted. Under this system a large part of the wealth produced exclusively by the labourer goes to the capitalist, while the labourer himself gets a pittance. Hence the class struggle. Marx also describes the tendency towards a growing impoverishment of the worker and a growing concentration of capital.*

He goes on to expound the key concept of 'alienated labour', thereby giving concrete form to the abstract *idea of alienation as developed by Hegel. All other forms of alienation (political, religious, etc.) can be understood only with reference to this central concept. The product of labour, Marx continues, is alienated by the capitalist. It follows that alienation can only be abolished if the system of private property is abolished.* Communism *is the abolition of private property. But communism is not the levelling-down or universalization of private property, as the 'crude communists' believe. 'Crude communism' is the product of envy and therefore* mirrors *the system of private property. The 'crude communists' want to bring everyone down to the situation the worker finds himself in under capitalism; 'true communism' aims rather at the 'positive transcendence' of private property by a 'fully developed humanism'. The final section of the* Manuscripts *deals with Hegel. Marx considers that Hegel correctly describes the process whereby man creates himself through his own labour. But he criticizes him for seeing labour only as 'mental labour',* that is, thought. *Alienation that takes place in thought can only be annulled in thought, that is, in imagination. Therefore Hegel is in effect forced to compromise with existing reality. Marx counterposes to Hegel's 'mental labour' the sensuous, practical activity of 'real, corporeal man'. He calls his standpoint 'consistent naturalism or humanism' and sees it as the unifying truth of both idealism and materialism.*]

Contents

PREFACE

In the *Deutsch–Französische Jahrbücher*[1] I announced a critique of jurisprudence and political science in the form of a critique of the *Hegelian* philosophy of right. While preparing this for

1. Marx is referring to his *Contribution to the Critique of Hegel's Philosophy of Right. Introduction*; see pp. 243–57 above.

publication, I found that to combine criticism directed only against speculation with criticism of the various subjects themselves was quite unsuitable; it hampered the development of the argument and made it more difficult to follow. Moreover, the wealth and diversity of the subjects to be dealt with would have fitted into *a single* work only if I had written in aphorisms, and an aphoristic presentation, for its part, would have given the *impression* of arbitrary systematization. I shall therefore publish the critique of law, morals, politics, etc., in a series of separate, independent pamphlets and finally attempt, in a special work, to present them once again as a connected whole, to show the relationship between the parts and to try to provide a critique of the speculative treatment of the material. That is why the present work only touches on the interconnection of political economy and the state, law, morals, civil life, etc., in so far as political economy itself particularly touches on these subjects.

It is hardly necessary to assure the reader who is familiar with political economy that I arrived at my conclusions through an entirely empirical analysis based on an exhaustive critical study of political economy.

It goes without saying that I have made use of German socialist works in addition to the French and English socialists. But the only *original* German works of any interest in this field – apart from those by Weitling – are the essays by Hess in *Einundzwanzig Bogen*[2] and Engels' *Outlines of a Critique of Political Economy*[3] in the *Deutsch–Französische Jahrbücher*; in the last-mentioned publication I too indicated in a very general way the basic elements of the present work.

It is only with *Feuerbach* that *positive* humanistic and naturalistic criticism begins. The less strident his writings are, the more certain, profound, comprehensive and lasting is their influence; they are the only writings since Hegel's *Phenomenology* and *Logic* to contain a real theoretical revolution.

In contrast to the *critical theologians*[4] of our time, I considered the concluding chapter of the present work (a critical analysis of the *Hegelian dialectic* and Hegelian philosophy in general) to be essential, since such a task has not yet been completed. Their

2. *Einundzwanzig Bogen aus der Schweiz*, First Part, Zürich and Winterthur, 1843.
3. See Engels, *Selected Writings*, Harmondsworth, 1967, pp. 148–77.
4. A reference to Bruno Bauer and his associates.

failure to go to the root of the matter is inevitable, since even the *critical* theologian is still a theologian. Either he must start out from certain presuppositions of philosophy which he considers authoritative or, if in the process of criticism and as a result of other people's discoveries he begins to doubt these philosophical presuppositions, he abandons them in a cowardly and indefensible way, he *abstracts* from them and he demonstrates his enthralment to them and his resentment of this enthralment purely in a negative, unconscious and sophistical way.

On close investigation *theological criticism*, although it was a truly progressive factor at the beginning of the movement, is in the final analysis nothing more than the culmination and consequence of the old *philosophical*, and especially *Hegelian, transcendence* distorted into a *theological caricature*. Elsewhere[5] I shall describe in detail this interesting example of historical justice, this Nemesis, which has now burdened theology – always philosophy's sore point – with the additional task of portraying in itself the negative dissolution of philosophy, i.e. its process of decay.

FIRST MANUSCRIPT

Wages of Labour

Wages are determined by the fierce struggle between capitalist and worker. The capitalist inevitably wins. The capitalist can live longer without the worker than the worker can without him. Combination among capitalists is habitual and effective, while combination among the workers is forbidden and has painful consequences for them. In addition to that, the landowner and the capitalist can increase their revenues with the profits of industry, while the worker can supplement his income from industry with neither ground rent nor interest on capital. This is the reason for the intensity of competition among the workers. It is therefore only for the worker that the separation of capital, landed property and labour is a necessary, essential and pernicious separation. Capital and landed property need not remain constant in this abstraction, as must the labour of the workers.

So for the worker the separation of capital, ground rent and labour is fatal.

5. Marx fulfilled this promise in *The Holy Family*, written jointly with Engels in 1845.

For wages the lowest and the only necessary rate is that required for the subsistence of the worker during work and enough extra to support a family and prevent the race of workers from dying out. According to Smith, the normal wage is the lowest which is compatible with common humanity, i.e. with a bestial existence.[1]

The demand for men necessarily regulates the production of men, as of every other commodity. If the supply greatly exceeds the demand, then one section of the workers sinks into beggary or starvation. The existence of the worker is therefore reduced to the same condition as the existence of every other commodity. The worker has become a commodity, and he is lucky if he can find a buyer. And the demand on which the worker's life depends is regulated by the whims of the wealthy and the capitalists. If supply exceeds demand, one of the elements which go to make up the price – profit, ground rent, wages – will be paid below its *price*. A part of these elements is therefore withdrawn from this application, with the result that the market price gravitates towards the natural price as the central point. But (1) it is very difficult for the worker to direct his labour elsewhere where there is a marked division of labour; and (2) because of his subordinate relationship to the capitalist, he is the first to suffer.

So the worker is sure to lose and to lose most from the gravitation of the market price towards the natural price. And it is precisely the ability of the capitalist to direct his capital elsewhere which either drives the worker, who is restricted to one particular branch of employment, into starvation or forces him to submit to all the capitalist's demands.

The sudden chance fluctuations in market price hit ground rent less than that part of the price which constitutes profit and wages, but they hit profit less than wages. For every wage which rises, there is generally one which remains *stationary* and another which *falls*.

The worker does not necessarily gain when the capitalist gains, but he necessarily loses with him. For example, the worker does not gain if the capitalist keeps the market price above the natural price by means of a manufacturing or trade secret, a monopoly or a favourably placed property.

Moreover, *the prices of labour are much more constant than the*

1. Adam Smith, *The Wealth of Nations*, 2 vols., Everyman edition, Vol. I, p. 61.

prices of provisions. They are often in inverse proportion. In a dear year, wages drop because of a drop in demand and rise because of an increase in the price of provisions. They therefore balance. In any case, some workers are left without bread. In cheap years wages rise on account of the rise in demand and fall on account of the fall in the price of provisions. So they balance.[2]

Another disadvantage for the worker:

The price of the labour of different kinds of workers varies much more than the *profits of the various branches in which capital is put to use*. In the case of labour, all the natural, spiritual and social variations in individual activity are manifested and variously rewarded, whereas dead capital behaves in a uniform way and is indifferent to *real* individual activity.

In general, we should note that where worker and capitalist both suffer, the worker suffers in his very existence while the capitalist suffers in the profit on his dead mammon.

The worker has not only to struggle for his physical means of subsistence; he must also struggle for work, i.e. for the possibility and the means of realizing his activity.

Let us consider the three main conditions which can occur in society and their effect on the worker.

(1) If the wealth of society is decreasing, the worker suffers most, for although the working class cannot gain as much as the property owners when society is prospering, *none suffers more cruelly from its decline than the working class*.[3]

(2) Let us now consider a society in which wealth is increasing. This condition is the only one favourable to the worker. Here competition takes place among the capitalists. The demand for workers outstrips supply. But:

In the first place the rise in wages leads to *overwork* among the workers. The more they want to earn the more they must sacrifice their time and freedom and work like slaves in the service of avarice. In doing so they shorten their lives. But this is all to the good of the working class as a whole, since it creates a renewed demand. This class must always sacrifice a part of itself if it is to avoid total destruction.

Furthermore, when is a society in a condition of increasing prosperity? When the capitals and revenues of a country are growing. But this is only possible

(a) as a result of the accumulation of a large quantity of labour,

2. Smith, op. cit., I, pp. 76–7.   3. ibid., p. 230.

for capital is accumulated labour; that is to say, when more and more of the worker's products are being taken from him, when his own labour increasingly confronts him as alien property and the means of his existence and of his activity are increasingly concentrated in the hands of the capitalist.

(b) The accumulation of capital increases the division of labour, and the division of labour increases the number of workers; conversely, the growth in the number of workers increases the division of labour, just as the growth in the division of labour increases the accumulation of capital. As a consequence of this division of labour on the one hand and the accumulation of capitals on the other, the worker becomes more and more uniformly dependent on labour, and on a particular, very one-sided and machine-like type of labour. Just as he is depressed, therefore, both intellectually and physically to the level of a machine, and from being a man becomes an abstract activity and a stomach, so he also becomes more and more dependent on every fluctuation in the market price, in the investment of capital and in the whims of the wealthy. Equally, the increase in that class of men who do nothing but work increases the competition among the workers and therefore lowers their price. In the factory system conditions such as these reach their climax.

(c) In a society which is becoming increasingly prosperous, only the very richest can continue to live from the interest on money. All the rest must run a business with their capital, or put it on the market. As a result the competition among the capitalists increases, there is a growing concentration of capital, the big capitalists ruin the small ones and a section of the former capitalists sinks into the class of the workers which, because of this increase in numbers, suffers a further depression of wages and becomes even more dependent on the handful of big capitalists. Because the number of capitalists has fallen, competition for workers hardly exists any longer, and because the number of workers has increased, the competition among them has become all the more considerable, unnatural and violent. Hence a section of the working class is reduced to beggary or starvation with the same necessity as a section of the middle capitalists ends up in the working class.

So even in the state of society most favourable to him, the inevitable consequence for the worker is overwork and early death, reduction to a machine, enslavement to capital which piles up in threatening opposition to him, fresh competition and starvation or beggary for a section of the workers.

An increase in wages arouses in the worker the same desire to get rich as in the capitalist, but he can only satisfy this desire by sacrificing his mind and his body. An increase in wages presupposes, and brings about, the accumulation of capital, and thus opposes the product of labour to the worker as something increasingly alien to him. Similarly, the division of labour makes him more and more one-sided and dependent, introducing competition from machines as well as from men. Since the worker has been reduced to a machine, the machine can confront him as a competitor. Finally, just as the accumulation of capital increases the quantity of industry and therefore the number of workers, so it enables the same quantity of industry to produce a *greater quantity of products*. This leads to overproduction and ends up either by putting a large number of workers out of work or by reducing their wages to a pittance.

Such are the consequences of a condition of society which is most favourable to the worker, i.e. a condition of *growing* wealth.

But in the long run the time will come when this state of growth reaches a peak. What is the situation of the worker then?

(3) 'In a country which had acquired that full complement of riches . . . both the wages of labour and the profits of stock would probably be very low . . . the competition for employment would necessarily be so great as to reduce the wages of labour to what was barely sufficient to keep up the number of labourers, and, the country being already fully peopled, that number could never be augmented.'[4]

The surplus population would have to die.

So in a declining state of society we have the increasing misery of the worker; in an advancing state, complicated misery; and in the terminal state, static misery.

Smith tells us that a society of which the greater part suffers is not happy.[5] But since even the most prosperous state of society leads to suffering for the majority and since the economic system [*Nationalökonomie*], which is a society based on private interests, brings about such a state of prosperity, it follows that society's distress is the goal of the economic system.

We should further note in connection with the relationship between worker and capitalist that the latter is more than com-

4. ibid., p. 84.   5. ibid., p. 70.

pensated for wage rises by a reduction in the amount of labour time, and that wage rises and increases in the interest on capital act on commodity prices like simple and compound interest respectively.

Let us now look at things from the point of view of the political economist and compare what he has to say about the theoretical and practical claims of the worker.

He tells us that originally, and in theory, the *whole produce* of labour belongs to the worker.[6] But at the same time he tells us that what the worker actually receives is the smallest part of the product, the absolute minimum necessary; just enough for him to exist not as a human being but as a worker and for him to propagate not humanity but the slave class of the workers.

The political economist tells us that everything is bought with labour and that capital is nothing but accumulated labour, but then goes on to say that the worker, far from being in a position to buy everything, must sell himself and his humanity.

While the ground rent of the indolent landowner generally amounts to a third of the product of the soil and the profit of the busy capitalist to as much as twice the rate of interest, the surplus which the worker earns amounts at best to the equivalent of death through starvation for two of his four children.[7]

According to the political economist labour is the only means whereby man can enhance the value of natural products, and labour is the active property of man. But according to this same political economy the landowner and the capitalist, who as such are merely privileged and idle gods, are everywhere superior to the worker and dictate the law to him.

According to the political economist labour is the only constant price of things. But nothing is more subject to chance than the price of labour, nothing exposed to greater fluctuations.

While the division of labour increases the productive power of labour and the wealth and refinement of society, it impoverishes the worker and reduces him to a machine. While labour gives rise to the accumulation of capital and so brings about the growing prosperity of society, it makes the worker increasingly dependent on the capitalist, exposes him to greater competition and drives him into the frenzied world of overproduction, with its subsequent slump.

According to the political economist the interest of the worker

6. ibid., p. 57.   7. ibid., p. 60.

is never opposed to the interest of society. But society is invariably and inevitably opposed to the interest of the worker.

According to the political economist the interest of the worker is never opposed to that of society (1) because the rise in wages is more than made up for by the reduction in the amount of labour time, with the other consequences explained above, and (2) because in relation to society the entire gross product is net product, and only in relation to the individual does the net product have any significance.

But it follows from the analyses made by the political economists, even though they themselves are unaware of the fact, that labour itself – not only under present conditions but in general in so far as its goal is restricted to the increase of wealth – is harmful and destructive.

*

In theory, ground rent and profit on capital are *deductions* made from wages. But in reality wages are a deduction which land and capital grant the worker, an allowance made from the product of labour to the worker, to labour.

The worker suffers most when society is in a state of decline. He owes the particular severity of his distress to his position as a worker, but the distress as such is a result of the situation of society.

But when society is in a state of progress the decline and impoverishment of the worker is the product of his labour and the wealth produced by him. This misery therefore proceeds from the very *essence* of present-day labour.

A society at the peak of its prosperity – an ideal, but one which is substantially achieved, and which is at least the goal of the economic system and of civil society – is *static misery* for the worker.

It goes without saying that political economy regards the *proletarian*, i.e. he who lives without capital and ground rent from labour alone, and from one-sided, abstract labour at that, as nothing more than a *worker*. It can therefore advance the thesis that, like a horse, he must receive enough to enable him to work. It does not consider him, during the time when he is not working, as a human being. It leaves this to criminal law, doctors, religion, statistical tables, politics and the beadle.

Let us now rise above the level of political economy and

examine the ideas developed above, taken almost word for word from the political economists, for the answers to these two questions:

(1) What is the meaning, in the development of mankind, of this reduction of the greater part of mankind to abstract labour?

(2) What mistakes are made by the piecemeal reformers, who either want to *raise* wages and thereby improve the situation of the working class, or – like Proudhon – see *equality* of wages as the goal of social revolution?

In political economy *labour* appears only in the form of *wage-earning activity*.

*

'It can be argued that those occupations which demand specific abilities or longer training have on the whole become more lucrative; while the commensurate wage for mechanically uniform activity, in which anyone can be quickly and easily trained, has fallen, and inevitably so, as a result of growing competition. And it is precisely *this* kind of labour which, under the present system of labour organization, is by far the most common. So if a worker in the first category now earns seven times as much as he did fifty years ago, while another in the second category continues to earn the same as he did then, then *on average* they earn four times as much. But if in a given country there are only a thousand workers in the first category and a million in the second, then 999,000 are no better off than fifty years ago, and they are *worse off* if the prices of staple goods have risen. And yet people are trying to deceive themselves about the most numerous class of the population with superficial *average* calculations of this sort. Moreover, the size of *wages* is only one factor in evaluating a *worker's income*: it is also essential to take into account the *length of time* for which such wages are guaranteed, and there is no question of guarantees in the anarchy of so-called free competition with its continual fluctuations and stagnation. Finally, we must bear in mind the *hours* of work which were usual earlier and those which are usual now. And for the English cotton workers the working day has been increased, as a result of the employers' greed, from twelve to sixteen hours during the past twenty-five years or so, i.e. since labour-saving machines were introduced. This increase in one country and in one branch of industry inevitably carried over to a greater or lesser degree into other areas, for the rights of the wealthy to subject the poor to boundless exploitation are still universally acknowledged.'[8]

'But even if it were as true as it is false that the average income of *all* classes of society has grown, the differences and *relative* intervals between incomes can still have grown bigger, so that the contrast between wealth and poverty becomes sharper. For it is precisely *because* total production rises that needs, desires and claims also increase, and they increase in the same measure as production rises; *relative* poverty can therefore grow while *absolute* poverty diminishes. The Samoyed is not poor with his blubber and rancid fish, for in *his* self-contained society everyone has the same needs. But in a *state which is making rapid headway*, which in the course of a decade increases its total production in relation to the population by a third, the worker who earns the same at the end of the ten years as he did at the beginning has not maintained his standard of living, he has grown poorer by a third.'[9]

But political economy knows the worker only as a beast of burden, as an animal reduced to the minimum bodily needs.

'If a people is to increase its spiritual freedom, it can no longer remain in thrall to its bodily needs, it can no longer be the servant of the flesh. Above all it needs *time* for intellectual exercise and recreation. This time is won through new developments in the organization of labour. Nowadays a single worker in the cotton mills, as a result of new ways of producing power and new machinery, can often do work that previously needed 100 or even 250–350 workers. All branches of industry have witnessed similar consequences, since external natural forces are increasingly being brought to bear on human labour. If the amount of time and human energy needed earlier to satisfy a given quantity of material needs was later reduced by half, then without any forfeiture of material comfort the margin for intellectual creation and recreation will have increased by half. But even the sharing of the spoils which we win from old Chronos[10] on his very own territory still depends on blind and unjust chance. In France it has been estimated that at the present stage of production an average working day of five hours from each person capable of work would be sufficient to satisfy all society's material needs ... In

8. Wilhelm Schulz, *Die Bewegung der Produktion, eine geschichtlich-statistische Abhandlung*, Zürich and Winterthur, 1843, p. 65.
9. ibid., pp. 65–6.   10. The Greek God of Time.

spite of the time saved through improvements in machinery, the time spent in slave labour in the factories has increased for many people.'[11]

'The transition from complicated handicrafts presupposes a breaking down of such work into the simple operations of which it consists. To begin with, however, only a *part* of the uniformly recurring operations falls to the machines, while another part falls to men. Permanently uniform activity of this kind is by its very nature harmful to both soul and body – a fact which is also confirmed by experience; and so when machinery is *combined* in this way with the mere division of labour among a larger number of men, all the shortcomings of the latter inevitably make their appearance. These shortcomings include the greater mortality of factory workers ... No attention has been paid to the essential distinction between how far men work *through* machines and how far they work *as* machines.'[12]

'In the future life of the nations, however, the mindless forces of nature operating in machines will be our slaves and servants.'[13]

'In the English spinning mills only 158,818 men are employed, compared with 196,818 women. For every hundred men workers in the Lancashire cotton mills there are 103 women workers; in Scotland the figure is as high as 209. In the English flax mills in Leeds there are 147 women for every 100 men workers; in Dundee and on the east coast of Scotland this figure is as high as 280. In the English silk-factories there are many women workers; in the wool factories, where greater strength is needed, there are more men. As for the North American cotton mills, in 1833 there were no fewer than 38,927 women alongside 18,593 men. So as a result of changes in the organization of labour, a wider area of employment opportunities has been opened up to members of the female sex ... more economic independence for women ... both sexes brought closer together in their social relations.'[14]

'Employed in the English spinning mills operated by steam and water in the year 1835 were: 20,558 children between 8 and 12 years of age; 35,867 between 12 and 13; and finally, 108,208 between 13 and 18 ... True, the advances in mechanization, which remove more and more of the monotonous tasks from human hands, are gradually eliminating these ills. But standing in the way of these more rapid advances is the fact that the

11. Schulz, op. cit., pp. 67–8.   12. ibid., p. 69.   13. ibid., p. 74.
14. ibid., pp. 71–2.

capitalists are in a position to make use of the energies of the lower classes, right down to children, very easily and very cheaply, and to use them *instead* of machinery.'[15]

'Lord Brougham's appeal to the workers: "Become capitalists!" ... The evil that millions are only able to eke out a living through exhausting, physically destructive and morally and intellectually crippling labour; that they are even forced to regard the misfortune of finding *such* work as fortunate.'[16]

'So in order to live, the non-owners are forced to place themselves directly or indirectly *at the service* of the owners, i.e. become dependent upon them.'[17]

'Servants – pay; workers – wages; clerks – salaries or emoluments.'[18]

'hire out one's labour', 'lend out one's labour at interest', 'work in another's place'.

'hire out the materials of labour', 'lend the materials of labour at interest', 'make another work in one's place'.[19]

'This economic constitution condemns men to such abject employments, such desolate and bitter degradation, that by comparison savagery appears like a royal condition.'[20] 'Prostitution of the non-owning class in all its forms.'[21] Rag-and-bone men.

Ch. Loudon, in his work *Solution du problème de la population*,[22] gives the number of prostitutes in England as 60–70,000. The number of women of 'doubtful virtue' is roughly the same.[23]

'The average life span of these unfortunate creatures on the streets, after they have embarked on their career of vice, is about six or seven years. This means that if the number of 60–70,000 prostitutes is to be maintained, there must be in the three kingdoms at least 8–9,000 women a year who take up this infamous trade, i.e. roughly twenty-four victims a day, which is an average of one an hour. So if the same proportion is true for the whole surface of the planet, then at all times there must be one and a half million of these unhappy creatures.'[24]

15. ibid., pp. 70–71.   16. ibid., p. 60.

17. C. Pecqueur, *Théorie nouvelle d'économie sociale et politique, ou études sur l'organisation des sociétés*, Paris, 1842, p. 409.

18. ibid., pp. 409–10.   19. ibid., p. 411.   20. ibid., pp. 417–18.
21. ibid., pp. 421 ff.

22. Charles Loudon, *Solution du problème de la population et de la subsistance, soumise à un médecin dans une série de lettres*, Paris, 1842, p. 229.

23. ibid., p. 228.   24. ibid., p. 229.

'The population of the poor grows with their poverty, and it is at the most extreme limit of need that human beings crowd together in the greatest numbers in order to fight among themselves for the right to suffer . . . In 1821 the population of Ireland was 6,801,827. By 1831 it had risen to 7,764,010; that is a 14 per cent increase in 10 years. In Leinster, the most prosperous of the provinces, the population only grew by 8 per cent, while in Connaught, the poorest of the provinces, the increase was as high as 21 per cent. (*Extract from Inquiries Published in England on Ireland*, Vienna, 1840.)'[25]

Political economy regards labour abstractly as a thing; labour is a commodity; if the price is high, the commodity is much in demand; if it is low, then it is much in supply; 'the price of labour as a commodity must fall lower and lower'.[26] This is brought about partly by the competition between capitalist and worker and partly by the competition among the workers themselves.

'. . . the working population, seller of labour, is forced to accept the smallest part of the product . . . Is the theory of labour as a commodity anything other than a disguised theory of slavery?'[27] 'Why then was labour regarded as nothing more than an exchange value?'[28]

The big workshops prefer to buy the labour of women and children, because it costs less than that of men.[29]

'*Vis-à-vis* his employer the worker is not at all in the position of a *free seller* . . . The capitalist is always free to employ labour, and the worker is always forced to sell it. The value of labour is completely destroyed if it is not sold at every instant. Unlike genuine commodities, labour can be neither accumulated nor saved.

'Labour is life, and if life is not exchanged every day for food it suffers and soon perishes. If human life is to be regarded as a commodity, we are forced to admit slavery.'[30]

So if labour is a commodity, it is a commodity with the most unfortunate characteristics. But even according to economic principles it is not one, for it is not the 'free product of a free market'.[31] The present economic regime 'reduces at the same time both the price and the remuneration of labour; it perfects the

25. Eugène Buret, *De la misère des classes laborieuses en Angleterre et en France*, 2 vols., Paris, 1840, Vol. I, pp. 36–7.

26. ibid., p. 43.   27. ibid.   28. ibid., p. 44.
29. ibid.   30. ibid., pp. 49–50.   31. ibid., p. 50.

worker and degrades the man'.[32] 'Industry has become a war, commerce a game.'[33]

'The machines for spinning cotton (in England) alone represent 84,000,000 handworkers.'[34]

Up to now industry has been in the situation of a war of conquest:

'it has squandered the lives of the men who composed its army with as much indifference as the great conquerors. Its goal was the possession of riches, and not human happiness.'[35] 'These interests (i.e. economic interests), left to their own free development, . . . cannot help coming into conflict; war is their only arbiter, and the decisions of war assign defeat and death to some and victory to others . . . It is in the conflict of opposing forces that science looks for order and equilibrium: *perpetual war*, in the view of science, is the only means of achieving peace; this war is called competition.'[36]

'The industrial war, if it is to be waged successfully, needs large armies which it can concentrate at one point and decimate at will. And neither devotion nor duty moves the soldiers of this army to bear the burdens placed upon them; what moves them is the need to escape the harshness of starvation. They feel neither affection nor gratitude for their bosses, who are not bound to their subordinates by any feeling of goodwill and who regard them not as human beings but as instruments of production which bring in as much and cost as little as possible. These groups of workers, who are more and more crowded together, cannot even be sure that they will always be employed; the industry which has summoned them together allows them to live only because it needs them; as soon as it can get rid of them it abandons them without the slightest hesitation; and the workers are forced to offer their persons and their labour for whatever is the going price. The longer, more distressing and loathsome the work which is given them, the less they are paid; one can see workers who toil their way non-stop through a sixteen hour day and who scarcely manage to buy the right not to die.'[37]

'We are convinced . . . as are the commissioners appointed to look into the conditions of the handloom weavers, that the large industrial towns would quickly lose their population of workers

32. ibid., p. 52–3.   33. ibid., p. 62.   34. ibid., p. 193.
35. ibid., p. 20.   36. ibid., p. 23.   37. ibid., pp. 68–9.

if they did not all the time receive a continual stream of healthy people and fresh blood from the surrounding country areas.'[38]

Profit of Capital

1. Capital

(1) What is the basis of *capital*, i.e. of private property in the products of another's labour?

'Even if capital cannot be reduced to simple theft or fraud, it still needs the assistance of legislation to sanctify inheritance.'[1]

How does one become an owner of productive stock? How does one become owner of the products created by means of this stock?

Through *positive law*.[2]

What does one acquire with capital, with the inheritance of a large fortune, for example?

'The person who either acquires, or succeeds to a great fortune, does not necessarily acquire or succeed to any political power ... The power which that possession immediately and directly conveys to him, is the power of purchasing; a certain command over all the labour, or over all the produce of labour, which is then in the market.'[3]

Capital is therefore the *power to command* labour and its products. The capitalist possesses this power not on account of his personal or human properties but in so far as he is an *owner* of capital. His power is the *purchasing* power of his capital, which nothing can withstand.

Later we shall see how the capitalist, by means of capital, exercises his power to command labour; but we shall then go on to see how capital, in its turn, is able to rule the capitalist himself.

What is capital?

'A certain quantity of *labour stocked* and stored up ...'[4]

Capital is *stored-up labour*.

(2) *Bonds*, or stock, is any accumulation of the products of the soil or of manufacture. Stock is only called *capital* when it yields its owner a revenue or profit.[5]

38. ibid., p. 362.
1. Jean-Baptiste Say, *Traité d'économie politique*, third edn, 2 vols., Paris, 1817, I, p. 136, footnote.
2. ibid., II, p. 4.   3. Smith, op. cit., I, pp. 26–7.
4. ibid., p. 295.   5. ibid., p. 243.

2. The Profit of Capital

The *profit or gain of capital* is altogether different from the *wages of labour*. This difference manifests itself in two ways: firstly, the profits of capital are regulated altogether by the value of the stock employed, although the labour of inspection and direction for different capitals may be the same. Furthermore, in many large factories the whole labour of this kind is committed to some principal clerk, whose wages never bear any regular proportion to the capital of which he oversees the management. And the owner of this capital, though he is thus discharged of almost all labour, still expects that his profits should bear a regular proportion to his capital.[6]

Why does the capitalist demand this proportion between profit and capital?

He could have no interest in employing these workers, unless he expected from the sale of their work something more than was sufficient to replace the stock advanced by him as wages; and he could have no interest to employ a great stock rather than a small one, unless his profits were to bear some proportion to the extent of his stock.[7]

So the capitalist makes a profit first on the wages and secondly on the raw materials advanced by him.

What relation, then, does profit have to capital?

It is not easy to ascertain what are the average wages of labour even in a particular place and at a particular time, and it is even more difficult to determine the profit on capital. Variations of price in the commodities which the capitalist deals in, the good or bad fortune both of his rivals and of his customers, a thousand other accidents to which his goods are liable in transit and in warehouses, all produce a daily, almost hourly, variation in profits.[8] But though it may be impossible to determine, with any degree of precision, the average profits of capital, some notion may be formed of them from the *interest of money*. Wherever a great deal can be made by the use of money, a great deal will be given for the use of it; wherever little can be made, little will be given.[9] 'The proportion which the usual market rate of interest ought to bear

6. ibid., p. 43. Note that this and many of the subsequent paragraphs are taken almost word for word, with a few minor omissions and changes, from Smith.

7. ibid., p. 42.   8. ibid., pp. 78–9.   9. ibid., p. 79.

to the ordinary rate of clear profit, necessarily varies as profit rises or falls. Double interest is in Great Britain reckoned what the merchants call a good, moderate, reasonable profit, terms which . . . mean no more than a *common and usual profit*.'[10]

What is the *lowest* rate of profit? And what is the *highest*?

The *lowest rate* of ordinary profit on capitals must always be *something more* than what is sufficient to compensate the occasional losses to which every employment of capital is exposed. It is this surplus only which is the neat or clear profit. The same holds for the lowest rate of interest.[11]

The *highest rate* to which ordinary profits can rise may be such as, in the price of the greater part of commodities, *eats up the whole of the rent of the land* and reduces the wages of labour expended in preparing the commodity and bringing it to market to the *lowest rate*, the bare subsistence of the labourer. The workman must always have been fed in some way or other while he was about the work; but the rent of land can disappear entirely. Example: the servants of the East India Company in Bengal.[12]

Besides all the advantages of limited competition which the capitalist can *exploit* in such a case, he can keep the market price above the natural price by quite honourable means.

Firstly, by *secrets in trade*, where the market is at a great distance from the residence of those who supply it; that is, by concealing a change in price, an increase above the natural level. The effect of this concealment is that other capitalists do not invest their capital in this branch of industry.

Secondly, by *secrets in manufacture*, which enable the capitalist to cut production costs and sell his goods at the same price, or even at a lower price than his competitors, while making a bigger profit. (Deceit by concealment is not immoral? Dealings on the Stock Exchange.) Furthermore, where production is confined to a particular locality (as in the case of select wines) and the *effective demand* can never be satisfied. Finally, through monopolies granted to individuals or companies. The price of monopoly is the highest which can be got.[13]

Other chance causes which can raise the profit on capital:

The acquisition of new territory, or of new branches of trade, may sometimes raise the profits of stock even in a wealthy country, because part of the capital is withdrawn from the old

10. ibid., p. 87. 11. ibid., p. 86. 12. ibid., pp. 86–7.
13. ibid., pp. 53–4.

branches of trade, competition comes to be less than before, and the market is less fully supplied with commodities, the prices of which then rise: those who deal in these commodities can then afford to borrow at a higher interest.[14]

As any particular commodity comes to be more manufactured, that part of the price which resolves itself into wages and profit comes to be greater in proportion to that which resolves itself into rent. In the progress of the manufacture of a commodity, not only the number of the profits increase, but every subsequent profit is greater than the preceding one; because the capital from which it is derived must always be greater. The capital which employs the weavers, for example, must be greater than that which employs the spinners; because it not only replaces that capital with its profits, but pays, besides, the wages of the weavers; and the profits must always bear some proportion to the capital.[15]

So the growing role played by human labour in fashioning the natural product increases not the wages of labour but partly the number of profitable capitals and partly the size of each capital in proportion to those that precede it.

More later about the profit which the capitalist derives from the division of labour.

He profits in two ways: firstly from the division of labour and secondly, and more generally, from the growing role played by human labour in fashioning the natural product. The larger the human share in a commodity, the larger the profit of dead capital.

In one and the same society the average rates of profit on capital are more nearly upon a level than are the wages of different kinds of labour.[16] In the different employments of capital, the ordinary rate of profit varies more or less with the certainty or uncertainty of the returns; '. . . the ordinary profit of stock, though it rises with the risk, does not always seem to rise in proportion to it'.[17]

Needless to say, profits also rise if the means of circulation (e.g. paper money) improve or become less expensive.

3. The Rule of Capital over Labour and the Motives of the Capitalist

'The consideration of his own private profit is the sole motive which determines the owner of any capital to employ it either in

14. ibid., p. 83. 15. ibid., p. 45. 16. ibid.
17. ibid., pp. 99–100.

agriculture, in manufactures, or in some particular branch of the wholesale or retail trade. The different quantities of productive labour which it may put into motion, and the different values which it may add to the annual produce of the land and labour of the society, according as it is employed in one or other of those different ways, never enter into his thoughts.'[18]

'The most useful employment of capital for the capitalist is that which, with the same degree of security, yields him the largest profit; but this employment is not always the most useful for society ... the most useful is that which ... stimulates the productive power of its land and labour.'[19]

'The plans and projects of the employers of stock regulate and direct all the most important operations of labour, and profit is the end proposed by all those plans and projects. But the rate of profit does not, like rent and wages, rise with the prosperity and fall with the declension of the society. On the contrary, it is naturally low in rich and high in poor countries, and it is always highest in the countries which are going fastest to ruin. The interest of this third order,[20] therefore, has not the same connection with the general interest of the society as that of the other two ... The interest of the dealers, however, in any particular branch of trade or manufactures, is always in some respects different from, and even opposite to, that of the public. To widen the market and to narrow the competition, is always the interest of the dealers ... an order of men whose interest is never exactly the same as that of the public, who have generally an interest to deceive and even to oppress the public ...'[21]

4. The Accumulation of Capitals and the Competition among the Capitalists

The *increase of capitals*, which raises wages, tends to lower profits, as a result of the competition among capitalists.[22]

If, for example, the capital which is necessary for the grocery trade of a particular town 'is divided between two different grocers, their competition will tend to make both of them sell cheaper than if it were in the hands of one only; and if it were divided among twenty, their competition would be just so much

18. ibid., p. 335.
20. i.e. those who live by profit.
22. ibid., p. 78.

19. Say, op. cit., II, pp. 130–31.
21. Smith, op. cit., I, pp. 231–2.

the greater, and the chance of their combining together, in order to raise the price, just so much the less'.[23]

Since we already know that monopoly prices are as high as possible, since the interest of the capitalists, even from a straight-forwardly economic point of view, is opposed to the interest of society, and since the growth of profits acts on the price of the commodity like compound interest,[24] it follows that the sole defence against the capitalists is *competition*, which in the view of political economy has the beneficial effect both of raising wages and cheapening commodities to the advantage of the consuming public.

But competition is possible only if capitals multiply and are held by many different people. It is only possible to generate a large number of capitals as a result of multilateral accumulation, since capital in general stems from accumulation. But multilateral accumulation inevitably turns into unilateral accumulation. Competition among capitalists increases accumulation of capitals. Accumulation, which under the rule of private property means *concentration* of capital in few hands, inevitably ensues if capitals are allowed to follow their own natural course. It is only through competition that this natural proclivity of capital begins to take shape.

We have already seen that the profit on capital is in proportion to its size. If we ignore deliberate competition for the moment, a large capital accumulates more rapidly, in proportion to its size, than does a small capital.

This means that, quite apart from competition, the accumulation of large capital takes place at a much faster rate than that of small capital. But let us follow this process further.

As capitals multiply, the profits on capitals diminish, as a result of competition. So the first to suffer is the small capitalist.

Furthermore, the increase of capitals and the presence of a large number of capitals presupposes growing prosperity in a country.

'In a country which had acquired its full complement of riches, . . . as the ordinary rate of clear profit would be very small, so the usual market rate of interest which could be afforded out of it would be so low as to render it impossible for any but the very wealthiest of people to live upon the interest of their money. All people of small or middling fortunes would be obliged to super-

23. ibid., p. 322.　　　24. ibid., pp. 87–8.

intend themselves the employment of their own stocks. It would be necessary that almost every man should be a man of business, or engage in some sort of trade.'[25]

This is the situation most dear to the heart of political economy.

'The proportion between capital and revenue, therefore, seems everywhere to regulate the proportion between industry and idleness. Wherever capital predominates, industry prevails: wherever revenue, idleness.'[26]

But what about the employment of capital in this increased competition?

'As the quantity of stock to be lent at interest increases, the interest, or the price which must be paid for the use of that stock, necessarily diminishes, not only from those general causes, which make the market price of things commonly diminish as their quantity increases, but from other causes which are peculiar to this particular case. As capitals increase in any country, the profits which can be made by employing them necessarily diminish. It becomes gradually more and more difficult to find within the country a profitable method of employing any new capital. There arises in consequence a competition between different capitals, the owner of one endeavouring to get possession of that employment which is occupied by another. But on most occasions he can hope to jostle that other out of this employment by no other means but by dealing upon more reasonable terms. He must not only sell what he deals in somewhat cheaper, but in order to get it to sell, he must sometimes, too, buy it dearer. The demand for productive labour, by the increase of the funds which are destined for maintaining it, grows every day greater and greater. Labourers easily find employment, but the owners of capitals find it difficult to get labourers to employ. Their competition raises the wages of labour and sinks the profits of stock.'[27]

The small capitalist therefore has two choices: he can either consume his capital since he can no longer live on the interest, i.e. cease to be a capitalist; or he can himself set up a business, sell his goods at a lower price and buy them at a dearer price than the richer capitalist, and pay higher wages, which means that he would go bankrupt, since the market price is already very low as a result of the intense competition we presupposed. If, on the other hand, the big capitalist wants to squeeze out the smaller one, he has all the same advantages over him as the capitalist has over the

25. ibid., p. 86.   26. ibid., p. 301.   27. ibid., p. 316.

worker. He is compensated for the smaller profits by the larger size of his capital, and he can even put up with short-term losses until the smaller capitalist is ruined and he is freed of this competition. In this way he accumulates the profits of the small capitalist.

Furthermore: the big capitalist always buys more cheaply than the small capitalist, because he buys in larger quantities. He can therefore afford to sell at a lower price.

But if a fall in the rate of interest turns the middle capitalists from rentiers into businessmen, conversely the increase in business capitals and the resulting lower rate of profit produce a fall in the rate of interest.

'But when the profits which can be made by the use of a capital are diminished . . . the price which can be paid for the use of it, . . . must necessarily be diminished with them.'[28]

'As riches, improvement, and population have increased, interest has declined', and consequently the profits of stock; '. . . after these are diminished, stock may not only continue to increase, but to increase much faster than before . . . A great stock, though with small profits, generally increases faster than a small stock with great profits. Money, says the proverb, makes money.'[29]

So if this large capital is opposed by small capitals with small profits, as is the case under the conditions of intense competition which we have presupposed, it crushes them completely.

The inevitable consequence of this competition is the deterioration in the quality of goods, adulteration, spurious production and universal pollution to be found in large towns.

Another important factor in the competition between big and small capitals is the relationship between *fixed capital* and *circulating capital*.

Circulating capital is capital 'employed in raising, manufacturing or purchasing goods, and selling them again with a profit. The capital employed in this manner yields no revenue or profit to its employer, while it either remains in his possession or continues in the same shape . . . His capital is continually going from him in one shape, and returning to him in another, and it is only by means of such circulation, or successive exchanges, that it can yield him any profit . . .' *Fixed capital* is capital 'employed in the

28. ibid.　　29. ibid., p. 83.

improvement of land, in the purchase of useful machines and instruments, or in such like things . . .'

'. . . every saving in the expense of supporting the fixed capital is an improvement of the net revenue of the society. The whole capital of the undertaker of every work is necessarily divided between his fixed and his circulating capital. While his whole capital remains the same, the smaller the one part, the greater must necessarily be the other. It is the circulating capital which furnishes the materials and wages of labour, and puts industry into motion. Every saving, therefore, in the expense of maintaining the fixed capital, which does not diminish the productive powers of labour, must increase the fund which puts industry into motion . . .'[30]

It is immediately clear that the relation between fixed capital and circulating capital is much more favourable to the big capitalist than it is to the smaller capitalist. The difference in volume between the amount of fixed capital needed by a very big banker and the amount needed by a very small one is insignificant. The only fixed capital they need is an office. The equipment needed by a big landowner does not increase in proportion to the extent of his land. Similarly, the amount of credit available to a big capitalist, compared with a smaller one, represents a bigger saving in fixed capital, namely in the amount of money which he must have available at all times. Finally, it goes without saying that where industrial labour is highly developed, i.e. where almost all manual crafts have become factory labour, the entire capital of the small capitalist is not enough to procure for him even the necessary fixed capital. It is well known that large-scale [agricultural] cultivation generally requires only a small number of hands.

The accumulation of large capitals is generally accompanied by a concentration and simplification of fixed capital, as compared with the smaller capitalists. The big capitalist establishes for himself some kind of organization of the instruments of labour.

'Similarly, in the sphere of industry every factory and every workshop is a more comprehensive combination of a larger material property with numerous and varied intellectual abilities and technical skills which have as their *shared* aim the development of production . . . Where legislation preserves the unity of large landed properties, the surplus quantity of a growing popula-

30. ibid., p. 257.

tion crowds together into industry, and it is therefore mainly in industry that the proletariat gathers in large numbers, as in Great Britain. But where legislation allows the continuous division of the land, as in France, the number of small, debt-ridden proprietors increases and many of them are forced into the class of the needy and the discontented. Should this division and indebtedness go far enough, the large estate will once again swallow up the small estates, in the same way as big industry destroys small industry; and since larger landholding complexes once more come into being, many propertyless workers no longer needed on the land are, in this case too, forced into industry.'[31]

'The character of commodities of the same sort changes as a result of changes in the nature of production, and in particular as a result of mechanization. Only by eliminating human labour has it become possible to spin from a pound of cotton worth 3s. 8d., 350 hanks worth 25 guineas and 167 miles in length.'[32]

'On average the prices of cotton goods have fallen by eleven twelfths over the past 45 years, and according to Marshall's calculations a quantity of manufacture costing 16s. in 1814 now costs 1s. 10d. The drop in prices of industrial products has meant both a rise in home consumption and an increase in the foreign market; as a result, the number of cotton workers in Great Britain not only did not fall after the introduction of machinery, but rose from 40,000 to one and a half million. As for the earnings of industrial employers and workers, the growing competition among factory owners has inevitably resulted in a drop in profits in proportion to the quantity of products. Between 1820 and 1833 the gross profit made by Manchester manufacturers on a piece of calico fell from 4s. 1½d. to 1s. 9d. But to make up for this loss, the rate of production has been correspondingly increased. The consequence is that there have been instances of overproduction in some branches of industry; that there are frequent bankruptcies, which create fluctuations of property *within* the class of capitalists and masters of labour, and force a number of those who have been ruined economically into the ranks of the proletariat; and that frequent and sudden reductions in employment are necessary, which gives rise to feelings of bitterness among the class of wage-earners.'[33]

'To hire out one's labour is to begin one's enslavement; to hire

31. Schulz, op. cit., pp. 58–9.   32. ibid., p. 62.
33. ibid., p. 63.

out the materials of labour is to achieve one's freedom ... Labour is man, while matter contains nothing human.'[34]

'The element of matter, which can do nothing to create wealth without the element of *labour*, acquires the magical property of being fruitful for them,[35] as if they themselves had provided this indispensable element.'[36] 'If we assume that a worker can earn an average of 400 francs a year from his daily labour, and that this sum is sufficient for one adult to eke out a living, then anyone who receives 2,000 francs in interest or rent is indirectly forcing 5 men to work for him; an income of 100,000 francs represents the labour of 250 men, and 1,000,000 francs the labour of 2,500 (300 million – Louis Philippe – therefore represents the labour of 750,000 workers).'[37]

'The property owners have received from human law the right to use and abuse the materials of all labour, i.e. to do as they wish with them ... There is no law which obliges them punctually and at all times to provide work for those who do not own property or to pay them a wage which is at all times adequate, etc.'[38] 'Complete freedom as to the nature, the quantity, the quality and the appropriateness of production, the use and consumption of wealth and the disposal of the materials of all labour. Everyone is free to exchange his possessions as he chooses, without any other consideration than his own interest as an individual.'[39]

'Competition is simply an expression of free exchange, which is itself the immediate and logical consequence of the right of any individual to use and abuse all instruments of production. These three economic moments, which are in reality only one – the right to use and abuse, freedom of exchange and unrestricted competition – have the following consequences: each produces what he wants, how he wants, when he wants, where he wants; he produces well or he produces badly, too much or not enough, too late or too early, too dear or too cheap; no one knows whether he will sell, to whom he will sell, how he will sell, when he will sell, where he will sell; the same goes for buying. The producer is acquainted with neither the needs nor the resources, neither the demand nor the supply. He sells when he wants, when he can, where he wants, to whom he wants and at the price he wants. The same goes for buying. In all this he is at all times the plaything of

34. Pecqueur, op. cit., pp. 411–12.
36. Pecqueur, op. cit., p. 412.
38. ibid., p. 413.

35. i.e. for the property owners.
37. ibid., pp. 412–13.
39. ibid.

chance, the slave of the law of the strongest, of the least pressed, of the richest . . . While at one point there is a shortage of wealth, at another there is a surfeit and squandering of the same. While one producer sells a great deal, or at high prices and with an enormous profit, another sells nothing or sells at a loss . . . Supply is ignorant of demand, and demand is ignorant of supply. You produce on the basis of a preference or a fashion prevalent among the consuming public; but by the time you are preparing to put your commodity on the market, the mood has passed and some other kind of product has come into fashion . . . The inevitable consequences are continual and spreading bankruptcies, mis-calculations, sudden collapses and unexpected fortunes; trade crises, unemployment, periodic surfeits and shortages; instability and decline of wages and profits; the loss or enormous waste of wealth, of time and of effort in the arena of fierce competition.'[40]

Ricardo in his book[41] (rent of land): Nations are merely work-shops for production, and man is a machine for consuming and producing. Human life is a piece of capital. Economic laws rule the world blindly. For Ricardo men are nothing, the product everything. In Chapter 26 of the French translation we read:

'To an individual with a capital of £20,000, whose profits were £2,000 per annum, it would be a matter quite indifferent whether his capital would employ a hundred or a thousand men . . . is not the real interest of the nation similar? Provided its net real income, its rents and profits, be the same, it is of no importance whether the nation consists of ten or twelve million inhabitants.'[42] 'In truth,' says M. de Sismondi, 'it remains only to desire that the king, who has been left quite alone on the island, should, by continuously cranking up a number of automatons, get all England's work done.'[43]

'The master who buys a worker's labour at a price so low that it is barely enough to meet his most pressing needs is responsible neither for the low wages nor the long hours of work: he himself

40. ibid., pp. 414–16.

41. David Ricardo, *On the Principles of Political Economy, and Taxation*, London, 1817.

42. Ricardo, op. cit. (Everyman edition), pp. 234–5.

43. J. C. L. Simonde de Sismondi, *Nouveaux principes d'économie politique*, 2 vols., Paris, 1819, II, p. 331. The whole of this paragraph, including the passage from Ricardo, is taken from Buret, op. cit., I, pp. 6–7.

is subject to the law which he imposes ... Misery is the product not so much of men as of the power of things.'[44]

'The inhabitants of many different parts of Great Britain have not capital sufficient to improve and cultivate all their lands. The wool of the southern counties of Scotland is, a great part of it, after a long land carriage through very bad roads, manufactured in Yorkshire, for want of capital to manufacture it at home. There are many little manufacturing towns in Great Britain, of which the inhabitants have not capital sufficient to transport the produce of their own industry to those distant markets where there is demand and consumption for it. If there are any merchants among them, they are properly only the agents of wealthier merchants who reside in some of the greater commercial cities.'[45] 'The annual produce of the land and labour of any nation can be increased in its value by no other means but by increasing either the *number of its productive labourers*, or *the productive powers of those labourers* who had before been employed ... In either case, an additional capital is almost always required.'[46]

'As the *accumulation* of stock must, in the nature of things, be previous to the division of labour, so labour can be more and more subdivided in proportion only as stock is previously more and more accumulated. The quantity of materials which the same number of people can work up, increases in a great proportion as labour comes to be more and more subdivided; and as the operations of each workman are gradually reduced to a greater degree of simplicity, a variety of new machines come to be invented for facilitating and abridging these operations. As the division of labour advances, therefore, in order to give constant employment to an equal number of workmen, an equal stock of provisions, and a greater stock of materials and tools than what would have been necessary in a ruder state of things, must be accumulated beforehand. But the number of workmen in every branch of business generally increases with the division of labour in that branch, or rather it is the increase of their number which enables them to class and subdivide themselves in this manner.'[47]

'As the accumulation of stock is previously necessary for carrying on this great improvement in the productive powers of labour, so that accumulation naturally leads to this improvement. The person who employs his stock in maintaining labour, neces-

44. Buret, op. cit., I, p. 82.   45. Smith, op. cit., I, pp. 326–7.
46. ibid., pp. 306–7.   47. ibid., pp. 241–2.

sarily wishes to employ it in such a manner as to produce as great a quantity of work as possible. He endeavours, therefore, both to make among his workmen the most proper distribution of employment, and to furnish them with the best machines which he can either invent or afford to purchase. His abilities in both these respects are generally in proportion to the extent of his stock, or to the number of people it can employ. The quantity of industry, therefore, not only increases in every country with the increase of the stock which employs it, but, in consequence of that increase, the same quantity of industry produces a much greater quantity of work.'[48]

Hence *overproduction*.

'More extensive combinations of productive forces . . . in trade and industry through the unification of more numerous and more varied human and natural forces for undertakings on a larger scale. Also there are already a number of cases of closer links among the main branches of production themselves. Thus large manufacturers will try to acquire large estates in order to avoid depending on others for at least a part of the raw materials they need for their industry; or they will set up a trading concern linked to their industrial enterprises and not only sell their own products but buy up and retail other sorts of goods to their workers. In England, where there are some factory owners who employ between ten and twelve thousand workers . . . similar combinations of different branches of production under the control of *one* man, small states or provinces within a state, are not uncommon. For example, the mine-owners near *Birmingham* recently took over the *entire* process of iron production, which was previously in the hands of several different entrepreneurs and owners. See "Der bergmännische Distrikt bei Birmingham", *Deutsche Vierteljahrsschrift*, no. 3, 1838. Finally, in the larger joint-stock companies which have become so numerous, we find extensive combinations of the financial resources of *many* shareholders with the scientific and technical knowledge and skills of others to whom the execution of the work is entrusted. In this way it is possible for many capitalists to apply their savings in a more diversified way and even to invest them simultaneously in agricultural, industrial and commercial production; as a result, their interests also become more diversified and the conflict between agricultural, industrial and commercial interests begins to

48. ibid., p. 242.

fade away. But the greater ease with which capital can be employed fruitfully in the most varied fields inevitably increases the conflict between the propertied and the propertyless classes.'[49]

The enormous profit which the landlords make out of misery. The greater the misery caused by industry, the higher the rent.

It is the same with the rate of interest on the vices of the proletariat. (Prostitution, drinking, the pawnbroker.)

The accumulation of capitals increases and the competition between them diminishes, as capital and landed property are united together in one hand and capital is enabled, because of its size, to combine different branches of production.

Indifference towards men. Smith's twenty lottery tickets.[50]

Say's net and gross revenue.

Rent of Land

The right of the landowners can be traced back to robbery.[1] Landowners, like all other men, love to reap where they never sowed, and demand a rent even for the natural produce of the land.[2]

'The rent of land, it may be thought, is frequently no more than a reasonable profit or interest for the stock laid out by the landlord upon its improvement. This, no doubt, may be partly the case upon some occasions ... The landlord demands a rent even for unimproved land, and the supposed interest or profit upon the expense of improvement is generally an addition to this original rent. Those improvements, besides, are not always made by the stock of the landlord, but sometimes by that of the tenant. When the lease comes to be renewed, however, the landlord commonly demands the same augmentation of rent as if they had been all made by his own.

'He sometimes demands rent for what is altogether incapable of human improvement.'[3]

Smith gives as an example of this last case kelp, a species of

49. Schulz, op. cit., pp. 40–41.
50. This is a reference to the following passage from Smith, op. cit., I, p. 94: 'In a perfectly fair lottery, those who draw the prizes ought to gain all that is lost by those that draw the blanks. In a profession where twenty fail for one that succeeds, that one ought to gain all that should have been gained by the unsuccessful twenty.'
1. Say, op. cit., I, p. 136, n. 2.   2. Smith, op. cit., I, p. 44.
3. ibid., p. 131.

seaweed which, when burnt, yields an alkaline salt useful for making glass, soap, etc. It grows in several parts of Great Britain, especially in Scotland, but only upon such rocks as lie within the high water mark, which are twice every day covered with the sea and of which the produce, therefore, was never augmented by human industry. The landlord, however, whose estate is bounded by a kelp shore of this kind, demands a rent for it as much as for his corn fields. The sea in the neighbourhood of the islands of Shetland is more than commonly abundant in fish, which make a great part of the subsistence of their inhabitants. But in order to profit by the produce of the water, they must have a habitation on the neighbouring land. The rent of the landlord is in proportion, not to what the farmer can make by the land, but by what he can make both by the land and by the water.[4]

'This rent may be considered as the produce of those powers of nature, the use of which the landlord lends to the farmer. It is greater or smaller according to the supposed extent of those powers, or in other words, according to the supposed natural or improved fertility of the land. It is the work of nature which remains after deducting or compensating everything which can be regarded as the work of man.'[5]

'The rent of land, therefore, considered as the price paid for the use of the land, is naturally a monopoly price. It is not at all proportioned to what the landlord may have laid out upon the improvement of the land, or to what he can afford to take; but to what the farmer can afford to give.'[6]

'They[7] are the only ones of the three orders[8] whose revenue costs them neither labour nor care, but comes to them, as it were, of its own accord, and independent of any plan or project of their own.'[9]

We have already seen how the volume of rent depends upon the degree of *fertility* of the land.

'The rent of land not only varies with its *fertility*, whatever be its produce, but with its situation, whatever be its fertility.'[10]

'The produce of lands, mines and fisheries, when their natural fertility is equal, is in proportion to the extent and proper applica-

4. ibid.   5. ibid., pp. 324–5.   6. ibid., p. 131.
7. i.e. the landlords.
8. Smith's 'three great, original, and constituent orders of civilised society', those who live by rent, those who live by wages, and those who live by profit.
9. Smith, op. cit., I, p. 230.   10. ibid., p. 133.

tion of the capitals employed about them. When the capitals are equal and equally well applied, it is in proportion to their natural fertility.'[11]

These propositions of Smith are important, because they reduce the rent of land, where costs of production and size are equal, to the degree of fertility of the soil. This clearly demonstrates the perversion of concepts in political economy, which turns the fertility of the soil into an attribute of the landlord.

But let us now consider the rent of land as it is actually formed.

The rent of land is established through the *struggle between tenant and landlord*. Throughout political economy we find that the hostile opposition of interests, struggle and war are acknowledged as the basis of social organization.

Let us now examine the relation between landlord and tenant.

'In adjusting the terms of the lease, the landlord endeavours to leave him no greater share of the produce than what is sufficient to keep up the stock from which he furnishes the seed, pays the labour, and purchases and maintains the cattle and other instruments of husbandry, together with the ordinary profits of farming stock in the neighbourhood. This is evidently the smallest share with which the tenant can content himself without being a loser, and the landlord seldom means to leave him any more. Whatever part of the produce, or, what is the same thing, whatever part of the price is over and above this share, he naturally intends to reserve himself as the rent of his land, which is evidently the highest the tenant can afford to pay in the actual circumstances of the land ... This portion ... may still be considered as the natural rent of land, or the rent for which it is actually meant that land should for the most part be let.'[12]

'The landlords,' says Say, 'operate a certain kind of monopoly against the tenants. The demand for their commodity, which is land, is capable of an infinite expansion; but the supply can only increase up to a certain point ... The agreement reached between landlord and tenant is always as advantageous as possible to the former ... Apart from the advantage which he derives from the nature of the case, he derives a further one from his position, his larger fortune, his credit and his standing; but the first of these advantages is in itself enough to enable him at all times to profit from the favourable circumstances of the land. The opening of a canal or a road and a growth in population and prosperity in a

11. ibid., p. 249.   12. ibid., pp. 130–31.

canton always raise the price of the rent . . . What is more, even if the tenant makes improvements on his plot of land at his own expense, he can only benefit from this capital for the duration of his lease; when his lease runs out, this capital remains in the hands of the landlord. From this moment on it is the latter who reaps the interest, even though it was not he who made the original outlay; for now the rent is raised proportionately.'[13]

'Rent, considered as the price paid for the use of land, is naturally the highest which the tenant can afford to pay in the actual circumstances of the land.'[14]

'The rent of an estate above ground commonly amounts to what is supposed to be a third of the gross produce; and it is generally a rent certain and independent of the occasional variations in the crop.'[15] Rent 'is seldom less than a fourth, and frequently more than a third of the whole produce'.[16]

Ground rent cannot be paid in the case of all commodities. For example, in many districts no rent is paid for stones.

'Such parts only of the produce of land can commonly be brought to market of which the ordinary price is sufficient to replace the stock which must be employed in bringing them thither, together with its ordinary profits. If the ordinary price is more than this, the surplus part of it will naturally go to the rent of the land. If it is not more, though the commodity may be brought to market, it can afford no rent to the landlord. Whether the price is or is not more depends upon the demand.'[17]

'Rent, it is to be observed, therefore, enters into the composition of the price of commodities in a different way from wages and profit. High or low wages and profit are the causes of high or low prices; high or low rent is the effect of it.'[18]

Among the *products* which always yield a rent is *food*.

'As men, like all other animals, naturally multiply in proportion to the means of their subsistence, food is always, more or less, in demand. It can always purchase or command a greater or smaller quantity of labour, and somebody can always be found who is willing to do something in order to obtain it. The quantity of labour, indeed, which it can purchase is not always equal to what it could maintain, if managed in the most economical manner, on account of the high wages which are sometimes given to

13. Say, op. cit., II, pp. 142–3.   14. Smith, op. cit., I, p. 130.
15. ibid., p. 153.   16. ibid., p. 325.   17. ibid., p. 132.
18. ibid.

labour. But it can always purchase such a quantity of labour as it can maintain, according to the rate at which that sort of labour is commonly maintained in the neighbourhood.

'But land, in almost any situation, produces a greater quantity of food than what is sufficient to maintain all the labour necessary for bringing it to market in the most liberal way in which that labour is ever maintained. The surplus, too, is always more than sufficient to replace the stock which employed that labour, together with its profits. Something, therefore, always remains for a rent to the landlord.'[19]

'Food is in this manner not only the original source of rent, but every other part of the produce of land which afterwards affords rent derives that part of its value from the improvement of the powers of labour in producing food by means of the improvement and cultivation of land.'[20] 'Human food seems to be the only produce of land which always and necessarily affords a rent to the landlord.'[21] 'Countries are populous not in proportion to the number of people whom their produce can clothe and lodge, but in proportion to that of those whom it can feed.'[22]

'After food, clothing and lodging are the two great wants of mankind.'[23] They generally yield a rent, but not necessarily.

Let us now see how the landlord exploits everything which is to the benefit of society.

(1) The rent of land increases with population.[24]

(2) We have already learnt from Say how ground rent rises with railways, etc., and with the improvement, security and multiplication of the means of communication.

(3) '... every improvement in the circumstances of the society tends either directly or indirectly to raise the real rent of land, to increase the real wealth of the landlord, his power of purchasing the labour, or the produce of the labour of other people.'

'The extension of improvement and cultivation tends to raise it directly. The landlord's share of the produce necessarily increases with the increase of the produce.'

'That rise in the real price of those parts of the rude produce of land ... the rise in the price of cattle, for example, tends too to raise the rent of land directly, and in a still greater proportion. The real value of the landlord's share, his real command of the labour of other people, not only rises with the real value of the

19. ibid., pp. 132–3.   20. ibid., p. 150.   21. ibid., p. 147.
22. ibid., p. 149.   23. ibid., p. 147.   24. ibid., p. 146.

produce, but the proportion of his share to the whole produce rises with it. That produce, after the rise in its real price, requires no more labour to collect it than before. A smaller proportion of it will, therefore, be sufficient to replace, with the ordinary profit, the stock which employs that labour. A greater proportion of it must, consequently, belong to the landlord.'[25]

The greater demand for raw products and the consequent rise in their value may partly be a result of the increase in population and the growth of their needs. But every new invention and every new application in manufacture of a raw material which was previously not used at all or only used rarely, makes for an increase in the ground rent. For example, the rent of coal-mines rose enormously when railways, steamships, etc., were introduced.

Besides this advantage which the landlord derives from manufacture, discoveries and labour, there is another that we shall see presently.

(4) 'All those improvements in the productive powers of labour, which tend directly to reduce the real price of manufactures, tend indirectly to raise the real rent of land. The landlord exchanges that part of his rude produce, which is over and above his own consumption, or what comes to the same thing, the price of that part of it, for manufactured produce. Whatever reduces the real price of the latter, raises that of the former. An equal quantity of the former becomes thereby equivalent to a greater quantity of the latter; and the landlord is enabled to purchase a greater quantity of the conveniences, ornaments or luxuries, which he has occasion for.'[26]

But it is foolish to conclude, as Smith does, that since the landlord exploits everything which is of benefit to society, the interest of the landlord is always identical with that of society.[27] In the economic system, under the rule of private property, the interest which any individual has in society is in inverse proportion to the interest which society has in him, just as the interest of the moneylender in the spendthrift is not at all identical with the interest of the spendthrift.

We mention only in passing the landlord's obsession with monopoly directed against the landed property of foreign countries, which is the reason, for example, for the corn laws. We shall similarly pass over medieval serfdom, slavery in the colonies and the distress of the rural population – the day-labourers – in Great

25. ibid., pp. 228–9.   26. ibid., p. 229.   27. ibid., p. 230.

Britain. Let us confine ourselves to the propositions of political economy itself.

(1) The landlord's interest in the well-being of society means, according to the principles of political economy, that he is interested in the growth of its population and its production and the increase of its needs, in a word, in the increase of wealth; and the increase of wealth is, if our previous observations are correct, identical with the growth of misery and slavery. The relationship of rising rents and rising misery is one example of the landlord's interest in society, for a rise in house rent also means a rise in ground rent – the interest on the land on which the house stands.

(2) According to the political economists themselves the interest of the landlord is fiercely opposed to that of the tenant, and therefore of a considerable section of society.

(3) The landlord is in a position to demand more rent from the tenant the less wages the tenant pays out, and the more rent the landlord demands the further the tenant pushes down the wages. For this reason the landlord's interest is just as opposed to that of the farm labourer as the manufacturer's is to that of the workers. It likewise pushes wages down to a minimum.

(4) Since a real reduction in the price of manufactured products puts up the rent of land, the landowner has a direct interest in depressing the wages of the factory worker, in competition among the capitalists, in overproduction and in all the misery occasioned by industry.

(5) So the interest of the landowner, far from being identical with the interest of society, is fiercely opposed to the interests of the tenants, the farm labourers, the factory workers and the capitalists. But as a result of competition the interest of one landowner is not even identical with that of another. We shall now take a look at competition.

Generally speaking, large landed property and small landed property are in the same relation to one another as large and small capital. In addition, however, there are special circumstances which lead without fail to the accumulation of large landed property and the swallowing up of small properties.

(1) Nowhere does the number of workers and the amount of equipment decline so greatly in proportion to the size of the stock as in landed property. Similarly, nowhere does the possibility of many-sided exploitation, the saving of production costs and the judicious division of labour increase more in proportion to that

stock than in this sphere. Whatever the size of the plot, there is a certain minimum of tools required – a plough, a saw, etc. – below which it is impossible to go, whereas there is no such lowermost limit to the size of the property.

(2) Large landed property accumulates for itself the interest on the capital which the tenant has invested in the improvement of the land. Small landed property must employ its own capital. The entire profit on this capital is lost to the investor.

(3) While every social improvement benefits the large landed property, it harms the small one, since it makes an increasingly large amount of ready money necessary.

(4) There are two further important laws of this competition to be considered:

(a) '. . . the rent of the cultivated land, of which the produce is human food, regulates the rent of the greater part of the other cultivated land'.[28]

In the long run only the large estate can produce sources of food such as cattle, etc. It is therefore in a position to regulate the rent of other land and force it down to a minimum.

The small landowner who works on his own account is therefore in the same relation to the big landowner as the craftsman who owns his *own* tools is to the factory owner. The small estate has become a mere tool. Ground rent disappears entirely for the small landowner; at the most there remains to him the interest on his capital and the wages of his labour, for ground rent can be forced so low by competition that it becomes nothing more than the interest on capital not invested by the owner himself.

(b) Furthermore, we have already seen that given equal fertility and equally effective exploitation of lands, mines and fisheries, the produce is in proportion to the extent of capital employed. Hence the victory of the large landowner. Similarly, where equal amounts of capital are invested the produce is in proportion to the degree of fertility. That is to say, where capitals are equal victory goes to the owner of the more fertile land.

(c) 'A mine of any kind may be said to be either fertile or barren, according as the quantity of mineral which can be brought from it by a certain quantity of labour is greater or less than what can be brought by an equal quantity from the greater part of other mines of the same kind.'[29]

'The most fertile coal-mine, too, regulates the price of coals at

28. ibid., p. 144.   29. ibid., p. 151.

all the other mines in its neighbourhood. Both the proprietor and the undertaker of the work find, the one that he can get a greater rent, the other that he can get a greater profit by somewhat underselling all their neighbours. Their neighbours are soon obliged to sell at the same price, though they cannot so well afford it, and though it always diminishes, and sometimes takes away altogether both their rent and their profit. Some works are abandoned altogether; others can afford no rent, and can be wrought only by the proprietor.'[30] 'After the discovery of the mines of Peru, the silver-mines of Europe were, the greater part of them, abandoned . . . This was the case, too, with the ancient mines of Peru, after the discovery of those of Potosi.'[31]

What Smith says here of mines is more or less true of landed property in general.

(d) 'The ordinary market price of land, it is to be observed, depends everywhere upon the ordinary market rate of interest . . . if the rent of land should fall short of the interest of money by a greater difference, nobody would buy the land, which would soon reduce its ordinary price. On the contrary, if the advantages should much more than compensate the difference, everybody would buy the land, which would soon raise its ordinary price.'[32]

It follows from this relation between ground rent and interest on money that ground rent must continue to fall until eventually only the richest people can afford to live from it. This means an increase in competition between those landowners who do not lease out their land. Some of them are ruined. There is once again an accumulation of large landed property.

This competition has the further consequence that a large part of landed property falls into the hands of the capitalists; thus the capitalists become landowners, just as the smaller landowners are in general nothing more than capitalists. In this way a part of large landed property becomes industrial.

So the final consequence is the abolition of the distinction between capitalist and landowner, which means that in general there remain only two classes in the population – the working class and the capitalist class. This selling off of landed property and transformation of such property into a commodity marks the final collapse of the old aristocracy and the final victory of the aristocracy of money.

(1) We refuse to join in the sentimental tears which romanticism

30. ibid., pp. 152–3.   31. ibid., p. 154.   32. ibid., p. 320.

sheds on this account. Romanticism always confuses the infamy of *selling off the land* with the entirely reasonable and, within the system of private property, inevitable and desirable consequence of the *selling off of private property* in land. In the first place, feudal landed property is already in essence land which has been sold off, land which has been estranged from man and now confronts him in the shape of a handful of great lords.

In feudal landownership we already find the domination of the earth as of an alien power over men. The serf is an appurtenance of the land. Similarly the heir through primogeniture, the first-born son, belongs to the land. It inherits him. The rule of private property begins with property in land, which is its basis. But in the system of feudal landownership the lord at least *appears* to be king of the land. In the same way, there is still the appearance of a relationship between owner and land which is based on something more intimate than mere *material* wealth. The land is individualized with its lord, it acquires his status, it is baronial or ducal with him, has his privileges, his jurisdiction, his political position, etc. It appears as the inorganic body of its lord. Hence the proverb *nulle terre sans maître*,[33] which expresses the blending of nobility and landed property. In the same way the rule of landed property does not appear directly as the rule of mere capital. Its relationship to those dependent upon it is more like that of a fatherland. It is a sort of narrow nationality.

In the same way feudal landed property gives its name to its lord, as does a kingdom to its king. His family history, the history of his house, etc. – all this individualizes his estate for him, and formally turns it into his house, into a person. Similarly, the workers on the estate are not in the position of *day-labourers*; rather, they are partly the property of the landowner, as are serfs, and they are partly linked to him through a relationship based on respect, submissiveness and duty. His relation to them is therefore directly political, and even has an *agreeable* aspect. Customs, character, etc., vary from one estate to another and appear to be one with their particular stretch of land; later, however, it is only a man's purse, and not his character or individuality, which ties him to the land. Finally, the feudal landowner makes no attempt to extract the maximum profit from his property. Rather, he consumes what is there and leaves the harvesting of it to his serfs

33. No land without its master.

and tenants. Such is the *aristocratic* condition of landownership, which sheds a romantic glory on its lords.

It is inevitable that this appearance should be abolished and that landed property, which is the root of private property, should be drawn entirely into the orbit of private property and become a commodity; that the rule of the property owner should appear as the naked rule of private property, of capital, divested of all political tincture; that the relationship between property owner and worker should be reduced to the economic relationship of exploiter and exploited; that the personal relationship between the property owner and his property should come to an end, and that the property itself should become purely *material* wealth; that the marriage of interest with the land should take over from the marriage of honour, and that land, like man, should sink to the level of a venal object. It is inevitable that the root of landed property – sordid self-interest – should also manifest itself in its cynical form. It is inevitable that immovable monopoly should become mobile and restless monopoly, competition; and that the idle enjoyment of the products of the sweat and blood of other people should become a brisk commerce in the same. Finally, it is inevitable under these conditions of competition that landed property, in the form of capital, should manifest its domination both over the working class and over the property owners themselves, inasmuch as the laws of the movement of capital are either ruining or raising them. In this way the medieval saying *nulle terre sans seigneur* gives way to the modern saying *l'argent n'a pas de maître*,[34] which is an expression of the complete domination of dead matter over men.

(2) The following observations can be made in connection with the controversy over whether or not to divide up landed property.

The *division of landed property* negates the *large-scale monopoly* of landed property, abolishes it, but only by *generalizing* it. It does not abolish the basis of monopoly, which is private property. It attacks the existence, but not the essence, of monopoly. The consequence is that it falls foul of the laws of private property. For to divide up landed property corresponds to the movement of competition in the industrial sphere. Apart from the economic disadvantages of this division of the instruments of labour and separation of labour (not to be confused with the division of

34. Money knows no master.

labour: this is not a case of dividing up work among a number of individuals, but of each individual doing the same work; it is a multiplication of the same work), this division of the land, like competition in industry, inevitably leads to further accumulation.

So wherever landed property is divided up, monopoly will inevitably reappear in an even more repulsive form – unless, that is, the division of landed property itself is negated or abolished. This does not mean a return to feudal property, but the abolition [*Aufhebung*] of private property in land altogether. The first step in the abolition of monopoly is always to generalize and extend its existence. The abolition of monopoly, when it has reached its broadest and most comprehensive existence, is its complete destruction. Association, when applied to the land, retains the benefits of large landed property from an economic point of view and realizes for the first time the tendency inherent in the division of land, namely equality. At the same time association restores man's intimate links to the land in a rational way, no longer mediated by serfdom, lordship and an imbecile mystique of property. This is because the earth ceases to be an object of barter, and through free labour and free enjoyment once again becomes an authentic, personal property for man. One great advantage of the division of the land is that its masses, who are no longer prepared to tolerate servitude, are destroyed by property in a different way from those in industry.

As for large landed property, its apologists have always sophistically identified the economic advantages inherent in large-scale agriculture with large landed property, as if these advantages would not on the one hand attain their fullest degree of development and on the other hand become socially useful for the first time once property was abolished. Similarly they have attacked the trading spirit of the small landowners, as if large-scale landownership, even in its feudal form, did not already contain within it the elements of barter – not to mention the modern English form, in which the feudalism of the landowner is combined with the huckstering and the industry of the tenant farmer.

Just as large-scale landed property can return the reproach of monopoly made against it by the advocates of division of the land, for the division of the land is also based on the monopoly of private property, so can the advocates of division return the reproach of partition, for partition of the land also exists – though in a rigid, ossified form – on the large estates. Indeed, division is the universal basis of private property. Besides, as the division of landed property leads once more to large landed property in the form of capital wealth, feudal landed property inevitably advances towards division or at least falls into the hands of the capitalists, however much it might twist and turn.

For large-scale landed property, as in England, drives the overwhelming majority of the population into the arms of industry and reduces its own workers to total misery. In this way it creates and increases the power of its enemy, capital and industry, by driving the poor and an entire range of activities over to the other side. It makes the majority of the country industrial, and hence antagonistic to landed property. Where industry has acquired great power, as in England, it gradually forces large landed property to give up its monopoly against foreign countries and obliges it to compete with foreign landed property. For under the rule of industry, landed property could maintain its feudal proportions only by means of a monopoly against foreign countries, so as to protect itself against the universal laws of trade which contradict its feudal nature. Once exposed to competition it is forced to obey the laws of competition, just like any other commodity which is subjected to them. It too begins to fluctuate, to increase and diminish, to fly from one hand into another, and no law is any longer capable of keeping it in a few predestined hands. The immediate consequence is its fragmentation into many hands, or at any event surrender to the power of the industrial capitalists.

Finally, large landed property which has been forcibly preserved in this way and which has given rise alongside itself to an extensive industry leads more rapidly to a crisis than does the division of landed property, alongside which the power of industry invariably takes second place.

It is clear from the case of England that large landed property has cast off its feudal character and assumed an industrial character in so far as it wants to make as much money as possible. It yields the owner the biggest possible rent and the tenant the biggest possible profit on his capital. As a consequence the agricultural workers have already been reduced to a minimum, and the class of tenant farmers already represents within landed property the might of industry and capital. As a result of foreign competition, ground rent more or less ceases to be an independent source of income. A large part of the landowners is forced to take over from the tenants, some of whom are consequently reduced to the proletariat. On the other hand, many tenants will take possession of landed property; for the big landowners, who have given themselves up for the most part to squandering their comfortable revenue and are generally not capable of large-scale agricultural management, in many cases have neither the capital nor the ability to exploit the land. Therefore a section of the big landowners is also ruined. Eventually wages, which have already been reduced to a minimum, must be reduced even further in order to meet the new competition. This then leads necessarily to revolution.

Landed property had to develop in each of these two ways, in order to experience in both of them its necessary decline; just as industry had to ruin itself both in the form of monopoly and in the form of competition before it could believe in man.

Estranged Labour

We have started out from the premises of political economy. We have accepted its language and its laws. We presupposed private property; the separation of labour, capital and land, and likewise of wages, profit and capital; the division of labour; competition; the concept of exchange value, etc. From political economy itself, using its own words, we have shown that the worker sinks to the level of a commodity, and moreover the most wretched commodity of all; that the misery of the worker is in inverse proportion to the power and volume of his production; that the necessary consequence of competition is the accumulation of capital in a few hands and hence the restoration of monopoly in a more terrible form; and that finally the distinction between capitalist and landlord, between agricultural worker and industrial worker, disappears and the whole of society must split into the two classes of *property owners* and propertyless *workers*.

Political economy proceeds from the fact of private property. It does not explain it. It grasps the *material* process of private property, the process through which it actually passes, in general and abstract formulae which it then takes as *laws*. It does not *comprehend* these laws, i.e. it does not show how they arise from the nature of private property. Political economy fails to explain the reason for the division between labour and capital, between capital and land. For example, when it defines the relation of wages to profit it takes the interests of the capitalists as the basis of its analysis; i.e. it assumes what it is supposed to explain. Similarly, competition is frequently brought into the argument and explained in terms of external circumstances. Political economy teaches us nothing about the extent to which these external and apparently accidental circumstances are only the expression of a necessary development. We have seen how exchange itself appears to political economy as an accidental fact. The only wheels which political economy sets in motion are *greed* and the *war of the avaricious – competition*.

Precisely because political economy fails to grasp the interconnections within the movement, it was possible to oppose, for example, the doctrine of competition to the doctrine of monopoly, the doctrine of craft freedom to the doctrine of the guild and the doctrine of the division of landed property to the doctrine of the great estate; for competition, craft freedom and division of landed property were developed and conceived only as accidental, deliberate, violent consequences of monopoly, of the guilds and of feudal property and not as their necessary, inevitable and natural consequences.

We now have to grasp the essential connection between private property, greed, the separation of labour, capital and landed property, exchange and competition, value and the devaluation [*Entwertung*] of man, monopoly and competition, etc. – the connection between this entire system of estrangement [*Entfremdung*] and the *money* system.

We must avoid repeating the mistake of the political economist, who bases his explanations on some imaginary primordial condition. Such a primordial condition explains nothing. It simply pushes the question into the grey and nebulous distance. It assumes as facts and events what it is supposed to deduce, namely the necessary relationship between two things, between, for example, the division of labour and exchange. Similarly, theology explains the origin of evil by the fall of man, i.e. it assumes as a fact in the form of history what it should explain.

We shall start out from a *present-day* economic fact.

The worker becomes poorer the more wealth he produces, the more his production increases in power and extent. The worker becomes an ever cheaper commodity the more commodities he produces. The *devaluation* of the human world grows in direct proportion to the *increase in value* of the world of things. Labour not only produces commodities; it also produces itself and the workers as a *commodity* and it does so in the same proportion in which it produces commodities in general.

This fact simply means that the object that labour produces, its product, stands opposed to it as *something alien*, as a *power independent* of the producer. The product of labour is labour embodied and made material in an object, it is the *objectification* of labour. The realization of labour is its objectification. In the sphere of political economy this realization of labour appears as a *loss of reality* for the worker, objectification as *loss of and bondage to the object*, and appropriation as *estrangement*, as *alienation* [*Entäusserung*].

So much does the realization of labour appear as loss of reality that the worker loses his reality to the point of dying of starvation. So much does objectification appear as loss of the object that the worker is robbed of the objects he needs most not only for life but also for work. Work itself becomes an object which he can only obtain through an enormous effort and with spasmodic interruptions. So much does the appropriation of the object appear as estrangement that the more objects the worker produces the fewer can he possess and the more he falls under the domination of his product, of capital.

All these consequences are contained in this characteristic, that the worker is related to the *product of his labour* as to an *alien* object. For it is clear that, according to this premise, the more the worker exerts himself in his work, the more powerful the alien, objective world becomes which he brings into being over against himself, the poorer he and his inner world become, and the less they belong to him. It is the same in religion. The more man puts into God, the less he retains within himself. The worker places his life in the object; but now it no longer belongs to him, but to the object. The greater his activity, therefore, the fewer objects the worker possesses. What the product of his labour is, he is not. Therefore, the greater this product, the less is he himself. The externalization [*Entäusserung*] of the worker in his product means not only that his labour becomes an object, an *external* existence, but that it exists *outside him*, independently of him and alien to him, and begins to confront him as an autonomous power; that the life which he has bestowed on the object confronts him as hostile and alien.

Let us now take a closer look at *objectification*, at the production of the worker, and the *estrangement*, the *loss* of the object, of his product, that this entails.

The worker can create nothing without *nature*, without the *sensuous external world*. It is the material in which his labour realizes itself, in which it is active and from which and by means of which it produces.

But just as nature provides labour with the *means of life* in the sense that labour cannot *live* without objects on which to exercise itself, so also it provides the *means of life* in the narrower sense, namely the means of physical subsistence of the *worker*.

The more the worker *appropriates* the external world, sensuous nature, through his labour, the more he deprives himself of the *means of life* in two respects: firstly, the sensuous external world becomes less and less an object belonging to his labour, a *means of life* of his labour; and secondly, it becomes less and less a *means of life* in the immediate sense, a means for the physical subsistence of the worker.

In these two respects, then, the worker becomes a slave of his object; firstly in that he receives an *object of labour*, i.e. he receives work, and secondly in that he receives *means of subsistence*. Firstly, then, so that he can exist as a *worker*, and secondly as a *physical subject*. The culmination of this slavery is that it is only as a *worker* that he can maintain himself as a *physical subject* and only as a *physical subject* that he is a worker.

(The estrangement of the worker in his object is expressed according to the laws of political economy in the following way: the more the worker produces, the less he has to consume; the more values he creates, the more worthless he becomes; the more his product is shaped, the more misshapen the worker; the more civilized his object, the more barbarous the worker; the more powerful the work, the more powerless the worker; the more intelligent the work, the duller the worker and the more he becomes a slave of nature.)

Political economy conceals the estrangement in the nature of labour by ignoring the **direct** *relationship between the* **worker** (labour) **and production**. It is true that labour produces marvels for the rich, but it produces privation for the worker. It produces palaces, but hovels for the worker. It produces beauty, but deformity for the worker. It replaces labour by machines, but it casts some of the workers back into barbarous forms of labour and turns others into machines. It produces intelligence, but it produces idiocy and cretinism for the worker.

The direct relationship of labour to its products is the relationship of the worker to the objects of his production. The relationship of the rich man to the objects of production and to production itself is only a *consequence* of this first relationship, and confirms it. Later we shall consider this second aspect. Therefore when we ask what is the essential relationship of labour, we are asking about the relationship of the worker to production.

Up to now we have considered the estrangement, the alienation of the worker only from one aspect, i.e. his *relationship to the products of his labour*. But estrangement manifests itself not only in the result, but also in the *act of production*, within the *activity of production* itself. How could the product of the worker's activity confront him as something alien if it were not for the fact that in the act of production he was estranging himself from himself? After all, the product is simply the résumé of the activity, of the production. So if the product of labour is alienation, production itself must be active alienation, the alienation of activity, the activity of alienation. The estrangement of the object of labour merely summarizes the estrangement, the alienation in the activity of labour itself.

What constitutes the alienation of labour?

Firstly, the fact that labour is *external* to the worker, i.e. does not belong to his essential being; that he therefore does not confirm himself in his work, but denies himself, feels miserable and not happy, does not develop free mental and physical energy, but mortifies his flesh and ruins his mind. Hence the worker feels himself only when he is not working; when he is working he does not feel himself. He is at home when he is not working, and not at home when he is working. His labour is therefore not voluntary but forced, it is *forced labour*. It is therefore not the satisfaction of a need but a mere *means* to satisfy needs outside itself. Its alien character is clearly demonstrated by the fact that as soon as no physical or other compulsion exists it is shunned like the plague. External labour, labour in which man alienates himself, is a labour of self-sacrifice, of mortification. Finally, the external character of labour for the worker is demonstrated by the fact that it belongs not to him but to another, and that in it he belongs not to himself but to another. Just as in religion the spontaneous activity of the human imagination, the human brain and the human heart detaches itself from the individual and reappears as the alien activity of a god or of a devil, so the activity of the worker is not his own spontaneous activity. It belongs to another, it is a loss of his self.

The result is that man (the worker) feels that he is acting freely only in his animal functions – eating, drinking and procreating, or at most in his dwelling and adornment – while in his human functions he is nothing more than an animal.

It is true that eating, drinking and procreating, etc., are also genuine human functions. However, when abstracted from other aspects of human activity and turned into final and exclusive ends, they are animal.

We have considered the act of estrangement of practical human activity, of labour, from two aspects: (1) the relationship of the worker to the *product of labour* as an alien object that has power over him. This relationship is at the same time the relationship to the sensuous external world, to natural objects, as an alien world confronting him in hostile opposition. (2) The relationship of labour to the *act of production* within *labour*. This relationship is the relationship of the worker to his own activity as something which is alien and does not belong to him, activity as passivity [*Leiden*], power as impotence, procreation as emasculation, the worker's *own* physical and mental energy, his personal life – for what is life but activity? – as an activity directed against himself, which is independent of him and does not belong to him. *Self-estrangement*, as compared with the estrangement of the *object* [*Sache*] mentioned above.

We now have to derive a third feature of *estranged labour* from the two we have already looked at.

Man is a species-being, not only because he practically and theoretically makes the species – both his own and those of other things – his object, but also – and this is simply another way of saying the same thing – because he looks upon himself as the present, living species, because he looks upon himself as a *universal* and therefore free being.

Species-life, both for man and for animals, consists physically in the fact that man, like animals, lives from inorganic nature; and because man is more universal than animals, so too is the area of inorganic nature from which he lives more universal. Just as plants, animals, stones, air, light, etc., theoretically form a part of human consciousness, partly as objects of science and partly as objects of art – his spiritual inorganic nature, his spiritual means of life, which he must first prepare before he can enjoy and digest them – so too in practice they form a part of human life and human activity. In a physical sense man lives only from these natural products, whether in the form of nourishment, heating, clothing, shelter, etc. The universality of man manifests itself in practice in that universality which makes the whole of nature his *inorganic* body, (1) as a direct means of life and (2) as the matter, the object and the tool of his life activity. Nature is man's *inorganic body,* that is to say nature in so far as it is not the human body. Man *lives* from nature, i.e. nature is his *body,* and he must maintain a continuing dialogue with it if he is not to die. To say that man's physical and mental life is linked to nature simply means that nature is linked to itself, for man is a part of nature.

Estranged labour not only (1) estranges nature from man and (2) estranges man from himself, from his own active function, from his vital activity; because of this it also estranges man from his *species*. It turns his *species-life* into a means for his individual life. Firstly it estranges species-life and individual life, and secondly it turns the latter, in its abstract form, into the purpose of the former, also in its abstract and estranged form.

For in the first place labour, *life activity, productive life* itself appears to man only as a *means* for the satisfaction of a need, the need to preserve physical existence. But productive life is species-life. It is life-producing life. The whole character of a species, its species-character, resides in the nature of its life activity, and free conscious activity constitutes the species-character of man. Life itself appears only as a *means of life.*

The animal is immediately one with its life activity. It is not distinct from that activity; it *is* that activity. Man makes his life activity itself an object of his will and consciousness. He has conscious life activity. It is not a determination with which he directly merges. Conscious life activity directly distinguishes man from animal life activity. Only because of that is he a species-being. Or rather, he is a conscious being, i.e. his own life is an object for him, only because he is a species-being. Only because of that is his activity free activity. Estranged labour reverses the relationship so that man, just because he is a conscious being, makes his life activity, his *being* [*Wesen*], a mere means for his *existence.*

The practical creation of an *objective world,* the *fashioning* of inorganic nature, is proof that man is a conscious species-being, i.e. a being which treats the species as its own essential being or itself as a species-being. It is true that animals also produce. They build nests and dwellings, like the bee, the beaver, the ant, etc. But they produce only their own immediate needs or those of their young; they produce one-sidedly, while man produces universally; they produce only when immediate physical need compels them to do so, while man produces even when he is free from physical need and truly produces only in freedom from such need; they produce only themselves, while man reproduces the whole of nature; their products belong immediately to their physical bodies, while man freely confronts his own product. Animals produce only according to the standards and needs of the species to which they belong, while man is capable of producing according to the standards of every species and of applying to each object its inherent standard; hence man also produces in accordance with the laws of beauty.

It is therefore in his fashioning of the objective that man really proves himself to be a *species-being*. Such production is his active species-life. Through it nature appears as *his* work and his reality. The object of labour is therefore the *objectification of the species-life of man*: for man reproduces himself not only intellectually, in his consciousness, but actively and actually, and he can therefore contemplate himself in a world he himself has created. In tearing away the object of his production from man, estranged labour therefore tears away from him his *species-life*, his true species-objectivity, and transforms his advantage over animals into the disadvantage that his inorganic body, nature, is taken from him.

In the same way as estranged labour reduces spontaneous and free activity to a means, it makes man's species-life a means of his physical existence.

Consciousness, which man has from his species, is transformed through estrangement so that species-life becomes a means for him.

(3) Estranged labour therefore turns *man's species-being* – both nature and his intellectual species-powers – into a being *alien* to him and a *means* of his *individual existence*. It estranges man from his own body, from nature as it exists outside him, from his spiritual essence [*Wesen*], his *human* essence.

(4) An immediate consequence of man's estrangement from the

product of his labour, his life activity, his species-being, is the *estrangement of man from man*. When man confronts himself, he also confronts *other* men. What is true of man's relationship to his labour, to the product of his labour and to himself, is also true of his relationship to other men, and to the labour and the object of the labour of other men.

In general, the proposition that man is estranged from his species-being means that each man is estranged from the others and that all are estranged from man's essence.

Man's estrangement, like all relationships of man to himself, is realized and expressed only in man's relationship to other men.

In the relationship of estranged labour each man therefore regards the other in accordance with the standard and the situation in which he as a worker finds himself.

We started out from an economic fact, the estrangement of the worker and of his production. We gave this fact conceptual form: *estranged, alienated* labour. We have analysed this concept, and in so doing merely analysed an economic fact.

Let us now go on to see how the concept of estranged, alienated labour must express and present itself in reality.

If the product of labour is alien to me and confronts me as an alien power, to whom does it then belong?

To a being *other* than me.

Who is this being?

The *gods*? It is true that in early times most production – e.g. temple building, etc., in Egypt, India and Mexico – was in the service of the gods, just as the product belonged to the gods. But the gods alone were never the masters of labour. The same is true of *nature*. And what a paradox it would be if the more man subjugates nature through his labour and the more divine miracles are made superfluous by the miracles of industry, the more he is forced to forgo the joy of production and the enjoyment of the product out of deference to these powers.

The *alien* being to whom labour and the product of labour belong, in whose service labour is performed and for whose enjoyment the product of labour is created, can be none other than *man* himself.

If the product of labour does not belong to the worker, and if it confronts him as an alien power, this is only possible because it belongs to *a man other than the worker*. If his activity is a torment for him, it must provide *pleasure* and enjoyment for someone else. Not the gods, not nature, but only man himself can be this alien power over men.

Consider the above proposition that the relationship of man to himself becomes *objective* and *real* for him only through his relationship to other men. If therefore he regards the product of his labour, his objectified labour, as an *alien, hostile* and powerful object which is independent of him, then his relationship to that object is such that another man – alien, hostile, powerful and independent of him – is its master. If he relates to his own activity as unfree activity, then he relates to it as activity in the service, under the rule, coercion and yoke of another man.

Every self-estrangement of man from himself and nature is manifested in the relationship he sets up between other men and himself and nature. Thus religious self-estrangement is necessarily manifested in the relationship between layman and priest, or, since we are here dealing with the spiritual world, between layman and mediator, etc. In the practical, real world, self-estrangement can manifest itself only in the practical, real relationship to other men. The medium through which estrangement progresses is itself a *practical* one. So through estranged labour man not only produces his relationship to the object and to the act of production as to alien and hostile powers[1]; he also produces the relationship in which other men stand to his production and product, and the relationship in which he stands to these other men. Just as he creates his own production as a loss of reality, a punishment, and his own product as a loss, a product which does not belong to him, so he creates the domination of the non-producer over production and its product. Just as he estranges from himself his own activity, so he confers upon the stranger an activity which does not belong to him.

Up to now we have considered the relationship only from the side of the worker. Later on we shall consider it from the side of the non-worker.

Thus through *estranged, alienated labour* the worker creates the relationship of another man, who is alien to labour and stands outside it, to that labour. The relation of the worker to labour creates the relation of the capitalist – or whatever other word one chooses for the master of labour – to that labour. *Private property* is therefore the product, result and necessary consequence of

1. In the original manuscript Marx wrote the word *Menschen* (men) and not *Mächten* (powers).

alienated labour, of the external relation of the worker to nature and to himself.

Private property thus derives from an analysis of the concept of *alienated labour*, i.e. *alienated man*, estranged labour, estranged life, *estranged man*.

It is true that we took the concept of *alienated labour* (*alienated life*) from political economy as a result of the *movement of private property*. But it is clear from an analysis of this concept that, although private property appears as the basis and cause of alienated labour, it is in fact its consequence, just as the gods were *originally* not the cause but the effect of the confusion in men's minds. Later, however, this relationship becomes reciprocal.

It is only when the development of private property reaches its ultimate point of culmination that this its secret re-emerges: namely, that it is (a) the *product* of alienated labour and (b) the *means* through which labour is alienated, the *realization of this alienation*.

This development throws light upon a number of hitherto unresolved controversies.

(1) Political economy starts out from labour as the real soul of production, and yet gives nothing to labour and everything to private property. Proudhon has dealt with this contradiction by deciding for labour and against private property.[2] But we have seen that this apparent contradiction is the contradiction of *estranged labour* with itself and that political economy has merely formulated the laws of estranged labour.

It therefore follows for us that *wages* and *private property* are identical: for where the product, the object of labour, pays for the labour itself, wages are only a necessary consequence of the estrangement of labour; similarly, where wages are concerned, labour appears not as an end in itself but as the servant of wages. We intend to deal with this point in more detail later on: for the present we shall merely draw a few conclusions.

An enforced *rise in wages* (disregarding all other difficulties, including the fact that such an anomalous situation could only be prolonged by force) would therefore be nothing more than better *pay for slaves* and would not mean an increase in human significance or dignity for either the worker or the labour.

Even the *equality of wages*, which Proudhon demands, would merely transform the relation of the present-day worker to his

2. In the pamphlet entitled *Qu'est-ce que la propriété?*, Paris, 1840.

work into the relation of all men to work. Society would then be conceived as an abstract capitalist.

Wages are an immediate consequence of estranged labour, and estranged labour is the immediate cause of private property. If the one falls, then the other must fall too.

(2) It further follows from the relation of estranged labour to private property that the emancipation of society from private property, etc., from servitude, is expressed in the *political* form of the *emancipation of the workers*. This is not because it is only a question of their emancipation, but because in their emancipation is contained universal human emancipation. The reason for this universality is that the whole of human servitude is involved in the relation of the worker to production, and all relations of servitude are nothing but modifications and consequences of this relation.

Just as we have arrived at the concept of *private property* through an *analysis* of the concept of *estranged, alienated labour*, so with the help of these two factors it is possible to evolve all economic *categories*, and in each of these categories, e.g. trade, competition, capital, money, we shall identify only a *particular* and *developed expression* of these basic constituents.

But before we go on to consider this configuration let us try to solve two further problems.

(1) We have to determine the general *nature* of *private property*, as it has arisen out of estranged labour, in its relation to *truly human* and *social property*.

(2) We have taken the *estrangement of labour*, its *alienation*, as a fact and we have analysed that fact. How, we now ask, does *man* come *to alienate his labour*, to estrange it? How is this estrangement founded in the nature of human development? We have already gone a long way towards solving this problem by *transforming* the question of the *origin* of *private property* into the question of the relationship of *alienated labour* to the course of human development. For in speaking of *private property* one imagines that one is dealing with something external to man. In speaking of labour one is dealing immediately with man himself. This new way of formulating the problem already contains its solution.

ad (1): The general nature of private property and its relationship to truly human property.

Alienated labour has resolved itself for us into two component parts which mutually condition one another, or which are merely different expressions of one and the same relationship. *Appropriation* appears as *estrangement*, as *alienation*; and *alienation* appears as *appropriation*, *estrangement* as true *admission to citizenship*.

We have considered the one aspect, *alienated* labour in relation to the *worker* himself, i.e. the *relation of alienated labour to itself*. And as product, as necessary consequence of this relationship we have found the *property relation of the non-worker* to the *worker and to labour. Private property* as the material, summarized expression of alienated labour embraces both relations – the *relation of the worker to labour and to the product of his labour and the non-worker* and the relation of the *non-worker to the worker* and to *the product of his labour*.

We have already seen that, in relation to the worker who *appropriates* nature through his labour, appropriation appears as estrangement, self-activity as activity for another and of another, vitality as a sacrifice of life, production of an object as loss of that object to an alien power, to an *alien* man. Let us now consider the relation between this man, who is *alien* to labour and to the worker, and the worker, labour, and the object of labour.

The first thing to point out is that everything which appears for the worker as an *activity of alienation, of estrangement*, appears for the non-worker as a *situation of alienation, of estrangement*.

Secondly, the *real, practical attitude* of the worker in production and to the product (as a state of mind) appears for the non-worker who confronts him as a *theoretical* attitude.

Thirdly, the non-worker does everything against the worker which the worker does against himself, but he does not do against himself what he does against the worker.

Let us take a closer look at these three relationships.[3]

SECOND MANUSCRIPT

The Relationship of Private Property

. . . forms the interest on his capital.[1] The worker is the subjective manifestation of the fact that capital is man completely lost to

3. The first manuscript breaks off at this point.
1. Page XL of the second manuscript begins with these words; the previous pages of the manuscript are missing.

himself, just as capital is the objective manifestation of the fact that labour is man lost to himself. But the *worker* has the misfortune to be a *living* capital, and hence a capital *with needs*, which forfeits its interest and hence its existence every moment it is not working. As capital, the *value* of the worker rises or falls in accordance with supply and demand, and even in a *physical* sense his *existence*, his *life*, was and is treated as a supply of a *commodity*, like any other commodity. The worker produces capital and capital produces him, which means that he produces himself; man as a *worker*, as a *commodity*, is the product of this entire cycle. The human properties of man as a worker – man who is nothing more than a *worker* – exist only in so far as they exist for a capital which is *alien* to him. But because each is alien to the other and stands in an indifferent, external and fortuitous relationship to it, this alien character inevitably appears as something *real*. So as soon as it occurs to capital – whether from necessity or choice – not to exist any longer for the worker, he no longer exists for himself; he has *no* work, and hence *no* wages, and since he exists not *as a man* but *as a worker*, he might just as well have himself buried, starve to death, etc. The worker exists as a worker only when he exists *for himself* as capital, and he exists as capital only when *capital* exists *for him*. The existence of capital is *his* existence, his *life*, for it determines the content of his life in a manner indifferent to him. Political economy therefore does not ɪecognize the unoccupied worker, the working man in so far as he is outside this work relationship. The swindler, the cheat, the beggar, the unemployed, the starving, the destitute and the criminal working man are *figures* which exist not *for it*, but only for other eyes – for the eyes of doctors, judges, grave-diggers, beadles, etc. Nebulous figures which do not belong within the province of political economy. Therefore as far as political economy is concerned, the requirements of the worker can be narrowed down to one: the *need to support him while he is working* and prevent the *race of workers* from dying out. Wages therefore have exactly the same meaning as the *maintenance and upkeep* of any other productive instrument, or as the *consumption* of *capital* in general which is necessary if it is to reproduce itself with interest (e.g. the oil which is applied to wheels to keep them turning). Wages therefore belong to the necessary *costs* of capital and of the capitalist, and must not be in excess of this necessary amount. It was therefore quite logical for the English factory owners, before the Amendment Bill of 1834,[2] to deduct from the worker's wages the public alms which he received from the Poor Rate, and to consider these alms as an integral part of those wages.

Production does not produce man only as a *commodity*, the *human commodity*, man in the form of a *commodity*; it also produces him as a *mentally* and physically *dehumanized* being ... Immorality, malformation, stupidity of workers and capitalists ... Its product is the *self-conscious* and *self-acting commodity* ... the *human* commodity ... A great advance by Ricardo, Mill, etc., on Smith and Say, to declare the *existence* of the human being – the greater or lesser human productivity of the commodity – to be *indifferent* and even *harmful*. The real aim of production is not how many workers a particular sum of capital can support, but how much interest it brings in and how much it *saves* each year. Similarly, English political economy took a big step forward, and a logical one, when – while acknowledging *labour* as the *sole* principle of political economy – it showed with complete clarity that wages and interest on capital are *inversely* related and that as a rule the capitalist can push up his profits *only* by forcing down wages, and vice-versa. Clearly the *normal* relationship is not one in which the customer is cheated, but in which the capitalist and the worker cheat each other. The relation of private property contains latent within itself the relation of private property as *labour*, the relation of private property as *capital* and the *connection* of these two. On the one hand we have the production of human activity as *labour*, i.e. as an activity wholly alien to itself, to man and to nature, and hence to consciousness and vital expression, the *abstract* existence of man as a mere *workman* who therefore tumbles day after day from his fulfilled nothingness into absolute nothingness, into his social and hence real non-existence; and on the other, the production of the object of human labour as *capital*, in which all the natural and social individuality of the object is *extinguished* and private property has lost its natural and social quality (i.e. has lost all political and social appearances and is not even *apparently* tainted with any human relationships), in which the *same* capital stays the *same* in the most varied natural and social circumstances, totally indifferent to its *real* content.

2. Better known as the Poor Law Amendment Act of 1834.

This contradiction, driven to its utmost limit, is necessarily the limit, the culmination and the decline of the whole system of private property.

It is therefore yet another great achievement of recent English political economy to have declared ground rent to be the difference between the interest on the worst and the best land under cultivation, to have confuted the romantic illusions of the landowner – his alleged social importance and the identity of his interest with the interest of society, which Adam Smith continued to propound after the Physiocrats – and to have anticipated and prepared the changes in reality which will transform the landowner into a quite ordinary and prosaic capitalist, thereby simplifying the contradiction, bringing it to a head and hastening its resolution. *Land* as *land* and *ground rent* as *ground rent* have thereby lost their *distinction in rank* and have become dumb *capital* and *interest* – or rather, capital and interest which only talk hard cash. The *distinction* between capital and land, between profit and ground rent, and the distinction between both and wages, *industry*, *agriculture*, and *immovable* and *movable* private property, is not one which is grounded in the nature of things, it is a *historical* distinction, a *fixed* moment in the formation and development of the opposition between capital and labour. In industry, etc., as opposed to immovable landed property, only the manner in which industry first arose and the opposition to agriculture within which industry developed, are expressed. As a *special* kind of work, as an *essential, important* and *life-encompassing* distinction, this distinction between industry and agriculture survives only as long as industry (town life) is developing *in opposition to* landed property (aristocratic feudal life) and continues to bear the feudal characteristics of its opposite in the form of monopoly, crafts, guilds, corporations, etc. Given these forms, labour continues to have an *apparently social* meaning, the meaning of *genuine* community, and has not yet reached the stage of *indifference* towards its content and of complete being-for-itself, i.e. of abstraction from all other being and hence of *liberated* capital.

But the necessary *development* of labour is liberated *industry*, constituted for itself as such, and *liberated capital*. The power of industry over its antagonist is at once manifested in the emergence of *agriculture* as an actual industry, whereas previously most of the work was left to the soil itself and to the *slave* of the soil, through whom the soil cultivated itself. With the transformation of the slave into a *free* worker, i.e. a *hireling*, the landowner himself is transformed into a master of industry, a capitalist. This transformation at first took place through the agency of the *tenant farmer*. But the tenant farmer is the representative, the revealed *secret*, of the landowner; only through him does the landowner have *his economic* existence, his existence as a property owner – for the ground rent of his land exists only because of the competition between the tenants. So in the person of the *tenant* the landowner *has* already essentially become a *common* capitalist. And this must also be effected in reality: the capitalist engaged in agriculture – the tenant – must become a landlord, or vice-versa. The *industrial trade* of the ,tenant is the industrial trade of the *landlord*, for the existence of the former posits the existence of the latter.

But remembering their conflicting origins and descent, the landowner sees the capitalist as his presumptuous, liberated and enriched slave of yesterday, and himself as a *capitalist* who is threatened by him; the capitalist sees the landowner as the idle, cruel and egotistical lord of yesterday; he knows that the landowner is harmful to him as a capitalist, and yet that he owes his entire present social position, his possessions and his pleasures, to industry; the capitalist sees in the landowner the antithesis of *free* industry and *free* capital which is independent of all natural forces – this opposition is extremely bitter, and each side tells the truth about the other. One only need read the attacks launched by immovable on movable property and vice-versa in order to gain a clear picture of their respective worthlessness. The landowner emphasizes the noble lineage of his property, the feudal reminiscences, the poetry of remembrance, his high-flown nature, his political importance, etc. When he is talking economics he avows that agriculture *alone* is productive. At the same time he depicts his opponent as a wily, huckstering, censorious, deceitful, greedy, mercenary, rebellious, heartless and soulless racketeer who is estranged from his community and busily trades it away, a profiteering, pimping, servile, smooth, affected trickster, a desiccated sharper who breeds, nourishes and encourages competition and pauperism, crime and the dissolution of all social ties, who is without honour, principles, poetry, substance or anything else. (See among others the Physiocrat *Bergasse*, whom Camille

Desmoulins has already flayed in his journal *Révolutions de France et de Brabant*; see also von Vincke, Lancizolle, Haller, Leo, Kosegarten[3] and *Sismondi*.)[4]

Movable property, for its part, points to the miracles of industry and change. It is the child, the legitimate, only-begotten son, of the modern age. It feels sorry for its opponent, whom it sees as a half-wit *unenlightened* as to his own nature (an assessment no one could disagree with) and eager to replace moral capital and free labour by brute, immoral force and serfdom. It paints him as a Don Quixote, who under a veneer of *directness*, *probity*, the *general interest* and *stability* hides an inability to develop, greedy craving for pleasure, self-seeking, sectional interest and evil intent. It brands him as a cunning *monopolist*. It discountenances his reminiscences, his poetry and his enthusiastic gushings by a historical and sarcastic recital of the baseness, cruelty, degradation, prostitution, infamy, anarchy and revolt forged in the workshops of his romantic castles.

Movable property itself claims to have won political freedom for the world, to have loosed the chains of civil society, to have linked together different worlds, to have given rise to trade which encourages friendship between peoples and to have created a pure morality and a pleasing culture; to have given the people civilized instead of crude wants and the means with which to satisfy them. The landowner, on the other hand – this idle and vexatious speculator in grain – puts up the price of the people's basic provisions and thereby forces the capitalist to put up wages without being able to raise productivity, so making it difficult and

3. See also the pompous Old Hegelian theologian *Funke*, who according to Herr Leo told with tears in his eyes how a slave had refused, when serfdom was abolished, to cease being a *noble possession*. See also Justus Möser's *Patriotische Phantasien*, which are distinguished by the fact that they never for one moment leave the staunch, petty bourgeois, 'home-baked', ordinary, narrow-minded horizon of the philistine, and yet still remain *pure* fantasy. It is this contradiction which has made them so plausible to the German mind. [*Marx's note*]

4. In these notes Marx is referring among others to the following writings: Camille Desmoulins, *Révolutions de France et de Brabant*, Second trimestre contenant mars, avril, mai, Paris, l'an Ier, no. 16, pp. 139 ff.; no. 23, pp. 425 ff; no. 26, pp. 580 ff. G. L. W. Funke, *Die aus der unbeschränkten Teilbarkeit des Grundeigentums hervorgehenden Nachteile*, Hamburg and Gotha, 1829, quoted by Heinrich Leo, *Studien und Skizzen zu einer Naturlehre des Staats*, I Abt., Halle, 1833. Justus Möser, *Patriotische Phantasien*, Berlin, 1775–8. J. C. L. Simonde de Sismondi, op. cit.

eventually impossible to increase the annual income of the nation
and to accumulate the capital which is necessary if work is to be
provided for the people and wealth for the country. As a result
the landowner brings about a general decline. Moreover, he
inordinately exploits *all* the advantages of modern civilization
without doing the least thing in return, and without mitigating a
single one of his feudal prejudices. Finally, the landlord – for
whom the cultivation of the land and the soil itself exist only as a
heaven-sent source of money – should take a look at the *tenant
farmer* and say whether he himself is not a *downright, fantastic,
cunning* scoundrel, who in his heart and in actual fact has for a
long time been a part of *free* industry and *well-loved* trade, however much he may resist them and prattle of historical memories
and moral or political goals. All the arguments he can genuinely
advance in his own favour are only true for the *cultivator of the
land* (the capitalist and the labourers), of whom the *landowner* is
rather the *enemy*; thus he testifies against himself. *Without*
capital, landed property is dead, worthless matter. The civilized
victory of movable capital has precisely been to reveal and create
human labour as the source of wealth in place of the dead thing.
(See Paul-Louis Courier, Saint-Simon, Ganilh, Ricardo, Mill,
MacCulloch, Destutt de Tracy and Michel Chevalier.)

The real course of development (to be inserted here) leads
necessarily to the victory of the *capitalist*, i.e. of developed private
property, over undeveloped, immature private property, the
landowner. In the same way, movement inevitably triumphs over
immobility, open and self-conscious baseness over hidden and
unconscious baseness, *greed* over *self-indulgence*, the avowedly
restless and versatile self-interest of *enlightenment* over the
parochial, worldly-wise, artless, lazy and deluded *self-interest of
superstition*, just as *money* must triumph over the other forms of
private property.

Those states which have a foreboding of the danger of allowing
the full development of free industry, pure morality, and that trade
which encourages friendship among peoples, attempt – although
quite in vain – to put a stop to the capitalization of landed
property.

Landed property, as distinct from capital, is private property,
capital, which is still afflicted with *local* and political prejudices,
which has not yet entirely emerged from its involvement with the
world and come into its own; it is capital which is *not yet fully*

developed. In the course of its *formation on a world scale* it must attain its abstract, i.e. *pure,* expression.

The relation of *private property* is labour, capital and the connections between these two. The movement through which these parts [*Glieder*] have to pass is:

First – Immediate or *mediated unity of the two.*

Capital and labour at first still united; later separated and estranged, but reciprocally developing and furthering each other as *positive* conditions.

Second – Opposition of the two. They mutually exclude each other; the worker sees in the capitalist his own non-existence, and vice-versa; each attempts to wrench from the other his existence.

Third – Opposition of each *to* itself. Capital = stored-up labour = labour. As such it divides into *itself* (capital) and its *interest*; this latter divides into *interest and profit.* Complete sacrifice of the capitalist. He sinks into the working class, just as the worker – but only by way of exception – becomes a capitalist. Labour as a moment of capital, its *costs.* I.e. wages a sacrifice of capital.

Labour divides into *labour itself* and *wages of labour.* The worker himself a capital, a commodity.

Hostile reciprocal opposition.

THIRD MANUSCRIPT

Private Property and Labour

ad page XXXVI.[1] The *subjective essence* of private property, *private property* as activity for itself, as *subject,* as *person,* is *labour.* It therefore goes without saying that only that political economy which recognized *labour* as its principle (Adam Smith) and which therefore no longer regarded private property as nothing more than a *condition* external to man, can be regarded as both a product of the real *energy* and *movement* of private property (it is the independent movement of private property become conscious for itself, it is modern industry as self), a product of modern *industry,* and a factor which has accelerated and glorified the energy and development of this *industry* and transformed it into

1. Marx numbered the pages of these manuscripts in roman numerals. The page referred to is one of those missing between the First and Second Manuscripts.

a power belonging to *consciousness*. Therefore the supporters of the monetary and mercantile system, who look upon private property as a *purely objective* being for man, appear as *fetish-worshippers*, as *Catholics*, to this enlightened political economy, which has revealed – within the system of private property – the *subjective* essence of wealth. Engels was therefore right to call Adam Smith the *Luther of political economy*.[2] Just as Luther recognized *religion* and *faith* as the essence of the external *world* and in consequence confronted Catholic paganism; just as he transcended *external* religiosity by making religiosity the *inner* essence of man; just as he negated the idea of priests as something separate and apart from the layman by transferring the priest into the heart of the layman; so wealth as something outside man and independent of him – and therefore only to be acquired and maintained externally – is abolished [*aufgehoben*]. I.e. its *external* and *mindless objectivity* is abolished inasmuch as private property is embodied in man himself and man himself is recognized as its essence – but this brings man himself into the province of private property, just as Luther brought him into the province of religion. So although political economy, whose principle is labour, appears to recognize man, it is in fact nothing more than the denial of man carried through to its logical conclusion: for man himself no longer stands in a relation of external tension to the external essence of private property – he himself has become the tense essence of private property. What was formerly *being-external-to-oneself*, man's material externalization, has now become the act of alienation, i.e. alienation through selling [*Veräusserung*]. This political economy therefore starts out by seeming to recognize man, his independence, his spontaneous activity, etc. Since it transfers private property into the very being of man, it can no longer be conditioned by local or national *features of private property* as *something existing outside it*. It (political economy) develops a *cosmopolitan*, universal energy which breaks through every limitation and bond and sets itself up as the *only* policy, the *only* universality, the *only* limitation and the *only* bond. But then, as it continues to develop, it is forced to cast off its *hypocrisy* and step forth in *all its cynicism*. This it does, without troubling its head for one moment about all the apparent contradictions to

2. In *Outlines of a Critique of Political Economy*, written during 1843, and published in February 1844 in the *Deutsch–Französische Jahrbücher*.

which this doctrine leads, by developing in a more one-sided way, and thus more sharply and more logically, the idea of *labour* as the sole *essence of wealth*, by showing that the conclusions of this doctrine, unlike the original conception, are *anti-human* and finally by delivering the death-blow to *ground rent* – that last *individual* and *natural* form of private property and source of wealth independent of the movement of labour, that expression of feudal property which has already become entirely economic and is therefore incapable of putting up any resistance to political economy. (The Ricardo school.) Not only does political economy become increasingly *cynical* from Smith through Say to Ricardo, Mill, etc., inasmuch as the consequences of *industry* appeared more developed and more contradictory to the latter; the latter also become more estranged – consciously estranged – from man than their predecessors. But this is *only* because their science develops more logically and more truly. Since they make private property in its active form the subject, thereby making man as a non-being [*Unwesen*] the essence [*Wesen*], the contradiction in reality corresponds entirely to the contradictory essence which they have accepted as their principle. The discordant *reality* of *industry*, far from refuting their *internally discordant* principle, actually confirms it. Their principle is in fact the principle of this discordance.

The physiocratic doctrine of Dr Quesnay forms the transition from the mercantile system to Adam Smith. *Physiocracy* is in a direct sense the *economic* dissolution of feudal property, but it is therefore just as directly the *economic transformation* and restoration of that property. The only difference is that its language is no longer feudal but economic. All wealth is resolved into *land* and *agriculture*. The land is not yet *capital*; it is still a *particular* mode of existence of capital whose value is supposed to lie in its natural particularity. But land is a universal natural *element*, whereas the mercantile system considered that wealth existed only in *precious metals*. The *object* of wealth, its matter, has therefore attained the greatest degree of universality possible within the *limits of nature* – in so far as it is directly objective wealth even as *nature*. And it is only through labour, through agriculture, that the land exists for *man*. Consequently, the subjective essence of wealth is already transferred to labour. But at the same time agriculture is the *only productive* labour. Labour is therefore not yet grasped in its universal and abstract form, but is still tied to a particular *element of nature as its matter* and is for that reason recognized only in a particular *mode of existence determined by nature*. It is therefore still only a *determinate, particular* externalization of man, just as its product is conceived as a determinate form of wealth, due more to nature than to itself. Here the land is still regarded as a part of nature which is independent of man, and not yet as capital, i.e. as a moment of labour itself. Rather, labour appears as a moment of *nature*. But since the fetishism of the old external wealth, which exists only as an object, has been reduced to a very simple element of nature, and since its essence has been recognized – even if only partially and in a particular way – in its subjective existence, the necessary advance has taken place in the sense that the *universal nature* of wealth has been recognized and *labour* has therefore been elevated in its absolute – i.e. abstract – form to the *principle*. It is possible to argue against the Physiocrats that *agriculture* is no different from an economic point of view – that is, from the only valid point of view – from any other industry, and that the *essence* of wealth is therefore not a *particular* form of labour tied to a particular element, a particular manifestation of labour, but *labour in general*.

Physiocracy denies *particular*, external, purely objective wealth by declaring labour to be its *essence*. But for physiocracy labour is in the first place merely the *subjective essence* of landed property (it starts out from the type of property which appears historically as the dominant and recognized type). It simply turns landed property into *alienated man*. It abolishes the feudal character of landed property by declaring *industry* (agriculture) to be its *essence*; but it sets its face against the world of industry and acknowledges the feudal system by declaring *agriculture* to be the *only* industry.

Clearly, once the *subjective essence* is grasped of industry constituting itself in opposition to landed property, i.e. as industry, this essence includes within it that opposition. For just as industry absorbs annulled landed property, so the *subjective* essence of industry at the same time absorbs the subjective essence of *landed property*.

Just as landed property is the first form of private property and industry at first confronts it historically as nothing more than a particular sort of private property – or rather, as the liberated slave of landed property – so this process is repeated in the scientific comprehension of the *subjective* essence of private property, of *labour*; labour appears at first only as *agricultural labour*, but later assumes the form of *labour in general*.

All wealth has become *industrial* wealth, *wealth* of labour, and *industry* is fully developed labour, just as the *factory system* is the perfected essence of *industry*, i.e. of labour, and *industrial capital* the fully developed objective form of private property.

Thus we see that it is only at this point that private property can perfect its rule over men and become, in its most universal form, a world-historical power.

Private Property and Communism

ad page xxxix.[1] But the antithesis between *propertylessness* and *property* is still an indifferent antithesis, not grasped in its *active connection*, its *inner* relation, not yet grasped as *contradiction*, as long as it is not understood as the antithesis between *labour* and *capital*. In its initial form this antithesis can manifest itself even without the advanced development of private property, as for example in ancient Rome, in Turkey, etc. In such cases it does not yet *appear* as established by private property itself. But labour, the subjective essence of private property as exclusion of property, and capital, objective labour as exclusion of labour, constitute *private property* in its developed relation of contradiction: a vigorous relation, therefore, driving towards resolution.

ad ibidem. The supersession [*Aufhebung*] of self-estrangement follows the same course as self-estrangement. *Private property* is first considered only in its objective aspect, but still with labour as its essence. Its form of existence is therefore *capital*, which is to be abolished 'as such' (Proudhon). Or the *particular form* of labour – levelled down, parcelled and therefore unfree – is taken as the source of the *harmfulness* of private property and its humanly estranged existence. For example, Fourier, like the Physiocrats, regarded agriculture as at least the *best* form of labour, while Saint-Simon on the other hand declared *industrial labour* as such to be the essence and consequently wants *exclusive* rule by the industrialists and the improvement of the condition of the workers. Finally, *communism*[2] is the *positive* expression of the

1. This section (pp. 345–58) formed an appendix to page xxxix of the incomplete Second Manuscript.

2. 'Communism' in this sense is, of course, the 'crude communism' of utopian thinkers such as Fourier, Proudhon and Babeuf, and is later contrasted with Marx's own conception of communism.

abolition of private property and at first appears as *universal* private property. In grasping this relation in its *universality*, communism is

(1) in its initial form only a *generalization* and *completion* of that relation (of private property). As such it appears in a dual form: on the one hand the domination of *material* property bulks so large that it threatens to destroy *everything* which is not capable of being possessed by everyone as private property; it wants to abstract from talent, etc., by *force*. Physical, immediate *possession* is the only purpose of life and existence as far as this communism is concerned; the category of *worker* is not abolished but extended to all men; the relation of private property remains the relation of the community to the world of things; ultimately this movement to oppose universal private property to private property is expressed in bestial form – *marriage* (which is admittedly a *form* of *exclusive private property*) is counterposed to the *community of women*, where women become *communal* and *common* property. One might say that this idea of a *community of women* is the *revealed secret* of this as yet wholly crude and unthinking communism. Just as women are to go from marriage into general prostitution, so the whole world of wealth – i.e. the objective essence of man – is to make the transition from the relation of exclusive marriage with the private owner to the relation of universal prostitution with the community. This communism, inasmuch as it negates the *personality* of man in every sphere, is simply the logical expression of the private property which is this negation. Universal *envy* constituting itself as a power is the hidden form in which *greed* reasserts itself and satisfies itself, but in *another* way. The thoughts of every piece of private property as such are *at least* turned against *richer* private property in the form of envy and the desire to level everything down; hence these feelings in fact constitute the essence of competition. The crude communist is merely the culmination of this envy and desire to level down on the basis of a *preconceived* minimum. It has a *definite, limited* measure. How little this abolition of private property is a true appropriation is shown by the abstract negation of the entire world of culture and civilization, and the return to the *unnatural* simplicity of the *poor*, unrefined man who has no needs and who has not even reached the stage of private property, let alone gone beyond it.

(For crude communism) the community is simply a community

of *labour* and equality of *wages*, which are paid out by the communal capital, the *community* as universal capitalist. Both sides of the relation are raised to an *imaginary* universality – *labour* as the condition in which everyone is placed and *capital* as the acknowledged universality and power of the community.

In the relationship with *woman*, as the *prey* and handmaid of communal lust, is expressed the infinite degradation in which man exists for himself, for the secret of this relationship has its *unambiguous*, decisive, *open* and revealed expression in the relationship of *man* to *woman* and in the manner in which the *direct*, *natural* species-relationship is conceived. The immediate, natural, necessary relation of human being to human being is the *relationship* of *man* to *woman*. In this *natural* species-relationship the relation of man to nature is immediately his relation to man, just as his relation to man is immediately his relation to nature, his own *natural* condition. Therefore this relationship *reveals* in a *sensuous* form, reduced to an observable *fact*, the extent to which the human essence has become nature for man or nature has become the human essence for man. It is possible to judge from this relationship the entire level of development of mankind. It follows from the character of this relationship how far *man* as a *species-being*, as *man*, has become himself and grasped himself; the relation of man to woman is the most *natural* relation of human being to human being. It therefore demonstrates the extent to which man's *natural* behaviour has become *human* or the extent to which his *human* essence has become a *natural* essence for him, the extent to which his *human nature* has become *nature* for him. This relationship also demonstrates the extent to which man's *needs* have become *human* needs, hence the extent to which the *other*, as a human being, has become a need for him, the extent to which in his most individual existence he is at the same time a communal being.

The first positive abolition of private property – *crude* communism – is therefore only a *manifestation* of the vileness of private property trying to establish itself as the *positive community*.

(2) Communism (a) still of a political nature, democratic or despotic; (b) with the abolition of the state, but still essentially incomplete and influenced by private property, i.e. by the estrangement of man. In both forms communism already knows itself as the reintegration or return of man into himself, the supersession

of man's self-estrangement; but since it has not yet comprehended the positive essence of private property or understood the *human* nature of need, it is still held captive and contaminated by private property. True, it has understood its concept, but not yet its essence.

(3) *Communism*[3] is the *positive* supersession of *private property* as *human self-estrangement*, and hence the true *appropriation* of the *human* essence through and for man; it is the complete restoration of man to himself as a *social*, i.e. human, being, a restoration which has become conscious and which takes place within the entire wealth of previous periods of development. This communism, as fully developed naturalism, equals humanism, and as fully developed humanism equals naturalism; it is the *genuine* resolution of the conflict between man and nature, and between man and man, the true resolution of the conflict between existence and being, between objectification and self-affirmation, between freedom and necessity, between individual and species. It is the solution of the riddle of history and knows itself to be the solution.

The entire movement of history is therefore both the *actual* act of creation of communism – the birth of its empirical existence – and, for its thinking consciousness, the *comprehended* and *known* movement of its *becoming*; whereas the other communism, which is not yet fully developed, seeks in isolated historical forms opposed to private property a historical proof for itself, a proof drawn from what already exists, by wrenching isolated moments from their proper places in the process of development (a hobby horse Cabet, Villegardelle, etc., particularly like to ride) and advancing them as proofs of its historical pedigree. But all it succeeds in showing is that by far the greater part of this development contradicts its assertions and that if it did once exist, then the very fact that it existed in the *past* refutes its claim to *essential being* [*Wesen*].

It is easy to see how necessary it is for the whole revolutionary movement to find both its empirical and its theoretical basis in the movement of *private property* or, to be more exact, of the economy.

This *material*, immediately *sensuous* private property is the

---

3. Having discussed the nature of 'crude communism', Marx now goes on to describe his own conception of communism.

material, sensuous expression of *estranged human* life. Its movement – production and consumption – is the sensuous revelation of the movement of all previous production, i.e. the realization or reality of man. Religion, the family, the state, law, morality, science, art, etc., are only *particular* modes of production and therefore come under its general law. The positive supersession of *private property*, as the appropriation of *human* life, is therefore the positive supersession of all estrangement, and the return of man from religion, the family, the state, etc., to his *human*, i.e. *social* existence. Religious estrangement as such takes place only in the sphere *of consciousness*, of man's inner life, but economic estrangement is that of *real life* – its supersession therefore embraces both aspects. Clearly the nature of the movement in different countries initially depends on whether the actual and *acknowledged* life of the people has its being more in consciousness or in the external world, in ideal or in real life. Communism begins with atheism (Owen), but atheism is initially far from being *communism*, and is for the most part an abstraction. The philanthropy of atheism is therefore at first nothing more than an abstract *philosophical* philanthropy, while that of communism is at once *real* and directly bent towards *action*.

We have seen how, assuming the positive supersession of private property, man produces man, himself and other men; how the object, which is the direct activity of his individuality, is at the same time his existence for other men, their existence and their existence for him. Similarly, however, both the material of labour and man as subject are the starting-point as well as the outcome of the movement (and the historical *necessity* of private property lies precisely in the fact that they must be this starting-point). So the *social* character is the general character of the whole movement; *just as* society itself produces *man* as *man*, so it is *produced* by him. Activity and consumption, both in their content and in their *mode of existence*, are *social* activity and *social* consumption. The *human* essence of nature exists only for *social* man; for only here does nature exist for him as a *bond* with other *men*, as his existence for others and their existence for him, as the vital element of human reality; only here does it exist as the *basis* of his own *human* existence. Only here has his *natural* existence become his *human* existence and nature become man for him. *Society* is therefore the perfected unity in essence of man with nature, the true resurrection of nature, the realized naturalism of man and the realized humanism of nature.[4]

Social activity and social consumption by no means exist *solely* in the form of a *directly* communal activity and a directly *communal* consumption, even though *communal* activity and *communal* consumption, i.e. activity and consumption that express and confirm themselves directly in *real association* with other men, occur wherever that *direct* expression of sociality [*Gesellschaftlichkeit*] springs from the essential nature of the content of the activity and is appropriate to the nature of the consumption.

But even if I am active in the field of science, etc. – an activity which I am seldom able to perform in direct association with other men – I am still *socially* active because I am active as a *man*. It is not only the material of my activity – including even the language in which the thinker is active – which I receive as a social product. My *own* existence *is* social activity. Therefore what I create from myself I create for society, conscious of myself as a social being.

My *universal* consciousness is only the *theoretical* form of that whose *living* form is the *real* community, society, whereas at present *universal* consciousness is an abstraction from real life and as such in hostile opposition to it. Hence the *activity* of my universal consciousness – as activity – is my *theoretical* existence as a social being.

It is above all necessary to avoid once more establishing 'society' as an abstraction over against the individual. The individual *is* the *social being*. His vital expression – even when it does not appear in the direct form of a *communal* expression, conceived in association with other men – is therefore an expression and confirmation of *social life*. Man's individual and species-life are not two *distinct things*, however much – and this is necessarily so – the mode of existence of individual life is a more *particular* or a more *general* mode of the species-life, or species-life a more *particular* or more *general* individual life.

As *species-consciousness* man confirms his real *social life* and merely repeats in thought his actual existence; conversely, species-

4. Prostitution is only a *particular* expression of the *universal* prostitution of the *worker*, and since prostitution is a relationship which includes not only the prostituted but also the prostitutor – whose infamy is even greater – the capitalist is also included in this category. [*This note was inserted by Marx at the bottom of his manuscript page without any further indication of reference*]

being confirms itself in species-consciousness and exists for itself in its universality, as a thinking being.

Man, however much he may therefore be a *particular* individual – and it is just this particularity which makes him an individual and a real *individual* communal being – is just as much the *totality*, the ideal totality, the subjective existence of thought and experienced society for itself; he also exists in reality as the contemplation and true enjoyment of social existence and as a totality of vital human expression.

It is true that thought and being are *distinct*, but at the same time they are in *unity* with one another.

Death appears as the harsh victory of the species over the particular individual, and seemingly contradicts their unity; but the particular individual is only a *particular species-being*, and as such mortal.

(4) Just as *private property* is only the sensuous expression of the fact that man becomes *objective* for himself and at the same time becomes an alien and inhuman object for himself, that his expression of life [*Lebensäusserung*] is his alienation of life [*Lebensentäusserung*], and that his realization is a loss of reality, an *alien* reality, so the positive supersession of private property, i.e. the *sensuous* appropriation of the human essence and human life, of objective man and of human *works* by and for man, should not be understood only in the sense of *direct*, one-sided *consumption*, of *possession*, of *having*. Man appropriates his integral essence in an integral way, as a total man. All his *human* relations to the world – seeing, hearing, smelling, tasting, feeling, thinking, contemplating, sensing, wanting, acting, loving – in short, all the organs of his individuality, like the organs which are directly communal in form, are in their *objective* approach or in their *approach to the object* the appropriation of that object. This appropriation of *human* reality, their approach to the object, is the *confirmation of human reality*.[5] It is human *effectiveness* and human *suffering*, for suffering, humanly conceived, is an enjoyment of the self for man.

Private property has made us so stupid and one-sided that an object is only *ours* when we have it, when it exists for us as capital or when we directly possess, eat, drink, wear, inhabit it, etc., in short, when we *use* it. Although private property conceives all

5. It is therefore just as varied as the *determinations* of the *human essence* and *activities*. [*Marx's note*]

these immediate realizations of possession only as *means of life*; and the life they serve is the *life* of *private property*, labour and capitalization.

Therefore *all* the physical and intellectual senses have been replaced by the simple estrangement of *all* these senses – the sense of *having*. So that it might give birth to its inner wealth, human nature had to be reduced to this absolute poverty. (On the category of *having* see Hess in *Einundzwanzig Bogen*.)[6]

The supersession of private property is therefore the complete *emancipation* of all human senses and attributes; but it is this emancipation precisely because these senses and attributes have become *human*, subjectively as well as objectively. The eye has become a *human* eye, just as its *object* has become a social, *human* object, made by man for man. The *senses* have therefore become *theoreticians* in their immediate praxis. They relate to the *thing* for its own sake, but the thing itself is an *objective human* relation to itself and to man,[7] and vice-versa. Need or enjoyment have therefore lost their *egoistic* nature, and nature has lost its mere *utility* in the sense that its use has become *human* use.

Similarly, the senses and enjoyment of other men have become my *own* appropriation. Apart from these direct organs, *social* organs are therefore created in the *form* of society; for example, activity in direct association with others, etc. has become an organ of my *life expression* and a mode of appropriation of *human* life.

Obviously the *human* eye takes in things in a different way from the crude non-human eye, the human *ear* in a different way from the crude ear, etc.

To sum up: it is only when man's object becomes a *human* object or objective man that man does not lose himself in that object. This is only possible when it becomes a *social* object for him and when he himself becomes a social being for himself, just as society becomes a being for him in this object.

On the one hand, therefore, it is only when objective reality universally becomes for man in society the reality of man's essential powers, becomes human reality, and thus the reality of his *own* essential powers, that all *objects* become for him the

6. Cf. Moses Hess, 'Philosophie der Tat', printed in *Einundzwanzig Bogen aus der Schweiz*, Erster Teil, Zürich, 1843, p. 329.

7. In practice I can only relate myself to a thing in a human way if the thing is related in a human way to man. [*Marx's note*]

objectification of himself, objects that confirm and realize his individuality, *his* objects, i.e. *he himself* becomes the object. The *manner* in which they become his depends on the *nature* of the *object* and the nature of the *essential power* that corresponds to *it*; for it is just the *determinateness* of this relation that constitutes the particular, *real* mode of affirmation. An object is different for the *eye* from what it is for the *ear*, and the eye's object *is* different from the *ear's*. The peculiarity of each essential power is precisely its *peculiar essence*, and thus also the peculiar mode of its objectification, of its *objectively real*, living *being*. Man is therefore affirmed in the objective world not only in thought but with *all* the senses.

On the other hand, let us look at the question in its subjective aspect: only music can awaken the musical sense in man and the most beautiful music has *no* sense for the unmusical ear, because my object can only be the confirmation of one of my essential powers, i.e. can only be for me in so far as my essential power exists for me as a subjective attribute (this is because the sense of an object for me extends only as far as *my* sense extends, only has sense for a sense that corresponds to that object). In the same way, and for the same reasons, the *senses* of social man are *different* from those of non-social man. Only through the objectively unfolded wealth of human nature can the wealth of subjective *human* sensitivity – a musical ear, an eye for the beauty of form, in short, *senses* capable of human gratification – be either cultivated or created. For not only the five senses, but also the so-called spiritual senses, the practical senses (will, love, etc.), in a word, the *human* sense, the humanity of the senses – all these come into being only through the existence of *their* objects, through *humanized* nature. The *cultivation* of the five senses is the work of all previous history. *Sense* which is a prisoner of crude practical need has only a *restricted* sense. For a man who is starving the human form of food does not exist, only its abstract form exists; it could just as well be present in its crudest form, and it would be hard to say how this way of eating differs from that of *animals*. The man who is burdened with worries and needs has no *sense* for the finest of plays; the dealer in minerals sees only the commercial value, and not the beauty and peculiar nature of the minerals; he lacks a mineralogical sense; thus the objectification of the human essence, in a theoretical as well as a practical respect, is necessary both in order to make man's *senses human* and to create an appropriate *human sense* for the whole of the wealth of humanity and of nature.

Just as in its initial stages society is presented with all the material for this *cultural development* through the movement of *private property* and of its wealth and poverty – both material and intellectual wealth and poverty – so the society that is *fully developed* produces man in all the richness of his being, the *rich* man who is *profoundly and abundantly endowed with all the senses*, as its constant reality. It can be seen how subjectivism and objectivism, spiritualism and materialism, activity and passivity [*Leiden*], lose their antithetical character, and hence their existence as such antitheses, only in the social condition; it can be seen how the resolution of the *theoretical* antitheses themselves is possible *only* in a *practical* way, only through the practical energy of man, and how their resolution is for that reason by no means only a problem of knowledge, but a *real* problem of life, a problem which *philosophy* was unable to solve precisely because it treated it as a *purely* theoretical problem.

It can be seen how the history of *industry* and the *objective* existence of industry as it has developed is the *open* book of the essential powers of man, man's psychology present in tangible form; up to now this history has not been grasped in its connection with the *nature* of man, but only in an external utilitarian aspect, for man, moving in the realm of estrangement, was only capable of conceiving the general existence of man – religion, or history in its abstract and universal form of politics, art, literature, etc. – as the reality of man's essential powers and as *man's species-activity*. In *everyday, material industry* (which can just as easily be considered as a part of that general development as that general development itself can be considered as a *particular* part of industry, since all human activity up to now has been labour, i.e. industry, self-estranged activity) we find ourselves confronted with the *objectified powers of the human essence*, in the form of *sensuous, alien, useful objects*, in the form of estrangement. A *psychology* for which this book, the most tangible and accessible part of history, is closed, can never become a *real* science with a genuine content. What indeed should we think of a science which *primly* abstracts from this large area of human labour, and fails to sense its own inadequacy, even though such an extended wealth of human activity says nothing more to it perhaps than what can be said in one word – 'need', 'common need'?

The *natural sciences* have been prolifically active and have gathered together an ever growing mass of material. But philosophy has remained just as alien to them as they have remained alien to philosophy. Their momentary union was only a *fantastic illusion*. The will was there, but not the means. Even historiography only incidentally takes account of natural science, which it sees as contributing to enlightenment, utility and a few great discoveries. But natural science has intervened in and transformed human life all the more *practically* through industry and has prepared the conditions for human emancipation, however much its immediate effect was to complete the process of dehumanization. *Industry* is the *real* historical relationship of nature, and hence of natural science, to man. If it is then conceived as the *exoteric* revelation of man's *essential powers*, the *human* essence of nature or the *natural* essence of man can also be understood. Hence natural science will lose its abstractly material, or rather idealist, orientation and become the basis of a *human* science, just as it has already become – though in an *estranged* form – the basis of actual human life. The idea of *one* basis for life and another for *science* is from the very outset a lie. Nature as it comes into being in human history – in the act of creation of human society – is the *true* nature of man; hence nature as it comes into being through industry, though in an *estranged* form, is true *anthropological* nature.

Sense perception (see Feuerbach) must be the basis of all science. Only when science starts out from sense perception in the dual form of *sensuous* consciousness and *sensuous* need – i.e. only when science starts out from nature – is it *real* science. The whole of history is a preparation, a development, for '*man*' to become the object of *sensuous* consciousness and for the needs of 'man as man' to become [sensuous] needs. History itself is a *real* part of *natural history* and of nature's becoming man. Natural science will in time subsume the science of man just as the science of man will subsume natural science: there will be *one* science.

Man is the immediate object of natural science; for immediate *sensuous nature* for man is, immediately, human sense perception (an identical expression) in the form of the *other* man who is present in his sensuous immediacy for him. His own sense perception only exists as human sense perception for himself through the *other* man. But *nature* is the immediate object of the *science of man*. Man's first object – man – is nature, sense perception; and the particular sensuous human powers, since they can find

objective realization only in *natural* objects, can find self-knowledge only in the science of nature in general. The element of
thought itself, the element of the vital expression of thought –
language – is sensuous nature. The *social* reality of nature and
human natural science or the *natural science of man* are identical
expressions.

It can be seen how the *rich man* and the wealth of *human* need
take the place of the *wealth* and *poverty* of political economy. The
rich man is simultaneously the man *in need of* a totality of vital
human expression; he is the man in whom his own realization
exists as inner necessity, as *need*. Given socialism, not only man's
wealth but also his *poverty* acquire a *human* and hence a social
significance. Poverty is the passive bond which makes man
experience his greatest wealth – the *other* man – as need. The
domination of the objective essence within me, the sensuous out-
burst of my essential activity, is *passion*, which here becomes the
activity of my being.

(5) A *being* sees himself as independent only when he stands on
his own feet, and he only stands on his own feet when he owes his
existence to himself. A man who lives by the grace of another
regards himself as a dependent being. But I live completely by the
grace of another if I owe him not only the maintenance of my life
but also its *creation*, if he is the *source* of my life. My life is
necessarily grounded outside itself if it is not my own creation. The
creation is therefore an idea which is very hard to exorcize from
the popular consciousness. This consciousness is *incapable of
comprehending* the self-mediated being [*Durchsichselbstsein*] of
nature and of man, since such a being contradicts all the *palpable
evidence* of practical life.

The creation of the *earth* received a heavy blow from the science
of *geogeny*, i.e. the science which depicts the formation of the
earth, its coming to be, as a process of self-generation. *Generatio
aequivoca*[8] is the only practical refutation of the theory of creation.

Now it is easy to say to a particular individual what Aristotle
said: You were begotten by your father and your mother, which
means that in you the mating of two human beings, a human
species-act, produced another human being. Clearly, then, man
also owes his existence to man in a physical sense. Therefore you
should not only keep sight of the *one* aspect, the *infinite* progression which leads you on to the question: 'Who begot my father,

8. Spontaneous generation.

his grandfather, etc.?' You should also keep in mind the *circular movement* sensuously perceptible in that progression whereby man reproduces himself in the act of begetting and thus always remains the subject. But you will reply: I grant you this circular movement, but you must also grant me the right to progress back to the question: Who begot the first man, and nature in general? I can only answer: Your question is itself a product of abstraction. Ask yourself how you arrived at that question. Ask yourself whether your question does not arise from a standpoint to which I cannot reply because it is a perverse one. Ask yourself whether that progression exists as such for rational thought. If you ask about the creation of nature and of man, then you are abstracting from nature and from man. You assume them as *non-existent* and want me to prove to you that they *exist*. My answer is: Give up your abstraction and you will then give up your question. But if you want to hold on to your abstraction, then do so consistently, and if you assume the non-existence of man and nature, then assume also your own non-existence, for you are also nature and man. Do not think and do not ask me questions, for as soon as you think and ask questions, your *abstraction* from the existence of nature and man has no meaning. Or are you such an egoist that you assume everything as non-existent and still want to exist yourself?

You can reply: I do not want to assume the nothingness of nature, etc. I am only asking how it *arose*, just as I might ask the anatomist about the formation of bones, etc.

But since for socialist man the *whole of what is called world history* is nothing more than the creation of man through human labour, and the development of nature for man, he therefore has palpable and incontrovertible proof of his self-mediated *birth*, of his *process of emergence*. Since the *essentiality* [*Wesenhaftigkeit*] of man and of nature, man as the existence of nature for man and nature as the existence of man for man, has become practically and sensuously perceptible, the question of an *alien* being, a being above nature and man – a question which implies an admission of the unreality of nature and of man – has become impossible in practice. *Atheism*, which is a denial of this unreality, no longer has any meaning, for atheism is a *negation of God*, through which negation it asserts the *existence of man*. But socialism as such no longer needs such mediation. Its starting-point is the *theoretically and practically sensuous consciousness* of man and of nature as *essential beings*. It is the *positive self-consciousness* of man, no longer mediated through the abolition of religion, just as *real life* is positive reality no longer mediated through the abolition of private property, through *communism*. Communism is the act of positing as the negation of the negation, and is therefore a *real* phase, necessary for the next period of historical development, in the emancipation and recovery of mankind. *Communism* is the necessary form and the dynamic principle of the immediate future, but communism is not as such the goal of human development – the form of human society.[9]

Need, Production and Division of Labour

We have seen what significance the *wealth* of human needs has, on the presupposition of socialism, and consequently what significance a *new mode of production* and a new *object* of production have. A fresh confirmation of *human* powers and a fresh enrichment of *human* nature. Under the system of private property their significance is reversed. Each person speculates on creating a *new* need in the other, with the aim of forcing him to make a new sacrifice, placing him in a new dependence and seducing him into a new kind of *enjoyment* and hence into economic ruin. Each attempts to establish over the other an alien power, in the hope of thereby achieving satisfaction of his own selfish needs. With the mass of objects grows the realm of alien powers to which man is subjected, and each new product is a new *potentiality* of mutual fraud and mutual pillage. Man becomes ever poorer as a man, and needs ever more *money* if he is to achieve mastery over the hostile being. The power of his *money* falls in inverse proportion to the volume of production, i.e. his need grows as the *power* of money increases. The need for money is for that reason the real need created by the modern economic system, and the only need it creates. The *quantity* of money becomes more and more its sole *important* property. Just as it reduces everything to its own form of abstraction, so it reduces itself in the course of its own movement to something *quantitative*. *Lack of moderation* and *intemperance* become its true standard. Subjectively this is

9. The meaning of this sentence is unclear. 'Communism ... as such' is sometimes taken as referring to the 'crude communism' discussed earlier. On the other hand, the sentence can be interpreted as meaning that communism is not the final stage in the development of humanity, but will in its turn be transcended by a richer and higher stage.

manifested partly in the fact that the expansion of production and needs becomes the *inventive* and ever *calculating* slave of inhuman, refined, unnatural and *imaginary* appetites – for private property does not know how to transform crude need into *human* need. Its *idealism* is *fantasy*, *caprice* and *infatuation*. No eunuch flatters his despot more basely or uses more infamous means to revive his flagging capacity for pleasure, in order to win a surreptitious favour for himself, than does the eunuch of industry, the manufacturer, in order to sneak himself a silver penny or two or coax the gold from the pocket of his dearly beloved neighbour. (Every product is a bait with which to entice the essence of the other, his money. Every real or potential need is a weakness which will tempt the fly onto the lime-twig. Universal exploitation of communal human nature. Just as each one of man's inadequacies is a bond with heaven, a way into his heart for the priest, so every need is an opportunity for stepping up to one's neighbour in sham friendship and saying to him: 'Dear friend, I can give you what you need, but you know the terms. You know which ink you must use in signing yourself over to me. I shall cheat you while I provide your pleasure.' He places himself at the disposal of his neighbour's most depraved fancies, panders to his needs, excites unhealthy appetites in him, and pounces on every weakness, so that he can then demand the money for his labour of love.

This estrangement partly manifests itself in the fact that the refinement of needs and of the means of fulfilling them gives rise to a bestial degeneration and a complete, crude and abstract simplicity of need; or rather, that it merely reproduces itself in its opposite sense. Even the need for fresh air ceases to be a need for the worker. Man reverts once more to living in a cave, but the cave is now polluted by the mephitic and pestilential breath of civilization. Moreover, the worker has no more than a precarious right to live in it, for it is for him an alien power that can be daily withdrawn and from which, should he fail to pay, he can be evicted at any time. He actually has to *pay* for this mortuary. A dwelling in the *light*, which Prometheus describes in Aeschylus as one of the great gifts through which he transformed savages into men, ceases to exist for the worker. Light, air, etc. – the simplest *animal* cleanliness – ceases to be a need for man. *Dirt* – this pollution and putrefaction of man, the *sewage* (this word is to be understood in its literal sense) of civilization – becomes an *element of life* for him. Universal *unnatural* neglect, putrefied nature, becomes an *element of life* for him. None of his senses exist any longer, either in their human form or in their *inhuman* form, i.e. not even in their animal form. The crudest *modes* (and *instruments*) of human labour reappear; for example, the *tread-mill* used by Roman slaves has become the mode of production and mode of existence of many English workers. It is not only human needs which man lacks – even his *animal* needs cease to exist. The Irishman has only one need left – the need to *eat*, to eat *potatoes*, and, more precisely, to eat *rotten potatoes*, the worst kind of potatoes. But England and France already have a *little* Ireland in each of their industrial cities. The savage and the animal at least have the need to hunt, to move about, etc., the need of companionship. The simplification of machinery and of labour is used to make workers out of human beings who are still growing, who are completely immature, out of *children*, while the worker himself becomes a neglected child. The machine accommodates itself to man's *weakness*, in order to turn *weak* man into a machine.

The fact that the multiplication of needs and of the means of fulfilling them gives rise to a lack of needs and of means is proved by the political economist (and by the capitalist – we invariably mean *empirical* businessmen when we refer to political economists, who are the *scientific* exposition and existence of the former) in the following ways:

(1) By reducing the worker's needs to the paltriest minimum necessary to maintain his physical existence and by reducing his activity to the most abstract mechanical movement. In so doing, the political economist declares that man has no other needs, either in the sphere of activity or in that of consumption. For even *this* life he calls *human* life and *human* existence.

(2) By taking as his standard – his *universal* standard, in the sense that it applies to the mass of men – the *worst possible state of privation* which life (existence) can know. He turns the worker into a being with neither needs nor senses and turns the worker's activity into a pure abstraction from all activity. Hence any *luxury* that the worker might enjoy is reprehensible, and anything that goes beyond the most abstract need – either in the form of passive enjoyment or active expression – appears to him as a luxury. Political economy, this science of *wealth*, is therefore at the same time the science of denial, of starvation, of *saving*, and it actually goes so far as to *save* man the *need* for fresh *air* or physical *exercise*. This science of the marvels of industry is at the same time

the science of *asceticism*, and its true ideal is the *ascetic* but *rapacious* skinflint and the *ascetic* but *productive* slave. Its moral ideal is the *worker* who puts a part of his wages into savings, and it has even discovered a servile *art* which can dignify this charming little notion and present a sentimental version of it on the stage. It is therefore – for all its worldly and debauched appearance – a truly moral science, the most moral science of all. Self-denial, the denial of life and of all human needs, is its principal doctrine. The less you eat, drink, buy books, go to the theatre, go dancing, go drinking, think, love, theorize, sing, paint, fence, etc., the more you *save* and the greater will become that treasure which neither moths nor maggots can consume – your *capital*. The less you *are*, the less you give expression to your life, the more you *have*, the greater is your *alienated* life and the more you store up of your estranged life. Everything which the political economist takes from you in terms of life and humanity, he restores to you in the form of *money* and *wealth*, and everything which you are unable to do, your money can do for you: it can eat, drink, go dancing, go to the theatre, it can appropriate art, learning, historical curiosities, political power, it can travel, it is *capable* of doing all those things for you; it can buy everything; it is genuine *wealth*, genuine *ability*. But for all that, it only *likes* to create itself, to buy itself, for after all everything else is its servant. And when I have the master I have the servant, and I have no need of his servant. So all passions and all activity are lost in *greed*. The worker is only permitted to have enough for him to live, and he is only permitted to live in order to have.

It is true that a controversy has arisen in the field of political economy. One school (Lauderdale, Malthus, etc.) advocates *luxury* and execrates thrift. The other (Say, Ricardo, etc.) advocates thrift and execrates luxury. But the former admits that it wants luxury in order to produce *labour*, i.e. absolute thrift; and the latter admits that it advocates thrift in order to produce *wealth*, i.e. luxury. The former has the *romantic* notion that greed alone should not regulate the consumption of the rich, and it contradicts its own laws when it forwards the idea of *prodigality* as a direct means of enrichment. The other side then advances earnest and detailed arguments to show that through prodigality I diminish rather than increase my *possessions*; but its supporters hypocritically refuse to admit that production is regulated by caprice and fancy; they forget the 'refined needs' and forget that

without consumption there can be no production; they forget
that through competition production inevitably becomes more
extensive and more luxurious; they forget that it is use which
determines the value of a thing, and that it is fashion which
determines use; they want only 'useful things' to be produced,
but they forget that the production of too many useful things
produces too many *useless* people. Both sides forget that prodigality and thrift, luxury and privation, wealth and poverty are
equal.

And you must not only be parsimonious in gratifying your
immediate senses, such as eating, etc. You must also be chary of
participating in affairs of general interest, showing sympathy and
trust, etc., if you want to be economical and if you want to avoid
being ruined by illusions.

You must make everything which is yours *venal*, i.e. useful. I
might ask the political economist: am I obeying economic laws if
I make money by prostituting my body to the lust of another (in
France the factory workers call the prostitution of their wives and
daughters the nth working hour, which is literally true), or if I
sell my friend to the Moroccans[1] (and the direct sale of men in
the form of trade in conscripts, etc., occurs in all civilized countries)? His answer will be: your acts do not contravene my laws,
but you should find out what Cousin Morality and Cousin
Religion have to say about it; the morality and religion of my
political economy have no objection to make, but ... But who
should I believe, then? Political economy or morality? The
morality of political economy is *gain*, labour and thrift, sobriety –
and yet political economy promises to satisfy my needs. The
political economy of morality is the wealth of a good conscience,
of virtue, etc. But how can I be virtuous if I do not exist? And
how can I have a good conscience if I am not conscious of anything? It is inherent in the very nature of estrangement that each
sphere imposes upon me a different and contrary standard: one
standard for morality, one for political economy, and so on. This
is because each of them is a particular estrangement of man and
each is centred upon one particular area of estranged essential
activity; each is related in an estranged way to the other ... Thus
M. Michel Chevalier accuses Ricardo of abstracting from morality.
But Ricardo allows political economy to speak its own language.

1. There were Christian slaves in Morocco until the early nineteenth
century.

If this language is not that of morality, it is not the fault of Ricardo. M. Chevalier abstracts from political economy in so far as he moralizes, but he really and necessarily abstracts from morality in so far as he deals with political economy. The relationship of political economy to morality is either an arbitrary and contingent one which is neither founded nor scientific, a *simulacrum*, or it is *essential* and can only be the relationship of economic laws to morality. If such a relationship does not exist, or if the opposite is rather the case, can Ricardo do anything about it? Moreover, the opposition between political economy and morality is only an *apparent* one. It is both an opposition and not an opposition. Political economy merely gives expression to moral laws *in its own way*.

Absence of needs as the principle of political economy is most strikingly apparent in its *theory of population*. There are *too many* people. Even the existence of man is a pure luxury, and if the worker is 'moral' he will be *economical* in procreation. (Mill suggests public commendation of those who show themselves temperate in sexual matters and public rebuke of those who sin against this barrenness of marriage ... Is this not the morality, the doctrine, of asceticism?)[2] The production of people appears as a public disaster.

The meaning which production has for the wealthy is *revealed* in the meaning which it has for the poor. At the top it always manifests itself in a refined, concealed and ambiguous way – as an appearance. At the bottom it manifests itself in a crude, straightforward and overt way – as a reality. The crude need of the worker is a much greater source of profit than the *refined* need of the rich. The basement dwellings in London bring in more for the landlords than the palaces, i.e. they constitute a *greater wealth* for him and, from an economic point of view, a greater *social* wealth.

Just as industry speculates on the refinement of needs, so too it speculates on their *crudity*. But the crudity on which it speculates is artificially produced, and its true manner of enjoyment is therefore *self-stupefaction*, this *apparent* satisfaction of need, this civilization *within* the crude barbarism of need. The English gin-shops are therefore the *symbolic* representation of private property. Their *luxury* demonstrates to man the true relation of

2. James Mill, *Éléments d'économie politique*, tr. J. T. Parisot, Paris, 1823, p. 59.

industrial luxury and wealth. For that reason they are rightly the only Sunday enjoyment of the English people, and are at least treated mildly by the English police.

We have already seen how the political economist establishes the unity of labour and capital in a number of different ways: (1) capital is *accumulated labour*; (2) the purpose of capital within production – partly the reproduction of capital with profit, partly capital as raw material (material of labour) and partly as itself a *working instrument* (the machine is capital directly identified with labour) – is *productive labour*; (3) the worker is a piece of capital; (4) wages belong to the costs of capital; (5) for the worker, labour is the reproduction of his life capital; (6) for the capitalist, it is a factor in the activity of his capital.

Finally, (7) the political economist postulates the original unity of capital and labour as the unity of capitalist and worker, which he sees as the original state of bliss. The fact that these two elements leap at each other's throats in the form of two persons is a *contingent* event for the political economist, and hence only to be explained by external factors (see Mill).

Those nations which are still dazzled by the sensuous glitter of precious metals and therefore make a fetish of metal money are not yet fully developed money nations. Compare England and France. The extent to which the solution of theoretical problems is a function of practice and is mediated through practice, and the extent to which true practice is the condition of a real and positive theory is shown, for example, in the case of *fetish-worship*. The sense perception of a fetish-worshipper is different from that of a Greek because his sensuous existence is different. The abstract hostility between sense and intellect is inevitable so long as the human sense [*Sinn*] for nature, the human significance [*Sinn*] of nature and hence the *natural* sense of *man*, has not yet been produced by man's own labour.

Equality is nothing but a translation into French, i.e. into political form, of the German '*Ich = Ich*'. Equality as the *basis* of communism is its *political* foundation. It is the same as when the German founds it on the fact that he sees man as *universal self-consciousness*. It goes without saying that the supersession of estrangement always emanates from the form of estrangement which is the *dominant* power – in Germany, *self-consciousness*; in France, *equality*, because politics; in England, real, material, *practical* need, which only measures itself against itself. It is from this point of view that Proudhon should be criticized and acknowledged.

If we characterize *communism* itself – which because of its character as negation of the negation, as appropriation of the human essence which is mediated with itself through the negation of private property, is not yet the *true*, self-generating position [*Position*], but one generated by private property [. . .]³ the real estrangement of human life remains and is all the greater the more one is conscious of it as such, it can only be attained once communism is established. In order to supersede the *idea* of private property, the *idea* of communism is enough. In order to supersede private property as it actually exists, *real* communist activity is necessary. History will give rise to such activity, and the movement which we already know *in thought* to be a self-superseding movement will in reality undergo a very difficult and protracted process. But we must look upon it as a real advance that we have gained at the outset an awareness of the limits as well as the goal of this historical movement and are in a position to see beyond it.

When communist *workmen* gather together, their immediate aim is instruction, propaganda, etc. But at the same time they acquire a new need – the need for society – and what appears as a means has become an end. This practical development can be most strikingly observed in the gatherings of French socialist workers. Smoking, eating and drinking, etc., are no longer means of creating links between people. Company, association, conversation, which in its turn has society as its goal, is enough for them. The brotherhood of man is not a hollow phrase, it is a reality, and the nobility of man shines forth upon us from their work-worn figures.

When political economy maintains that supply and demand always balance each other, it immediately forgets its own assertion that the supply of *people* (the theory of population) always exceeds the demand and that therefore the disproportion between supply and demand finds its most striking expression in what is the essential goal of production – the existence of man.

The extent to which money, which appears to be a means, is the true *power* and the sole *end* – the extent to which in general the *means* which gives me being and which appropriates for me alien

3. At this point a corner of the page is missing and only the fragments of six sentences remain. The meaning of the missing passage is impossible to reconstruct.

and objective being, is an *end in itself* . . . is apparent from the fact
that landed property, where the soil is the source of life, and the
horse and the *sword*, where they are the *true means of life*, are also
recognized as the actual political powers. In the Middle Ages an
Estate becomes emancipated as soon as it is allowed to bear a
sword. Among nomadic peoples it is the *horse* which makes me
into a free man and a participant in the life of the community.

We said above that man is regressing to the *cave dwelling*, etc.,
but in an estranged, repugnant form. The savage in his cave – an
element of nature which is freely available for his use and shelter
– does not experience his environment as alien; he feels just as
much at home as a *fish* in water. But the poor man's basement
dwelling is an uncongenial element, an 'alien, restrictive power
which only surrenders itself to him at the expense of his sweat and
blood'. He cannot look upon it as his home, as somewhere he can
call his own. Instead he finds himself in someone else's house, in
an *alien* house, whose owner lies in wait for him every day, and
evicts him if he fails to pay the rent. At the same time he is aware
of the difference in quality between his own dwelling and those
other-worldly human dwellings which exist in the heaven of
wealth.

Estrangement appears not only in the fact that the means of
my life belong to *another* and that *my* desire is the inaccessible
possession of *another*, but also in the fact that all things are *other*
than themselves, that my activity is *other* than itself, and that
finally – and this goes for the capitalists too – an *inhuman* power
rules over everything.

There is one form of inactive and extravagant wealth, given
over exclusively to pleasure, the owner of which is *active* as a
merely *ephemeral* individual, rushing about erratically. He looks
upon the slave labour of others, their human *sweat and blood*,
as the prey of his desires, and regards man in general – including
himself – as a futile and sacrificial being. He arrogantly looks down
upon mankind, dissipating what would suffice to keep alive a
hundred human beings, and propagates the infamous illusion that
his unbridled extravagance and ceaseless, unproductive consumption is a condition of the *labour* and hence *subsistence* of
the others. For him, the realization of man's *essential powers* is
simply the realization of his own disorderly existence, his whims
and his capricious and bizarre notions. But this wealth, which
regards wealth as a mere means, worthy only of destruction, and

which is therefore both slave and master, both generous and mean, capricious, conceited, presumptuous, refined, cultured and ingenious – this wealth has not yet experienced *wealth* as an entirely *alien power* over itself; it sees in wealth nothing more than its own power, the final aim of which is not wealth but consumption . . .[4]

. . . and the glittering illusion about the nature of wealth – an illusion which derives from its sensuous appearance – is confronted by the *working, sober, prosaic, economical* industrialist who is enlightened about the nature of wealth and who not only provides a wider range of opportunities for the other's self-indulgence and flatters him through his products – for his products are so many base compliments to the appetites of the spendthrift – but also manages to appropriate for himself in the only *useful* way the other's dwindling power. So if industrial wealth at first appears to be the product of extravagant, fantastic wealth, in its inherent course of development it actively supplants the latter. For the fall in the *interest on money* is a necessary consequence and result of industrial development. Therefore the means of the extravagant rentier diminish daily in *inverse* proportion to the growing possibilities and temptations of pleasure. He must therefore either consume his capital himself, and in so doing bring about his own ruin, or become an industrial capitalist . . . On the other hand, it is true that there is a direct and constant rise in the *rent of land* as a result of industrial development, but as we have already seen there inevitably comes a time when landed property, like every other kind of property, falls into the category of capital which reproduces itself with profit – and this is a result of the same industrial development. Therefore even the extravagant landlord is forced either to consume his capital, i.e. ruin himself, or become the tenant farmer of his own property – an agricultural industrialist.

The decline in the rate of interest – which Proudhon regards as the abolition of capital and as a tendency towards the socialization of capital – is therefore rather a direct symptom of the complete victory of working capital over prodigal wealth, i.e. the transformation of all private property into industrial capital. It is the complete victory of private property over all those of its

4. At this point the bottom of the page is torn and three or four lines are missing.

qualities which are still *apparently* human and the total subjuga-
tion of the property owner to the essence of private property –
labour. To be sure, the industrial capitalist also seeks enjoyment.
He does not by any means regress to an unnatural simplicity of
need, but his enjoyment is only incidental, a means of relaxation;
it is subordinated to production, it is a calculated and even an
economical form of pleasure, for it is charged as an expense of
capital; the sum dissipated may therefore not be in excess of what
can be replaced by the reproduction of capital with profit. Enjoyment is therefore subsumed under capital, and the pleasure-
seeking individual under the capitalizing individual, whereas
earlier the contrary was the case. The decline in the rate of interest
is therefore a symptom of the abolition of capital only in so far
as it is a symptom of the growing domination of capital, of that
growing estrangement which is hastening towards its own
abolition. This is the only way in which that which exists affirms
its opposite.

The wrangle among political economists about luxury and
saving is therefore merely a wrangle between that section of
political economy which has become aware of the nature of
wealth and that section which is still imprisoned within romantic
and anti-industrial memories. But neither of them knows how to
express the object of the controversy in simple terms, and neither
of them is therefore in a position to clinch the argument.

Furthermore, the *rent of land* qua rent of land has been abolished,
for the argument of the Physiocrats, who say that the landowner
is the only true producer, has been demolished by the political
economists, who show that the landowner as such is the only
completely unproductive rentier. Agriculture is a matter for the
capitalist, who invests his capital in this way when he can expect
to make a normal profit. The argument of the Physiocrats that
landed property, as the only productive property, should alone
pay state taxes and should therefore alone give its consent to them
and take part in state affairs, is turned into the opposite argument
that the tax on rent of land is the only tax on unproductive
income and hence the only tax which does not harm national
production. Naturally it follows from this argument that the
landowner can no longer derive political privileges from his
position as principal tax-payer.

Everything which Proudhon interprets as the growing power of
labour as against capital is simply the growing power of labour in

the form of capital, *industrial capital*, as against capital which is not consumed *as* capital, i.e. industrially. And this development is on its way to victory, i.e. the victory of *industrial* capital.

Clearly, then, it is only when *labour* is grasped as the essence of private property that the development of the economy as such can be analysed in its real determinateness.

Society, as it appears to the political economist, is *civil society*, in which each individual is a totality of needs and only exists for the other as the other exists for him – in so far as each becomes a means for the other. The political economist, like politics in its *rights of man*, reduces everything to man, i.e. to the individual, whom he divests of all his determinateness in order to classify him as a capitalist or a worker.

The *division of labour* is the economic expression of the *social nature of labour* within estrangement. Or rather, since *labour* is only an expression of human activity within alienation, an expression of life as alienation of life, the *division of labour* is nothing more than the *estranged, alienated* positing of human activity as a *real species-activity* or as *activity of man as a species-being*.

Political economists are very unclear and self-contradictory about the *essence* of the *division of labour*, which was naturally seen as one of the main driving forces in the production of wealth as soon as *labour* was seen to be the *essence* of *private property*. That is to say, they are very unclear about *human activity as species activity in this its estranged and alienated form*.

Adam Smith: 'The division of labour ... is not originally the effect of any human wisdom ... It is the necessary, though very slow and gradual consequence of the propensity to truck, barter and exchange one thing for another. Whether this propensity be one of those original principles of human nature ... or whether, as seems more probable, it be the necessary consequence of the faculties of reason and of speech it belongs not to our present subject to inquire. It is common to all men, and to be found in no other race of animals ... In almost every other race of animals the individual when it is grown up to maturity is entirely independent ... But man has almost constant occasion for the help of his brethren, and it is in vain for him to expect it from their benevolence only. He will be more likely to prevail if he can interest their self-love in his favour, and show them that it is for their own advantage to do for him what he requires of them ... We address ourselves not to their *humanity* but to their *self-love*, and never talk to them of *our own necessities* but of *their advantages*.'⁵

'As it is by treaty, by barter, and by purchase that we obtain from one another the greater part of those mutual good offices that we stand in need of, so it is this same *trucking* disposition which originally gives occasion to the *division of labour*. In a tribe of hunters or shepherds a particular person makes bows and arrows, for example, with more readiness and dexterity than any other. He frequently exchanges them for cattle or for venison with his companions; and he finds at last that he can in this manner get more cattle and venison than if he himself went to the field to catch them. From a regard to his own interest, therefore, the making of bows and arrows grows to be his chief business . . .'⁶

'The difference of *natural talents* in different men . . . is not . . . so much the *cause* as the *effect* of the division of labour . . . Without the disposition to truck, barter and exchange, every man must have procured to himself every necessary and conveniency of life which he wanted. All must have had . . the *same work* to do, and there could have been no such *difference* of *employment* as could alone give occasion to any great difference of talent.'⁷

'As it is this disposition which forms that difference of talents . . . among men, so it is this same disposition which renders that difference useful. Many tribes of animals . . . of the same species derive from nature a much more remarkable distinction of genius than what, antecedent to custom and education, appears to take place among men. By nature a philosopher is not in genius and in disposition half so different from a street-porter, as a mastiff is from a greyhound, or a greyhound from a spaniel, or this last from a shepherd's dog. Those different tribes of animals, however, though all of the same species, are of scarce any use to one another. The strength of the mastiff is not, in the least, supported for example by the swiftness of the greyhound . . . The effects of those different geniuses and talents, for want of the power or disposition to barter and exchange, cannot be brought into a common stock, and do not in the least contribute to the *better accommodation* and *conveniency* of the *species*. Each animal is still obliged to support and defend itself, separately and independently, and derives no sort of advantage from that variety of talents with

5. Adam Smith, op. cit., I, pp. 12–13. In this and the following passages the emphasis is by Marx.

6. ibid., pp. 13–14.   7. ibid., I, p. 14.

which nature has distinguished its fellows. Among men, on the contrary, the most dissimilar geniuses are of use to one another; the *different produces* of their respective talents, by the general disposition to truck, barter and exchange, being brought, as it were, into a common stock, where every man may purchase whatever part of the produce of other men's talents he has occasion for.'[8]

'As it is the power of *exchanging* that gives occasion to the *division of labour*, so the *extent of this division* must always be limited by the *extent* of that *power*, or, in other words, by the *extent of the market*. When the market is very small, no person can have any encouragement to dedicate himself entirely to one employment, for want of the power to exchange all that surplus part of the produce of his own labour, which is over and above his own consumption, for such parts of the produce of other men's labour as he has occasion for.'[9]

In an *advanced* state of society 'every man thus lives by exchanging, or becomes in some measure a *merchant*, and the *society itself* grows to be what is properly a *commercial* society'.[10] (See Destutt de Tracy: 'Society is a series of reciprocal exchanges; *commerce* contains the whole essence of society.'[11]) The accumulation of capitals increases with the division of labour, and vice-versa.

Thus far Adam Smith.

'If every family produced all that it consumed, society could keep going even if no exchange of any sort took place ... Although it is not *fundamental*, exchange is indispensable in our advanced state of society ... The division of labour is a skilful application of the powers of man; it increases society's production – its power and its pleasures – but it robs the individual, reduces the capacity of each person taken individually. Production cannot take place without exchange.'[12]

Thus J.-B. Say.

'The powers inherent in man are his intelligence and his physical capacity for work. Those which spring from the condition of society consist of the capacity to *divide labour* and to *distribute different tasks among different people* ... and the *power* to ex-

8. ibid., I, pp. 14–15.   9. ibid., p. 15.   10. ibid., p. 20.
11. Destutt de Tracy, *Éléments d'idéologie. IVe et V^e parties. Traité de la volonté et de ses effets*, Paris, 1826, pp. 68 and 78.
12. Say, op. cit., I, pp. 76–7.

change *mutual services* and the products which constitute these means . . . The motive which induces a man to give his services to another is self-interest – he demands a recompense for the services rendered. The right of exclusive private property is indispensable to the establishment of exchange among men.' 'Exchange and division of labour mutually condition each other.'[13]

Thus Skarbek.

Mill presents developed exchange, *trade*, as a *consequence* of the *division of labour*.

'. . . the agency of man can be traced to very simple elements. He can, in fact, do nothing more than produce motion. He can move things towards one another; and he can separate them from one another: the properties of matter perform all the rest . . . In the employment of labour and machinery, it is often found that the effects can be increased by skilful distribution, by separating all those operations which have any tendency to impede one another, by bringing together all those operations which can be made in any way to aid one another. As men in general cannot perform many different operations with the same quickness and dexterity with which they can by practice learn to perform a few, it is always an advantage to limit as much as possible the number of operations imposed upon each. For dividing labour, and distributing the power of men and machinery, to the greatest advantage, it is in most cases necessary to operate upon a large scale; in other words, to produce the commodities in great masses. It is this advantage which gives existence to the great manufactories; a few of which, placed in the most convenient situations, sometimes supply not one country, but many countries, with as much as they desire of the commodity produced.'[14]

Thus Mill.

But all the modern political economists agree that division of labour and volume of production, division of labour and accumulation of capital, are mutually determining, and that only *liberated* private property, left to itself, is capable of producing the most effective and comprehensive division of labour.

Adam Smith's argument can be summed up as follows: the

13. F. Skarbek, *Théorie des richesses sociales, suivie d'une bibliographie de l'économie politique*, Paris, 1829, Vol. 1, p. 25 f.

14. James Mill, *Elements of Political Economy*, London, 1821, pp. 5–9. Marx quotes as usual from the French translation by J. T. Parisot, published in Paris in 1823.

division of labour gives labour an infinite capacity to produce. It has its basis in the *propensity* to *exchange* and *barter*, a specifically human propensity which is probably not fortuitous but determined by the use of reason and of language. The motive of those engaged in exchange is not *humanity* but *egoism*. The diversity of human talents is more the effect than the cause of the division of labour, i.e. of exchange. Moreover, it is only on account of the latter that this diversity is useful. The particular qualities of the different races within a species of animal are by nature more marked than the differences between human aptitudes and activities. But since animals are not able to *exchange*, the diversity of qualities in animals of the same species but of different races does not benefit any individual animal. Animals are unable to combine the different qualities of their species; they are incapable of contributing anything to the *common* good and the *common* comfort of their species. This is not the case with *men*, whose most disparate talents and modes of activity are of benefit to each other, *because* they can gather together their *different* products in a common reserve from which each can make his purchases. Just as the division of labour stems from the propensity to *exchange*, so it grows and is limited by the *extent* of *exchange*, of the *market*. In developed conditions each man is a *merchant* and society is a *trading association*.

Say regards *exchange* as fortuitous and not basic. Society could exist without it. It becomes indispensable in an advanced state of society. Yet *production* cannot take place *without it*. The division of labour is a *convenient*, *useful* means, a skilful application of human powers for social wealth, but it is a diminution of the *capacity of each man* taken *individually*. This last remark is an advance on Say's part.

Skarbek distinguishes the *individual* powers *inherent* in man – intelligence and physical capacity for work – from those powers which are *derived* from society – *exchange* and *division of labour*, which mutually condition each other. But the necessary precondition of exchange is *private property*. Skarbek is here giving expression in objective form to what Smith, Say, Ricardo, etc., say when they designate *egoism* and *private self-interest* as the basis of exchange and *haggling* as the *essential* and *adequate* form of exchange.

Mill presents *trade* as a consequence of the *division of labour*. For him, *human* activity is reduced to *mechanical movement*. The division of labour and the use of machinery promote abundance of production. Each person must be allocated the smallest possible sphere of operations. The division of labour and the use of machinery, for their part, require the production of wealth *en masse*, which means a concentration of production. This is the reason for the big factories.

The consideration of the *division of labour* and *exchange* is of the highest interest, because they are the *perceptibly alienated* expressions of human *activity* and *essential powers* as *species*-activity and *species*-powers.

To say that the *division of labour* and *exchange* are based on *private property* is simply to say that *labour* is the essence of private property – an assertion that the political economist is incapable of proving and which we intend to prove for him. It is precisely in the fact that the *division of labour* and *exchange* are configurations of private property that we find the proof, both that *human* life needed *private property* for its realization and that it now needs the abolition of private property.

The *division of labour* and *exchange* are the two *phenomena* on whose account the political economist brags about the social nature of his science, while in the same breath he unconsciously expresses the contradiction which underlies his science – the establishment of society through unsocial, particular interests.

The factors we have to consider are these: the *propensity* to *exchange*, which is grounded in egoism, is regarded as the cause or the reciprocal effect of the division of labour. Say regards exchange as not *fundamental* to the nature of society. Wealth and production are explained by the division of labour and exchange. The impoverishment and denaturing [*Entwesung*] of individual activity by the division of labour are admitted. Exchange and division of labour are acknowledged as producers of the great *diversity of human talents*, a diversity which becomes *useful* because of exchange. Skarbek divides man's powers of production or essential powers into two parts: (1) those which are individual and inherent in him, his intelligence and his special disposition or capacity for work; and (2) those which are *derived* not from the real individual but from society, the division of labour and exchange. Furthermore, the division of labour is limited by the *market*. Human labour is simply *mechanical* movement; most of the work is done by the material properties of the objects. Each individual must be allocated the smallest number of operations possible. Fragmentation of labour and concentration of capital; the nothingness of individual production and the production of wealth *en masse*. Meaning of free private property in the division of labour.

Money

If man's *feelings*, passions, etc., are not merely anthropological characteristics in the narrower sense, but are truly *ontological* affirmations of his essence (nature), and if they only really affirm themselves in so far as their *object* exists *sensuously* for them, then it is clear:

(1) That their mode of affirmation is by no means one and the same, but rather that the different modes of affirmation constitute the particular character of their existence, of their life. The mode in which the object exists for them is the characteristic mode of their *gratification*.

(2) Where the sensuous affirmation is a direct annulment [*Aufheben*] of the object in its independent form (eating, drinking, fashioning of objects, etc.), this is the affirmation of the object.

(3) In so far as man, and hence also his feelings, etc., are *human*, the affirmation of the object by another is also his own gratification.

(4) Only through developed industry, i.e. through the mediation of private property, does the ontological essence of human passion come into being, both in its totality and in its humanity; the science of man is therefore itself a product of the self-formation of man through practical activity.

(5) The meaning of private property, freed from its estrangement, is the *existence* of *essential objects* for man, both as objects of enjoyment and of activity.

Money, inasmuch as it possesses the *property* of being able to buy everything and appropriate all objects, is the *object* most worth possessing. The universality of this *property* is the basis of money's omnipotence; hence it is regarded as an omnipotent being ... Money is the *pimp* between need and object, between life and man's means of life. But *that* which mediates *my* life also *mediates* the existence of other men for me. It is for me the *other* person.

What, man! confound it, hands and feet
And head and backside, all are yours!
And what we take while life is sweet,
Is that to be declared not ours?
   Six stallions, say, I can afford,
Is not their strength my property?
I tear along, a sporting lord,
As if their legs belonged to me.

(Goethe, *Faust* – Mephistopheles)[1]

Shakespeare in *Timon of Athens*:

Gold? Yellow, glittering, precious gold? No, gods,
I am no idle votarist: roots, you clear heavens!
Thus much of this will make black, white; foul, fair;
Wrong, right; base, noble; old, young; coward, valiant.
... Why, this
Will lug your priests and servants from your sides;
Pluck stout men's pillows from below their heads:
This yellow slave
Will knit and break religions; bless th'accurst;
Make the hoar leprosy adored; place thieves,
And give them title, knee, and approbation,
With senators on the bench: this is it
That makes the wappen'd widow wed again;
She whom the spital-house and ulcerous sores
Would cast the gorge at, this embalms and spices
To th' April day again. Come, damned earth,
Thou common whore of mankind, that putt'st odds
Among the rout of nations, I will make thee
Do thy right nature.[2]

And later on:

O thou sweet king-killer, and dear divorce
'Twixt natural son and sire! Thou bright defiler
Of Hymen's purest bed! Thou valiant Mars!
Thou ever young, fresh, loved and delicate wooer,
Whose blush doth thaw the consecrated snow
That lies on Dian's lap! Thou *visible god*,
That solder'st close *impossibilities*,
And mak'st them kiss! That speak'st with every tongue,
To every purpose! O thou touch of hearts!
Think, thy slave man rebels; and by thy virtue
Set them into confounding odds, that beasts
May have the world in empire![3]

1. Part I, scene 4. Tr. P. Wayne, Harmondsworth, 1949.
2. Act IV, scene 3.   3. ibid.

Shakespeare paints a brilliant picture of the nature of *money*. To understand him, let us begin by expounding the passage from Goethe.

That which exists for me through the medium of *money*, that which I can pay for, i.e. which money can buy, that *am I*, the possessor of the money. The stronger the power of my money, the stronger am I. The properties of money are my, the possessor's, properties and essential powers. Therefore what I *am* and what I *can do* is by no means determined by my individuality. I *am* ugly, but I can buy the *most beautiful* woman. Which means to say that I am not *ugly*, for the effect of *ugliness*, its repelling power, is destroyed by money. As an individual, I am *lame*, but money procures me twenty-four legs. Consequently, I am not lame. I am a wicked, dishonest, unscrupulous and stupid individual, but money is respected, and so also is its owner. Money is the highest good, and consequently its owner is also good. Moreover, money spares me the trouble of being dishonest, and I am therefore presumed to be honest. I am *mindless*, but if money is the *true mind* of all things, how can its owner be mindless? What is more, he can buy clever people for himself, and is not he who has power over clever people cleverer than them? Through money I can have anything the human heart desires. Do I not therefore possess all human abilities? Does not money therefore transform all my incapacities into their opposite?

If *money* is the bond which ties me to *human* life and society to me, which links me to nature and to man, is money not the bond of all *bonds*? Can it not bind and loose all bonds? Is it therefore not the universal *means of separation*? It is the true *agent of separation* and the true *cementing agent*, it is the *chemical* power of society.

Shakespeare brings out two properties of money in particular:

(1) It is the visible divinity, the transformation of all human and natural qualities into their opposites, the universal confusion and inversion of things; it brings together impossibilities.

(2) It is the universal whore, the universal pimp of men and peoples.

The inversion and confusion of all human and natural qualities, the bringing together of impossibilities, the *divine* power .of money lies in its *nature* as the estranged and alienating *species-essence* of man which alienates itself by selling itself. It is the alienated *capacity* of *mankind*.

What I as a man cannot do, i.e. what all my individual powers cannot do, I can do with the help of *money*. Money therefore transforms each of these essential powers into something which it is not, into its *opposite*.

If I desire a meal or want to take the mail coach because I am not strong enough to make the journey on foot, money can procure me both the meal and the mail coach, i.e. it transfers my wishes from the realm of imagination, it translates them from their existence as thought, imagination and desires into their *sensuous*, *real* existence, from imagination into life, and from imagined being into real being. In this mediating role money is the *truly creative* power.

Demand also exists for those who have no money, but their demand is simply a figment of the imagination. For me or for any other third party it has no effect, no existence. For me it therefore remains *unreal* and *without an object*. The difference between effective demand based on money and ineffective demand based on my need, my passion, my desire, etc., is the difference between *being* and *thinking*, between a representation which merely *exists* within me and one which exists outside me as a *real object*.

If I have no money for travel, I have no *need*, i.e. no real and self-realizing need, to travel. If I have a vocation to study, but no money for it, I have *no* vocation to study, i.e. no *real, true* vocation. But if I really do not have any vocation to study, but have the will *and* the money, then I have an *effective* vocation to do so. *Money*, which is the external, universal *means* and *power* – derived not from man as man and not from human society as society – to turn *imagination into reality* and *reality into mere imagination*, similarly turns *real human and natural powers* into purely abstract representations, and therefore *imperfections* and tormenting phantoms, just as it turns *real imperfections and phantoms* – truly impotent powers which exist only in the individual's fantasy – into *real essential powers* and *abilities*. Thus characterized, money is the universal inversion of *individualities*, which it turns into their opposites and to whose qualities it attaches contradictory qualities.

Money therefore appears as an *inverting* power in relation to the individual and to those social and other bonds which claim to be *essences* in themselves. It transforms loyalty into treason, love into hate, hate into love, virtue into vice, vice into virtue, servant into master, master into servant, nonsense into reason and reason into nonsense.

Since money, as the existing and active concept of value, confounds and exchanges everything, it is the universal *confusion* and *exchange* of all things, an inverted world, the confusion and exchange of all natural and human qualities.

He who can buy courage is brave, even if he is a coward. Money is not exchanged for a particular quality, a particular thing, or for any particular one of the essential powers of man, but for the whole objective world of man and of nature. Seen from the standpoint of the person who possesses it, money exchanges every quality for every other quality and object, even if it is contradictory; it is the power which brings together impossibilities and forces contradictions to embrace.

If we assume *man* to be *man*, and his relation to the world to be a human one, then love can be exchanged only for love, trust for trust, and so on. If you wish to enjoy art you must be an artistically educated person; if you wish to exercise influence on other men you must be the sort of person who has a truly stimulating and encouraging effect on others. Each one of your relations to man – and to nature – must be a *particular expression*, corresponding to the object of your will, of your *real individual* life. If you love unrequitedly, i.e. if your love as love does not call forth love in return, if through the *vital expression* of yourself as a loving person you fail to become a *loved person*, then your love is impotent, it is a misfortune.

Critique of Hegel's Dialectic and General Philosophy

This is perhaps the place to make a few remarks, by way of explanation and justification, about the Hegelian dialectic, both in general, and in particular as expounded in the *Phenomenology* and *Logic*, as well as about its relation to the modern critical movement.

Modern German criticism was so preoccupied with the old world and so entangled during the course of its development with its subject-matter that it had a completely uncritical attitude to the method of criticism and was completely unaware of the *seemingly formal* but in fact *essential* question of how we now stand in relation to the Hegelian *dialectic*. The lack of awareness about the relation of modern criticism to Hegelian philosophy in general and to the dialectic in particular has been so pronounced that critics like Strauss and Bruno Bauer are still, at least implicitly, imprisoned within Hegelian logic, the first completely so and the second in his *Synoptiker*[1] (where, in opposition to Strauss, he substitutes the 'self-consciousness' of abstract man for the substance of abstract nature) and even in his *Das entdeckte Christentum*.[2] For example, in *Das entdeckte Christentum* we find the following passage:

'As if self-consciousness, in positing the world, that which is different, and in producing itself in that which it produces, since it then does away with the difference between what it has produced and itself and since it is only in the producing and in the movement that it is itself – as if it did not have its purpose in this movement,' etc.[3] Or again: 'They (the French Materialists) could not yet see that the movement of the universe only really comes to exist for itself and enters into unity with itself as the movement of self-consciousness.'[4]

These expressions are not even different in their language from the Hegelian conception. They reproduce it word for word.

How little awareness there was of the relation to Hegel's dialectic while this criticism was under way (Bauer's *Synoptiker*), and how little even the completed criticism of the subject-matter contributed to such an awareness, is clear from Bauer's *Gute Sache der Freiheit*,[5] where he dismisses Herr Gruppe's impertinent question 'and now what will happen to logic?' by referring him to future Critics.

But now that Feuerbach, both in his 'Thesen' in the *Anekdota*[6] and in greater detail in his *Philosophie der Zukunft*,[7] has destroyed the foundations of the old dialectic and philosophy, that very

1. Bruno Bauer, *Kritik der evangelischen Geschichte der Synoptiker*, Vols. 1–2, Leipzig, 1841; Vol. 3, Brunswick, 1842.

2. Bruno Bauer, *Das entdeckte Christentum. Eine Erinnerung an das achtzehnte Jahrhundert und ein Beitrag zur Krisis des neunzehnten*, Zürich and Winterthur, 1843.

3. ibid., p. 113.   4. ibid., pp. 114 f.

5. Bauer, *Die gute Sache der Freiheit und meine eigene Angelegenheit*, Zürich and Winterthur, 1842, pp. 193 ff.

6. Arnold Ruge (ed.), *Anekdota zur neuesten deutschen Philosophie und Publizistik*, Zürich and Winterthur, 1843, Vol. 2, p. 62. Ludwig Feuerbach, 'Vorläufige Thesen zur Reformation der Philosophie'.

7. Ludwig Feuerbach, *Grundsätze der Philosophie der Zukunft*, Zürich and Winterthur, 1843.

school of Criticism, which was itself incapable of taking such a step but instead watched while it was taken, has proclaimed itself the pure, resolute, absolute Criticism which has achieved self-clarity, and in its spiritual pride has reduced the whole process of history to the relation between the rest of the world, which comes into the category of the 'masses', and itself. It has assimilated all dogmatic antitheses into the *one* dogmatic antithesis between its own sagacity and the stupidity of the world, between the critical Christ and mankind – the '*rabble*'. It has daily and hourly demonstrated its own excellence against the mindlessness of the masses and has finally announced that the critical *Day of Judgement* is drawing near, when the whole of fallen humanity will be arrayed before it and divided into groups, whereupon each group will receive its certificate of poverty. The school of Criticism has made known in print its superiority to human feelings and the world, above which it sits enthroned in sublime solitude, with nothing but an occasional roar of sarcastic laughter from its Olympian lips. After all these delightful capers of idealism (Young Hegelianism) which is expiring in the form of Criticism, it (the critical school) has not once voiced so much as a suspicion of the need for a critical debate with its progenitor, the Hegelian dialectic. It has not even indicated a critical attitude to Feuerbach's dialectic. A completely uncritical attitude towards itself.

Feuerbach is the only person who has a *serious* and a *critical* attitude to the Hegelian dialectic and who has made real discoveries in this field. He is the true conqueror of the old philosophy. The magnitude of his achievement and the quiet simplicity with which he presents it to the world are in marked contrast to the others.

Feuerbach's great achievement is:

(1) To have shown that philosophy is nothing more than religion brought into thought and developed in thought, and that it is equally to be condemned as another form and mode of existence of the estrangement of man's nature.

(2) To have founded *true materialism* and *real science* by making the social relation of 'man to man' the basic principle of his theory.

(3) To have opposed to the negation of the negation, which claims to be the absolute positive, the positive which is based upon itself and positively grounded in itself.

Feuerbach explains the Hegelian dialectic, and in so doing

justifies taking the positive, that is sensuously ascertained, as his starting-point, in the following way:

Hegel starts out from the estrangement of substance (in logical terms: from the infinite, the abstractly universal), from the absolute and fixed abstraction. In ordinary language, he starts out from religion and theology.

Secondly, he supersedes the infinite and posits the actual, the sensuous, the real, the finite, the particular. (Philosophy as supersession of religion and theology.)

Thirdly, he once more supersedes the positive, and restores the abstraction, the infinite. Restoration of religion and theology.

Feuerbach therefore conceives the negation of the negation *only* as a contradiction of philosophy with itself, as philosophy which affirms theology (supersession, etc.) after having superseded it and hence affirms it in opposition to itself.

The positing or self-affirmation and self-confirmation present in the negation of the negation is regarded as a positing which is not yet sure of itself, which is still preoccupied with its opposite, which doubts itself and therefore stands in need of proof, which does not prove itself through its own existence, which is not admitted. It is therefore directly counterposed to that positing which is sensuously ascertained and grounded in itself. (Feuerbach sees negation of the negation, the concrete concept, as thought which surpasses itself in thought and as thought which strives to be direct awareness, nature, reality.)[8]

But since he conceives the negation of the negation from the aspect of the positive relation contained within it as the true and only positive and from the aspect of the negative relation contained within it as the only true act and self-realizing act of all being, Hegel has merely discovered the *abstract*, *logical*, *speculative* expression of the movement of history. This movement of history is not yet the *real* history of man as a given subject, it is simply the *process of his creation*, the *history of his emergence*. We shall explain both the abstract form of this movement and the difference between Hegel's conception of this process and that of modern criticism as formulated in Feuerbach's *Das Wesen des Christentums* or rather, the *critical* form of a movement which in Hegel is still uncritical.

Let us take a look at Hegel's system. We must begin with his

---

8. ibid., paras. 29 and 30.

Phenomenology, which is the true birthplace and secret of the Hegelian philosophy.

Phenomenology[9]

A. *Self-consciousness*

I. *Consciousness*. (a) Certainty in sense experience, or the 'this' and *meaning*. (b) *Perception* or the thing with its properties and *illusion*. (c) Power and understanding, phenomena and the super-sensible world.

II. *Self-consciousness*. The truth of certainty of oneself. (a) Independence and dependence of self-consciousness, lordship and servitude. (b) Freedom of self-consciousness. Stoicism, scepticism, the unhappy consciousness.

III. *Reason*. Certainty and truth of reason. (a) Observational reason; observation of nature and of self-consciousness. (b) Realization of rational self-consciousness through itself. Pleasure and necessity. The law of the heart and the madness of self-conceit. Virtue and the way of the world. (c) Individuality which is real in and for itself. The spiritual animal kingdom and deception or the thing itself. Legislative reason. Reason which tests laws.

B. *Mind*.

I. *True* mind, morality.

II. Self-estranged mind, culture.

III. Mind certain of itself, morality.

C. *Religion*.

Natural religion, the *religion of art*, *revealed* religion.

D. *Absolute knowledge*

Hegel's *Encyclopaedia* begins with logic, with *pure speculative thought*, and ends with *absolute knowledge*, with the self-conscious, self-comprehending philosophical or absolute mind, i.e. super-human, abstract mind. In the same way, the whole of the *Encyclopaedia* is nothing but the *extended being* of philosophical mind, its self-objectification; and the philosophical mind is nothing but the estranged mind of the world thinking within its self-estrangement, i.e. conceiving itself abstractly. *Logic* is the *currency* of the mind, the speculative *thought-value* of man and of nature, their essence which has become completely indifferent to all real determinateness and hence unreal, *alienated* thought, and therefore thought which abstracts from nature and from real man;

9. What follows are the chapter and section headings of Hegel's *Phenomenology of Mind*.

abstract thought. The *external character of this abstract thought* ... *nature* as it is for this abstract thought. Nature is external to it, its loss of self; it grasps nature externally, as abstract thought, but as alienated abstract thought. Finally *mind*, which is thought returning to its birthplace and which as anthropological, phenomenological, psychological, moral, artistic-religious mind is not valid for itself until it finally discovers and affirms itself as *absolute* knowledge and therefore as absolute, i.e. abstract mind, receives its conscious and appropriate existence. For its real existence is *abstraction*.

Hegel commits a double error.

The first appears most clearly in the *Phenomenology*, which is the birthplace of Hegelian philosophy. When, for example, Hegel conceives wealth, the power of the state, etc., as entities estranged from the being of man, he conceives them only in their thought form ... They are entities of thought, and therefore simply an estrangement of *pure*, i.e. abstract, philosophical thought. Therefore the entire movement ends with absolute knowledge. What these objects are estranged from and what they confront with their claim to reality is none other than abstract thought. The *philosopher*, himself an abstract form of estranged man, sets himself up as the *yardstick* of the estranged world. The entire *history of alienation* and the entire *retraction* of this alienation is therefore nothing more than the *history of the production* of abstract, i.e. absolute, thought, of logical, speculative thought. *Estrangement*, which thus forms the real interest of this alienation and its supersession, is the opposition of *in itself* and *for itself*, of *consciousness* and *self consciousness*, of *object* and *subject*, i.e. the opposition within thought itself of abstract thought and sensuous reality or real sensuousness. All other oppositions and the movements of these oppositions are only the *appearance*, the *mask*, the *exoteric* form of these two opposites which are alone important and which form the *meaning* of these other, profane oppositions. It is not the fact that the human essence *objectifies* itself in an *inhuman* way, in opposition to itself, but that it *objectifies* itself in *distinction* from and in *opposition* to abstract thought, which constitutes the essence of estrangement as it exists and as it is to be superseded.

The appropriation of man's objectified and estranged essential powers is therefore firstly only an *appropriation* which takes place in *consciousness*, in pure thought, i.e. in *abstraction*. In the *Phenomenology*, therefore, despite its thoroughly negative and critical appearance and despite the fact that its criticism is genuine and often well ahead of its time, the uncritical positivism and equally uncritical idealism of Hegel's later works, the philosophical dissolution and restoration of the empirical world, is already to be found in latent form, in embryo, as a potentiality and a secret. Secondly, the vindication of the objective world for man – e.g. the recognition that *sensuous* consciousness is not *abstractly* sensuous consciousness, but *humanly* sensuous consciousness; that religion, wealth, etc., are only the estranged reality of *human* objectification, of *human* essential powers born into work, and therefore only the *way* to true *human* reality – this appropriation, or the insight into this process, therefore appears in Hegel in such a way that *sense perception, religion*, the power of the state, etc., are spiritual entities, for *mind* alone is the *true* essence of man, and the true form of mind is the thinking mind, the logical, speculative mind. The *humanity* of nature and of nature as produced by history, of man's products, is apparent from the fact that they are *products* of abstract mind and therefore factors of the *mind, entities of thought*. The *Phenomenology* is therefore concealed and mystifying criticism, criticism which has not attained self-clarity; but in so far as it grasps the *estrangement* of man – even though man appears only in the form of mind – *all* the elements of criticism are concealed within it, and often *prepared* and *worked out* in a way that goes far beyond Hegel's own point of view. The 'unhappy consciousness', the 'honest consciousness', the struggle of the 'noble and base consciousness', etc. etc., these separate sections contain the *critical* elements – but still in estranged form – of entire spheres, such as religion, the state, civil life and so forth. Just as the *entity*, the *object*, appears as a thought-entity, so also the *subject* is always *consciousness* or *self-consciousness*; or rather, the object appears only as *abstract* consciousness and man only as *self-consciousness*. The various forms of estrangement which occur are therefore merely different forms of consciousness and self-consciousness. Since abstract consciousness, which is how the object is conceived, is *in itself* only one moment in the differentiation of self-consciousness, the result of the movement is the identity of self-consciousness and consciousness, absolute knowledge, the movement of abstract thought no longer directed outwards but proceeding only within itself; i.e., the result is the dialectic of pure thought.

The importance of Hegel's *Phenomenology* and its final result –

the dialectic of negativity as the moving and producing principle –
lies in the fact that Hegel conceives the self-creation of man as a
process, objectification as loss of object [*Entgegenständlichung*],
as alienation and as supersession of this alienation; that he
therefore grasps the nature of *labour* and conceives objective man
– true, because real man – as the result of his *own labour*. The
real, *active* relation of man to himself as a species-being, or the
realization of himself as a real species-being, i.e. as a human
being, is only possible if he really employs all his *species-powers* –
which again is only possible through the cooperation of mankind
and as a result of history – and treats them as objects, which is at
first only possible in the form of estrangement.

We shall now demonstrate in detail the one-sidedness and the
limitations of Hegel, as observed in the closing chapter of the
Phenomenology. This chapter ('Absolute Knowledge') contains
the concentrated essence of the *Phenomenology*, its relation to the
dialectic, and Hegel's *consciousness* of both and their interrela-
tions.

For the present, let us observe that Hegel adopts the standpoint
of modern political economy. He sees *labour* as the *essence*, the
self-confirming essence, of man; he sees only the positive and not
the negative side of labour. Labour is *man's coming to be for himself* within *alienation* or as an *alienated man*. The only labour
Hegel knows and recognizes is *abstract mental* labour. So that
which above all constitutes the *essence* of philosophy – the
alienation of man who knows himself or *alienated* science that
thinks itself – Hegel grasps as its essence, and is therefore able to
bring together the separate elements of previous philosophies and
present his philosophy as *the* philosophy. What other philosophers
did – that they conceived separate moments of nature and of man's
life as moments of self-consciousness, indeed, of abstract self-
consciousness – this Hegel *knows* by *doing* philosophy. Therefore
his science is absolute.

Let us now proceed to our subject.

'Absolute Knowledge'. The last chapter of the Phenomenology.

The main point is that the *object* of *consciousness* is nothing
else but *self-consciousness*, or that the object is only *objectified
self-consciousness*, self-consciousness as object. (The positing of
man = self-consciousness.)

It is therefore a question of surmounting the *object of consciousness*. *Objectivity* as such is seen as an *estranged* human

relationship which does not correspond to *human nature*, to self-consciousness. The *reappropriation* of the objective essence of man, produced in the form of estrangement as something alien, therefore means transcending not only *estrangement* but also *objectivity*. That is to say, man is regarded as a *non-objective, spiritual* being.

Hegel describes the process of *surmounting the object of consciousness* in the following way:

The *object* does not only show itself as *returning* into the *self*, (according to Hegel that is a *one-sided* conception of the movement, a conception which grasps only one side). Man is equated with self. But the self is only *abstractly* conceived man, man produced by abstraction. Man *is* self [*selbstisch*]. His eyes, his ears, etc., have the *quality of self*; each one of his essential powers has this quality of *self*. But therefore it is quite wrong to say that *self-consciousness* has eyes, ears, essential powers. *Self-consciousness* is rather a quality of human nature, of the human eye, etc.; human nature is not a quality of *self-consciousness*.

The self abstracted and fixed for itself is man as *abstract egoist, egoism* raised to its pure abstraction in thought. (We shall come back to this later.)

For Hegel *human nature, man*, is equivalent to *self-consciousness*. All estrangement of human nature is therefore *nothing* but *estrangement of self-consciousness*. Hegel regards the estrangement of self-consciousness not as the *expression*, reflected in knowledge and in thought, of the *real* estrangement of human nature. On the contrary, *actual* estrangement, estrangement which appears real, is in its innermost hidden nature – which philosophy first brings to light – nothing more than the *appearance* of the estrangement of real human nature, of *self-consciousness*. The science which comprehends this is therefore called *phenomenology*. All reappropriation of estranged objective being therefore appears as an incorporation into self-consciousness; the man who takes hold of his being is *only* the self-consciousness which takes hold of objective being. The return of the object into the self is therefore the reappropriation of the object.

Expressed *comprehensively*, the *surmounting of the object of consciousness* means:

(1) That the object as such presents itself to consciousness as something disappearing.

(2) That it is the alienation of self-consciousness which establishes thingness [*Dingheit*].

(3) That this alienation has not only a *negative* but also a *positive* significance.

(4) That this significance is not only *for us* or in itself, but *for self-consciousness itself*.

(5) *For self-consciousness* the negative of the object, its own supersession of itself, has a *positive* significance – or self-consciousness *knows* the nullity of the object – in that self-consciousness alienates itself, for in this alienation it establishes *itself* as object or establishes the object as itself, for the sake of the indivisible unity of *being-for-itself*.

(6) On the other hand, this other moment is also present in the process, namely, that self-consciousness has superseded and taken back into itself this alienation and objectivity, and is therefore *at home* in *its* other-being *as such*.

(7) This is the movement of *consciousness*, and consciousness is therefore the totality of its moments.

(8) Similarly, consciousness must have related itself to the object in terms of the totality of its determinations, and have grasped it in terms of each of them. This totality of determinations makes the object *intrinsically* [*an sich*] a *spiritual being*, and it becomes that in reality for consciousness through the apprehending of each one of these determinations as determinations of *self* or through what we earlier called the spiritual attitude towards them.[10]

ad (1) That the object as such presents itself to consciousness as something disappearing is the above-mentioned *return of the object into the self*.

ad (2) The *alienation of self-consciousness* establishes *thingness*. Because man is equivalent to self-consciousness, his alienated objective being or *thingness* (that which is an *object for him*, and the only true object for him is that which is an essential object, i.e. his *objective* essence; since it is not *real man*, and therefore not *nature*, for man is *human nature*, who becomes as such the subject, but only the abstraction of man, self-consciousness, thingness can only be alienated self-consciousness) is the equivalent of *alienated self-consciousness*, and *thingness* is established by this alienation. It is entirely to be expected that a living, natural being equipped and endowed with objective, i.e. material essential powers should have *real* natural *objects* for the objects of its being,

10. These eight points are taken almost word for word from the chapter 'Absolute Knowledge' of Hegel's *Phenomenology of Mind*.

and that its self-alienation should take the form of the establishment of a *real*, objective world, but as something *external* to it, a world which does not belong to its being and which overpowers it. There is nothing incomprehensible or mysterious about that. It would only be mysterious if the contrary were true. But it is equally clear that a *self-consciousness*, through its alienation, can only establish *thingness*, i.e. an abstract thing, a thing of abstraction and not a *real* thing. It is also clear that thingness is therefore in no way something *independent* or *substantial vis-à-vis* self-consciousness; it is a mere creature, a *postulate* of self-consciousness. And what is postulated, instead of confirming itself, is only a confirmation of the act of postulating; an act which, for a single moment, concentrates its energy as product and *apparently* confers upon that product – but only for a moment – the role of an independent, real being.

When real, corporeal *man*, his feet firmly planted on the solid earth and breathing all the powers of nature, establishes his real, objective *essential powers* as alien objects by externalization [*Entäusserung*], it is not the *establishing* [*Setzen*] which is subject; it is the subjectivity of *objective* essential powers whose action must therefore be an *objective* one. An objective being acts objectively, and it would not act objectively if objectivity were not an inherent part of its essential nature. It creates and establishes only objects because it is established by objects, because it is fundamentally *nature*. In the act of establishing it therefore does not descend from its 'pure activity' to the *creation* of *objects*; on the contrary, its *objective* product simply confirms its *objective* activity, its activity as the activity of an objective, natural being.

Here we see how consistent naturalism or humanism differs both from idealism and materialism and is at the same time their unifying truth. We also see that only naturalism is capable of comprehending the process of world history.

Man is directly a *natural being*. As a natural being and as a living natural being he is on the one hand equipped with *natural powers*, with *vital powers*, he is an *active* natural being; these powers exist in him as dispositions and capacities, as *drives*. On the other hand, as a natural, corporeal, sensuous, objective being he is a *suffering*, conditioned and limited being, like animals and plants. That is to say, the *objects* of his drives exist outside him as *objects* independent of him; but these objects are objects of his *need*, essential objects, indispensable to the exercise and confirmation of his essential powers. To say that man is a *corporeal*, living, real, sensuous, objective being with natural powers means that he has *real, sensuous objects* as the object of his being and of his vital expression, or that he can only *express* his life in real, sensuous objects. To *be* objective, natural and sensuous and to have object, nature and sense outside oneself, or to be oneself object, nature and sense for a third person is one and the same thing. *Hunger* is a natural *need*; it therefore requires a *nature* and an *object* outside itself in order to satisfy and still itself. Hunger is the acknowledged need of my body for an *object* which exists outside itself and which is indispensable to its integration and to the expression of its essential nature. The sun is an *object* for the plant, an indispensable object which confirms its life, just as the plant is an object for the sun, an *expression* of its life-awakening power and its *objective* essential power.

A being which does not have its nature outside itself is not a natural being and plays no part in the system of nature. A being which has no object outside itself is not an objective being. A being which is not itself an object for a third being has no being for its *object*, i.e. it has no objective relationships and its existence is not objective.

A non-objective being is a *non-being*.

Imagine a being which is neither an object itself nor has an object. In the first place, such a being would be the *only* being; no other being would exist outside it, it would exist in a condition of solitude. For as soon as there are objects outside me, as soon as I am not *alone*, I am *another*, a reality *other* than the object outside me. For this third object I am therefore a *reality* other than it, i.e. *its* object. A being which is not the object of another being therefore presupposes that *no* objective being exists. As soon as I have an object, this object has me for its object. But a non-objective being is an unreal, non-sensuous, merely thought, i.e. merely conceived being, a being of abstraction. To be *sensuous*, i.e. to be real, is to be an object of sense, a *sensuous* object, and thus to have sensuous objects outside oneself, objects of one's sense perception. To be sensuous is to *suffer* (to be subjected to the actions of another).

Man as an objective sensuous being is therefore a *suffering* being, and because he feels his suffering [*Leiden*], he is a *passionate* [*leidenschaftliches*] being. Passion is man's essential power vigorously striving to attain its object.

But man is not only a natural being; he is a *human* natural being; i.e. he is a being for himself and hence a *species-being*, as which he must confirm and realize himself both in his being and in his knowing. Consequently, *human* objects are not natural objects as they immediately present themselves, nor is *human sense*, in its immediate and objective existence, *human* sensibility and human objectivity. Neither objective nor subjective nature is immediately present in a form adequate to the *human* being. And as everything natural must *come into being*, so man also has his process of origin in *history*. But for him history is a conscious process, and hence one which consciously supersedes itself. History is the true natural history of man. (We shall return to this later.)

Thirdly, since this establishing of thingness is itself only an appearance, an act which contradicts the nature of pure activity, it must be superseded once again and thingness must be denied.

ad 3, 4, 5, 6.

(3) This alienation of consciousness has not only a *negative* but also a *positive* significance, and (4) it has this positive significance not only *for us* or in itself, but for consciousness itself.

(5) *For self-consciousness* the negative of the object or its own supersession of itself has a *positive* significance – or self-consciousness *knows* the nullity of the object – in that self-consciousness alienates *itself*, for in this alienation it *knows* itself as object or, for the sake of the indivisible unity of *being-for-itself*, the object as itself. (6) On the other hand the other moment is also present in the process, namely, that self-consciousness has superseded and taken back into itself this alienation and objectivity, and is therefore *at home* in its *other-being as such*.

To recapitulate. The appropriation of estranged objective being or the supersession of objectivity in the form of *estrangement* – which must proceed from indifferent otherness to real, hostile estrangement – principally means for Hegel the supersession of *objectivity*, since it is not the *particular* character of the object but its *objective* character which constitutes the offence and the estrangement as far as self-consciousness is concerned. The object is therefore negative, self-superseding, a *nullity*. This nullity of the object has not only a negative but also a *positive* significance for consciousness, for it is precisely the *self-confirmation* of its non-objectivity and *abstraction*. For *consciousness itself* the nullity of the object therefore has a positive significance because it *knows* this nullity, the objective being, as its *self-alienation*; because it knows that this nullity exists only as a result of its own self-alienation . . .

The way in which consciousness is, and in which something is for it, is *knowing*. Knowing is its only act. Hence something comes to exist for consciousness in so far as it *knows* that *something*. Knowing is its only objective relationship. It knows the nullity of the object, i.e. that the object is not distinct from it, the non-existence of the object for it, in that it knows the object as its own *self-alienation*; that is, it knows itself – i.e. it knows knowing, considered as an object – in that the object is only the *appearance* of an object, an illusion, which in essence is nothing more than knowing itself which has confronted itself with itself and hence with a *nullity*, a something which has *no* objectivity outside knowing. Knowing knows that when it relates itself to an object it is only *outside* itself, alienates itself; that it only *appears* to itself as an object, or rather, that what appears to it as an object is only itself.

On the other hand, says Hegel, this other moment is also present in the process, namely, that self-consciousness has superseded and taken back into itself this alienation and objectivity, and is therefore *at home* in its *other-being as such*.

This discussion is a compendium of all the illusions of speculation.

Firstly, consciousness – self-consciousness – is *at home* in its *other-being as such*. It is therefore, if we here abstract from Hegel's abstraction and talk instead of self-consciousness, of the self-consciousness of man, *at home in its other-being as such*. This implies, for one thing, that consciousness – knowing as knowing, thinking as thinking – claims to be the direct *opposite* of itself, claims to be the sensuous world, reality, life – thought over-reaching itself in thought (Feuerbach).[11] This aspect is present in so far as consciousness as mere consciousness is offended not by estranged objectivity but by *objectivity as such*.

Secondly it implies that self-conscious man, in so far as he has acknowledged and superseded the spiritual world, or the general spiritual existence of his world, as self-alienation, goes on to re-affirm it in this alienated form and presents it as his true existence, restores it and claims to be *at home in his other-being as such*.

11. In his *Grundsätze der Philosophie der Zukunft* (§30) Feuerbach writes: 'Hegel is a thinker who *over-reaches* himself in thought'.

Thus, for example, having superseded religion and recognized it as a product of self-alienation, he still finds himself confirmed in *religion* as *religion*. Here *is* the root of Hegel's *false* positivism or of his merely *apparent* criticism: it is what Feuerbach calls the positing, negating and re-establishing of religion or theology, but it needs to be conceived in a more general way. So reason is at home in unreason as unreason. Man, who has realized that in law, politics, etc., he leads an alienated life, leads his true human life in this alienated life as such. Self-affirmation, self-confirmation in *contradiction* with itself and with the knowledge and the nature of the object is therefore true *knowledge* and true *life*.

Therefore there can no longer be any question about a compromise on Hegel's part with religion, the state, etc., since this untruth is the untruth of his principle.

If I *know* religion as *alienated* human self-consciousness, then what I know in it as religion is not my self-consciousness but my alienated self-consciousness confirmed in it. Thus I know that the self-consciousness which belongs to the essence of my own self is confirmed not in *religion* but in the *destruction* and *supersession* of religion.

In Hegel, therefore, the negation of the negation is not the confirmation of true being through the negation of apparent being. It is the confirmation of apparent being or self-estranged being in its negation, or the negation of this apparent being as an objective being residing outside man and independent of him and its transformation into the subject.

The act of superseding therefore plays a special role in which negation and preservation (affirmation) are brought together.

Thus, for example, in Hegel's *Philosophy of Right*, *private right* superseded equals *morality*, morality superseded equals *family*, family superseded equals *civil society*, civil society superseded equals *state* and state superseded equals *world history*. In *reality* private right, morality, family, civil society, state, etc., continue to exist, but have become *moments* and modes of human existence which are meaningless in isolation but which mutually dissolve and engender one another. They are *moments of movement*.

In their real existence this character of *mobility* is hidden. It first appears, is first revealed, in thought and in philosophy. Hence my true religious existence is my existence in the *philosophy of religion*, my true political existence is my existence in the *philosophy of right*, my true natural existence is my existence in the *philosophy of nature*, my true artistic existence is my existence in the *philosophy of art* and my true *human* existence is my *existence in philosophy*. Similarly, the true existence of religion, state, nature and art is the *philosophy* of religion, nature, the state and art. But if the philosophy of religion, etc., is for me the true existence of religion, then I am truly religious only as a *philosopher of religion*, and I therefore deny *real* religiosity and the really *religious* man. But at the same time I *confirm* them, partly in my own existence or in the alien existence which I oppose to them – for this *is* merely their *philosophical* expression – and partly in their particular and original form, for I regard them as merely *apparent* other-being, as allegories, forms of their own true existence concealed under sensuous mantles, i.e. forms of my *philosophical* existence.

Similarly, *quality* superseded equals *quantity*, quantity superseded equals *measure*, measure superseded equals *essence*, essence superseded equals *appearance*, appearance superseded equals *reality*, reality superseded equals the *concept*, the concept superseded equals *objectivity*, objectivity superseded equals the *absolute idea*, the absolute idea superseded equals *nature*, nature superseded equals *subjective* spirit, subjective spirit superseded equals *ethical* objective spirit, ethical spirit superseded equals *art*, art superseded equals *religion*, religion superseded equals *absolute knowledge*.

On the one hand this act of superseding is the act of superseding an entity of thought; thus, private property as *thought* is superseded in the *thought* of morality. And because thought imagines itself to be the direct opposite of itself, i.e. *sensuous reality*, and therefore regards its own activity as *sensuous, real* activity, this supersession in thought, which leaves its object in existence in reality, thinks it has actually overcome it. On the other hand, since the object has now become a moment of thought for the thought which is doing the superseding, it is regarded in its real existence as a confirmation of thought, of self-consciousness, of abstraction.

From one aspect the existence which Hegel *supersedes* in philosophy is therefore not *real* religion, state, nature, but religion already in the form of an object of knowledge, i.e. *dogmatics*; hence also *jurisprudence, political science* and *natural science*. From this aspect he therefore stands in opposition both to the *actual* being and to the immediate non-philosophical *science* or non-philosophical *concepts* of this being. He therefore contradicts their current conceptions.

From the other aspect the man who is religious, etc., can find his final confirmation in Hegel.

We should now examine the *positive* moments of the Hegelian dialectic, within the determining limits of estrangement.

(a) *The act of superseding* as an objective movement which *re-absorbs* alienation into itself. This is the insight, expressed within estrangement, into the *appropriation* of objective being through the supersession of its alienation; it is the estranged insight into the *real objectification* of man, into the real appropriation of his objective being through the destruction of the *estranged* character of the objective world, through the supersession of its estranged mode of existence, just as atheism as the supersession of God is the emergence of theoretical humanism, and communism as the supersession of private property the vindication of real human life as man's property, the emergence of practical humanism. Atheism is humanism mediated with itself through the supersession of religion; communism is humanism mediated with itself through the supersession of private property. Only when we have superseded this mediation – which is, however, a necessary precondition – will *positive* humanism, positively originating in itself, come into being.

But atheism and communism are no flight, no abstraction, no loss of the objective world created by man or of his essential powers projected into objectivity, no impoverished regression to unnatural, primitive simplicity. They are rather the first real emergence, the realization become real for man, of his essence as something real.

Therefore, in grasping the *positive* significance of the negation which has reference to itself, even if once again in estranged form, Hegel grasps man's self-estrangement, alienation of being, loss of objectivity and loss of reality as self-discovery, expression of being, objectification and realization. In short, he sees labour – within abstraction – as man's *act of self-creation* and man's relation to himself as an alien being and the manifestation of himself as an alien being as the emergence of *species-consciousness* and *species-life*.

(b) But in Hegel, apart from or rather as a consequence of the inversion we have already described, this act appears, firstly, to be *merely formal* because it is abstract and because human nature itself is seen only as *abstract thinking being*, as self-consciousness.

And secondly, because the conception is *formal* and *abstract*, the supersession of alienation becomes a confirmation of alienation. In other words, Hegel sees this movement of *self-creation* and *self-objectification* in the form of *self-alienation* and *self-estrangement* as the *absolute* and hence the final *expression of human life* which has itself as its aim, is at rest in itself and has attained its own essential nature.

This movement in its abstract form as dialectic is therefore regarded as *truly human life*. And since it is still an abstraction, an estrangement of human life, it is regarded as a *divine process*, but as the divine process of man. It is man's abstract, pure, absolute being (as distinct from himself), which itself passes through this process.

Thirdly, this process must have a bearer, a subject; but the subject comes into being only as the result; this result, the subject knowing itself as absolute self-consciousness, is therefore *God, absolute spirit, the self-knowing and self-manifesting idea*. Real man and real nature become mere predicates, symbols of this hidden, unreal man and this unreal nature. Subject and predicate therefore stand in a relation of absolute inversion to one another; a *mystical subject–object* or *subjectivity encroaching upon the object*, the *absolute subject* as a *process*, as a *subject* which *alienates* itself and returns to itself from alienation, while at the same time re-absorbing this alienation, and the subject as this process; pure, *ceaseless* revolving within itself.

First, the formal and abstract conception of man's act of self-creation or self-objectification.

Because Hegel equates man with self-consciousness, the estranged object, the estranged essential reality of man is nothing but consciousness, nothing but the thought of estrangement, its *abstract* and hence hollow and unreal expression, *negation*. The supersession of alienation is therefore likewise nothing but an abstract, hollow supersession of that hollow abstraction, the *negation of the negation*. The inexhaustible, vital, sensuous, concrete activity of self-objectification is therefore reduced to its mere abstraction, *absolute negativity*, an abstraction which is then given permanent form as such and conceived as independent activity, as activity itself. Since this so-called negativity is nothing more than the *abstract, empty* form of that real living act, its content can only be a *formal* content, created by abstraction from all content. Consequently there are general, abstract *forms of abstraction* which fit every content and are therefore indifferent to all content; forms of thought and logical categories torn away from *real* mind and *real* nature. (We shall expound the *logical* content of absolute negativity later.)

Hegel's positive achievement in his speculative logic is to present *determinate concepts*, the universal *fixed thought-forms* in their independence of nature and mind, as a necessary result of the universal estrangement of human existence, and thus also of human thought, and to comprehend them as moments in the process of abstraction. For example, *being* superseded is essence, essence superseded is the concept, the concept superseded is . . . the absolute idea. But what is the absolute idea? It is compelled to supersede its own self again, if it does not wish to go through the whole act of abstraction once more from the beginning and to reconcile itself to being a totality of abstractions or a self-comprehending abstraction. But the abstraction which comprehends itself as abstraction knows itself to be nothing; it must relinquish itself, the abstraction, and so arrives at something which is its exact opposite, *nature*. Hence the whole of the *Logic* is proof of the fact that abstract thought is nothing for itself, that the absolute idea is nothing for itself and that only *nature* is something.

The absolute idea, the abstract idea which '*considered* from the aspect of its unity with itself is *intuition* [*Anschauen*]',[12] and which 'in its own absolute truth *resolves* to let the moment of its particularity or of initial determination and other-being, the *immediate idea*, as its reflection, *issue freely from itself as nature*',[13] this whole idea, which conducts itself in such a strange and baroque fashion, and which has caused the Hegelians such terrible headaches, is purely and simply *abstraction*, i.e. the abstract thinker; abstraction which, taught by experience and enlightened as to its own truth, resolves under various conditions – themselves false and still abstract – to *relinquish itself* and to establish its other-being, the particular, the determinate, in place of its self-pervasion [*Beisichsein*], non-being, universality and indeterminateness; to let *nature*, which it concealed within itself as a mere abstraction, as a thing of thought, *issue freely from itself*, i.e. to

12. G. W. F. Hegel, *Encyclopädie der philosophischen Wissenschaften in Grundrisse*, 3rd edn, Heidelberg, 1830, p. 222.

13. ibid.

abandon abstraction and to take a look at nature, which exists *free* from abstraction. The abstract idea, which directly becomes *intuition*, is quite simply nothing more than abstract thought which relinquishes itself and decides to engage in *intuiting*. This entire transition from logic to philosophy of nature is nothing more than the transition – so difficult for the abstract thinker to effect, and hence described by him in such a bizarre manner – from *abstracting* to *intuiting*. The *mystical* feeling which drives the philosopher from abstract thinking to intuition is *boredom*, the longing for a content.

The man estranged from himself is also the thinker estranged from his *essence*, i.e. from his natural and human essence. His thoughts are therefore fixed phantoms existing outside nature and man. In his *Logic* Hegel has locked up all these phantoms, conceiving each of them firstly as negation, i.e. as *alienation* of *human* thought, and secondly as negation of the negation, i.e. as supersession of this alienation, as a *real* expression of human thought. But since this negation of the negation is itself still trapped in estrangement, what this amounts to is in part the restoration of these fixed phantoms in their estrangement and in part a failure to move beyond the final stage, the stage of self-reference in alienation, which is the true existence of these phantoms.[14] In so far as this abstraction apprehends itself and experiences an infinite boredom with itself, we find in Hegel an abandonment of abstract thought which moves solely within thought, which has no eyes, teeth, ears, anything, and a resolve to recognize *nature* as being and to go over to intuition.

But *nature* too, taken abstractly, for itself, and fixed in its separation from man, is *nothing* for man. It goes without saying that the abstract thinker who decides on intuition, intuits nature abstractly. Just as nature lay enclosed in the thinker in a shape

14. That is, Hegel substitutes the act of abstraction revolving within itself for these fixed abstractions; in so doing he has the merit, first of all, of having revealed the source of all these inappropriate concepts which originally belonged to separate philosophers, of having combined them and of having created as the object of criticism the exhaustive range of abstraction rather than one particular abstraction. We shall later see why Hegel separates thought from the *subject*; but it is already clear that if man is not human, then the expression of his essential nature cannot be human, and therefore that thought itself could not be conceived as an expression of man's being, of man as a human and natural subject, with eyes, ears, etc., living in society, in the world and in nature. [*Marx's note*]

which even to him was shrouded and mysterious, as an absolute idea, a thing of thought, so what he allowed to come forth from himself was simply this *abstract nature*, nature as a thing of thought – but with the significance now of being the other-being of thought, real, intuited nature as distinct from abstract thought. Or, to put it in human terms, the abstract thinker discovers from intuiting nature that the entities which he imagined he was creating out of nothing, out of pure abstraction, in a divine dialectic, as the pure products of the labour of thought living and moving within itself and never looking out into reality, are nothing more than *abstractions* from *natural forms*. The whole of nature only repeats to him in a sensuous, external form the abstractions of logic. He *analyses* nature and these abstractions again. His intuiting of nature is therefore only the act of confirmation of his abstraction from the intuition of nature, a conscious re-enactment of the process by which he produced his abstraction. Thus, for example, Time is equated with Negativity referred to itself.[15] In the natural form, superseded Movement as Matter corresponds to superseded Becoming as Being. Light is the *natural* form of *Reflection-in-itself*. Body as *Moon* and *Comet* is the *natural* form of the *antithesis* which, according to the *Logic*, is the *positive grounded upon itself* and the *negative* grounded upon itself. The Earth is the *natural* form of the logical *ground*, as the negative unity of the antithesis, etc.

Nature as nature, i.e. in so far as it is sensuously distinct from the secret sense hidden within it, nature separated and distinct from these abstractions is *nothing*, a *nothing proving itself to be nothing*, it is *devoid of sense*, or only has the sense of an externality to be superseded.

'In the finite-*teleological* view is to be found the correct premise that nature does not contain the absolute end within itself.'[16]

Its end is the confirmation of abstraction.

'Nature has revealed itself as the idea in the *form* of *other-being*. Since the *idea* in this form is the negative of itself or *external to itself*, nature is not only external relative to this idea, but *externality* constitutes the form in which it exists as nature.'[17]

Externality here should not be understood as *self-externalizing sensuousness* accessible to light and to sensuous man. It is to be taken in the sense of alienation, a flaw, a weakness, something which ought not to be. For that which is true is still the idea.

15. Hegel, op. cit., p. 225.   16. ibid.   17. ibid., p. 227.

Nature is only the *form* of its *other-being*. And since abstract thought is the *essence*, that which is external to it is in essence something merely *external*. The abstract thinker recognizes at the same time that *sensuousness, externality* in contrast to thought which moves and lives *within itself*, is the essence of nature. But at the same time he expresses this antithesis in such a way that this *externality of nature*, its *antithesis* to thought, is its *defect* and that in so far as it is distinct from abstraction it is a defective being. A being which is defective not only for me, not only in my eyes, but in itself, has something outside itself which it lacks. That is to say, its essence is something other than itself. For the abstract thinker nature must therefore supersede itself, since it is already posited by him as a potentially *superseded* being.

'*For us*, mind has *nature* as its *premise*, since it is nature's *truth* and therefore its *absolute primus*. In this truth nature has *disappeared*, and mind has yielded as the idea which has attained being-for-itself, whose *object* as well as *subject* is *the concept*. This identity is *absolute negativity*, for whereas in nature the concept has its perfect external objectivity, in this its alienation has been superseded and the concept has become identical with itself. It is this identity only in that it is a return from nature.'[18]

'*Revelation*, as the *abstract idea*, is unmediated transition to, the *coming-to-be* of, nature; as the revelation of the mind which is free it is the *establishing* of nature as *its own* world; an establishing which, as reflection, is at the same time a *presupposing* of the world as independently existing nature. Revelation in its concept is the creation of nature as the mind's being, in which it procures the affirmation and truth of its freedom.' 'The *absolute is mind*: this is the highest definition of the absolute.'[19]

18. ibid., p. 392.   19. ibid., p. 393.

Critical Notes on the Article 'The King of Prussia and Social Reform. By a Prussian'[1]

[*This article, written in August 1844 for the Paris* Vorwärts!, *is a reply to an article by Arnold Ruge published in* Vorwärts! *No. 60. Ruge, inaccurately signing himself 'a Prussian', belittles the importance of the Silesian weavers' rising and goes on to issue a call for a political party through which to campaign for social reform within the existing state system. Marx's scathing reply represents a final break with Ruge.*

Marx's aim in writing the 'Notes' was twofold. Firstly, he wanted to make it quite plain that he was not the anonymous 'Prussian' and secondly he wanted to criticize Ruge's ideas on the state, social reform and the prospects for the German working class. He develops his earlier theory of the split between the state (political society) and civil society (that is, economic life). The state, he argues, is by nature incapable of removing the social roots of misery in civil life. This is because its jurisdiction ends where civil society begins. The contradiction between public and private life is the very basis of the state.

This is not to say that socialists should reject the idea of political activity. But it is essential to avoid substituting *political action, which is action from the standpoint of the state, for social revolution. A social revolution involves the 'whole', which is excluded from political life. Through social revolution the individual once more becomes part of a real human community. Socialism certainly requires political activity. But as soon as its 'goal, its* soul emerges, *socialism throws its political mask aside'.*

Marx bases his hopes for a socialist revolution on the growing awareness of the German working class, as seen in the Silesian uprising. He calls the German proletariat the 'theoretician of the European proletariat'.]

---

1. Particular circumstances make it necessary for me to declare that the present article is my first contribution to *Vorwärts!* [*Marx's note*]

[*Vorwärts!*,[2] No. 63, 7 August 1844]

An article has appeared in the sixtieth issue of the *Vorwärts!* with the title 'The King of Prussia and Social Reform' and it is signed by '*A Prussian*'.

This so-called Prussian begins by reporting the contents of the Royal Prussian Order in Council on the subject of the *workers' uprising in Silesia*[3] and goes on to give the opinion of the French journal *La Réforme*[4] of that same Prussian Order in Council. The *Réforme*, he says, discerns the origins of the Order in Council in the King's '*panic* and his *religious sentiments*'. It even hails this document as a *presentiment* of the great reforms imminent in bourgeois society. The 'Prussian' delivers the following lecture to the *Réforme*.

Neither the King nor German society has had any 'presentiment of its reform'[5]; not even the uprisings in Bohemia and Silesia have managed to arouse such feelings. In an *unpolitical* country like Germany it is not possible to represent the sporadic misery of the factory districts as a matter of universal concern, let alone as a disaster to the whole civilized world. As far as the Germans are concerned, these events belong in the same category as any *local* shortage of food or water. In accordance with this the King views it as a *failure* of the *administration or of charitable institutions*. For this reason and because but few troops were needed to deal with the feeble weavers the destruction of factories and machines does not make the King and the authorities '*panic*'. Nor were *religious sentiments* responsible for the Order in Council; it was instead a very sober expression of Christian statesmanship and of a doctrine which does not permit any obstacles to stand in the way of its only remedy: the 'good intentions of Christian hearts'. Poverty and crime are two great evils; who can provide a cure for them? The state and the authorities? By no means. But the union of all Christian hearts can do so.

2. A German newspaper published twice weekly in Paris from January to December 1844. Under the influence of Marx, who clearly co-operated in editing the paper from the summer of 1844 onwards, *Vorwärts!* began to take on a communistic character. The paper mercilessly criticized the situation in Prussia. At the request of the Prussian government, the Guizot ministry ordered the expulsion from France of Marx and the principal collaborators on the paper in January 1845.

3. This is a reference to the uprising of 4–6 June 1844 – the first great struggle between workers and capitalists that Germany had ever seen.

4. A French democratic republican newspaper, published 1843–50 in Paris.

5. Note the stylistic and grammatical nonsense. 'Neither the King nor German society has had any presentiment of its reform.' (To whom does 'its' refer?) [*Marx's note*]

Our so-called Prussian denies that the King '*panicked*' for a number of reasons, among them being the fact that few troops were needed to deal with the feeble weavers.

, This means that in a country where banquets with liberal toasts and liberal champagne froth provoke Royal Orders in Council (as we saw in the case of the Düsseldorf banquet),[6] where the burning desire of the entire liberal bourgeoisie for freedom of the press and a constitution could be suppressed without the aid of *a single soldier*, in a country where passive obedience is the order of the day, can it be anything but an *event* and indeed a *terrifying* event when armed troops have to be called out against feeble weavers? And in the first encounter the feeble weavers even gained a victory. They were only suppressed when reinforcements were brought up. Is the uprising of a mass of workers less dangerous because it can be defeated without the aid of a whole army? Our sharp-witted Prussian should compare the revolt of the Silesian weavers with the uprisings of English workers. The Silesians will then stand revealed as *strong* weavers.

A consideration of the *general* relationship between *politics* and the *defects of society* will enable us to explain why the weavers could not induce any great '*panic*' in the King. For the present, however, we will only point out that the uprising was directed in the first instance not against the King of Prussia but against the bourgeoisie. As an aristocrat and an absolute monarch the King of Prussia can have no love of the bourgeoisie; even less can he feel any anxiety if the submissiveness and impotence of the bourgeoisie is increased by its tense and difficult relationship with the proletariat. Similarly, an orthodox Catholic will feel a greater hostility towards an orthodox Protestant than towards an atheist, just as a legitimist will dislike a liberal more than a communist. This is not because atheists are closer to Catholics or communists closer to legitimists than they are to Protestants or liberals respectively, but, on the contrary, because they are more remote from them, because the latter do not impinge on their sphere of interests. The direct political antagonist of the King of Prussia, in his role as politician, is to be found in liberalism. For the King,

6. A reference to the decree of the Prussian king Frederick William IV (18 July 1843) in connection with the participation of government employees in a banquet given in Düsseldorf by some liberals in honour of the Seventh Flemish Parliament. State employees were henceforth forbidden to take part in such Rhenish events.

the antagonism of the proletariat exists no more than does the King for the proletariat. This means that if the proletariat has contrived to eliminate such antipathies and political antagonisms, and to attract the entire hostility of the political powers towards itself, it must have acquired a very definite power. Lastly, the King's appetite for *interesting* and *significant* phenomena is well known and it must have been a very pleasant surprise for him to discover such an '*interesting*' and '*much discussed*' *pauperism* within his very own frontiers and thus to find yet another opportunity to appear in the public eye. How he must have rejoiced to hear the news that he too now possessed his '*own*' Royal Prussian *pauperism*!

Our 'Prussian' is even less fortunate when he *denies* that '*religious sentiment*' was responsible for the Royal Order in Council.

Why is 'religious sentiment' not the source of this Order in Council? Because the latter 'was the very *sober* expression of Christian statesmanship', a 'sober' expression of the doctrine whose 'only remedy, the good intentions of Christian hearts . . . does not permit any obstacles to stand in its way'.

Is not *religious sentiment* the source of Christian statesmanship? Is it not true that a doctrine which possesses a universal panacea in the good intentions of Christian hearts is founded on religious sentiments? Is it true that the expression of religious feelings ceases to be the expression of religious feelings if it is *sober*? I would go even further! I would maintain that any religious feelings that contest the ability of 'the state and the authorities' to 'remedy great evils' while they themselves seek a cure in the 'union of Christian hearts' must be conceited and *drunk* in the extreme. Only very *drunk* religious feelings could locate the source of the evil – as does our 'Prussian' – in the absence of the Christian spirit. Such feelings alone could suggest that the authorities should resort to '*exhortation*' as the only means whereby the Christian spirit might be fortified. According to the 'Prussian' *Christian sentiment* is the sole end and aim of the Order in Council. Religious sentiment, when it is drunk, of course, not when it is sober, considers itself to be the only good. Whenever it comes across evil it attributes it to its own *absence*, for, if it is the only good, then it alone can create the good. Therefore, an Order in Council, dictated by religious feelings, logically enough itself decrees religious feelings. A politician with *sober* religious feelings would not attempt to find a 'cure' for his own 'perplexity' in the 'exhortations of the pious Preacher to cultivate Christian sentiments'.

How then does our so-called 'Prussian' demonstrate to the *Réforme* that the Order in Council is not an emanation of religious feeling? By describing it as an emanation of religious feeling. What insight into social movements can be expected from such an *illogical* mind? Let us listen to him *gossiping* about the relationship of *German society* to the workers' movement and social reform in general.

Let us *distinguish* – as our 'Prussian' fails to do – let us distinguish between the various categories subsumed by the expression 'German society': government, bourgeoisie, the press and finally the workers themselves. These are the *various* masses we are concerned with here. The 'Prussian' merges them all into one mass and condemns them *en masse* from his exalted standpoint. According to him *German society* has 'not even had a *presentiment* of its reform'.

Why is it so lacking in this instinct? Because, the Prussian explains,

In an *unpolitical* country like Germany it is not possible to represent the sporadic misery of the factory districts as a matter of *universal concern*, let alone as a disaster to the whole civilized world. As far as the Germans are concerned, these events belong in the same category as any *local* shortage of food or water. In accordance with this the King views it as a *failure* of the *administration or of charitable institutions*.

The 'Prussian' thus explains this *absurd* interpretation of the plight of the workers with reference to the *peculiar nature* of an unpolitical country.

It will be granted that England is a *political* nation. It will further be granted that England is the *nation of pauperism*; the word itself is English in origin. An examination of the situation in England is thus the most certain way whereby to discover the *relation* of a *political* nation to *pauperism*. In England the misery of the workers is not sporadic but *universal*; it is not confined to the factory districts but extends to country districts too. Workers' movements are not in their infancy but have recurred periodically for close on a century.

What then is the view of pauperism taken by the English bourgeoisie and the government and the press connected with it?

In so far as the English bourgeoisie regards pauperism as the *fault of politics* the Whigs put the blame on the Tories and the Tories put it on the Whigs. According to the Whigs the chief cause of pauperism is to be discovered in the monopoly of landed property and in the laws prohibiting the import of grain. In the Tory view the source of the trouble lies in liberalism, in competition and the excesses of the factory system. Neither party discovers the explanation in politics itself but only in the politics of the other party. Neither party would even dream of a reform of society as a whole.

The most decisive expression of the insight of the English into pauperism – and by the English we mean the English bourgeoisie and the government – is to be found in *English Political Economy*, i.e. the scientific reflection of the state of the economy in England.

MacCulloch, a pupil of the cynic Ricardo and one of the best and most celebrated of the English economists, is familiar with the present state of affairs and has an overall view of the movement of bourgeois society. In a public lecture, amidst applause, he had the temerity to apply to political economy what Bacon had said of philosophy:

The man who suspends his judgement with true and untiring wisdom, who progresses gradually, and who successively surmounts obstacles which impede the course of study like mountains, will in time reach the summit of knowledge where rest and pure air may be enjoyed, where Nature may be viewed in all her beauty, and whence one may descend by an easy path to the final details of practice.[7]

The *pure air* of the pestilential atmosphere of English basement dwellings! The *great natural beauty* of the fantastic rags in which the English poor are clothed and of the faded, shrivelled flesh of the women worn out by work and want; the children lying on dung-heaps; the stunted monsters produced by overwork in the mechanical monotony of the factories! The most charming *final details of practice*: prostitution, murder and the gallows!

Even that section of the English bourgeoisie which is conscious of the dangers of pauperism regards both the dangers and the means for remedying them not merely as *particular* problems, but – to put it bluntly – in a *childish* and *absurd* manner.

7. Marx is quoting Bacon from the French translation (Geneva, Paris, 1825, pp. 131–2) of John Ramsay MacCulloch's *A Discourse on the Rise, Progress, Peculiar Objects and Importance of Political Economy* (Edinburgh, 1824).

Thus, for example, in his pamphlet 'Recent Measures for the Promotion of Education in England', Dr Kay reduces the whole question to the *neglect of education*. It is not hard to guess the reason! He argues that the worker's lack of education prevents him from understanding the 'natural laws of trade', laws which *necessarily* reduce him to pauperism. For this reason the worker rises up in rebellion. And this rebellion may well '*cause embarrassment* to the prosperity of English manufactures and English commerce, *impair* the mutual confidence of businessmen and *diminish* the stability of political and social institutions'.

This is the extent of the insanity of the English bourgeoisie and its press on the subject of pauperism, the national epidemic of England.

Let us assume for the moment that the criticisms levelled by our 'Prussian' at *German* society are justified. Is it true that their explanation is to be found in the *unpolitical* nature of Germany? But if the bourgeoisie of an *unpolitical* Germany is unable to achieve clarity about the general significance of *sporadic* misery, it does not lag behind the bourgeoisie of a *political* England which has managed to overlook the general significance of universal misery, of misery whose general meaning has become apparent partly by virtue of its periodic recurrence in time, partly by its extension in space and partly by the failure of every attempt to eliminate it.

The 'Prussian' heaps further obloquy on the *unpolitical* nature of Germany because the King of Prussia has located the cause of pauperism in 'failures of the administration or of charitable *institutions*' and has therefore looked to administrative or charitable *measures* to provide a cure for pauperism.

Is this analysis peculiar to the King of Prussia? Let us again look briefly at England, the only country where there has been any large-scale action against pauperism worth mentioning.

The present English Poor Laws date from Act 43 of the reign of Elizabeth.[8] How does this legislation propose to deal with pauperism? By obliging the parishes to support their own poor workers, by the Poor Rate, by legal charity. Charity dispensed by the administration: this has been the method in force for two centuries. After long and painful experiences what view is adopted by Parliament in its Bill of Amendment in 1834?

8. It is not necessary for our purposes here to go back to the labourers' Statute of Edward III. [*Marx's note*]

It begins by explaining the frightening increase in pauperism as the result of a '*defect in the administration*'.

It therefore provides for a reform of the administration of the Poor Rate by officials of the different parishes. *Unions* of about twenty parishes are to be set up under a central administration. On a specified day the Board of Guardians, consisting of officials elected by the tax-payers, are to assemble at the headquarters of the union and decide on eligibility for relief. These Boards are presided over and controlled by government representatives from the Central Commission at Somerset House, the *Ministry of Pauperism*, to use the phrase aptly coined by a Frenchman.[9] The capital so administered is almost equal to the sum required by the War Office in France. The number of local offices thus maintained amounts to 500 and each of these local offices keeps at least twelve officials busy.

The English Parliament did not rest content with the *formal* reform of the administration.

The chief cause of the *acute* condition of English pauperism was found to lie in the *Poor Law* itself. It was discovered that charity, the legal method of combating social evils, itself fostered social evils. As for pauperism in *general*, it was held to be an *eternal law of nature* in accordance with Malthus's theory:

Since the population threatens unceasingly to exceed the available means of subsistence, benevolence is folly, an open encouragement to misery. The state, therefore, can do nothing but leave misery to its fate, and, at best, facilitate the death of those in want.

The English Parliament combined this philanthropic theory with the view that pauperism is a *state of misery brought on by the workers themselves*, and that in consequence it should not be regarded as a misfortune to be prevented but as a crime to be suppressed and punished.

In this way the system of the workhouse came into being, i.e. houses for the poor whose internal arrangements were devised to *deter* the indigent from seeking a refuge from starvation. In the workhouses charity has been ingeniously combined with the *revenge* of the bourgeoisie on all those wretched enough to appeal to their charity.

Initially England attempted to eliminate pauperism by means of *charity* and *administrative measures*. It then came to regard the

9. Eugène Buret.

progressive increase in pauperism not as the inevitable consequence of modern *industry* but rather as the consequence of the *English Poor Law*. It construed the state of universal need as merely a *particular* feature of English law. What was formerly attributed to a *deficiency of charity* was now ascribed to the *superabundance of charity*. Lastly, need was regarded as the fault of the needy and punishable as such.

The general lesson learnt by political England from its experience of pauperism is none other than that, in the course of history and despite all administrative measures, pauperism has developed into a *national institution* which has inevitably become the object of a highly ramified and extensive administrative system, a system however which *no longer* sets out to eliminate it, but which strives instead to *discipline* and *perpetuate* it. This administrative system has abandoned all attempts to stop pauperism at its source through positive measures; it confines itself to preparing a grave for it with true police mildness as soon as it erupts on the surface of officialdom. Far from advancing beyond administrative and charitable measures, the English state has regressed to a far more primitive position. It dispenses its administrative gifts only to *that* pauperism which is induced by despair to allow itself to be caught and incarcerated.

Thus far the 'Prussian' has failed to show that the procedure adopted by the King of Prussia has any features peculiar to it. But *why*, our great man now exclaims with *rare naïvety*: 'Why does the King not *decree the education of all deprived children at a stroke*?' Why must he turn first to the authorities with requests for their plans and proposals?

Our all-too-clever 'Prussian' will regain his composure when he realizes that in acting thus the King of Prussia is just as unoriginal as in all his other actions. In fact he has taken the only course of action open to the head of a state.

Napoleon wished to do away with begging at a single stroke. He instructed his officials to prepare plans for the abolition of beggary throughout the whole of France. The project was subject to delay; Napoleon became impatient, he wrote to Crétet, his Minister of the Interior; he commanded him to get rid of begging within a month. He said, 'One should not depart this life without leaving traces which commend our memory to posterity. Do not ask me for another three or four months to obtain information; you have young advocates, clever prefects, expert engineers of bridges and roads. Set them all in motion, do not fall into the sleepy inactivity of routine office work.'

Within a few months everything was ready. On 5 July 1808 the law to suppress begging was enacted. By what means? By means of the *dépôts* which were so speedily transformed into penal institutions that in a short time the poor man could gain access to one only via a *police court*. Nevertheless, M. Noailles du Gard, a member of the legislative body, was able to declare, 'Eternal gratitude to the hero who has found a refuge for the needy and the means of life for the poor. Childhood will no longer be abandoned, poor families will no longer lack resources, nor will workers go without encouragement and employment. *Nos pas ne seront plus arrêtés par l'image dégoûtante des infirmités et de la honteuse misère.*'[10]

This last cynical statement is the only truth contained in this eulogy.

If Napoleon can turn to his advocates, prefects and engineers for counsel, why should not the King of Prussia turn to his authorities?

Why did not Napoleon simply decree the abolition of beggary *at a stroke*? This question is just as valid as that of our 'Prussian' who asks: 'Why does the King not decree the education of all deprived children at a stroke?' Does the 'Prussian' understand what the King would have to decree? Nothing other than the *abolition of the proletariat*. To educate children it is necessary to *feed* them and free them from the *need to earn a livelihood*. The feeding and educating of destitute children, i.e. the feeding and educating of the *entire future* proletariat, would mean the abolition of the proletariat and of pauperism.

For a moment the *Convention* had the courage to *decree* the abolition of pauperism, not indeed '*at a stroke*', as the 'Prussian' requires of his King, but only after instructing the Committee of Public Safety to draw up the necessary plans and proposals and after the latter had made use of the extensive investigation by the Constituent Assembly into the state of poverty in France and, through Barère, had proposed the establishment of the 'Livre de la bienfaisance nationale'[11] etc. What was achieved by the decree of the Convention? Simply that there was now one decree more

10. We will no longer be hampered by the disgusting sight of illness and shameful misery.
11. Book of national charity.

in the world and that *one* year later starving women besieged the Convention.

The Convention, however, represented the *maximum of political energy, political power* and *political understanding*.

No government in the whole world has issued *decrees* about pauperism *at a stroke* and without consulting the authorities. The English Parliament even sent emissaries to all the countries in Europe in order to discover the different administrative remedies in use. But in their attempts to come to grips with pauperism every government has stuck fast at *charitable* and *administrative measures* or even regressed to a more primitive stage than that.

Can the state do otherwise?

The *state* will never discover the source of *social* evils *in the 'state and the organization of society'*, as the Prussian expects of his King. Wherever there are political parties each party will attribute *every* defect of society to the fact that its rival is at the helm of the state instead of itself. Even the radical and revolutionary politicians look for the causes of evil not in the *nature* of the state but in a specific *form of the state* which they would like to replace with *another* form of the state.

From a *political* point of view the *state* and the *organization of society* are not *two* different things. The state is the organization of society. In so far as the state acknowledges the existence of *social* grievances it locates their origins either in the *laws of nature* over which no human agency has control, or in *private life*, which is independent of the state, or else in *malfunctions of the administration* which is dependent on it. Thus England finds poverty to be based on the *law of nature* according to which the population must always outgrow the available means of subsistence. From another point of view it explains *pauperism* as the consequence of the *bad will of the poor*, just as the King of Prussia explains it in terms of the *unchristian feelings of the rich* and the Convention explains it in terms of the *counter-revolutionary and suspect attitudes* of the *proprietors*. Hence England punishes the poor, the King of Prussia exhorts the rich and the Convention beheads the proprietors.

Lastly, *all* states seek the cause in *fortuitous* or *intentional defects in the administration* and hence the cure is sought in administrative measures. Why? Because the *administration* is the *organizing* agency of the state.

The contradiction between the vocation and the good intentions of the administration on the one hand and the means and powers at its disposal on the other cannot be eliminated by the state, except by abolishing itself; for the state is based on this contradiction. It is based on the contradiction between *public* and *private life*, between *universal* and *particular interests*. For this reason, the state must confine itself to *formal, negative* activities, since the scope of its own power comes to an end at the very point where civil life and work begin. Indeed, when we consider the consequences arising from the asocial nature of civil life, of private property, of trade, of industry, of the mutual plundering that goes on between the various groups in civil life, it becomes clear that the *law of nature* governing the administration is *impotence*. For, the fragmentation, the depravity and the *slavery of civil society* is the natural foundation of the *modern* state, just as the civil society of slavery was the natural foundation of the state in *antiquity*. The existence of the state is inseparable from the existence of slavery. The state and slavery in antiquity – frank and open *classical* antitheses – were not more closely *welded* together than the modern state and the cut-throat world of modern business – sanctimonious *Christian* antitheses. If the modern state desired to abolish the *impotence* of its administration it would have to abolish contemporary *private life*. And to abolish private life it would have to abolish itself, since it exists *only* as the antithesis of private life. However, no *living* person believes the defects of his existence to be based on the *principle*, the essential nature of his own life; they must instead be grounded in circumstances *outside* his own life. *Suicide* is contrary to nature. Hence the state cannot believe in the *intrinsic* impotence of its administration, i.e. of itself. It can *only* perceive formal, contingent defects in it and try to remedy them. If these modifications are inadequate, well, that just shows that social ills are natural imperfections, independent of man, they are a *law of God*, or else, the will of private individuals is too degenerate to meet the good intentions of the administration halfway. And how [perverse private individuals are! They grumble about the government when it places limits on freedom and yet demand that the government should prevent the inevitable consequences of that freedom!

The more powerful a state and hence the *more political* a nation, the less inclined it is to explain the *general* principle governing *social* ills and to seek out their causes by looking at the *principle of the state*, i.e. at the *actual organization of society* of which the state is the active, self-conscious and official expression. *Political* understanding is just *political* understanding because its thought does not transcend the limits of politics. The sharper and livelier it is, the more incapable is it of comprehending social problems. The *classical* period of political understanding is the *French Revolution*. Far from identifying the principle of the state as the source of social ills, the heroes of the French Revolution held social ills to be the source of political problems. Thus Robespierre regarded great wealth and great poverty as an obstacle to *pure democracy*. He therefore wished to establish a universal system of *Spartan* frugality. The principle of politics is the *will*. The more one-sided, i.e. the more perfect, *political* understanding is, the more completely it puts its faith in the *omnipotence* of the will; the blinder it is towards the *natural* and spiritual *limitations* of the will, the more incapable it becomes of discovering the real source of the evils of society. No further arguments are needed to prove that when the 'Prussian' claims that 'the political understanding' is destined 'to uncover the roots of social want in Germany' he is indulging in vain illusions.

It was foolish to expect the King of Prussia to exhibit a power not possessed by the Convention and Napoleon combined; it was foolish to expect him to possess a vision which could cross *all* political frontiers, a vision with which our clever 'Prussian' is no better endowed than is his King. The entire declaration was all the more foolish as our 'Prussian' admits:

Fine words and fine sentiments are *cheap*, insight and successful actions are *dear*; in this case they are *more than dear*, they are quite *unobtainable*.

If they are quite unobtainable then we should acknowledge the efforts of everyone who does what is possible in a given situation. For the rest I leave it to the reader's tact to determine whether the commercial jargon of 'cheap', 'dear', 'more than dear', 'unobtainable', are to be included in the category of '*fine* words' and '*fine* sentiments'.

Even if we assume then that the 'Prussian's' remarks about the German government and the German bourgeoisie – the latter is presumably to be included in 'German society' – are well-founded, does this mean that this segment of society is more perplexed in Germany than in England and France? Is it possible to be more perplexed than in England, for example, where *perplexity* has been erected into a system? If workers' uprisings were to break out today all over England the bourgeoisie and the government would not have any better solutions than those that were open to them in the last third of the eighteenth century. Their only solution is physical force and since the efficacy of physical force declines in geometric proportion to the growth of pauperism and of the proletariat's understanding, the perplexity of the English necessarily increases in geometric proportion too.

Lastly, it is *false, factually false,* that the German bourgeoisie wholly fails to appreciate the general significance of the Silesian revolt. In a number of towns the masters are making attempts to associate themselves with the journeymen. All the *liberal* German papers, the organs of the liberal bourgeoisie, are overflowing with statements about the organization of labour, the reform of society, criticism of monopolies and competition, etc. All as a result of the workers' movements. The newspapers of Trier, Aachen, Cologne, Wesel, Mannheim, Breslau and even Berlin are publishing often quite sensible articles on social questions from which our 'Prussian' could well profit. Indeed, letters from Germany constantly express surprise at the lack of bourgeois resistance to *social* ideas and tendencies.

If the 'Prussian' were more conversant with the history of the social movement he would have asked the opposite question. Why does the German bourgeoisie attribute such relatively universal significance to sporadic and particular problems? How are we to explain why the proletariat should be shown such *animosity* and *cynicism* by the *political* bourgeoisie and such *sympathy* and *lack of resistance* by the unpolitical bourgeoisie?

[*Vorwärts!,* No. 64, 10 August 1844]

Now for the oracular utterances of the 'Prussian' concerning the *German workers.*

The German poor (he observes wittily) *are no cleverer than the poor Germans,* i.e. they *never* look beyond their hearth, their factory or their district: they remain as yet untouched by the all-pervading spirit of politics.

In order to compare the situation of the German workers with that of the English and French workers, the 'Prussian' should have compared the *first formation,* the *beginnings* of the French and English workers' movements with the *new-born* German movement. He fails to do this. Hence his entire argument amounts only to the trivial observation that, e.g., industry in Germany is less advanced than in England, or that the start of a movement looks different from its later development. He had wished to speak of the specific nature of the German workers' movement, but does not say a single word on the subject.

He should consider the matter from the correct vantage-point. He would then realize that *not a single one* of the French and English insurrections has had the same *theoretical* and *conscious* character as the Silesian weavers' rebellion.

Think first of the *Weavers' Song*,[12] that intrepid battle-cry which does not even mention hearth, factory or district but in which the proletariat at once proclaims its antagonism to the society of private property in the most decisive, aggressive, ruthless and forceful manner. The Silesian rebellion *starts* where the French and English workers' *finish*, namely with an understanding of the nature of the proletariat. This *superiority* stamps the whole episode. Not only were machines destroyed, those competitors of the workers, but also the *account books*, the titles of ownership, and whereas all other movements had directed their attacks primarily at the visible enemy, namely the *industrialists*, the Silesian workers turned also against the hidden enemy, the bankers. Finally, not one English workers' uprising was carried out with such courage, foresight and endurance.

As for the German workers' level of education or capacity for it, I would point to *Weitling's* brilliant writings which surpass *Proudhon's* from a theoretical point of view, however defective they may be in execution. What single work on the emancipation of the bourgeoisie, that is, political emancipation, can the bourgeoisie – for all their philosophers and scholars – put beside Weitling's *Guarantees of Harmony and Freedom*? If we compare the meek, sober mediocrity of German political literature with this *titanic* and brilliant literary debut of the German workers; if we compare these *gigantic* children's shoes of the proletariat with the dwarf-like proportions of the worn-out political shoes of the German bourgeoisie, we must predict a vigorous future for this German Cinderella. It must be granted that the German proletariat is the *theoretician* of the European proletariat just as the English proletariat is its *economist* and the French its *politician*. It must be granted that the vocation of Germany for *social*

12. Written by Heine.

revolution is as *classical* as its incapacity for *political* revolution. For just as the impotence of the German bourgeoisie is the *political* impotence of Germany, so too the capacity of the German proletariat – even apart from German theory – is the *social* capacity of Germany. The disparity between the philosophical and political development of Germany is nothing *abnormal*. It is a necessary disparity. Only in socialism can a philosophical nation discover the praxis consonant with its nature and only in the *proletariat* can it discover the active agent of its emancipation.

For the moment, however, I have neither time nor the will to lecture the 'Prussian' on the relationship between German society and the social revolution and to show how this relationship explains, on the one hand, the feeble reaction of the German bourgeoisie to socialism and, on the other hand, the brilliant talents of the German proletariat for socialism. He can find the first rudiments necessary for an understanding of this phenomenon in my Introduction to the *Critique of Hegel's Philosophy of Right* (in the *Franco–German Yearbooks*).

Thus the cleverness of the *German poor* stands in *inverse* ratio to the cleverness of the *poor Germans*. But people who make every object the occasion for stylistic exercises in public are misled by such *formal* activities into perverting the content, while for its part the perverted content stamps the imprint of vulgarity upon the form. Thus the 'Prussian's' attempt to discuss the workers' unrest in Silesia in formal antitheses has led him into the greatest antitheses to the truth. Confronted with the initial outbreak of the Silesian revolt no man who thinks and who loves the truth could regard the duty to play *schoolmaster* to the event as his primary task. On the contrary, his duty would rather be to study it to discover its *specific* character. Of course, this requires scientific understanding and a certain love of mankind, while the other procedure needs only a ready-made phraseology saturated in an overweening love of oneself.

Why does the 'Prussian' treat the German workers with such disdain? Because he believes the 'whole problem' – namely the problem of the plight of the workers – 'to have been *as yet* untouched by the all-pervading spirit of *politics*'. He dilates on his platonic love for the spirit of *politics* as follows:

All rebellions that are sparked off by the disastrous *isolation of men from the community* and *of their thoughts from social principles* are bound to be suppressed amid a welter of blood and incomprehension. But once need produces understanding and once the *political* understanding of the Germans discovers the roots of social need then even in Germany these events will be felt to be the symptoms of a great upheaval.

First of all, we hope that the 'Prussian' will permit us to make a *stylistic* comment. His antithesis is incomplete. The first half asserts: Once *need* produces *understanding*. The second half states: Once the *political understanding* discovers the *roots of social need*. The *simple* understanding of the first half of the anti-thesis becomes *political* understanding in the second, just as the simple *need* of the first half becomes the *social* need of the second. Why has our master of style weighted the two halves of his anti-thesis so unequally? I do not think that he has reflected on the matter. I shall reveal his correct *instinct* to him. Had he written: 'Once *social* need produces *political* understanding and once *political understanding* has discovered the roots of *social need*' no impartial reader could have failed to see that this antithesis was *nonsensical*. To begin with everyone would have wondered why the anonymous author did not link social understanding with social need and political understanding with political need as the most elementary logic would require? But let us proceed to the issue itself!

It is entirely false that *social* need produces *political* under-standing. Indeed, it is nearer the truth to say that *political* under-standing is produced by social *well-being*. Political understanding is something spiritual, that is given to him that hath, to the man who is already sitting on velvet. Our 'Prussian' should take note of what M. Michel Chevalier, a French economist, has to say on the subject:

In 1789 when the bourgeoisie rose in rebellion the only thing lacking to its freedom was the right to participate in the government of the country. Emancipation meant the removal of the control of public affairs, the high civic, military and religious functions from the hands of the privileged classes who had a monopoly of these functions. *Wealthy* and *enlightened*, self-sufficient and able to manage their own affairs, they wished to evade the clutches of arbitrary rule.

We have already demonstrated to our 'Prussian' how inade-quate *political* understanding is to the task of discovering the source of social need. *One* last word on his view of the matter. The more developed and the more comprehensive is the *political* understanding of a nation, the more the proletariat will squander its energies – at least in the initial stages of the movement – in senseless, futile uprisings that will be drowned in blood. Because it thinks in political terms it regards the *will* as the cause of all evils and *force* and the *overthrow of a particular* form of the state as the universal remedy. Proof: the first outbreaks of the *French* proletariat.[13] The workers in Lyons imagined their goals were entirely political, they saw themselves purely as soldiers of the republic, while in reality they were the soldiers of socialism. Thus their political understanding obscured the roots of their social misery, it falsified their insight into their real goal, their *political understanding deceived* their *social instincts*.

But if the 'Prussian' expects understanding to be the result of misery why does he identify '*suppression in blood*' with '*suppression in incomprehension*'? If misery is a means whereby to produce understanding, then a bloody slaughter must be a *very extreme* means to that end. The 'Prussian' would have to argue that suppression in a welter of blood will stifle incomprehension and bring a breath of fresh air to the understanding.

The 'Prussian' predicts the suppression of the insurrections which are sparked off by the '*disastrous isolation of man from the community* and *of their thoughts from social principles*'.

We have shown that in the Silesian uprising there was no separation of thoughts from social principles. That leaves '*the disastrous isolation of men from the community*'. By community is meant here the *political community, the state*. It is the old song about *unpolitical Germany*.

But do not *all* rebellions without exception have their roots in *the disastrous isolation of man from the community*? Does not every rebellion necessarily presuppose isolation? Would the revolution of 1789 have taken place if French citizens had not felt disastrously isolated from the community? The abolition of this isolation was its very purpose.

But the community from which the worker is *isolated* is a community of quite different reality and scope than the *political* community. The community from which *his own labour* separates him is *life* itself, physical and spiritual life, human morality, human activity, human enjoyment, *human nature*. *Human nature*

13. A reference to the uprisings of the Lyons workers in November 1831 and April 1834.

is the true community of men. Just as the disastrous isolation from this nature is disproportionately more far-reaching, unbearable, terrible and contradictory than the isolation from the political community, so too the transcending of this isolation and even a partial reaction, a *rebellion* against it, is so much greater, just as the *man* is greater than the *citizen* and *human life* than *political life*. Hence, however limited an industrial revolt may be, it contains within itself a *universal* soul: and however universal a political revolt may be, its *colossal* form conceals a *narrow* spirit.

The 'Prussian' brings his essay to a close worthy of it with the following sentence:

A social revolution without a political soul (i.e. without a central insight organizing it from the point of view of the totality) is impossible.

We have seen: a social revolution possesses a *total* point of view because – even if it is confined to only one factory district – it represents a protest by man against a dehumanized life, because it proceeds from the point of view of the *particular, real individual*, because the *community* against whose separation from himself the individual is reacting, is the *true* community of man, *human* nature. In contrast, the *political soul* of revolution consists in the tendency of the classes with no political power to put an end to their *isolation from the state* and from *power*. Its point of view is that of the state, of an abstract *totality* which exists *only* through its separation from real life and which is *unthinkable* in the absence of an organized antithesis between the universal idea and the individual existence of man. In accordance with the *limited* and *contradictory* nature of the political soul a revolution inspired by it organizes a dominant group within society at the cost of society.

We shall let the 'Prussian' in on the secret of the nature of a '*social* revolution with a *political* soul': we shall thus confide to him the secret that not even his *phrases* raise him above the level of political narrow-mindedness.

A '*social*' revolution with a *political* soul is either a composite piece of nonsense, if by 'social' revolution the 'Prussian' understands a 'social' revolution as *opposed* to a political one, while at the same time he endows the social revolution with a political, rather than a social soul. Or else a '*social revolution with a political soul*' is nothing but a paraphrase of what is usually called a '*political revolution*' or a '*revolution pure and simple*'. Every revolution dissolves the *old order of society*; to that extent it is *social*. Every revolution brings down the *old ruling power*; to that extent it is *political*.

The 'Prussian' must choose between this *paraphrase* and *nonsense*. But whether the idea of a *social revolution* with a *political soul* is paraphrase or nonsense there is no doubt about the rationality of a *political revolution* with a *social soul*. All revolution – the *overthrow* of the existing ruling power and the *dissolution* of the old order – is a *political act*. But without revolution *socialism* cannot be made possible. It stands in need of this political act just as it stands in need of *destruction* and *dissolution*. But as soon as its *organizing functions* begin and its *goal*, its *soul* emerges, socialism throws its *political* mask aside.

Such lengthy perorations were necessary to break through the *tissue* of errors concealed in a single newspaper column. Not every reader possesses the education and the time necessary to get to grips with such *literary swindles*. In view of this does not our anonymous 'Prussian' owe it to the reading public to give up writing on political and social themes and to refrain from making declamatory statements on the situation in Germany, in order to devote himself to a conscientious analysis of his own situation?

Paris, 31 July 1844

Appendix

[*This appendix contains two short but extremely famous texts by Marx which, although they fall outside the temporal limits of this volume, are of obvious relevance to it. The first, best known by Engels' title of the 'Theses on Feuerbach', was written in the spring of 1845. The second, Marx's preface to his* A Contribution to the Critique of Political Economy, *was written fourteen years later in 1859. As Lucio Colletti mentions in his introduction to this volume, these brief texts – together with the postface to the second German edition of* Capital, volume I – *are all that Marx left to explain the 'reasons, philosophical as well as practical, which had induced [him] to give up philosophy after his break with Hegel and Feuerbach; induced him to devote himself to the analysis of modern capitalist society, instead of going on to write a philosophical treatise of his own'.*]

A. CONCERNING FEUERBACH

I

The chief defect of all hitherto existing materialism (that of Feuerbach included) is that the thing, reality, sensuousness, is conceived only in the form of the *object or of contemplation*, but not as *sensuous human activity, practice*, not subjectively. Hence, in contradistinction to materialism, the *active* side was developed abstractly by idealism – which, of course, does not know real, sensuous activity as such. Feuerbach wants sensuous objects, really distinct from the thought objects, but he does not conceive human activity itself as *objective* activity. Hence, in *Das Wesen des Christentums*, he regards the theoretical attitude as the only genuinely human attitude, while practice is conceived and fixed only in its dirty-judaical manifestation. Hence he does not grasp the significance of 'revolutionary', of 'practical-critical', activity.

II

The question whether objective truth can be attributed to human thinking is not a question of theory but is a *practical* question. Man must prove the truth, i.e. the reality and power, the this-sidedness of his thinking in practice. The dispute over the reality or non-reality of thinking that is isolated from practice is a purely *scholastic* question.

III

The materialist doctrine concerning the changing of circumstances and upbringing forgets that circumstances are changed by men and that it is essential to educate the educator himself. This doctrine must, therefore, divide society into two parts, one of which is superior to society.

The coincidence of the changing of circumstances and of human activity or self-changing can be conceived and rationally understood only as *revolutionary practice*.

IV

Feuerbach starts out from the fact of religious self-alienation, of the duplication of the world into a religious world and a secular one. His work consists in resolving the religious world into its secular basis. But that the secular basis detaches itself from itself and establishes itself as an independent realm in the clouds can only be explained by the cleavages and self-contradictions within this secular basis. The latter must, therefore, in itself be both understood in its contradiction and revolutionized in practice. Thus, for instance, after the earthly family is discovered to be the secret of the holy family, the former must then itself be destroyed in theory and in practice.

V

Feuerbach, not satisfied with *abstract thinking*, wants *contemplation*; but he does not conceive sensuousness as *practical*, human-sensous activity.

VI

Feuerbach resolves the religious essence into the *human* essence. But the human essence is no abstraction inherent in each single individual. In its reality it is the ensemble of the social relations.

Feuerbach, who does not enter upon a criticism of this real essence, is consequently compelled:

1. To abstract from the historical process and to fix the religious sentiment as something by itself and to presuppose an abstract – *isolated* – human individual.

2. Essence, therefore, can be comprehended only as 'genus', as an internal, dumb generality which *naturally* unites the many individuals.

VII

Feuerbach, consequently, does not see that the 'religious sentiment' is itself a social product, and that the abstract individual whom he analyses belongs to a particular form of society.

VIII

All social life is essentially *practical*. All mysteries which lead theory to mysticism find their rational solution in human practice and in the comprehension of this practice.

IX

The highest point reached by contemplative materialism, that is, materialism which does not comprehend sensuousness as practical activity, is the contemplation of single individuals and of civil society.

X

The standpoint of the old materialism is civil society; the standpoint of the new is human society, or social humanity.

XI

The philosophers have only *interpreted* the world, in various ways; the point is to *change* it.

B. PREFACE
(to *A Contribution to the Critique of Political Economy*)

I examine the system of bourgeois economy in the following order: *capital, landed property, wage-labour; the State, foreign trade, world market*. The economic conditions of existence of the three great classes into which modern bourgeois society is divided are analysed under the first three headings; the interconnection of the other three headings is self-evident. The first part of the first book, dealing with Capital, comprises the following chapters: 1. The commodity; 2. Money or simple circulation; 3. Capital in general. The present part consists of the first two chapters. The entire material lies before me in the form of monographs, which were written not for publication but for self-clarification at widely separated periods; their remoulding into an integrated whole according to the plan I have indicated will depend upon circumstances.

A general introduction,[1] which I had drafted, is omitted, since on further consideration it seems to me confusing to anticipate results which still have to be substantiated, and the reader who really wishes to follow me will have to decide to advance from the particular to the general. A few brief remarks regarding the course of my study of political economy may, however, be appropriate here.

Although I studied jurisprudence, I pursued it as a subject subordinated to philosophy and history. In the year 1842–3, as editor of the *Rheinische Zeitung*, I first found myself in the embarrassing position of having to discuss what is known as material interests. The deliberations of the Rhenish Landtag on forest thefts and the division of landed property; the official polemic started by Herr von Schaper, then Oberpräsident of the Rhine Province, against the *Rheinische Zeitung* about the condition of the Moselle peasantry, and finally the debates on free trade and protective tariffs caused me in the first instance to turn my attention to economic questions. On the other hand, at that time when good intentions 'to push forward' often took the place of factual knowledge, an echo of French socialism and communism, slightly tinged by philosophy, was noticeable in the *Rheinische Zeitung*. I objected to this dilettantism, but at the

1. '1857 Introduction', in *Grundrisse*, The Pelican Marx Library, 1973, pp. 81–111.

same time frankly admitted in a controversy with the *Allgemeine Augsburger Zeitung* that my previous studies did not allow me to express any opinion on the content of the French theories. When the publishers of the *Rheinische Zeitung* conceived the illusion that by a more compliant policy on the part of the paper it might be possible to secure the abrogation of the death sentence passed upon it, I eagerly grasped the opportunity to withdraw from the public stage to my study.

The first work which I undertook to dispel the doubts assailing me was a critical re-examination of the Hegelian philosophy of law; the introduction to this work being published in the *Deutsch–Französische Jahrbücher* issued in Paris in 1844. My inquiry led me to the conclusion that neither legal relations nor political forms could be comprehended whether by themselves or on the basis of a so-called general development of the human mind, but that on the contrary they originate in the material conditions of life, the totality of which Hegel, following the example of English and French thinkers of the eighteenth century, embraces within the term 'civil society'; that the anatomy of this civil society, however, has to be sought in political economy. The study of this, which I began in Paris, I continued in Brussels, where I moved owing to an expulsion order issued by M. Guizot. The general conclusion at which I arrived and which, once reached, became the guiding principle of my studies can be summarized as follows. In the social production of their existence, men inevitably enter into definite relations, which are independent of their will, namely relations of production appropriate to a given stage in the development of their material forces of production. The totality of these relations of production constitutes the economic structure of society, the real foundation, on which arises a legal and political superstructure and to which correspond definite forms of social consciousness. The mode of production of material life conditions the general process of social, political and intellectual life. It is not the consciousness of men that determines their existence, but their social existence that determines their consciousness. At a certain stage of development, the material productive forces of society come into conflict with the existing relations of production or – this merely expresses the same thing in legal terms – with the property relations within the framework of which they have operated hitherto. From forms of development of the productive forces these relations turn into their fetters. Then begins an era of social revolution. The changes in the economic foundation lead sooner or later to the transformation of the whole immense superstructure. In studying such transformations it is always necessary to distinguish between the material transformation of the economic conditions of production, which can be determined with the precision of natural science, and the legal, political, religious, artistic or philosophic – in short, ideological forms in which men become conscious of this conflict and fight it out. Just as one does not judge an individual by what he thinks about himself, so one cannot judge such a period of transformation by its consciousness, but, on the contrary, this consciousness must be explained from the contradictions of material life, from the conflict existing between the social forces of production and the relations of production. No social order is ever destroyed before all the productive forces for which it is sufficient have been developed, and new superior relations of production never replace older ones before the material conditions for their existence have matured within the framework of the old society. Mankind thus inevitably sets itself only such tasks as it is able to solve, since closer examination will always show that the problem itself arises only when the material conditions for its solution are already present or at least in the course of formation. In broad outline, the Asiatic, ancient, feudal and modern bourgeois modes of production may be designated as epochs marking progress in the economic development of society. The bourgeois mode of production is the last antagonistic form of the social process of production – antagonistic not in the sense of individual antagonism but of an antagonism that emanates from the individuals' social conditions of existence – but the productive forces developing within bourgeois society create also the material conditions for a solution of this antagonism. The prehistory of human society accordingly closes with this social formation.

Frederick Engels, with whom I maintained a constant exchange of ideas by correspondence since the publication of his brilliant essay on the critique of economic categories[2] (printed in the *Deutsch–Französische Jahrbücher*), arrived by another road (compare his *Lage der arbeitenden Klasse in England*[3]) at the same

2. 'Outlines of a Critique of Political Economy'. (For this and following footnote references, see 'Chronology of Works by Marx and Engels' (pp. 439–42 below) for details of editions in English).
3. 'The Condition of the Working Class in England'.

result as I, and when in the spring of 1845 he too came to live in Brussels, we decided to set forth together our conception as opposed to the ideological one of German philosophy, in fact to settle accounts with our former philosophical conscience. The intention was carried out in the form of a critique of post-Hegelian philosophy.[4] The manuscript, two large octavo volumes, had long ago reached the publishers in Westphalia when we were informed that owing to changed circumstances it could not be printed. We abandoned the manuscript to the gnawing criticism of the mice all the more willingly since we had achieved our main purpose – self-clarification. Of the scattered works in which at that time we presented one or another aspect of our views to the public, I shall mention only the *Manifesto of the Communist Party*, jointly written by Engels and myself, and a *Discours sur le libre échange,* which I myself published. The salient points of our conception were first outlined in an academic, although polemical, form in my *Misère de la philosophie . . .*[5] this book which was aimed at Proudhon appeared in 1847. The publication of an essay on *Wage-Labour*[6] written in German in which I combined the lectures I had held on this subject at the German Workers' Association in Brussels, was interrupted by the February Revolution and my forcible removal from Belgium in consequence.

The publication of the *Neue Rheinische Zeitung* in 1848 and 1849 and subsequent events cut short my economic studies, which I could only resume in London in 1850. The enormous amount of material relating to the history of political economy assembled in the British Museum, the fact that London is a convenient vantage-point for the observation of bourgeois society, and finally the new stage of development which this society seemed to have entered with the discovery of gold in California and Australia, induced me to start again from the very beginning and to work carefully through the new material. These studies led partly of their own accord to apparently quite remote subjects on which I had to spend a certain amount of time. But it was in particular the imperative necessity of earning my living which reduced the time at my disposal. My collaboration, continued now for eight years, with the *New York Tribune*, the leading Anglo-American newspaper, necessitated an excessive fragmentation of my studies, for I wrote only exceptionally newspaper correspondence in the strict

4. *The German Ideology.*   5. *The Poverty of Philosophy.*
6. 'Wage-Labour and Capital'.

sense. Since a considerable part of my contributions consisted of articles dealing with important economic events in Britain and on the Continent, I was compelled to become conversant with practical details which, strictly speaking, lie outside the sphere of political economy.

This sketch of the course of my studies in the domain of political economy is intended merely to show that my views – no matter how they may be judged and how little they conform to the interested prejudices of the ruling classes – are the outcome of conscientious research carried on over many years. At the entrance to science, as at the entrance to hell, the demand must be made:

> *Qui si convien lasciare ogni sospetto*
> *Ogni viltà convien che qui sia morta.*[7]

Karl Marx

London, January 1859

7. Dante, *Divina Commedia*, Canto III, lines 14–15. ('Here all distrust must be abandoned; here all cowardice must die.')

Glossary of Key Terms

This glossary aims at dealing with two problems. On the one hand, readers not familiar with Marx or more particularly with his early writings might find it useful as a broad 'map' to the works contained in this volume. It should be borne in mind that in some cases the interpretation of the individual terms draws on material which slightly postdates the present texts (e.g. the *Theses on Feuerbach* – see Appendix above – which furnish a concise outline of many of Marx's ideas). On the other hand, the glossary provides an opportunity to explain some of the terms (e.g. *Wesen* and *Aufhebung*) which in German have layers of meaning not found together in any one English word. The reader should bear these further layers of meaning in mind whenever he finds such words in the text.

Alienation and Estrangement

Hegel and others equated alienation with objectification (q.v.). Marx was the first thinker to disentangle the two meanings from one another. He saw alienation rather as an aberrant form of objectification, which in itself is neither positive nor negative, but neutral. Alienation, for Marx, arises only under specific social conditions – conditions under which man's objectification of his natural powers, e.g. through work, takes on forms which bring his human *essence* (q.v.) into conflict with his existence.

Alienation always arises as the *result* of something (it is not a 'human condition') and it is always alienation or estrangement *from* something. The alienation which is founded in capitalism has four main aspects:

(1) man is alienated from the products of his activity, which belong to another (the capitalist);

(2) man is alienated from his productive activity itself (i.e. work), which is not an affirmation but rather a negation of his essential nature;

(3) man is alienated from his own essential nature, his humanity;

(4) man is alienated from other men, from the community.

The term *Entäusserung* is chiefly translated as 'alienation'. Both words have the same commercial connotations. *Entäusserung*, unlike 'alienation', can also mean 'externalization' and is translated as such whenever this aspect of its meaning is to the fore.

The term *Entfremdung* is translated as 'estrangement'. *Entfremdung* suggests more strongly than *Entäusserung* that man is opposed by an alien power which he himself has produced but which now governs him.

Finally the term *Veräusserung*, which occurs only rarely, means the 'praxis' or 'activity' of alienation, or alienation through selling.

Critique

This is a crucial concept for understanding Marx's relationship to bourgeois thought. He uses it to signify the act of 'tearing away the veil' of mystification that surrounds the 'moment of truth' present in every theory. This 'moment of truth' is then subsumed or superseded (q.v.) within a truer theory.

Essence, nature of man

Marx criticized theories that depict man's essence or nature as a fixed and immutable abstraction inhering in each single individual. For Marx, the individual is 'social being' and his essence is the 'aggregate of social relations'. The individual is thus alienated from his essential nature if he is alienated from the social process as a whole, i.e. if he is detached from or opposed to, rather than the focus of, the community. Marx's view of the human essence is paralleled in the three main semantic dimensions of the German word *Wesen*. *Wesen* can mean 'essence' or 'substance', as in *menschliches Wesen* (human nature); it can mean a 'being' or a 'living thing', as in *menschliches Wesen* (human being); and lastly it is used, compounded mostly with other nouns, to signify a complex, a collection or a whole, as in *Schulwesen* (the educational system). Marx regularly exploits the fact that the word carries these diverse meanings, and in doing so enters territory where the translator cannot follow.

Fetishism

The worship of inanimate objects vested with magical properties. In the religious world 'the products of the human head acquire life of their own . . . It is the same in the world of commodities with the products of the human hand.' The social action of the producers 'takes the form of the action of objects, which rule the producers instead of being ruled by them'.

(Marx first treats the notion of fetishism in detail in the first volume of *Capital*, but it is prefigured a number of times in the present texts, e.g. when Marx analyses primogeniture, pp. 164ff.)

Objectification (Vergegenständlichung)

Objectification is man's natural means of projecting himself through his productive activity into nature. Before Marx, no strict separation was made of the terms objectification and alienation. Marx's concept of praxis (q.v.), however, enabled him to extricate them from one another. Objectification affords a free man the possibility of contemplating himself in a world of his own making.

Praxis or 'productive activity'

Marx considered both Hegel's idea of the contemplative, *knowing* subject and Feuerbach's 'materialism' as abstract and one-sided interpretations of the world – Hegel because he reduced history to emanation of the spirit, and Feuerbach because he disregarded the active element, the practical activity which fashions the object. Marx's concept of praxis – man's forming and grasping of himself and of nature by producing objects – is the bridge between 'idealism' and 'materialism'.

Praxis is also the foundation of the 'science of man' which supersedes both traditional speculative philosophy and political economy, abolishing the opposition between them. Using this concept, Marx analyses the history of mankind, which has formed itself through its social and economic activity.

Species-being (Gattungswesen)

The notion of 'species-being', which was first developed by Ludwig Feuerbach, is basic to Marx's thought. Feuerbach saw the 'essential difference between man and the brute' in the fact that man is not only 'conscious of himself an an individual' (as animals are) but also aware of himself as a member of a species, i.e. a species-being. 'Man is in fact at once I and Thou; he can put himself in the place of another, for this reason, that to him his species, his essential nature, and not merely his individuality, is an object of thought' (Feuerbach, *The Essence of Christianity*). For this reason, an atomized and competitive society in which the individual and the universal are in conflict is at odds with what is specifically human in man.

Supersession, Transcendence (Aufhebung)

There is no one English word to render accurately the meaning of *Aufhebung* in the technical sense given it by Hegel and Marx. *Aufheben* normally has two main meanings, one negative (annul, abolish) and the other positive (supersede, transcend). Hegel exploited this duality of meaning and used the word to describe that action whereby a higher form of thought or nature supersedes a lower form, while at the same time 'preserving' some of its moments. Marx's concept of 'critique' is an instance of this positive–negative movement of supersession.

Chronology of Marx's Life 1818 to August 1844

1818

5 May   Born at Trier (Treves), Rhineland Prussia.

1835

September   Leaves school. Writes in his *Abitur* essay: 'Our relationship with society started, to a certain extent, even before we could determine it ... Man's nature is such that he can achieve perfection only when working for the good and perfection of his fellows.'

October   Studies law at Bonn university. He also follows the course in classical mythology and the history of art.

1836

October   Moves to Berlin. Continues his law studies, and attends lectures in philosophy, history and the history of art. He becomes a friend of Bruno Bauer and other Young Hegelian writers. He writes verse and attempts novels and plays. In a letter to his father (10 November 1837) he writes: 'From idealism, which I equated by the way with Kant and Fichte, having drawn it from those sources, I went on to seek the Idea in the real (*im Wirklichen*) itself. If in earlier times the gods lived above the earth, now they have become its centre.' He had read 'fragments of Hegel, and did not relish its grotesque and craggy melody'. He studied the Hegelian system: 'This work, for the purposes of which I familiarized myself with natural science, Schelling and history ... caused me an endless headache ... This, my dearest child, cherished by the light of the moon, is carrying me like a false siren into the enemy's [i.e. Hegel's] arms.'

1839–41

Studies Greek philosophy. In his doctoral dissertation – 'On the Difference between the Democritean and Epicurean Philosophy of Nature' – he champions the Epicurean principle of the freedom of consciousness and man's capacity to act upon nature, as against the strict determinism of Democritus. He finishes his studies at Berlin in

March 1841, and goes to Bonn with the intention of taking up a professorship. In Bonn he studies Feuerbach's *Essence of Christianity* and decides that 'there is no other path to truth and freedom except that through the fiery stream [*Feuer-Bach*].' He gives up his idea of an academic chair when a number of progressive academics are forced to leave their teaching posts.

1842

April   Starts writing for the *Rheinische Zeitung*, which represents the industrial, liberal interests. In October he becomes the paper's editor. During this time he deepens his knowledge of practical politics and the economic realities of capitalism. In Cologne he meets Engels for the first time and studies the French utopian socialists (Fourier, Proudhon, etc.). He announces that the *Rheinische Zeitung* will submit the views of these latter to a 'thorough-going critique'.

November Breaks publicly with the Berlin circle of Young Hegelians.

1843

January–   The Prussian government steps up its censorship and
April   finally orders the suppression of the *Rheinische Zeitung*. In March, Marx resigns the editorship, disgusted with the timorous attitude of the shareholders in the face of the government's ban.

May   Together with Arnold Ruge, he plans to publish the *Franco-German Yearbooks* in either Paris or Strasbourg. He writes to Ruge of his hatred for the monarchy and 'the system of industry and commerce, of property and the exploitation of man'. 'It is our task' – he writes – 'to drag the old world into the full light of day and give positive shape to the new one.'

Summer   Writes his *Critique of Hegel's Doctrine of the State*.

October   Writes to Feuerbach, asking him to join in working on the *Yearbooks*. Later in the month he moves to Paris.

Autumn   Writes *On the Jewish Question* and *A Contribution to the*
1843–   *Critique of Hegel's Philosophy of Right. Introduction* for the
January   *Yearbooks*.
1844

November Makes contact with the French democrats and socialists
1843–   and starts going to meetings of German and French
January   workers. Becomes friends with Heinrich Heine.
1845

Late 1843– Makes an intensive study of the French Revolution of 1789
March   and begins a systematic study of political economy
1844   through the writings of Adam Smith, Jean-Baptiste Say and others.

1844

February   The first and last edition of the *Yearbooks* is published, and includes two articles by Friedrich Engels.

March   Meets Bakunin and other Russian revolutionary leaders and the French democrats and socialists Pierre Levoux, Louis Blanc and others. Breaks with Ruge because of the latter's attitude to the communistic direction in Marx's writings for the *Yearbooks*.

April–
August   Continues his study of the writings of the bourgeois economists and makes the first drafts of a critique of bourgeois political economy for his *Economic and Philosophical Manuscripts*.

June   Welcomes the rising of the Silesian weavers, which he sees as a demonstration of the growing maturity of the German working class.

July   Meets Pierre-Joseph Proudhon. Writes *Critical Notes to the Article 'The King of Prussia and Social Reform. By a Prussian'* in order to answer Ruge's views on the Silesian events.

Note on Previous Editions of the Works of Marx and Engels

Until recently there existed no complete edition of the works of Marx and Engels in any language. The Marx–Engels Institute, under its director D. Riazanov, began to produce such an edition in the late 1920s; the collapse of the project in 1935 was no doubt connected with Riazanov's dismissal and subsequent disappearance. However, eleven indispensable volumes did emerge between 1927 and 1935, under the title *Karl Marx–Friedrich Engels: Historisch–Kritische Gesamtausgabe*, commonly referred to as the *MEGA* edition. The *MEGA* contains works of both men down to 1848, and their correspondence, but nothing more. For the next thirty years, the field was held by the almost inaccessible Russian edition, the Marx-Engels *Sochineniya* (twenty-nine volumes, 1928–46).

Only in 1968 did the East Germans complete the first German definitive edition, the forty-one volume *Marx–Engels Werke* (*MEW*). Until then, the works of Marx and Engels existed only in separate editions and smaller collections on specific themes. For this reason, the translations into English have followed the same pattern – the only general selection being the *Marx–Engels Selected Works* (*MESW*), now expanded to a three-volume edition. Recently, however, the major gaps in the English translations have begun to be filled. Lawrence and Wishart have produced a complete translation of *Theories of Surplus Value*, as well as the first adequate translation of *A Contribution to the Critique of Political Economy* and Marx's book on *The Cologne Communist Trial*. They plan to issue a complete English-language edition of even greater scope than the *MEW*, though this will inevitably take many years to complete. The Pelican Marx Library occupies an intermediate position between the *MESW* and the complete edition. It brings together the most important of Marx's larger works, the three volumes of *Capital* and the *Grundrisse*, as well as three volumes of political writings and a volume of early writings.

Chronology of Works by Marx and Engels

Date[1]	Author[2]	Title	English edition[3]
1843	M	*Critique of Hegel's Doctrine of the State*	P *EW*
1843	M	*On the Jewish Question*	P *EW*
1843–4	M	*A Contribution to the Critique of Hegel's Philosophy of Right. Introduction*	P *EW*
1844	M	*Excerpts from James Mill's* Elements of Political Economy	P *EW*
1844	E	*Outlines of a Critique of Political Economy*	P. Engels
1844	M	*Economic and Philosophical Manuscripts*	P *EW*
1844	M	*Critical Notes on the Article 'The King of Prussia and Social Reform. By a Prussian'*	P *EW*
1844	M & E	*The Holy Family, or a Critique of Critical Critique*	LW 1957
1844–5	E	*Condition of the Working Class in England*	Blackwell 1958

1. Date of composition, except for *Capital*, where the date of first publication is given.

2. M = Marx, E = Engels.

3. The following abbreviations are used:

P. Engels: Engels, *Selected Writings*, Harmondsworth, 1967.

LW: Lawrence and Wishart.

MESW: Karl Marx and Frederick Engels, Selected Works in Three Volumes, Progress Publishers, 1969.

P: Pelican Marx Library.

P *EW: Early Writings* (Pelican Marx Library).

P *FI: The First International and After* (Pelican Marx Library).

P *R1848: The Revolutions of 1848* (Pelican Marx Library).

P *SE: Surveys from Exile* (Pelican Marx Library).

Date	Author	Title	English edition
1845	M	Theses on Feuerbach	P EW
1845–6	M & E	The German Ideology	LW 1964
1846–7	M	The Poverty of Philosophy	LW 1956
1847	M & E	Speeches on Poland	P R1848
1847	M	Wage Labour and Capital	MESW I
1847–8	M & E	Manifesto of the Communist Party	P R1848
1848	M & E	Speeches on Poland	P R1848
1848	M & E	Demands of the Communist Party in Germany	P R1848
1848–9	M & E	Articles in the Neue Rheinische Zeitung	P R1848 (selection)
1850 (March)	M & E	Address of the Central Committee to the Communist League	P R1848
1850 (June)	M & E	Address of the Central Committee to the Communist League	P R1848
1850	M & E	Reviews from the Neue Rheinische Zeitung Revue	P R1848
1850	M	The Class Struggles in France: 1848 to 1850	P SE
1850	E	The Peasant War in Germany	LW 1956
1851–2	E	Revolution and Counter-Revolution in Germany	MESW I
1852	M	The Eighteenth Brumaire of Louis Bonaparte	P SE
1852	M	Revelations on the Cologne Communist Trial	LW 1970
1856	M	Speech at the Anniversary of the People's Paper	P SE
1857–8	M	Grundrisse	P
1859	M	A Contribution to the Critique of Political Economy	LW 1971
1852–61	M & E	Articles in the New York Daily Tribune	P SE (selections)
1861	M	Articles in Die Presse on the Civil War in the United States	P SE (selections)
1861–3	M	Theories of Surplus Value, Vol. 1	LW 1967
		Vol. 2	LW 1970
		Vol. 3	LW 1972
1863	M	Proclamation on Poland	P SE
1864	M	Inaugural Address of the International Working Men's Association	P FI
1864	M	Provisional Rules of the International Working Men's Association	P FI

Date	Author	Title	English edition
1865	E	*The Prussian Military Question and the German Workers Party*	P *FI* (extract)
1865	M	*Wages, Prices, and Profit*	*MESW II*
1866	E	*What Have the Working Classes to Do with Poland?*	P *FI*
1867	M	*Capital,* Vol. 1	P
1867	M	*Instructions for Delegates to the Geneva Congress*	P *FI*
1868	M	*Report to the Brussels Congress*	P *FI*
1869	M	*Report to the Basel Congress*	P *FI*
1870	M	*The General Council to the Federal Council of French Switzerland* (a circular letter)	P *FI*
1870	M	*First Address of the General Council on the Franco-Prussian War*	P *FI*
1870	M	*Second Address of the General Council on the Franco-Prussian War*	P *FI*
1871	M	First draft of *The Civil War in France*	P *FI*
1871	M & E	*On the Paris Commune*	LW 1971
1871	M	*The Civil War in France*	P *FI*
1871	M & E	*Resolution of the London Conference on Working-Class Political Action*	P *FI*
1872	M & E	*The Alleged Splits in the International*	P *FI*
1872	M	*Report to the Hague Congress*	P *FI*
1872–3	E	*The Housing Question*	*MESW II*
1874	M	*Political Indifferentism*	P *FI*
1874	E	*On Authority*	*MESW II*
1874–5	M	*Conspectus of Bakunin's Book* Statism and Anarchy	P *FI* (extract)
1875	M & E	*For Poland*	P *FI*
1875	M	*Critique of the Gotha Programme*	P *FI*
1876–8	E	*Anti-Dühring*	LW 1955
1879	M & E	*Circular Letter to Bebel, Liebknecht, Bracke, et al.*	P *FI*
1879–80	M	*Marginal Notes on Adolph Wagner's* Lehrbuch der politischen Ökonomie	P *Capital*
1880	E	*Socialism: Utopian and Scientific*	*MESW III*
1880	M	*Introduction to the Programme of the French Worker's Party*	P *FI*
1873–83	E	*Dialectics of Nature*	LW 1954
1884	E	*The Origin of the Family, Private Property, and the State*	*MESW III*

Date	Author	Title	English edition
1885	M	*Capital*, Vol. 2	P
1886	E	*Ludwig Feuerbach and the End of Classical German Philosophy*	*MESW III*
1894	M	*Capital*, Vol. 3	P

Index

About the Author

KARL MARX was born at Trier in 1818 of a (German) Jewish family converted to Christianity. As a student in Bonn and Berlin he was influenced by Hegel's dialectic, but he later reacted against idealist philosophy and began to develop his theory of historical materialism. He related the state of society to its economic foundations and means of production, and recommended armed revolution on the part of the proletariat. In Paris in 1844 Marx met Frederick Engels, with whom he formed a lifelong partnership. Together they prepared the *Manifesto of the Communist Party* (1848) as a statement of the Communist League's policy. In 1848 Marx returned to Germany and took an active part in the unsuccessful democratic revolution. The following year he arrived in England as a refugee and lived in London until his death in 1883. Helped financially by Engels, Marx and his family nevertheless lived in great poverty. After years of research (mostly carried out at the British Museum), he published in 1867 the first volume of his great work, *Capital*. From 1864 to 1872 Marx played a leading role in the International Working Men's Association, and his last years saw the development of the first mass workers' parties founded on avowedly Marxist principles. Besides the two posthumous volumes of *Capital* compiled by Engels, Karl Marx's other writings include *The German Ideology, The Poverty of Philosophy, A Contribution to the Critique of Political Economy,* and *Theories of Surplus Value.*

About the Editor

QUINTIN HOARE is the General Editor of the Vintage Marx Library and Editor of the British journal, *New Left Review.*

LUCIO COLLETTI, Professor of Philosophy at the University of Rome, is the author of *From Rousseau to Lenin* (awarded the Isaac Deutscher Memorial Prize in 1973), and *Marxism and Hegel.*

V-285   PARKES, HENRY B.   *Gods and Men*
V-719   REED, JOHN   *Ten Days That Shook the World*
V-176   SCHAPIRO, LEONARD   *The Government and Politics of the Soviet Union* (Revised Edition)
V-745   SCHAPIRO, LEONARD   *The Communist Party of the Soviet Union*
V-375   SCHURMANN, F. and O. SCHELL (eds.)   *The China Reader: Imperial China*, I
V-376   SCHURMANN, F. and O. SCHELL (eds.)   *The China Reader: Republican China*, II
V-377   SCHURMANN, F. and O. SCHELL (eds.)   *The China Reader: Communist China*, III
V-681   SNOW, EDGAR   *Red China Today*
V-312   TANNENBAUM, FRANK   *Ten Keys to Latin America*
V-322   THOMPSON, E. P.   *The Making of the English Working Class*
V-724   WALLACE, SIR DONALD MACKENZIE   *Russia: On the Eve of War and Revolution*
V-206   WALLERSTEIN, IMMANUEL   *Africa: The Politics of Independence*
V-298   WATTS, ALAN   *The Way of Zen*
V-557   WEINSTEIN, JAMES   *The Decline of Socialism in America 1912-1925*
V-106   WINSTON, RICHARD   *Charlemagne: From the Hammer to the Cross*
V-627   WOMACK, JOHN JR.   *Zapata and the Mexican Revolution*
V-81   WOOCK, ROGER R. and ARTHUR I. BLAUSTEIN (eds.)   *Man against Poverty: World War III*
V-486   WOOLF, S. J. (ed.)   *European Fascism*
V-545   WOOLF, S. J. (ed.)   *The Nature of Fascism*
V-495   YGLESIAS, JOSE   *In the Fist of Revolution: Life in a Cuban Country Town*

VINTAGE POLITICAL SCIENCE
AND SOCIAL CRITICISM